T0257672

IET MATERIALS, CIRCUITS AND DEVICES SERIES 55

Hardware Architectures for Deep Learning

Other volumes in this series:

Volume 2	**Analogue IC Design: The current-mode approach** C. Toumazou, F.J. Lidgey and D.G. Haigh (Editors)
Volume 3	**Analogue–Digital ASICs: Circuit techniques, design tools and applications** R.S. Soin, F. Maloberti and J. France (Editors)
Volume 4	**Algorithmic and Knowledge-Based CAD for VLSI** G.E. Taylor and G. Russell (Editors)
Volume 5	**Switched Currents: An analogue technique for digital technology** C. Toumazou, J.B.C. Hughes and N.C. Battersby (Editors)
Volume 6	**High-Frequency Circuit Engineering** F. Nibler *et al.*
Volume 8	**Low-Power High-Frequency Microelectronics: A unified approach** G. Machado (Editor)
Volume 9	**VLSI Testing: Digital and mixed analogue/digital techniques** S.L. Hurst
Volume 10	**Distributed Feedback Semiconductor Lasers** J.E. Carroll, J.E.A. Whiteaway and R.G.S. Plumb
Volume 11	**Selected Topics in Advanced Solid State and Fibre Optic Sensors** S.M. Vaezi-Nejad (Editor)
Volume 12	**Strained Silicon Heterostructures: Materials and devices** C.K. Maiti, N.B. Chakrabarti and S.K. Ray
Volume 13	**RFIC and MMIC Design and Technology** I.D. Robertson and S. Lucyzyn (Editors)
Volume 14	**Design of High Frequency Integrated Analogue Filters** Y. Sun (Editor)
Volume 15	**Foundations of Digital Signal Processing: Theory, algorithms and hardware design** P. Gaydecki
Volume 16	**Wireless Communications Circuits and Systems** Y. Sun (Editor)
Volume 17	**The Switching Function: Analysis of power electronic circuits** C. Marouchos
Volume 18	**System on Chip: Next generation electronics** B. Al-Hashimi (Editor)
Volume 19	**Test and Diagnosis of Analogue, Mixed-Signal and RF Integrated Circuits: The system on chip approach** Y. Sun (Editor)
Volume 20	**Low Power and Low Voltage Circuit Design with the FGMOS Transistor** E. Rodriguez-Villegas
Volume 21	**Technology Computer Aided Design for Si, SiGe and GaAs Integrated Circuits** C.K. Maiti and G.A. Armstrong
Volume 22	**Nanotechnologies** M. Wautelet *et al.*
Volume 23	**Understandable Electric Circuits** M. Wang
Volume 24	**Fundamentals of Electromagnetic Levitation: Engineering sustainability through efficiency** A.J. Sangster
Volume 25	**Optical MEMS for Chemical Analysis and Biomedicine** H. Jiang (Editor)
Volume 26	**High Speed Data Converters** A.M.A. Ali
Volume 27	**Nano-Scaled Semiconductor Devices** E.A. Gutiérrez-D (Editor)
Volume 28	**Security and Privacy for Big Data, Cloud Computing and Applications** L. Wang, W. Ren, K.R. Choo and F. Xhafa (Editors)
Volume 29	**Nano-CMOS and Post-CMOS Electronics: Devices and modelling** Saraju P. Mohanty and Ashok Srivastava
Volume 30	**Nano-CMOS and Post-CMOS Electronics: Circuits and design** Saraju P. Mohanty and Ashok Srivastava
Volume 32	**Oscillator Circuits: Frontiers in design, analysis and applications** Y. Nishio (Editor)
Volume 33	**High Frequency MOSFET Gate Drivers** Z. Zhang and Y. Liu
Volume 34	**RF and Microwave Module Level Design and Integration** M. Almalkawi
Volume 35	**Design of Terahertz CMOS Integrated Circuits for High-Speed Wireless Communication** M. Fujishima and S. Amakawa
Volume 38	**System Design with Memristor Technologies** L. Guckert and E.E. Swartzlander Jr.
Volume 39	**Functionality-Enhanced Devices: An alternative to Moore's law** P.-E. Gaillardon (Editor)
Volume 40	**Digitally Enhanced Mixed Signal Systems** C. Jabbour, P. Desgreys and D. Dallett (Editors)

Volume 43   **Negative Group Delay Devices: From concepts to applications** B. Ravelo (Editor)

Volume 45   **Characterisation and Control of Defects in Semiconductors** F. Tuomisto (Editor)

Volume 47   **Understandable Electric Circuits: Key concepts, 2nd Edition** M. Wang

Volume 51   **Modelling Methodologies in Analogue Integrated Circuit Design** G. Dundar and M.B. Yelten (Editors)

Volume 53   **VLSI Architectures for Future Video Coding** M. Martina (Editor)

Volume 54   **Advances in High-Power Fiber and Diode Laser Engineering** Ivan Divliansky (Editor)

Volume 58   **Magnetorheological Materials and their Applications** S. Choi and W. Li (Editors)

Volume 60   **IP Core Protection and Hardware-Assisted Security for Consumer Electronics** A. Sengupta and S. Mohanty

Volume 64   **Phase-Locked Frequency generation and Clocking: Architectures and circuits for modem wireless and wireline systems** W. Rhee (Editor)

Volume 67   **Frontiers in Securing IP Cores: forensic detective control and obfuscation techniques** A Sengupta

Volume 68   **High-Quality Liquid Crystal Displays and Smart Devices: Vol. 1 and Vol. 2** S. Ishihara, S. Kobayashi and Y. Ukai (Editors)

Volume 69   **Fibre Bragg Gratings in Harsh and Space Environments: Principles and applications** B. Aïssa, E.I. Haddad, R.V. Kruzelecky, and W.R. Jamroz

Volume 70   **Self-Healing Materials: From fundamental concepts to advanced space and electronics applications, 2nd Edition** B. Aïssa, E.I. Haddad, R.V. Kruzelecky, and W.R. Jamroz

Volume 71   **Radio Frequency and Microwave Power Amplifiers: Vol. 1 and Vol. 2** A. Grebennikov (Editor)

Volume 73   **VLSI and Post-CMOS Electronics Volume 1: VLSI and Post-CMOS Electronics and Volume 2: Materials, devices and interconnects** R. Dhiman and R. Chandel (Editors)

Hardware Architectures for Deep Learning

Edited by
Masoud Daneshtalab and Mehdi Modarressi

The Institution of Engineering and Technology

Published by The Institution of Engineering and Technology, London, United Kingdom

The Institution of Engineering and Technology is registered as a Charity in England & Wales (no. 211014) and Scotland (no. SC038698).

© The Institution of Engineering and Technology 2020

First published 2020

This publication is copyright under the Berne Convention and the Universal Copyright Convention. All rights reserved. Apart from any fair dealing for the purposes of research or private study, or criticism or review, as permitted under the Copyright, Designs and Patents Act 1988, this publication may be reproduced, stored or transmitted, in any form or by any means, only with the prior permission in writing of the publishers, or in the case of reprographic reproduction in accordance with the terms of licenses issued by the Copyright Licensing Agency. Enquiries concerning reproduction outside those terms should be sent to the publisher at the undermentioned address:

The Institution of Engineering and Technology
Michael Faraday House
Six Hills Way, Stevenage
Herts, SG1 2AY, United Kingdom

www.theiet.org

While the authors and publisher believe that the information and guidance given in this work are correct, all parties must rely upon their own skill and judgement when making use of them. Neither the authors nor publisher assumes any liability to anyone for any loss or damage caused by any error or omission in the work, whether such an error or omission is the result of negligence or any other cause. Any and all such liability is disclaimed.

The moral rights of the authors to be identified as authors of this work have been asserted by them in accordance with the Copyright, Designs and Patents Act 1988.

British Library Cataloguing in Publication Data
A catalogue record for this product is available from the British Library

ISBN 978-1-78561-768-3 (hardback)
ISBN 978-1-78561-769-0 (PDF)

Typeset in India by MPS Limited
Printed in the UK by CPI Group (UK) Ltd, Croydon

Contents

About the editors		**xv**
Preface		**xvii**
Acknowledgments		**xxi**
Part I	**Deep learning and neural networks: concepts and models**	**1**
1	**An introduction to artificial neural networks**	**3**
	Ahmad Kalhor	
1.1	Introduction	3
	1.1.1 Natural NNs	3
	1.1.2 Artificial neural networks	6
	1.1.3 Preliminary concepts in ANNs	7
1.2	ANNs in classification and regression problems	11
	1.2.1 ANNs in classification problems	11
	1.2.2 ANNs in regression problems	12
	1.2.3 Relation between classification and regression	13
1.3	Widely used NN models	14
	1.3.1 Simple structure networks	14
	1.3.2 Multilayer and deep NNs	16
1.4	Convolutional neural networks	20
	1.4.1 Convolution layers	21
	1.4.2 Pooling layers	22
	1.4.3 Learning in CNNs	23
	1.4.4 CNN examples	24
1.5	Conclusion	25
	References	25
2	**Hardware acceleration for recurrent neural networks**	**27**
	Sima Sinaei and Masoud Daneshtalab	
2.1	Recurrent neural networks	28
	2.1.1 Long short-term memory	30
	2.1.2 Gated recurrent units	36

	2.2	Hardware acceleration for RNN inference	37
		2.2.1 Software implementation	37
		2.2.2 Hardware implementation	38
	2.3	Hardware implementation of LSTMs	39
		2.3.1 Model compression	40
		2.3.2 Datatype and Quantization	44
		2.3.3 Memory	46
	2.4	Conclusion	48
	References		48

3 Feedforward neural networks on massively parallel architectures   53
Reza Hojabr, Ahmad Khonsari, Mehdi Modarressi,
and Masoud Daneshtalab

	3.1	Related work	55
	3.2	Preliminaries	57
	3.3	ClosNN: a customized Clos for neural network	59
	3.4	Collective communications on ClosNN	60
	3.5	ClosNN customization and area reduction	62
	3.6	Folded ClosNN	65
	3.7	Leaf switch optimization	67
	3.8	Scaling to larger NoCs	67
	3.9	Evaluation	68
		3.9.1 Performance comparison under synthetic traffic	69
		3.9.2 Performance evaluation under realistic workloads	70
		3.9.3 Power comparison	71
		3.9.4 Sensitivity to neural network size	72
	3.10	Conclusion	73
	References		73

Part II   Deep learning and approximate data representation   77

**4 Stochastic-binary convolutional neural networks with deterministic
bit-streams   79**
M. Hassan Najafi, S. Rasoul Faraji, Bingzhe Li, David J. Lilja,
and Kia Bazargan

	4.1	Overview	79
	4.2	Introduction	79
	4.3	Background	81
		4.3.1 Stochastic computing	81
		4.3.2 Deterministic low-discrepancy bit-streams	82
		4.3.3 Convolutional neural networks	84
	4.4	Related work	84

	4.5	Proposed hybrid binary-bit-stream design	85
		4.5.1 Multiplications and accumulation	86
		4.5.2 Handling negative weights	86
	4.6	Experimental results	88
		4.6.1 Performance comparison	88
		4.6.2 Cost comparison	90
	4.7	Summary	92
	Acknowledgment		92
	References		92

5 Binary neural networks 95

Najmeh Nazari and Mostafa E. Salehi

	5.1	Introduction	95
	5.2	Binary neural networks	96
		5.2.1 Binary and ternary weights for neural networks	97
		5.2.2 Binarized and ternarized neural networks	100
	5.3	BNN optimization techniques	109
	5.4	Hardware implementation of BNNs	111
	5.5	Conclusion	112
	References		113

Part III Deep learning and model sparsity 117

6 Hardware and software techniques for sparse deep neural networks 119

Ali Shafiee, Liu Liu, Lei Wang, and Joseph Hassoun

	6.1	Introduction	119
	6.2	Different types of sparsity methods	120
	6.3	Software approach for pruning	122
		6.3.1 Hard pruning	122
		6.3.2 Soft pruning, structural sparsity, and hardware concern	122
		6.3.3 Questioning pruning	122
	6.4	Hardware support for sparsity	123
		6.4.1 Advantages of sparsity for dense accelerator	124
		6.4.2 Supporting activation sparsity	125
		6.4.3 Supporting weight sparsity	125
		6.4.4 Supporting both weight and activation sparsity	131
		6.4.5 Supporting output sparsity	137
		6.4.6 Supporting value sparsity	140
	6.5	Conclusion	143
	References		143

7   Computation reuse-aware accelerator for neural networks   147
      Hoda Mahdiani, Alireza Khadem, Ali Yasoubi, Azam Ghanbari,
      Mehdi Modarressi, and Masoud Daneshtalab

      7.1   Motivation   148
      7.2   Baseline architecture   150
             7.2.1   Computation reuse support for weight redundancy   151
             7.2.2   Computation reuse support for input redundancy   152
      7.3   Multicore neural network implementation   153
             7.3.1   More than K weights per neuron   153
             7.3.2   More than N neurons per layer   153
      7.4   Experimental results   154
      7.5   Conclusion and future work   156
      References   156

Part IV   Convolutional neural networks for embedded systems   159

**8   CNN agnostic accelerator design for low latency
      inference on FPGAs**   161
      Sachin Kumawat, Mohammad Motamedi, and Soheil Ghiasi

      8.1   Introduction   161
      8.2   Brief review of efforts on FPGA-based acceleration of CNNs   162
      8.3   Network structures and operations   163
             8.3.1   Convolution   163
             8.3.2   Inner product   163
             8.3.3   Pooling   165
             8.3.4   Other operations   166
      8.4   Optimizing parallelism sources   166
             8.4.1   Identifying independent computations   166
             8.4.2   Acceleration strategies   167
      8.5   Computation optimization and reuse   168
             8.5.1   Design control variables   168
             8.5.2   Partial sums and data reuse   169
             8.5.3   Proposed loop coalescing for flexibility with
                      high efficiency   170
      8.6   Bandwidth matching and compute model   171
             8.6.1   Resource utilization   171
             8.6.2   Unifying off-chip and on-chip memory   172
             8.6.3   Analyzing runtime   174
      8.7   Library design and architecture implementation   176
             8.7.1   Concurrent architecture   176
             8.7.2   Convolution engine   178
             8.7.3   Restructuring fully connected layers   179
             8.7.4   Zero overhead pooling   179
             8.7.5   Other layers   180

8.8   Caffe integration   180
8.9   Performance evaluation   181
         8.9.1   Optimizer results   181
         8.9.2   Onboard runs   182
         8.9.3   Architecture comparison   185
References   187

**9   Iterative convolutional neural network (ICNN): an iterative CNN
       solution for low power and real-time systems   191**
       Katayoun Neshatpour, Houman Homayoun, and Avesta Sasan

9.1   Motivation   191
9.2   Background on CNN   194
9.3   Optimization of CNN   195
9.4   Iterative learning   196
         9.4.1   Case study: iterative AlexNet   199
9.5   ICNN training schemes   200
         9.5.1   Sequential training   200
         9.5.2   Parallel Training   200
9.6   Complexity analysis   203
9.7   Visualization   204
         9.7.1   Background on CNN visualization   204
         9.7.2   Visualizing features learned by ICNN   204
9.8   Contextual awareness in ICNN   208
         9.8.1   Prediction rank   209
         9.8.2   Pruning neurons in FC layers   211
         9.8.3   Pruning filters in CONV layers   211
9.9   Policies for exploiting energy-accuracy trade-off in ICNN   212
         9.9.1   Dynamic deadline (DD) policy for real-time applications   212
         9.9.2   Thresholding policy (TP) for dynamic complexity
                     reduction   213
         9.9.3   Context-aware pruning policy   214
         9.9.4   Pruning and thresholding hybrid policy   216
         9.9.5   Variable and dynamic bit-length selection   217
9.10 ICNN implementation results   218
         9.10.1 Implementation framework   218
         9.10.2 Dynamic deadline policy for real-time applications   219
         9.10.3 Thresholding policy for dynamic complexity reduction   220
         9.10.4 Context-aware pruning policy for parameter reduction   223
9.11 Pruning and thresholding hybrid policy   225
         9.11.1 Fixed percentage PTHP   225
         9.11.2 Confidence-tracking PTHP   226
         9.11.3 Run-time and overall accuracy   227
9.12 Conclusions   229
References   229

Part V   **Deep learning on analog accelerators**   **233**

10 **Mixed-signal neuromorphic platform design for streaming**
    biomedical signal processing   **235**
    Sandeep Pande, Federico Corradi, Jan Stuijt, Siebren Schaafsma, and
    Francky Catthoor

    10.1 Introduction   236
    10.2 Related work   237
          10.2.1 Mixed-signal neuromorphic architectures – brief review   237
          10.2.2 Biomedical signal processing challenges for ECG
                  application   240
    10.3 NeuRAM3 mixed-signal neuromorphic platform   241
          10.3.1 Analog neural components including local synapse
                  array   242
          10.3.2 Global synapse communication network realized with
                  TFT-based switches   242
          10.3.3 NeuRAM3 mixed-signal neuromorphic platform FPGA
                  architecture   246
    10.4 ECG application mapping on non-scaled neuromorphic platform
          instance   248
          10.4.1 ECG classification and overall setup   248
          10.4.2 ECG signal compression and encoding in spikes   249
          10.4.3 Recurrent spiking neural network   252
          10.4.4 Recurrent neural network implemented in VLSI spiking
                  neurons   252
          10.4.5 Training LIF classifiers   254
          10.4.6 VLSI implementation of the recurrent spiking neural
                  network   256
    10.5 Results and discussion   257
          10.5.1 Classification accuracy   257
          10.5.2 Discussion on results for ECG application   258
          10.5.3 NeuRAM3 hardware platform results   259
    10.6 Summary and conclusions   260
    Acknowledgments   260
    References   261

11 **Inverter-based memristive neuromorphic circuit for**
    ultra-low-power IoT smart applications   **265**
    Arash Fayyazi, Mohammad Ansari, Mehdi Kamal, Ali Afzali-Kusha,
    and Massoud Pedram

    11.1 Introduction   265
    11.2 Literature review   267
    11.3 Inverter-based memristive neuromorphic circuit   270
          11.3.1 Neuron circuit with memristive synapse   271

11.3.2 Input interface (DAC) 274
11.3.3 Training scheme 276
11.3.4 Output interface (ADC) 280
11.4 Results and discussion 282
11.4.1 Input interface (DAC) 282
11.4.2 Output interface (ADC) 284
11.4.3 Inverter-based memristive neuromorphic circuit 285
11.4.4 Impact of unideal condition 289
11.5 Conclusion 291
References 292

Index **297**

About the editors

Masoud Daneshtalab is a tenured associate professor at Mälardalen University (MDH) in Sweden, an adjunct professor at Tallinn University of Technology (Tal-Tech) in Estonia, and sits on the board of directors of Euromicro. His research interests include interconnection networks, brain-like computing, and deep learning architectures. He has published over 300-refereed papers.

Mehdi Modarressi is an assistant professor at the Department of Electrical and Computer Engineering, University of Tehran, Iran. He is the founder and director of the *Parallel and Network-based Processing* research laboratory at the University of Tehran, where he leads several industrial and research projects on deep learning-based embedded system design and implementation.

Preface

Deep learning has greatly affected our everyday life by providing novel IT services and also changing the ways we interact with computers and other technology. In particular, deep learning has brought an unprecedented increase in the quality and accuracy of computer vision and speech recognition which serve as the base of many smart applications and services.

Computer vision is perhaps the most important area that benefits from deep learning. Deep learning enables computers to detect objects of interest in images and classify or identify categories of objects with higher precision. These advances in computer vision have translated to improvements in robotics, autonomous drones, drive-assisted systems, and self-driving cars (with early prototypes are currently under-test by Tesla and Google). Face detection and recognition can be included in many services (e.g., security and authentication) in smart environments and Internet of Things (IoT) solutions.

Further, recent innovations in deep learning are completely reshaping the future of computer-aided diagnosis, disease detection procedures, and medical decision support tools. With deep learning-based computer vision, computers are expected to read and analyze X-rays, magnetic resonance imaging (MRI), electrocardiogram (ECG) waveforms, and computed tomography (CT) scan images more rapidly and accurately than doctors to diagnose diseases earlier and less invasively. Another emerging application of deep learning in medicine is healthcare monitoring, where biometric monitoring services are implemented on either wearable or implantable devices to enable the measurement and analysis of patient data in real time.

Furthermore, deep learning has enabled developing novel and accurate speech recognition functions on smartphones and computers. The popular examples include the voice-enabled features of Android and Windows, Amazon's Alexa, Apple's Siri, and Microsoft's Cortana.

Smart text and language processing is another field that has been revolutionized by deep learning. Google Translate service now supports text-to-text and spoken-to-spoken translation for more than 100 pairs of languages. Online subtitle generation for video streams is another capability that is now viable by deep learning.

This rapid growth of the server, desktop, and embedded applications/services based on deep learning has brought about a renaissance in the practical and theoretical aspects of neural networks as the basis of any deep learning system.

However, the superior accuracy and efficiency of neural networks come at the cost of high computational complexity, power consumption, and memory bandwidth demand. State-of-the-art neural networks in many practical applications, such as real-time object recognition in an autonomous vehicle or data analysis in a server, are orders of magnitude larger than conventional simple neural networks that have long been used since the 1990s. Generally, the size and complexity of neural networks are proportional to the problem complexity. For example, while a few hundred neurons can implement a simple digit classifier, an accurate image processing convolutional neural network needs thousands of neurons, with several hundred millions of arithmetic operations, to recognize objects of interest in a single picture or video frame.

Modern graphics processing units (GPUs), with tens of Teraflops throughput, often have enough processing power for real-time execution of such large neural networks. However, the power consumption of powerful GPUs (100–200 W) is far beyond the tight power budget of a typical embedded system. Even if dissipating 200 W in a self-driving car, which receives power from the car's battery, is not a serious issue, the cost of modern GPUs (>1000$) may be quite prohibitive.

Due to the limited computation capabilities and power budget of embedded and mobile edge devices, some deep learning-based services on such systems rely on cloud-centric architectures to offload deep learning tasks to cloud-side servers. This way, the raw or pre-processed data is sent to the cloud to be processed, and the results are sent back to the device. However, this model causes different problems like high latency, high energy consumption of continuous data transmission, loss of data privacy and security, and the need for an always-on network connection. Therefore, there is always a strong demand to move the deep learning execution to embedded devices to improve latency, power, and privacy issues.

Even for desktop and server computers that employ high-performance central processing units (CPUs) and GPUs with a larger power budget, running a large neural network with millions of neurons and several gigabytes of model parameters is a challenging task. In particular, power- and performance-efficient deep learning implementation in cloud-side servers is critical to reduce power delivery and cooling expenses, which constitute one of the largest components of the total cost of ownership (TCO).

To meet the excessive computational power demand of deep learning applications, the semiconductor industry has introduced deep learning hardware accelerators and domain-specific processors in recent years. These accelerators are special-purpose processors, in which the data path, instruction set, and register configuration are tailored to the specific processing requirements and dataflow model of neural networks. In this way, a customized processor can run neural networks with higher throughput and power efficiency than a general-purpose processor, where a piece of software code runs on a general-purpose architecture.

Starting from 2016, almost all major players in the semiconductor industry have fabricated their deep learning accelerators. The example deep learning processors include Google TPU, IBM TrueNorth, Nvidia Volta, AMD Radeon Instinct, Samsung M1, HiSilicon Kirin, Qualcomm Cloud-AI100, Intel Nervana, Intel EyeQ, Apple A12-Bionic, Huawei Ascend310, and Cadence C5, to name a few. There are also a stunning number of smaller companies and start-ups that design hardware and software solutions for deep learning.

The academic research follows the same trend as the industrial efforts, with a large body of research work targeting efficient hardware implementation for different deep learning models. This trend is reflected in the growing number of research papers on neural networks published in flagship conferences and journals in recent years.

This book provides an overview of the basic concepts and recent advances in some of the key deep learning hardware research areas.

The book is structured into five parts. Part I of the book contains three chapters to introduce the fundamental concepts of neural networks. This part first provides a background on the neural network concepts and models (Chapter 1) and then reviews in more detail some design issues of two important neural network classes, i.e., recurrent neural network (RNN) (Chapter 2) and feedforward (Chapter 3) models.

Part II has two chapters devoted to low-precision data representation for neural networks. The chapters review and introduce some state-of-the-art proposals to simplify neural network execution by using stochastic (Chapter 4) and binary (Chapter 5) data representations. The chapters show that due to their inherent error-tolerance property, neural networks experience negligible or sublinear accuracy degradation when these approximate data representations are employed.

In addition to error tolerance, recent hardware accelerators exploit some other interesting properties of the weights and intermediate activations of neural networks to boost performance and energy efficiency. High degree of weight and intermediate data sparsity is one of these properties that neural networks demonstrate. This property suggests that a considerable portion of neural network weights are very small, even equal to zero, or redundant. Furthermore, many intermediate data values propagated throughout the network during evaluation become zero. Part III of the book addresses this sparsity issue and its potential capabilities to simplify neural network models. It contains two chapters that first survey some effective techniques, from both software and hardware sides, to exploit model sparsity for efficient neural network implementation (Chapter 6), and then introduces in more detail a method that exploits redundant weight values to reduce neural network power consumption (Chapter 7). Convolutional neural network (CNN) is a very popular deep neural network model, which is primarily used for image processing. Part IV is devoted to hardware and software techniques for efficient CNN implementation in power-limited embedded systems. This part first introduces a novel field-programmable gate arrays (FPGA)-based architecture for embedded CNN implementation (Chapter 8). Chapter 9 shows how a large convolutional neural network can be broken into a sequence of smaller networks to reduce the model complexity and make it more amenable to hardware acceleration. The final part of the book, Part V, covers the emerging and ever-growing trend of accelerating neural networks on analog hardware. This part presents a mixed-signal neuromorphic platform for always-on biomedical signal processing (Chapter 10), followed by introducing novel mersister-based analog neural network architectures for IoT platforms (Chapter 11).

The rapidly expanding field of deep learning hardware is a popular research topic in electrical/computer engineering and computer science, appearing as part of the syllabus in undergraduate and postgraduate courses at many universities.

This book aims to complement the research and teaching and serve as a reference for researchers, postgraduate students, and engineers who work on learning-based services and hardware platforms.

Acknowledgments

First and foremost, we would like to thank all the contributing authors of this book who shared their knowledge and experience in their respective chapters.

We also acknowledge the financial support from the Swedish Foundation for International Cooperation in Research and Higher Education (STINT). The STINT's *Initiation Grant* program supported the mobility between our research groups and facilitated managing and developing this book.

Finally, we would like to thank the IET editors and production team for their continued assistance in managing the process of editing the book during this project.

Part I

Deep learning and neural networks: concepts and models

An introduction to artificial neural networks

Ahmad Kalhor[1]

In this chapter, an introduction to neural networks (NNs) with an emphasis on classification and regression applications is presented. In this chapter, some preliminaries about natural and artificial neural networks (ANNs) are introduced first. Then, by giving initial concepts about classification and regression problems, appropriate overall structures of ANNs for such applications are explained. The simple structures of NNs and their limitations as well as some more powerful multilayer and deep learning models are introduced in the next part of this chapter. Finally, convolutional NNs and some of their well-known developments are briefly explained.

1.1 Introduction

A conventional computing paradigm solves a problem by an algorithmic way, in which programs provide every step that had to be taken, in the form of deterministic algorithms, to carry out the tasks. In some domains, however, designing an explicit algorithm is not always possible (or is very difficult), particularly when system has to deal with situations and data that did not fit within the explicit parameters provided by the programmers (e.g., for recognizing emotions or answering new questions). Machine learning is a subset of artificial intelligence that actually takes the way in which our brain solves these problems: learn to solve a problem by analyzing training examples. It trains a machine how to perform a particular task using large amounts of data and routines that provide the ability to learn from the data. Deep learning is a subset of machine learning that uses deep NNs to solve complex problems.

A NN is a set of simple processing units, called neurons, that are arranged in multiple layers, through which a desired outputs result is generated from exogenous or stimulating inputs. Figure 1.1 shows a simple diagram of a NN.

1.1.1 Natural NNs

NNs have been emerged naturally in the body of animals to provide their perception from the environment and to learn to take appropriate reactions against external

[1]School of Electrical and Computer Engineering, University of Tehran, Tehran, Iran

Figure 1.1   A simple diagram of a NN as a set of wired neurons in layers

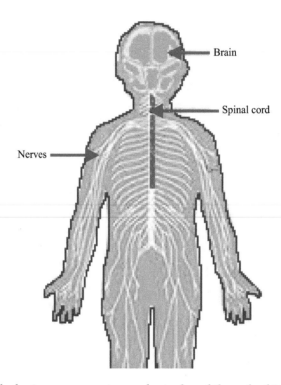

*Figure 1.2   The brain, nervous system and spinal cord through which the
intelligence of a creature emerges*

stimuli. Such networks are the source of the intelligence, through which creatures
can understand the outside world, make their habitation, and take suitable reactions
in the environment. To answer an important question that how such intelligence
emerges, biologists and scientists have discovered, and still exploring, the brain,
nervous system, and spinal cord (Figure 1.2).

They have continuously developed their knowledge about the nervous systems.
Neuroscientists currently research about the structure and function of the brain to

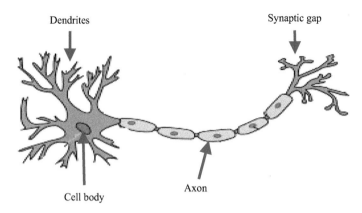

Figure 1.3   Structure of a nerve cell (neuron) including dendrites, cell body, axon, cell nucleus and synaptic gap

find out how the human brain models and learns the real world. Figure 1.3 shows the structure of a nerve cell, or neuron, which includes dendrites, cell body, axon, cell nucleus, and synaptic gaps [1].

A certain neuron includes plenty of dendrites that absorb the incoming electro-chemical signals from adjacent neurons and accumulate them within its cell body. In the kernel of the cell, the accumulated signal will be compared with a threshold and if it is bigger than the threshold, it will activate. By neuron activation, it spikes and sends a chemical signal to adjacent neurons through the axon. A synaptic gap plays an important role in giving weights to the transformed signal between the axons and dendrites of connected neurons.

There are three types of neurons in the nervous system. *Sensory* neurons get information about what is going on inside and outside of the body and bring that information into the central nervous system (CNS), so as to be processed by the neural system. *Interneurons* connect one neuron to another and are found only in the CNS. Most of the interneurons are in the brain. *Motor* neurons get information from other neurons and convey commands to the muscles, organs, and glands.

We can consider an input–output layer-based structure between the input data (stimulus) received by the input sensory neurons (input layer) and the data generated by motor neurons (output layer), the set of interneurons from the hidden layers. Figure 1.4 shows a simplified input–output scheme of a nervous system.

The NN is the source of some imperative learning capabilities in the human body. The humankind can learn to classify all different types of signals received from their senses including visual (seeing), auditory (hearing), tactile (touch), gustatory (taste), olfactory (smell), vestibular (movement), and proprioceptive (body awareness). They can make long and short memories about different events and senses that they have experienced or learned in the past. They can provide skills to do different complicated tasks and actions, which they have learned or experienced.

Perhaps the computational intelligence, including logic, mathematics, and inference, is the most significant exclusive capability of the human's NN.

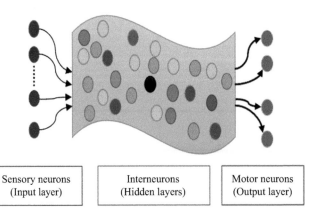

| Sensory neurons (Input layer) | Interneurons (Hidden layers) | Motor neurons (Output layer) |

Figure 1.4 An input–output model for the human nervous system

There are some interesting facts about the brain. There are about 100 billion neurons in a normal human brain with about 100 trillion total connections that give 1,000 connections for each neuron, on average. The learning processes and the interconnections among neurons are mainly due to the functionality of synaptic gaps. The communication speed (electrochemical signal transition) for each neuron is low but since the communications are done massively and in parallel, the total processing speed of the brain is high. The robustness of the natural NNs is high in learning and even if some parts of the brain damaged, the learning and inference processes will proceed. Due to high-level abstraction and inference in the brain, its generalization is high.

1.1.2 Artificial neural networks

Inspired by natural NNs, from the beginning of the twentieth century, scientists and engineers have intended to design ANNs in order to provide solutions for challenging and real-world problems in the same way as the human brain operates. These efforts led to the emergence of ANNs.

The range of engineering or nonengineering problems solved by ANNs has been continually increased through time. Among different applications, classification and regression are more investigated by ANNs. Classification and categorizing different objects, images, texts, speeches, signatures, videos, and so forth are performed appropriately by ANNs. Fault detection in industrial systems and fraud and anomaly detection in social and finance systems are critical examples of classification problems that are efficiently solved by ANNs. In regression problems, function approximation, simulation of natural and cosmic phenomena, time series prediction, signal recovery and repair are some examples that can be solved by NNs.

Some application classes are developed through memory NNs: identification by biometric signals, character recognition, machine translation, word prediction in a writing or speech process, walking and moving modeling, training social robots to interact with the environment, image captioning, and enriching video or image with descriptions. Besides supervised applications, there are some unsupervised applications which are developed by mechanism-based NNs. The basic applications include pattern optimization, pattern clustering, and pattern sorting and pattern generation. These solutions are used in noise cancellation, super-resolution techniques, and recommender systems, to name a few.

1.1.3 Preliminary concepts in ANNs

In this section, some initial important concepts in ANNs are explained. At first, a simple mathematical model of a biological neuron is introduced. Then, some frequently used activation functions, feedforward, recurrent NNs, and supervised and unsupervised learning approaches in ANN are introduced.

1.1.3.1 Mcculloch and Pitz neuron

Here, a simple mathematical model of a biological neuron, which was proposed by McCulloch and Walter Pitz in 1943, is introduced. This model, referred to as M&P hereinafter, is inspired from the biological neuron. As explained earlier, a biological neuron becomes active when the sum of weighted inputs is greater than a threshold. Figure 1.5 shows a diagram of M&P neuron.

The following equation shows the relation between the output of the neuron and the stimulating inputs $\{x_i\}_{i=1}^n$:

$$y_{in} = w_1x_1 + w_2x_2 + \ldots + w_nx_n$$
$$y = f(y_{in}) = \begin{cases} 1 & y_{in} \geq \theta \\ 0 & y_{in} < \theta \end{cases} \tag{1.1}$$

where $\{w_i\}_{i=1}^n$ denotes the weights of inputs and θ denotes the threshold according to which the neuron becomes active or inactive. The suggested activation function in an M&P neuron is a conditional step function with binary outputs. Another representation for the M&P is shown in Figure 1.6, with the corresponding input–output relation presented by (1.2):

$$y_{in} = w_1x_1 + w_2x_2 + \ldots + w_nx_n + b$$
$$y = f(y_{in}) = \begin{cases} 1 & y_{in} \geq 0 \\ 0 & y_{in} < 0 \end{cases} \tag{1.2}$$

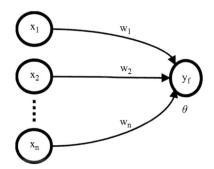

Figure 1.5   A diagram of M&P neuron

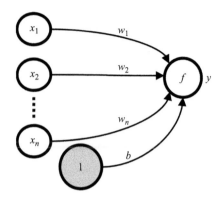

Figure 1.6   A generalized form of M&P neuron

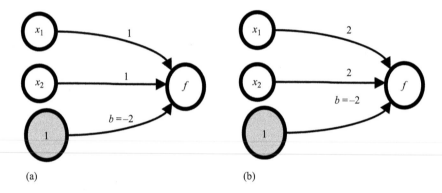

(a)   (b)

Figure 1.7   Two M&P neurons which represent "AND" and "OR" logic gates in (a) and (b), respectively

In the new representation, the threshold parameter is considered as a new weight ($b = \theta$), which is called the bias parameter. Actually, in the new form of an M&P neuron, the parameter of the activation function can be learned in much the same way as the other weight parameters.

Using suitable weights and threshold (bias), an M&P neuron can represent the operations of some simple logic gates. Figure 1.7 shows how the "AND" and "OR" logic gates are produced.

To model logic gates, the input must be applied to the network in the binary or bipolar formats. It has been shown that by using a sufficient number of M&P neurons, large circuits (with many logic gates) can be modeled and the reactions of natural NNs against environment stimulations can be mimicked [2].

1.1.3.2   Widely used activation functions

Each node (neuron) in an ANN has an activation function by which the final output of the neuron for a given sum of weighted inputs is calculated. Inspiring from biological

Table 1.1   Some typical activation functions used in ANN

Name	Plot	Equation	Derivative (with respect to x)	Range
Identity		$f(x) = x$	$f'(x) = 1$	$(-\infty, +\infty)$
Binary step		$f(x) = \begin{cases} 0 & \text{for } x < 0 \\ 1 & \text{for } x \geq 0 \end{cases}$	Non-derivable	$\{0, 1\}$
Bipolar step		$f(x) = \begin{cases} -1 & \text{for } x < 0 \\ 1 & \text{for } x \geq 0 \end{cases}$	Non-derivable	$\{-1, 1\}$
Logistic (soft binary step)		$f(x) = \dfrac{1}{1 + e^{-x}}$	$f'(x) - f(x)(1 - f(x))$	$(0, +1)$
tan H (soft bipolar step)		$f(x) = \dfrac{e^x - e^{-x}}{e^x + e^{-x}}$	$f'(x) = 1 - f(x)^2$	$(-1, +1)$
Rectified linear unit (ReLU)		$f(x) = \begin{cases} 0 & \text{for } x < 0 \\ x & \text{for } x \geq 0 \end{cases}$	$f(x) = \begin{cases} 0 & \text{for } x < 0 \\ 1 & \text{for } x \geq 0 \end{cases}$	$[0, +\infty)$

neurons, the activation function causes a neuron spike while the sum of weighted stimulation inputs is bigger than a threshold. Some crisp or soft step functions such as binary or bipolar steps or soft steps such as logistic or bipolar sigmoid function can provide such responses. Table 1.1 presents some typical activation functions utilized in neurons.

1.1.3.3   Feedforward and recurrent architectures in ANN

Depending on the data that passes from the input layer to the output layer (through the hidden layers), ANNs are categorized into two groups: (1) feedforward NNs and (2) recurrent NNs (RNNs). In feedforward networks, data moves in the forward direction from the input layer to the output layer and connections between the nodes do not form a cycle. In such architectures, each output is a static function of the inputs. In RNNs, at least in one node (i.e., a neuron in a layer), the data returns to the same neuron or to a neuron in the previous layers. To allow feedback, RNNs have a notion of time: for some nodes, the input at time step t depends on an output from

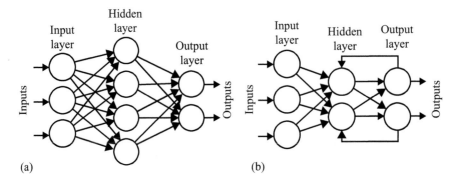

Figure 1.8   Two examples of (a) feedforward and (b) recurrent networks

time step $t - 1$. These networks, by providing nonhomogeneous nonlinear difference equations among inputs, outputs and hidden states, provide the required complexity for memory-based applications. This feature enables them to learn and predict the dynamic behavior of nonlinear complicated systems. Figure 1.8 displays the general structure of (a) feedforward and (b) recurrent NNs.

1.1.3.4   Supervised and unsupervised learning in ANN

In order to learn an ANN for a target application, the parameters, i.e., weights and bias values, and hyper-parameters, including the number of layers and neurons, the type of activation functions, the type of the network (feedforward or recurrent) should be specified and optimized during a learning or training procedure.

There are two general approaches to learn NNs. In the supervised learning approach, for each explicit or implicit training input data, the corresponding output is also provided. In this model, the outputs generated by the network should make high equivalency with the golden output. In such problems, after considering a good initial architecture for the network and an appropriate loss function for the output quality, the parameters are adjusted in such a way that the loss function becomes minimized. For this purpose, plenty of learning strategies, including local search methods (such as various versions of the gradient descent method) and intelligent or evolutionary-based global search methods (such as simulated annealing or genetic algorithms) have been suggested.

In contrast, in the unsupervised learning approach, there is no target output for the training data. In fact, it is not known exactly that the outputs of the network must converge to which targets. However, it is desired that the generated outputs satisfy some geometric or statistical properties, defined by the designer. Usually, in unsupervised learning problems, updating rules come from a predesigned mechanism. Figure 1.9 outlines the supervised and unsupervised learning strategies.

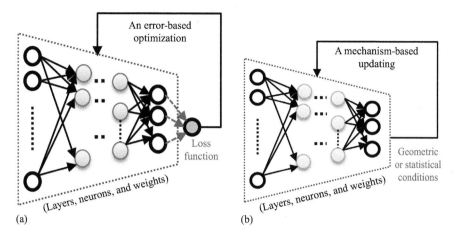

Figure 1.9   Diagrams for two learning strategies: (a) supervised learning and (b) unsupervised learning

1.2   ANNs in classification and regression problems

In this section, after giving some concepts about classification and regression problems, the required structure of ANN, for such applications, is explained.

1.2.1   ANNs in classification problems

Classification is the process of identifying to which set of classes a new object belongs. When applying ANNs to a classification problem, it is desired to learn network in such a way that it assigns each new input pattern, x to its corresponding target class label, $l(x)$. In supervised learning, the learning is done by a training set of data containing objects whose class membership is known.

In real-world classification problems, there are various disturbances, nullities, and distortions in input patterns. Thus, it is essential that the input space (x) is transferred to an effective feature space, $z(x)$ where the undesirable nullities, disturbances, and distortions are removed. In an effective feature space, the feature points of each class are expected to be within a close proximity and separated (and far enough) from feature points of other classes. By carrying out the partitioning task based on the patterns of the classes, feature points of each class will be located in one or more separated certain regions, and hence the target labels can be generated. Consequently, a NN carries out classification in two steps: feature extraction and partitioning. Figure 1.10 shows a diagram for such a network applied to classification problems.

Figure 1.11 shows a two-dimensional (2D) illustrative example indicating how a NN solves a classification problem. As Figure 1.11 indicates, at the entrance of the network, Q feature points with different labels (indicated by stars, bullets, and squares)

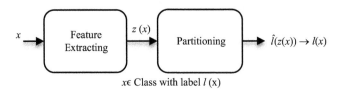

Figure 1.10   *Classification steps by NNs*

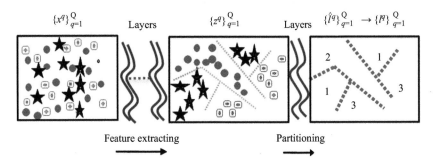

Figure 1.11   *An illustrative example that shows how a NN acts in a classifying process*

are in causal positions. However, by designing an appropriate feature extraction part, including a sufficient number of layers, the feature points with the same labels come closer and lie in some local regions in the feature space. Now, by using the partitioning part, the target labels are revealed at the output.

1.2.2   ANNs in regression problems

In statistical modeling, regression analysis is a set of statistical processes for estimating the relationships among variables and between the input variables and the function output. Actually, in applying an ANN to a regression problem, it is desired that the network be learned by a supervised learning approach in order to map the input space (x) to its target value, $y(x)$. However, similar to the classification problems, the input space (x) is required to be transferred to an ineffective feature space, $z(x)$, where nullities, disturbances, and distortions of the input patterns are removed. It is expected that by providing the effective feature space, the target outputs (y) make a smooth and valid map on $z(x)$. After feature extraction, in the second part, the feature space, z, is mapped to $\widehat{y}(z(x))$ which has high equivalency with the target output ($y(x)$). Figure 1.12 shows these steps.

Figure 1.13 shows a 2D illustrative example that explains how a NN solves a regression problem.

As shown in Figure 1.13, Q feature points are intake initially. From the initial disturbed input space and by designing an appropriate "feature extraction" methods,

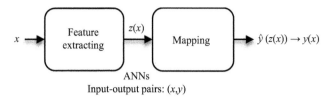

Figure 1.12   *A simple diagram of a NN applied in a regression problem*

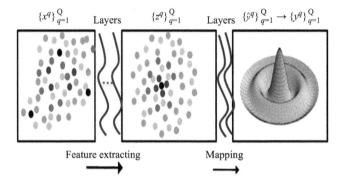

Figure 1.13   *An illustrative example that shows how a NN acts in a regression process*

an effective feature space is obtained. It is expected that by designing an appropriate mapping part, a regression function with sufficient degree of smoothness and equivalency with the target samples is obtained.

1.2.3 Relation between classification and regression

By imposing some constraints, a regression problem can be converted to a classification problem. Actually, by quantizing the output of a regression problem and considering each quantized level as an individual class (while there is no nearness among different classes), a regression problem is represented as a classification problem. Assume that the output of the regression function is scalar, and consider that $y_{\min}$ and $y_{\sup}$ denote the minimum and the supremum of the output, respectively. The output can be quantized to n_C sequenced levels with equal distance $\rho = (y_{\max} - y_{\min})/n_C$. Consequently, each output y^q can be indicated by label $l^q \in \{1, 2, \ldots, n_C\}$, which is computed as

$$l^q = \text{label}(y^q) \quad \text{if} \quad y_{\min} + (l^q - 1)\rho \leq y^q < y_{\min} + l^q \tag{1.3}$$

Figure 1.14 shows a simple example where the real output signal (dot line) has been quantized into $n_c = 5$ levels (solid line). From Figure 1.14, it is understood that the classification problem converges to a regression problem if $n_C \to \infty$.

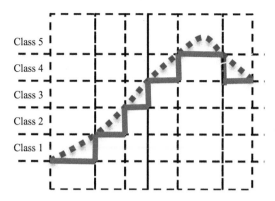

Figure 1.14   A quantized regression problem by $n_c = 5$ levels

1.3   Widely used NN models

In this section, well-known and widely used NN models are introduced and their potentials and limitations are discussed.

1.3.1   Simple structure networks

A simple structure network is a network without any hidden layers. The activation functions of the output neurons are bipolar or binary step functions. Actually, a simple structure network can include a set of modified M&P neurons having equal number of inputs. Figure 1.15 shows a simple structure network with one M&P neuron, where the input–output function of the network is defined as

$$y_{in} = \sum_{i=1}^{n} w_i x_i + b \quad y = f(y_{in}) = \begin{cases} 1 & y_{in} \geq 0 \\ 0 \, (or - 1) & y_{in} < 0 \end{cases} \tag{1.4}$$

Since the simple network structure does not provide enough high complexity, it cannot be used for feature extracting purposes in a classification problem. However, considering the sign of y_{in} as the equation of a hyperplane, in (2.2), each M&P neuron can partition the input (n-dimensional) space into two parts. Therefore, simple structure networks can be used for patriating purposes. Figure 1.16 shows a simple 2D illustrative example where a simple structure network by specifying a line in the 2D space has separated circles and triangle patterns.

Generally, simple structure networks are capable to perform the classification problems, when all patterns with equal labels are linearly separable. In this way, if the number of classes is more than 1, an individual M&P neuron is required for each output class. There are several learning methods for this class of NNs. Table 1.2 summarizes these methods and outlines their convergence and generalization properties.

"Hebb Net" uses a modified version of the earliest and simplest learning rule, which was proposed by Donald Hebb in natural NNs [3]. Although this learning rule is important in studying natural NNs, it practically works in a few examples.

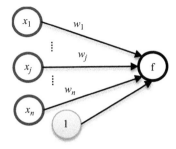

Figure 1.15   A simple structure network with one M&P neuron

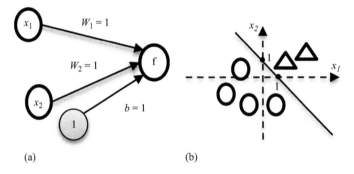

(a)   (b)

Figure 1.16   A simple structure network that (a) by making a line separates circles and (b) triangle patterns

Table 1.2   Some learning methods for simple structure networks

Network	Learning method	Convergence	Generalization
Hebb Net [3]	Hebb rule	No	No
Perceptron [4, 5]	Perceptron rule	Yes	No
Adaline [6]	Delta rule (least mean square)	Conditional*	Conditional*

* If pattern distribution of two classes is similar in shape and density

The Perceptron rule is one of the common methods in learning simple structure networks and is backed by a convergence theorem that shows a separable hyperplane between patterns of a certain class and other classes will be found in a limited number updating rule iterations [4, 5], provided that they are linearly separable. However, its drawback is that it stops by finding any separable hyperplane, so it cannot maximize the margins of the separating hyperplane with training patterns. Therefore, its generalization for new patterns is not guaranteed. Adaline (adaptive linear neuron) is another suggested method to tune parameters of a simple structure network [6]. This method minimizes the square error between the target labels of each pattern and the arguments of neurons. Adaline finds a separating hyperplane between the patterns of two classes, when their pattern distributions are similar in shape and density.

1.3.2   *Multilayer and deep NNs*

Simple structure networks cannot offer any solution for the challenges and constraints of real-world classification or regression problems. Some major challenges are:

- Patterns of each class are not necessarily linearly separable from patterns of other classes. In this case, the patterns are localized in some convex- or non-convex-shaped regions.
- The dimension of many real-world input patterns is high and there are nonlinear correlations among them.
- In real-world input patterns, there are plenty of disturbances with different scales
- The input patterns of the same class have distortions in size, shape, position, and perspective.
- In some cases when there are certain sequences between input patterns, the applied input itself may not be sufficient to determine the output of the network and it is necessary to consider former input patterns for getting the right output.

The above-mentioned challenges render the input patterns insufficient for the partitioning and mapping purposes, and hence the NN must have a feature extraction part before any partitioning or mapping. This requirement led to the emergence of multilayer NNs and deep learning NNs.

1.3.2.1   Multilayer perceptron

To handle the case when the class patterns are not linearly separable, it is required to add one or two hidden layers to the NN. Actually, adding one hidden layer provides the required complexity to generate the label of patterns of a class, which are localized in a convex-shaped region. Furthermore, adding two hidden layers enables the network to generate label for patterns that are localized in a non-convex-shaped region or some isolated local regions. Figure 1.17 shows two ANNs with one hidden layer and two hidden layers.

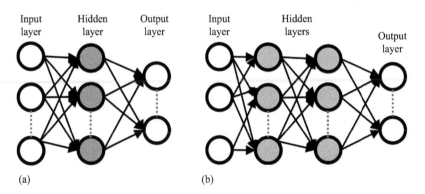

Figure 1.17   ANNs with (a) one hidden layer and (b) two hidden layers

To learn such networks, the former learning rules (developed for simple structure networks) cannot be applied for this model. For this purpose, it has been shown that applying gradient-based methods (e.g., error back propagation [7]) or evolutionary-based methods (such as genetic algorithms [8]) can train the network appropriately. In gradient-based methods, it is essential to use derivable activation functions such as bipolar or binary sigmoid functions.

1.3.2.2 Autoencoders and stacked RBMs

To handle the case when there are correlations among different dimensions of the input patterns, it is required that the network encodes input patterns to some space with a sufficiently lower dimension. In certain cases, if the dimension reduction is not applied, the partitioning and mapping of the input patterns may suffer from overfitting and the network misses its generalization for new incoming patterns. Autoencoder networks [9] and stacked restricted Boltzmann machine (RBM) [10] are two networks with the data-encoding capability. In these networks, in order to remove correlations, a variant of nonlinear principal component analysis (PCA, [11]) is performed, where the nullity spaces are removed to get a maximum variance space. Figure 1.18 shows a diagram of a typical autoencoder.

In the autoencoder model, the network includes two sequenced parts: encoding and decoding. The encoding part performs the dimension reduction. The decoding part is added to reconstruct the former inserted patterns and ensure that no information from input patterns is lost due to encoding.

Another alternative network for dimension reduction is RBM. An RBM is a simple two-layered network (including visible and hidden layers) by which an encoding algorithm is performed. The model RBM is trained in a bidirectional state. Actually, the given input pattern (as a visible layer) should make a hidden layer with a lower dimension that can retrieve the initial input pattern. By stacking some sequenced RMBs, the dimension of the input patterns is reduced accordingly [12]. Figure 1.19 shows a sample RBMs encoding flow.

To train autoencoders in an unsupervised manner, the encoding and decoding parts are trained first. Then, the encoding part is added to a partitioning or mapping

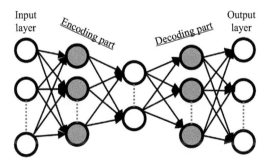

Figure 1.18   Diagram of an autoencoder network with encoding and decoding parts

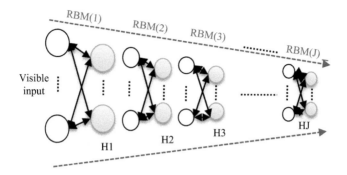

Figure 1.19   Diagram of some stacked RBM

part. The new network can be trained in a supervised manner for a classification or regression problem. Such a learning procedure can be utilized for stacked RBMs, too. However, to train stacked RBMs, each RBM should be trained independently from the previously trained RBMs. Then, after a sufficient number of stacked RBMs, they can be added to a partitioning or mapping part for classification or regression problems, respectively.

Deep-belief NNs are one of the most widely used examples of ANNs which use autoencoders or stacked RBMs for classification or regression problems [13].

1.3.2.3   Convolutional neural networks

In many challenging classification and regression problems, particularly in classifying different categories of images and speech signals, there are different sources of disturbance and distortions in input patterns. To have a successful classification or regression in such cases, the deeper networks with many hidden layers are required. Actually, the newly adding layers in the networks should act as a variant nonlinear filter, which can remove all disturbances and distortions from input patterns. Convolutional neural networks (CNNs) are successful networks that have been developed to achieve this goal [14,15]. Actually, CNNs by presenting a sufficient number of convolutional layers allow passing frequent patterns from small to large kernel sizes. In this model, each convolution layer, by considering some shared-weight filters and applying "ReLU" activation functions, makes new feature maps from feature maps of the preceding layer. In addition to convolution layers, CNNs use pooling layers to reduce the size of feature maps. The role of pooling layers is to remove different distortions from input patterns and to provide more scaled feature space with a sufficiently low dimension. Actually, a pooling layer subsamples the feature maps provided by convolutional layers. In CNNs, the number of convolutional or pooling layers may exceed 100 layers. Figure 1.20 shows a diagram of a CNN including one convolutional, one pooling, and two fully connected layers.

To learn CNNs, the error backpropagation method is used. To have successful training and generalization, some learning tricks and technique, such as using

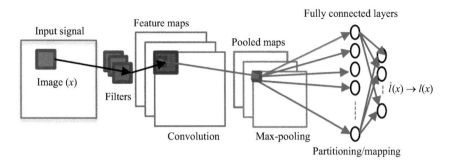

Figure 1.20   Diagram of a CNN including convolutional, pooling, and fully connected layer

stochastic mini-batch gradient approach, batch normalization, and drop out, are utilized.

1.3.2.4   Recurrent neural networks

In some applications, such as language modeling, word prediction, speech recognition, translation machines, and time series prediction, the sequence at which the input patterns are received is important and should be considered to solve the problem. For such applications, a memory is implemented in the NN by adding some layers and also modifying the direction of the data flow inside the network. These modifications led to the emergence of RNNs. Actually, a nonlinear difference equation is trained on a RNN that can convey the effects of former related patterns in the output.

RNNs and their hardware implementation issues will be introduced in more detail in Chapter 2.

The classic RNN models, however, suffer from the problem of vanishing gradient, so cannot keep long-term memory [16]. To address this issue, the long short-term memory (LSTM) modules is designed to convey effective information from previous steps by (1) providing an information belt within recurrent units and (2) adding some special gates to the model [16]. Gated recurrent unit (GRU) module is another successful network that implements the LSTM functionality with less number of gates [17]. Figure 1.21 shows the diagrams of the (a) classic RNN, (b) LSTM, and (c) GRU models

As shown in Figure 1.21(a), in a simple RNN module, the input and the former outputs of the module are concatenated to generate the outputs of the module. For the other two models, as shown in Figure 1.21(b) and (c), the network structure is more complex, containing more interconnected layers and switching gates. Such complex structures allow establishing long-term dependency between former inputs and the current output. To learn the RNN, the network should be unfolded in time to get an equivalent feedforward NN. Error backpropagation through time (BPTT) is the most widely used training method for RNNs [18].

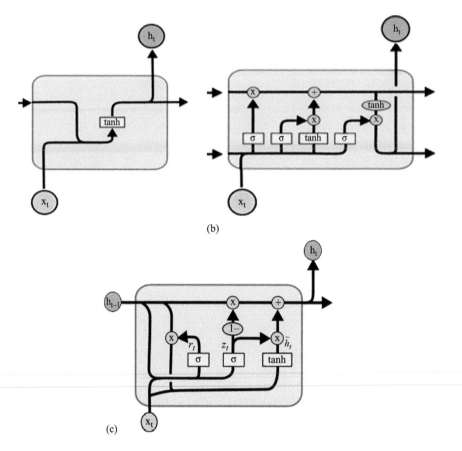

Figure 1.21   Diagrams of (a) classic RNN, (b) LSTM, and (c) GRU modules

1.4   Convolutional neural networks

CNNs, as the heart of many image and speech processing applications, have attracted considerable attention in recent years. This model can filter various disturbances and reduce distortions by applying a sequence of convolutional and pooling layers.

In many real-world patterns, the effective features are a highly nonlinear transformation from their original unique form. For example, in classification of objects in an optic image, the effective features of objects (e.g., cars and trees) have different sizes, colors, textures, positions, and perspectives. In addition, different backgrounds, nonrelevant objects, and different intensities of the light make the problem even more difficult. These disturbances and distortions make the patterns of cars and trees absolutely nonseparable in the vector space. To address this issue, the convolutional and pooling layers of CNNs perform a sequence of filtering and scaling tasks on effective features. Eventually, a new space of features formed in which the vectors of different objects (e.g., cars and trees) are separable and by using one or two dense layers (fully connected layers), the feature space is partitioned (or mapped) and the desired labels (or target map) are revealed in a classification (or regression) problem.

In the following sections, we briefly explain the structure of the convolutional and pooling layers and introduce some successful CNN implementations. Some more CNN examples and explanations can be found in Chapters 8 and 9.

1.4.1 Convolution layers

Convolution in CNN is a variant of convolution operation in the LTI systems. Here, the convolution of a patch of the input signal (x) through a filter with parameters (w, b) is defined as follows:

$$z = f\,(x.w + b) \tag{1.5}$$

where b denotes the filter scalar bias w denotes the main parameter of the filter, and f denotes a nonlinear activation function such as ReLU. Actually, after appropriate learning on the filters, such operation can amplify all relevant patches and remove nonrelevant ones. By repeating the above procedure on a set of chosen patches on the initial signal, a feature map is extracted.

CNNs select patches by swiping through different dimensions of the signal by a certain step (stride) and putting the generated units in a position corresponded to the initial spatial position of the patch. Figure 1.22 shows the diagrams of a convolution operation on a 6 ∗ 6 2D signal by a 3 ∗ 3 filter with the stride of 1. Figure 1.23 shows how the set of patches is chosen by swiping on the whole signal.

By defining more filters in a convolutional layer, more feature maps are extracted from the input. Figure 1.24 shows how a 2D $a * b$ input signal is convolved by four, $c * l$ filters to generate four $(a - c + 1) * (b - l + 1)$ feature maps (stride=1).

This 2D convolution operation can be generalized to signals with different dimensions: one-dimensional signals such as time series or three-dimensional signals such as colored images or multichannel images.

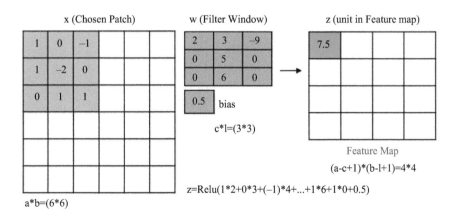

*Figure 1.22   Diagrams of convolution through a 3*3 filter on a 6*6 signal by stride 1*

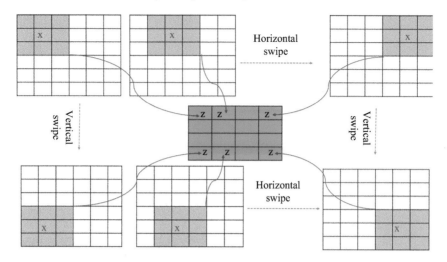

Figure 1.23   Diagrams showing how the patches are chosen by swiping on the two dimensions of the input signal

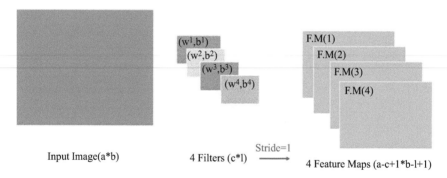

Figure 1.24   Diagrams show that by applying four filters, four feature maps are generated from a 2D signal

1.4.2   Pooling layers

According to the special convolution model, presented in the previous section, neighboring cells of the output feature map have some shared information from the input. Consequently, the feature maps can be subsampled to reduce their size and also get some degrees of disturbance rejection. This subsampling procedure is done by pooling layers. In a pooling operation on an $a*b$ feature map, the feature map is first partitioned into multiple tiled rectangles of size $c*d$ and each tile is replaced by a single value in the output. The output value can take the maximum value of the tile (Max-pooling) or the mean value across all cells of the tile (Mean-pooling). This way,

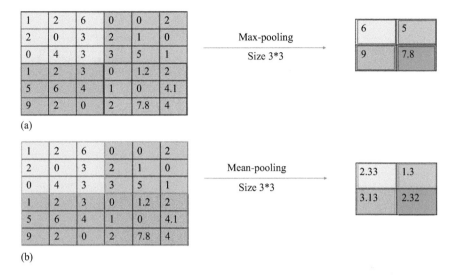

Figure 1.25   Operation of (a) Max-pooling and (b) Mean-pooling, both of which have been applied to a 2D signal

a new feature map of size ($[a/c]*[d/b]$) is generated which is evidently smaller than the input. Figure 1.25 shows how "Max-pooling" and "Mean-pooling" on a 6*6 image with the tile size of 3*3 can reduce the feature map size.

It is shown that by using pooling layers, the data is encoded to space with smaller size and the network becomes more tolerant to the distortion of the input signal.

1.4.3   Learning in CNNs

Like other classification and regression networks, a CNN consists of two major parts: sequenced convolutional and pooling layers for feature extraction, and one or two fully connected layers for partitioning or mapping purpose. In the learning process of a CNN, the number of convolution and pooling layers and their parameters, as well as the number of fully connected layers and the neuron weights are set and adjusted.

In an appropriately designed and learned CNN, the sequencing of the convolutional and pooling layers removes the disturbances and reduces the distortions gradually from lower scales to higher scales. For example, in a typical image classification CNN, the former convolutional and pooling layers detect, scale, and extract edges and corners but the latter convolutional and pooling layers detect scale sub-skeletons with various sizes. Such sub-skeletons are frequent in different classes and finally they will be revealed as the main features. For instance, Figure 1.26 shows a CNN that categorizes various images of cars. A set of scaled sub-skeletons of wheels, windows, copouts, and so on comprises the effective features. Next, the fully connected layers partition the feature space to classify objects or generate the desired output in regression problems.

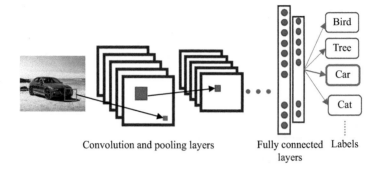

Figure 1.26   An example of image classification by a CNN

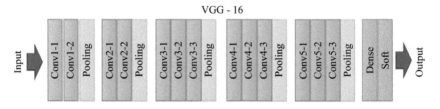

Figure 1.27   Structure of "VGG 16" network

A typical training algorithm for CNNs defines a loss function (e.g., mean squared error or cross entropy), and then minimizes it in order to get equivalency between the outputs generated by the network and the golden target outputs. For this purpose, different gradient and error backpropagation methods have been introduced. In addition, to overcome some drawbacks of the gradient methods, such as stuck in local optimal points and sensitivity to initial values, plenty of techniques, such as regulation, stochastic gradient through mini batch data sets, batch normalization, and dropout, have been developed. These methods also help to increase the generalization of CNNs.

1.4.4   CNN examples

AlexNet is one of the most well-known CNN models. It was introduced in 2012 and was first to achieve a top-5 classification error rate of 15.4%. The network is made up of five convolutional, Max-pooling, and dropout layers, and three fully connected layers. It applies ReLU for the nonlinearity functions. The network was designed for classification with 1,000 possible categories. AlexNet was trained on ImageNet data with about 15 million images by total of 22,000 categories.

VGGNet is another successful CNN implementation introduced in 2014 [19]. It uses 19 CNN layers with 3*3 filters and the stride and pad of 1, along with 2*2 Max-pooling layers with stride 2. Figure 1.27 shows the structure of the shortened version of VGGNet.

GoogleNet was introduced in 2015 [20]. It was designed after the idea that CNN layers should not necessarily be stacked up sequentially. The GoogleNet designers showed that a creative structure of layers may give better performance than the baseline stacked models. GoogleNet adds 1*1 convolutional operations before the 3*3 and 5*5 layers. The 1*1 convolutions (or network in network layer) provide a method of dimension reduction. It uses nine inception modules in the whole architecture, with over 100 layers in total. Using an average-pooling approach, GoogleNet eliminates the fully connected layers. With these innovations, GoogleNet has $12\times$ fewer parameters than AlexNet.

Residual neural network (ResNet) is a 152-layer network, which was introduced in 2015, and set new records in classification, detection, and localization accuracy [21]. Using residual blocks, ResNet features a novel architecture with "skip connections" and heavy batch normalization.

1.5 Conclusion

In this chapter, an introduction to the NNs with emphasis on the classification and regression problems was presented. At first, natural and ANNs were introduced and then appropriate structures of ANNs in classification and regression problems were explained. Next, simple structure NNs and their restrictions were explained and then some developed multilayer and deep learning NNs were introduced. At the end, the emerging CNN model and some well-known CNN structures were explained briefly.

References

[1] K. Gurney, *An Introduction to Neural Networks*, Routledge: CRC Press; 1st edition, 1997.

[2] L. Fausett, *Fundamentals of Neural Networks: Architectures, Algorithms, and Applications*, Pearson; 1st edition, 1993.

[3] J. L. McClelland and D. E. Rumelhart, *Computational Models of Cognition and Perception. Explorations in Parallel Distributed Processing: A Handbook of Models, Programs, and Exercises*, MIT Press, Cambridge, MA, 1988.

[4] F. Rosenblatt, *Principles of Neurodynamics; Perceptrons and the Theory of Brain Mechanisms*, Spartan Books, Washington, 1962.

[5] M. L. Minsky and S. A. Papert, *Perceptrons*, MIT Press, Cambridge; expanded edition, 1988.

[6] B. Widrow and M. E. Hoff, Jr., "Adaptive switching circuits," *IRE WESCON Convention Record*, 4: 9–104, 1960.

[7] D. E. Rumelhart, G. E. Hinton, and R. J. Williams, "Learning representations by back-propagating errors," *Nature*, 323 (6088): 53–536, 1986.

[8] A. E. Eiben and J. E. Smith, *Introduction to Evolutionary Computing*, Vol. 53. Springer, Heidelberg, 2003.

[9] G. E. Hinton and R. S. Zemel, "Autoencoders, minimum description length, and Helmholtz free energy," *NIPS'93 Proceedings of the 6th International Conference on Neural Information Processing Systems*, Pages 3–10, 1993.

[10]   C.-Y. Liou, J.-C. Huang, and W.-C. Yang, "Modeling word perception using the Elman network," *Neurocomputing*, 71 (16–18): 3150, 2008.

[11]   H. Abdi and L. J. Williams, "Principal component analysis," *Wiley Interdisciplinary Reviews: Computational Statistics*, 2 (4): 433–459, 2010.

[12]   G. E. Hinton and R. R. Salakhutdinov, "Reducing the dimensionality of data with neural networks," *Science*, 313 (5786): 50–507, 2006.

[13]   G. E. Hinton, "Deep belief networks," *Scholarpedia*, 4 (5): 5947, 2009.

[14]   K. Fukushima, "Neocognitron," *Scholarpedia*, 2 (1): 1717, 2007.

[15]   A. Krizhevsky, I. Sutskever, and G. E. Hinton, "ImageNet classification with deep convolutional neural networks," *Advances in Neural Information Processing Systems*, 1097–1105, 2012.

[16]   S. Hochreiter and J. Schmidhuber, "Long short-term memory," *Neural Computation*, 9 (8): 1735–1780, 1997.

[17]   R. Dey and F. M. Salem, "Gate-variants of gated recurrent unit (GRU) neural networks," arXiv:1701.05923 [cs.NE], 2017.

[18]   M. C. Mozer, "A focused backpropagation algorithm for temporal pattern recognition," *Complex Systems*, 3: 34–381, 1989.

[19]   O. Russakovsky, J. Deng, H. Su *et al.*, "ImageNet large scale visual recognition challenge," *International Journal of Computer Vision*, 115: 21–252, 2015.

[20]   C. Szegedy, W. Liu, Y. Jia *et al.*, "Going deeper with convolutions," arXiv:1409.4842 [cs.CV], 2014.

[21]   K. He, X. Zhang, S. Ren, and J. Sun, "Deep residual learning for image recognition," arXiv:1512.03385 [cs.CV], 2015.

Chapter 2

Hardware acceleration for recurrent neural networks

Sima Sinaei[1] and Masoud Daneshtalab[1]

Sequence learning refers to an important subset of machine learning tasks that deal with data for which order is important—that is, the data is arranged in a specific order, and this order is relevant to the task at hand. For example, a sequence learning task might be to predict the next-day closing price of a stock, given the closing price of that stock from the past 60 days. This is a *regression* task, in which the goal is to predict an unknown continuous-valued output. Another example of a sequence learning task would be to predict the next word in a sentence, given a sample phrase like "I went to the gym to exercise." This is a *classification task*, where the goal is to predict an unknown, but discrete-valued output. Another example would be to label the word being spoken in a segment of audio; this is also a classification task, but the goal is to produce the correct label for the entire sequence, rather than for the next item in the sequence. There is a wide range of sequence learning problems, for which a special class of neural networks, called recurrent neural networks (RNN), often yield state-of-the-art results.

One of the most widely used and effective RNN models used for sequence learning is called *long short-term memory* (LSTM) [1]. This model is derived from a basic modification to the baseline RNNs for more efficient handling of sequential data. LSTM is a powerful neural network algorithm that has been shown to provide state-of-the-art performance in various sequence learning tasks, including natural language processing (NLP) [2], video classification [3], and speech recognition [4].

Implementing a deep learning task often takes place in two stages: training and inference. During the training phase, a large amount of data is fed to the model in a recurring fashion. By examining the difference between the desired output and the actual output returned by the model, small incremental adjustments are made to the model's parameters until it can perform the task with an acceptable level of accuracy over the training dataset. Then, in the inference stage, the trained neural network is employed to perform the target task under real-world workloads. An appropriately trained neural network can generate accurate output for the input data, including the data that were not in the training data set.

[1]Division of Intelligent Future Technologies, Mälardalen University, Västerås, Sweden

It is the inference stage that carries the utility of a deep learning model—it is what is implemented and deployed to the end user. The details of this implementation are determined by the application. Often, the application brings demanding real-time requirements in terms of latency and number of concurrent users. Complex models require a large amount of memory resources, high computation load, and high energy consumption. For all of these reasons, realizing a deep learning inference system can be a challenging task. Consequently, instead of the conventional software-based approach, neural networks are often implemented as a special-purpose hardware accelerator.

In a cloud-based data analytics system, the benefits of augmenting servers with efficient neural network hardware accelerator are clear. First, faster computation improves system throughput, effectively lowering the number of server resources required to handle the workload or increasing the maximum workload the system can handle. Second, better energy efficiency reduces the operating cost of the system. Some big IT companies like Google and Microsoft have begun deploying custom ASICs and FPGAs for neural networks in their data centers to enhance the performance of the analytics applications [5,6].

For mobile and Internet-of-things (IoT) platforms, which already come with many deep learning-based applications, sometimes the neural network execution may not be performed on the embedded device; rather, data is offloaded to a cloud server to be processed. However, there are many benefits with performing inference on the edge device instead. As an example, consider Amazon Alexa, a home voice assistant service. Using an Alexa-enabled device, users can speak voice commands to initiate different services such as playing music, checking the weather, ordering food, and controlling other smart devices. The system processes voice commands by having the local device send a recorded voice audio stream to Amazon's servers, where it is processed using a speech recognition algorithm [7]. If voice recognition happens on the device instead, there would be a number of benefits. The service provider (Amazon) benefits from decreased server load, and thus lower operating costs. The user would benefit from increased privacy, as only the directives from their voice commands, rather than the raw audio, would be shared with the server. Additionally, the system could provide limited functionality even without an Internet connection if information could be downloaded to the device in advance.

This chapter focuses on the LSTM model and is concerned with the design of a high-performance and energy-efficient solution to implement deep learning inference.

The chapter is organized as follows: Section 2.1 introduces Recurrent Neural Networks (RNNs). In this section Long Short Term Memory (LSTM) and Gated Recurrent Unit (GRU) network models are discussed as special kind of RNNs. Section 2.2 discusses inference acceleration with hardware. In Section 2.3, a survey on various FPGA designs is presented within the context of the results of previous related works and after which Section 2.4 concludes the chapter.

2.1   Recurrent neural networks

RNNs have a strong adaptability to time series analysis because they introduce the concept of sequences into the structure design of the neural network units. In a RNN, the output activations are stored from one or more of the layers of the network which are called hidden later activations. Next time an input is fed to the network, and the previously stored outputs are considered as additional inputs concatenated with the normal inputs. For example, if a hidden layer has 10 regular input nodes and 128 hidden nodes in the layer, it would actually receive 138 total inputs.

A chunk of neural network A with input x_t and outputs h_t is shown in Figure 2.1. In this model, information is passed from one step of the network to the next via a loop. This information is the *hidden state*, which is a representation of previous inputs. This iterative invocation of a layer is the main difference of RNNs with a normal feedforward model. In fact, the RNN can be considered as multiple copies of the same network replicated in time. RNN treats the hidden layers as successive recurrent layers (Figure 2.2, left). This structure can be unfolded to produce the outputs of a neuron component sequence at discrete time steps corresponding to the input time series (Figure 2.2, right). With this architecture, RNN has a strong capability of capturing the historical information embedded in the past elements of the input for some amount of time.

This chained structure shows that RNNs are closely suited to lists and sequences of data. The unique feature of RNNs is the fact that they are able to connect previous information to the current layer. An example application is video processing in which by using previous video frames the understanding of the current frame may be increased. The feedback loop in the recurrent layer allows RNN maintain information in "memory" over time. But, it can be difficult to train standard RNNs to solve problems that involve learning long-term temporal dependencies. This is because the gradient of the loss function decays exponentially with time; a challenge that is known as the vanishing gradient problem.

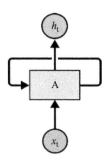

Figure 2.1   Recurrent neural networks

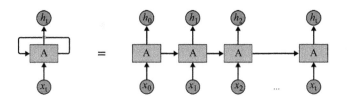

Figure 2.2   Unfolding structure of an RNN

In some problems, it only needs to consider recent information to perform the present task, but it is very likely for the gap between the relevant information and the point where it is needed to be large. When that gap grows, RNNs become unable to learn to connect the information, because they usually keep a short memory, in which *long-term dependencies* may not fit. This shortcoming is explored and analyzed in-depth in [8,9]. This problem of the baseline RNNs led to the emergence of LSTM and GRU. We will describe the basics of these models in the following sections.

2.1.1   Long short-term memory

LSTMs are a special kind of RNN, which allows the network to capture information from inputs for a long time using a special hidden unit, called the LSTM cell [10]. LSTMs have emerged as an effective and scalable model for several learning problems related to sequential data. Earlier RNN models for attacking these problems have either been tailored toward a specific problem or did not scale to long-time dependencies. LSTMs, on the other hand, are both general and effective in capturing long-term temporal dependencies.

All repeated neural networks have the shape of a series of repeating neural network modules. As shown in Figure 2.3, in a baseline RNN, these repeating modules have a simple structure, similar to one tan*h* layer.

LSTMs inherit this chain-like structure, but implement the repeating module in a different and more complex way (Figure 2.4). Instead of a single neural network layer, there are four layers interacting in a special way. Figure 2.4 shows the internal structure of an LSTM and how the current instance, the middle box, interact with the instances at the previous and next time steps. An LSTM has a similar control flow as a RNN. It processes data as it propagates forward. The major differences are the operations within the LSTM cells. These operations are used to allow the LSTM to keep or forget information.

Figure 2.5 shows the notations used in LSTM dataflow. Each line carries an entire vector, from the output of one node to the inputs of others. The circles represent pointwise operations, such as vector addition, while the boxes are learned neural network layers. A line merging indicates concatenation, whereas a line forking denotes content copy, with each copy going to a different way.

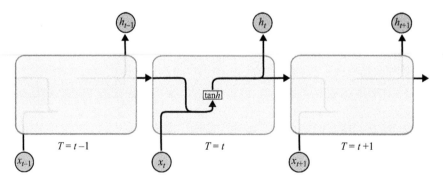

Figure 2.3   The repeating module in a standard RNN

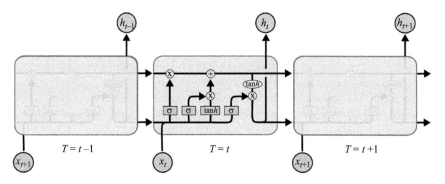

Figure 2.4   The repeating module in an LSTM

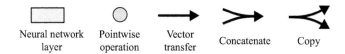

Figure 2.5   Notations in LSTM dataflow

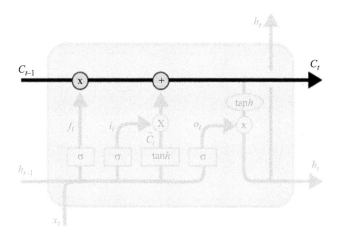

Figure 2.6   The core idea behind LSTM

2.1.1.1   Main concept of LSTMs

In addition to standard RNN units, LSTM adds some special units to the network. The units that are unique to LSTM include a *memory cell* that can maintain information in memory for long periods of time. A set of gates is used to control when information enters the memory, when it goes to output, and when it is forgotten. These extra parts allow LSTMs learn longer-term dependencies. The main idea of LSTM network is the *cell state* which is a piece of intermediate information (or result) stored in memory cell and represented by the horizontal line running through the top of Figure 2.6.

LSTM can remove or add the information to the cell state, regulated by the gate structures. Gates are composed of a sigmoid neural network layer and a multiplication operation. The sigmoid layer returns numbers between "0" and "1" as output, describing how much of each component should be let through. At the two extreme points, "0" value means "let nothing through," while a "1" value means "let everything through." In order to control the cell state, the repeating module in an LSTM (Figure 2.4) has three kinds of sigmoid gates. A typical sigmoid gate used in LSTM cells for removing or adding information is shown in Figure 2.7.

2.1.1.2 Steps in LSTM

The first step in the LSTM is to decide what information we need to throw away from the cell state. Figure 2.8 represents the *forget operation*. Information from the previous hidden state (h_{t-1}) and information from the current input (x_t) are passed through the sigmoid function and the layer generates a number between "0" and "1." If the generated value is "0," the corresponding data is eliminated from the previous

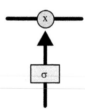

Figure 2.7   Sigmoid layer in LSTM for removing or adding information

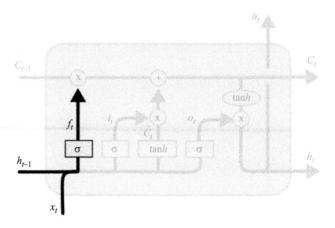

Figure 2.8   Forget operation

state (C_{t-1}) and if the value is "1," the associated data completely goes through. Equation (2.1) represents the forget operation formula:

$$f_t = \sigma(W_f.[h_{t-1}, x_t] + b_f) \tag{2.1}$$

where W_f is *forget* weight vector and b_f is the bias value for forget operation.

The next step in the LSTM is to decide what new information is needed to be stored in the cell state. Figure 2.9 represents the *update gate operation*. This step has two parts. First, a sigmoid layer called the "input gate layer" decides which values should be updated. Next, a tan$h$ layer creates a vector of new candidate values $\tilde{C}_t$ that can be added to the state. Finally, these two layers will be combined to create an update to the state, as represented in (2.2) and (2.3):

$$i_t = \sigma(W_i.[h_{t-1}, x_t] + b_i) \tag{2.2}$$

$$\tilde{C}_t = \tanh(W_c.[h_{t-1}, x_t] + b_c) \tag{2.3}$$

where W_i and W_c are weight vectors and b_i and b_c are bias values.

The next step is to update the old cell state C_{t-1} into the new cell state C_t (Figure 2.10). First, the cell state (C_{t-1}) goes through a pointwise multiplication by the forget vector (f_t). This introduces a possibility of dropping values in the cell state if it gets multiplied by values near "0." Then we take the output from the input gate (i_t) multiplied by current memory value $(\tilde{C}_t)$ and do a pointwise addition which updates the cell state to new values that the neural network finds relevant. Equation (2.4) shows how the new cell state is calculated:

$$C_t = f_t \times C_{t-1} + i_t \times \tilde{C}_t \tag{2.4}$$

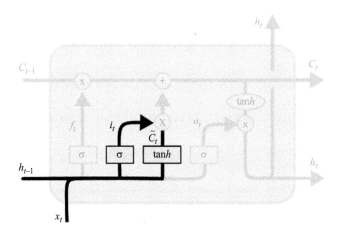

Figure 2.9   Update operation

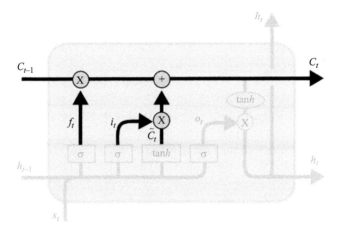

Figure 2.10   Updating the values

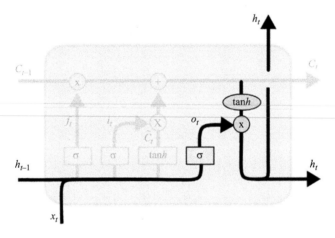

Figure 2.11   Output operation

Finally, it should be decided what to deliver as output (Figure 2.11). This will actually be a filtered version of the cell state. First, a sigmoid layer is run on the cell state to specify what parts of the cell state should appear in the output. Then, the cell state is passed through the tanh function and multiplied by the output of the sigmoid gate (to push the value to be between -1 and 1) as

$$o_t = \sigma(W_o.[h_{t-1}, x_t] + b_o) \tag{2.5}$$

$$h_t = o_t \times \tanh(C_t) \tag{2.6}$$

where o_t is the output value of sigmoid gate, W_o is the weight vector, and b_o is the bias value.

2.1.1.3 Variants on the LSTM model

In several researches, different variants of LSTMs are proposed. In [10], a comprehensive comparison of popular variants of LSTM is presented.

One of the most popular LSTM variants, introduced in [3], adds a set of the so-called peephole connections to the base architecture. Peephole connections provide feedback from the cell to the gates, allowing the gates to carry out their operations as a function of both the incoming inputs and the previous state of the cell. Figure 2.12 and (2.7) show how peepholes are added to all gates:

$$f_t = \sigma(W_f.[C_{t-1}, h_{t-1}, x_t] + b_f)$$
$$i_t = \sigma(W_i.[C_{t-1}, h_{t-1}, x_t] + b_i) \qquad (2.7)$$
$$o_t = \sigma(W_o[C_t, h_{t-1}, x_t] + b_o)$$

Another important variation couples forget and input gates, as shown in Figure 2.13. Instead of separately deciding about what to forget and what new

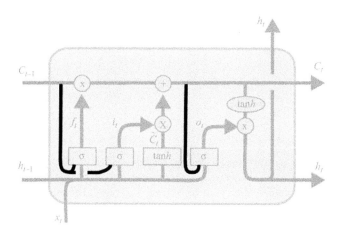

Figure 2.12   Peephole connections

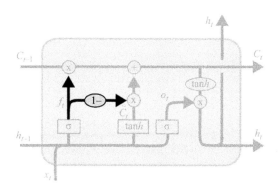

Figure 2.13   Input new values to the state when something older is forgotten

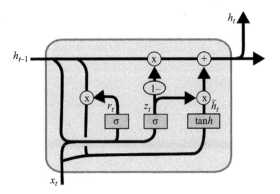

Figure 2.14   Gated recurrent unit

information to add, those decisions can now be made together. In this method, the information is forgotten only when its place is required to store a new input data. In other words, a new value enters the state when an older item is forgotten. Equation (2.8) describes how the cell state would be calculated using this method:

$$C_t = f_t * C_{t-1} + (1 - f_t) * \tilde{C}_t \qquad (2.8)$$

2.1.2   Gated recurrent units

The GRU model [11] is one the most widely used RNN models that can be considered as a variation of the LSTM. Among several changes that GRU makes on the baseline LSTM, its major modifications is twofold. First, it combines *forget* and *input* gates into a single *update* gate. Second, it also merges the cell state and hidden state. The resulting model (Figure 2.14) is simpler than standard LSTM models. GRUs have two gates: reset gate and update gate. *Reset* gate determines how to combine new input to the previous memory and *update* gate decides what information to throw away and what new information to add.

Equation (2.9) describes the behavior of this model, where x_t, h_t, z_t, r_t, and $\tilde{h}_t$ represent input vector, output vector, update gate vector, rest fate vector, and current memory state, respectively:

$$
\begin{aligned}
z_t &= \sigma(W_z.[h_{t-1}, x_t]) \\
r_t &= \sigma(W_r.[h_{t-1}, x_t]) \\
h_t &= \tanh(W.[r_t * h_{t-1}, x_t]) \\
h_t &= (1 - z) * h_{t-1} + z_t * h_t
\end{aligned}
\qquad (2.9)
$$

Simply stated, unlike the LSTM model, the GRU is not required to use a memory unit to control the flow of information. Rather, it can directly use all hidden states without any control. GRUs have fewer parameters and so may learn faster and need less data for generalization. Nonetheless, with large data, the LSTMs with higher expressiveness may still lead to better results. In [12], more than 10,000 RNN architectures are tested and it turned out that LSTMs outperform many other RNN models on certain tasks. In this chapter, we will focus more on LSTM which was presented in the previous subsection.

2.2 Hardware acceleration for RNN inference

As mentioned earlier, implementing a deep learning application is a two-step process: training and inference. Training is a time-consuming process that may take even days. However, it is *one-time cost*, because once a model is trained to return accurate enough output, this step is finished and usually will not be revisited. Inference, on the other hand, carries the *recurring cost* of the deep learning application. In this stage, new data is fed to the model, and only the forward pass through the network is computed. "Cost," in this case, carries two implications. The first is the actual monetary cost due to the energy consumption of the system. It is in the best interest of the application maintainer to minimize the amount of energy required to compute inference because this cost is incurred every time the system processes a new input. The second is the inference delay that the user experiences. For a mobile application, for example, this means the time the user waits to get a response from the system.

Most accelerators target the inference time, as it has to be done on edge devices or cloud-side servers every time a new input data is received. Therefore, the methods we review in this section are inference-time accelerators.

2.2.1 Software implementation

The most straightforward way to implement neural networks is the software-based approach. This strategy is appealing because it is the simplest, in terms of development time, design effort, and design complexity. It also provides flexibility, as a high-level software solution can run on any platform. The develop–debug feedback loop for software is short, compared with that of hardware design, so a robust solution can be implemented in relatively short order. When using a machine learning framework like Theano or TensorFlow, it is feasible to simply take the same code used for training and adapt it to implement inference. TensorFlow Lite [13] was developed specifically for adapting TensorFlow codes to mobile applications. The cost of software-based inference implementation is often low, so this approach is often the first to be taken by application designers—especially if there are no tight real-time latency constraints.

However, for applications with low-latency and high-throughput requirements, a pure software-based approach may be insufficient. For a basic scalar processor, the computations must be performed sequentially. Modern superscalar, multicore processor architectures with powerful SIMD units, as well as low-level linear algebra libraries (such as BLAS [14]) introduce some degrees to facilitate matrix–vector computations, but fundamentally there is a limit to computational performance when a pure software-based approach is taken.

One promising approach is to run neural networks on graphics processing units (GPU). Containing thousands of processing cores, GPUs provide massive parallelism that can speed up matrix–vector operations by multiple orders of magnitude. GPUs have become a popular tool in the deep learning community; in fact, major GPU manufacturers have begun adapting the design of their GPUs specifically to deep learning applications [10]. Many machine learning frameworks support GPUs and offer seamless GPU integration through their back-end computational engines. At run time, if the engine sees that a GPU is present on the machine, it will automatically offload the neural computations to it. Although neural networks can be implemented on the GPU by writing custom CUDA code, but due to highly optimized GPU libraries for deep learning, such as cuDNN [15], many parts of the design flow can now be done automatically.

There are few disadvantages associated with the GPU-based approach. The first is the high cost of the device—high-end GPUs can cost thousands of dollars [16]. While this is a non-recurring cost, it may simply be too high of a barrier to entry, especially for individuals. The other main drawback is the high power usage of GPUs. For a complex neural network-based speech recognition algorithm, a GPU implementation required almost twice the amount of power required by its CPU-only counterpart [17]. While total energy consumption for a particular task may be lower on a GPU than on a CPU, the high-power requirement of a GPU may be prohibiting for some platforms—especially for embedded systems. In order to meet performance requirements while meeting the cost and energy/power consumption constraints, it is often necessary to design custom hardware for accelerating inference.

2.2.2 Hardware implementation

In general terms, a custom hardware solution that is designed after the computation pattern of a specific application is called an application-specific integrated circuit (ASIC). In contrast with general purpose CPUs and GPUs, which are designed to handle a large variety of tasks, ASICs are designed to perform a specific function or a specific class of functions. ASICs contain only the data paths required to perform their specified function, and for this reason, ASICs can be highly optimized, in terms of computational throughput and energy efficiency. For example, a recent study shows that an ASIC designed for accelerating a neural network-based computer vision application achieved $13\times$ faster computation and $3,400\times$ less energy consumption than a GPU-based solution [18].

In general, the less variability in an algorithm, the better and simpler hardware implementation can be obtained. Inference in all neural network models has several properties that make it well-suited for a hardware-optimized implementation:

1. There are a fixed number of computations performed in each forward pass through the network. This allows the hardware designer to choose the appropriate amount and type of computational units, such as adders and multipliers.
2. Matrix–vector multiplications of the neural networks is easily parallelizable—each element of the vector product relies on a separate row of the parameter

matrix, and so these output terms can be computed independently of one another.

3. The model parameter values are fixed and known at run-time. This opens up the opportunity for various compression schemes and quantization approaches, which reduce the amount and size of the parameters in memory.

4. In addition to the number of computations being fixed, the order in which they are performed, and thus the order in which data is accessed, can be fixed. Having a predictable data-access pattern allows memory operations to be optimized, either through the interface to off-chip DRAM or in the properties of on-chip SRAM.

Once an architecture is developed, the process of designing digital hardware involves writing in a hardware description language (HDL) to describe the structure and behavior of a circuit. Unlike most software languages, which describe a sequential procedure to be executed by a CPU, an HDL adopts a concurrent model of computation, i.e., describes operations being done in parallel. The process of writing and testing HDL can be both difficult and time-consuming, requiring a special skill set and domain knowledge. Because of this, designing custom hardware to accelerate inference carries a high nonrecurring engineering cost. Additionally, once an ASIC has been fabricated, its design and functionality is fixed. Any modification to the design requires a full re-fabrication cycle and replacement of existing devices, which can be quite expensive.

Field-programmable gate arrays (FPGAs) present a solution to hardware design that offers more flexibility than an ASIC. These devices contain a large, interconnected array of programmable units, which can be reconfigured to implement complex digital circuits. These programmable units are given different names in different products, among them configurable logic blocks (CLBs) is the most common. They also contain memory (RAM) and multiply-add units (also known as DSP units) that are connected to the CLBs. The architecture of a typical FPGA is shown in Figure 2.15. While they offer lower energy efficiency and performance than ASICs, they still significantly outperform CPUs and GPUs in energy efficiency (and in some cases performance). In a prior work, it has been shown that the FPGA-based hardware accelerator for a speech recognition application achieved $43\times$ and $197\times$ better speed and energy efficiency, respectively, than a CPU implementation and $3\times$ and $14\times$ better speed and energy efficiency, respectively, than a GPU implementation [17].

The rest of this chapter will present a survey on some recent custom hardware accelerators for the LSTMs model.

2.3   Hardware implementation of LSTMs

Several previous studies have addressed the problem of implementing LSTM network inference in a hardware-friendly manner. Complete solutions to this problem should address three issues: reduce the amount of data and parameters by compressing the model, optimize the dataflow for the target hardware platform, and finally optimize the memory usage.

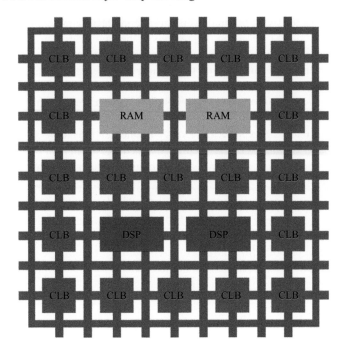

Figure 2.15   FPGA device architecture

2.3.1   Model compression

The first step in the design of a hardware architecture is selecting the data format and bit precision of the numbers and, if needed, a model compression strategy. This step determines the required computational elements, the memory requirements, and ultimately the performance and throughput of the system.

Parameter compression can significantly reduce the memory footprint and computational complexity of the inference computations. Several methods have been proposed for neural network model compression. These methods are generally classified into parameter reduction and parameter quantization approaches. The former approach reduces the number of parameters needed to run the model, while the latter reduces the number of bits needed to represent model parameters.

The *pruning* technique reduces the number of parameters by removing (i.e., setting to zero) unnecessary weight connections. After training, model parameters with an absolute value below some threshold are removed. Then, the sparse model is retrained using the remaining connections. The retrained model may be pruned and retrained again in order to achieve the desired level of sparsity.

Pruning is a well-studied method in feedforward and convolutional neural networks. Using this technique, Han *et al.* demonstrated 9× and 13× reduction in number of parameters for two well-known convolutional networks [19]. Building upon this approach, Han *et al.* also proposed a hardware-friendly pruning method, called load-balance aware pruning [17]. This method facilitates the distribution of the processing workload by constraining regions of the parameter matrices to contain an equal number of nonzero connections. After pruning, the memory footprint of the model parameters is reduced using sparse matrix encoding methods, such as compressed sparse column (CSC) or compressed sparse row (CSR). Some accelerators have been designed to operate directly on sparse encoded models and efficiently skip zero-valued connections [17,18].

Singular value decomposition (SVD) is another technique for reducing the number of model parameters. By keeping just the largest singular values, the dimensionality of model parameter matrices can be reduced while maintaining an acceptable level of accuracy. In [20], SVD is applied to a fully connected layer of a convolutional network and achieved a compression rate of $7\times$ with only a 0.04% loss in prediction accuracy. In [21], this technique is applied to a five-layer LSTM for speech processing and reduced the model size by $3\times$ with only a 0.5% loss in prediction accuracy. An advantage of this approach is that it does not require special encoding (and consequently more memory) to store the compressed model; this translates to simplified accelerator architecture because the parameter matrix structure does not have to be decoded.

A common technique to quantize parameters is *weight sharing*. With this approach, a small number of effective weight values are used [19]. After training, similar weights are identified using k-means clustering. The centroid of a cluster is then chosen to be the shared weight value. The quantized model can then be retrained using only the shared weights. This technique allows parameter matrices to be stored as indices into the shared weight codebook, thus reducing the memory footprint. For example, a weight sharing scheme with 32 shared weights requires only 5 bits to store an individual weight. Han *et al.* utilize weight sharing to enable on-chip parameter storage in their hardware accelerator for fully connected layers [18]. A benefit to this approach is that is does not restrict the datatype of the actual weights; high-precision datatypes can be used for computation with minimal storage requirements.

Another quantization technique is called *binarization*. This method constrains all weight values during training to $+1$ or -1, thus requiring only a single bit to represent. An extension of this technique applies the same quantization on layer activations as well. Various approaches have been proposed for training a neural network with binary weights and activations [22–24]. The approach detailed in [24] was applied to an LSTM model for text prediction and resulted in better power and performance efficiency with negligible loss in prediction accuracy, compared with that of the full-precision model. Binarization comes with significant advantages for hardware implementation. In a weight-only binarization scheme, multiplication is reduced to a two's complement operation, thus eliminating the need for expensive hardware multipliers. Weight and activation binarization simplifies hardware implementation even further, requiring only XNOR and bit-count operations in place of multiply accumulation. In both schemes, model parameter storage size is drastically reduced.

For many deployed deep learning applications, the costliest operation in terms of both time and power consumption is off-chip memory access. Han *et al.* propose a three-stage model compression and quantization method that dramatically reduces the storage requirement of model parameters and allows many deep learning models to be stored in on chip SRAM [19]. The authors show that, for a small number of example feedforward and convolutional networks, this method can reduce parameter storage requirements by $35\times$ to $49\times$ without loss in prediction accuracy. The three compression stages are as follows. First, pruning removes all model parameters that have an absolute value below some threshold. Next, parameters are quantized through weight sharing, in which weight values are binned through k-means clustering. This allows only the weight indices to be stored. Finally, the pruned and quantized parameters are stored in memory using Huffman coding.

In [17], Han *et al.* present a model compression method called *load balance-aware pruning*. This method extends the standard pruning technique by optimizing the workload across parallel processing elements, resulting in reduced computation time. The technique works by first dividing the parameter matrix into submatrices based on the number of processing elements available. These submatrices are then constrained to have the same sparsity, such that they contain an equal number of nonzero parameters after pruning. The authors show that for a sample speech recognition model, the prediction performance of load balance-aware pruning does not differ much from that of the standard pruning. Linear quantization is used to further compress the model, with the fixed-point fraction length set by analyzing the dynamic range of each layer. The authors found that quantizing to 12-bits did not reduce the prediction performance from that of the 32-bit floating point model. However, 8-bit fixed point quantization caused prediction performance to deteriorate significantly.

In [20], compression of fully connected layers in a convolutional network is explored using SVD. For some example CNN model, SVD is performed on the first fully connected layer weights. The first 500 singular values are chosen. This results in a compression rate of $7\times$ and a prediction accuracy loss of only 0.04%. The authors also proposed a data quantization flow in which the fixed-point fractional length of both the model parameters and the layer inputs are optimized. First, the dynamic range of parameter matrices for each layer is analyzed in order to determine the fractional length which yields the smallest total error between the floating-point versions of the parameters. Then, the same process is applied to the input data at each layer. Fractional lengths are static in a single layer but dynamic in-between layers. The authors found that for an example CNN model, 16-bit static fixed-point precision resulted in negligible prediction performance loss compared with that of the floating-point model. The 8-bit static precision resulted in significantly worse performance, but an 8-bit dynamic precision model resulted in a performance loss of only 1.52%.

In [21], SVD for LSTM model compression is applied. First, the authors present the compression technique for a general recurrent network. Input and recurrent parameter matrices for each layer are factored jointly to produce a recurrent projection matrix. The compression ratio for a given layer can then be controlled by setting the rank of the projection matrix. This method is extended to LSTM by concatenating the four-gate parameter matrices and treating them as a single matrix. For an example speech recognition model, the authors showed that they were able to compress the original network to a third of its original size only with a small degradation in accuracy.

Chen *et al.* investigated the effect of various quantization strategies during training and inference in [25]. The authors found that for a CNN trained on MNIST using 32-bit floating point parameters, quantizing to 16-bit fixed point for inference results in a loss of only 0.01% in prediction accuracy.

In [26], Shin *et al.* applied a weight-sharing quantization approach to large-scale LSTM models. After an initial model training stage using floating-point parameters, uniform quantization and retraining are applied iteratively in order to find an optimal quantization step size. This approach is applied to two multilayer LSTMs for NLP applications. The authors found that due to the wide dynamic range across layers of the model, an optimal approach is to group parameter values by layer and connection type (i.e., separate feedforward and recurrent parameter matrices) and perform quantization of each group separately.

In [22], a method for training very low-precision (1-bit) neural networks is introduced. The so-called binary neural networks drastically reduce both memory and computational requirements for deployed models. With this model compression scheme, weights are constrained to values of $+1$ or -1 during training. Thus, inference computation includes only addition and subtraction, which is simpler and more efficient to implement in hardware than multiplication. The authors applied this technique to a three-layer feedforward network for MNIST classification and achieved 0.01% better prediction accuracy than that of a full-precision version of the model.

In [23], an alternative approach for model binarization is proposed. This training method constrains not only the network weights to binary values, but layer activations as well. This provides even more of an advantage for hardware implementation, as all computational operations involve only $+1$ or -1. By mapping -1 to 0, multiply-accumulate operations can be replaced with XNOR and bit-count operations, which can be computed very quickly and efficiently in hardware. As in [22], the authors applied this approach to a three-layer feedforward network for MNIST classification. This demonstrated only a 0.1% loss in prediction accuracy compared with that of the full-precision implementation of the model.

Building upon previous works on model binarization, in [24] an algorithm called loss-aware binarization is proposed. Unlike previous approaches, this algorithm directly minimizes training loss with respect to the binarized weights. The algorithm can also be extended to binarizing both weights and activations by using a simple sign function for binarizing activations. The authors experimented with a four-layer feedforward network for MNIST classification. Compared with the prediction accuracy of the full-precision version of the model, results showed a 0.01% improvement using binary weights only, and a 0.19% loss in accuracy using binary weights and activations. Unique to this work, a method for binarizing RNNs is proposed. An example LSTM model for text prediction is used to evaluate the method. Compared with the full-precision model, the binarized model achieves 0.02% loss in accuracy using binary weights only and 0.11% loss in accuracy using binary weights and activations. Compared with two other cited binarization methods for both weight-only and weight and activation binarization, the approach proposed in this work achieves the best prediction performance.

In [27], the efficient RNN (E-RNN) framework for FPGA implementations of the automatic speech recognition (ASR) application is presented. The overall goal of this work is to improve performance/energy efficiency under tight accuracy requirements. Taking the block-circulant matrix-based approach, E-RNN uses the *alternating direction method of multipliers* (ADMM) technique for more accurate block-circulant training. Two design explorations are also presented to provide guidance on block size and reducing RNN training trials. Based on the two observations, E-RNN is decomposed in two phases: (1) determining the RNN model to reduce computation and storage subject to accuracy requirement and (2) hardware implementations of RNN model, including processing element design optimization and quantization.

2.3.2   Datatype and Quantization

The datatype used for hardware implementation affects many of the decisions made during the FPGA design process—ultimately impacting energy efficiency and processing throughput. While full-precision floating-point data is often used during the training phase, research has shown that fixed-point datatypes with reduced word length can be used for inference with minimal loss in accuracy [25,28,29]. Besides the benefit of reduced memory footprint compared with floating-point datatypes, this quantization approach has a number of advantages. First, it is simple to implement using a linear quantization approach, and tools that automate this process are freely available [28]. Second, fixed point quantization can be used in conjunction with a parameter-reduction compression approach, such as pruning or SVD [18,20]. Finally, fixed-point multiplication and addition map can be used directly to dedicated DSP hardware units, such as the Xilinx DSP48 and its variants. When using a short enough word length, data can be packed such that DSP units are able to process two multiply-accumulate operations concurrently [30].

When specifying a fixed-point datatype, there is a trade-off among word length (the total number of bits), fractional part length (the location of the decimal point), and the supported dynamic range. In general, larger word lengths allow for larger dynamic range but come at the cost of increased memory footprint. It can be a challenge to find a balance between reducing word length and maintaining computational accuracy. A simple approach is to use a *static* fixed-point representation for all datatypes. Given a large enough word length, an appropriately set fraction length can allow enough room for the integer component to grow while maintaining an acceptable level of fractional precision. Many accelerator architectures have taken this approach due to its straightforward implementation in hardware [18,31–33]. However, a multilayer model with a large number of parameters may have a wide dynamic range that is difficult to represent using a reduced word length. A solution to this issue is to use a *dynamic* fixed-point representation [28]. With this approach, the dynamic range of each layer is analyzed separately in order to select an appropriate fraction length. In hardware implementation, this translates to extra bit shift operations between layers to align decimal points. The impact of dynamic fixed point on convolutional networks has been widely studied and shown to yield minimal loss in prediction accuracy, even with word lengths as short as 4 or 8 bits [20,28]. Studies related to LSTM are limited, but Shin *et al.* found that for dynamic quantization of multilayer LSTMs should be separated not only by layer but also by connection type (i.e., feedforward vs. recurrent) as well. Dynamic fixed point has successfully been implemented in FPGA hardware accelerators [17,20].

Li *et al.* proposed an FPGA accelerator for the basic RNN model in [33]. The authors noted that for NLP applications, the number of nodes in the output layer (i.e., the vocabulary size) is usually much larger than the number of hidden-layer nodes. As such, the computation of the output layer is often the dominating factor in the computational complexity of RNNs. To balance the computational workload of processing elements in an RNN accelerator, the proposed architecture unrolls the network in time: the computation of the hidden layer is done serially, while the output layer computation for a window of time is done in parallel. Additionally, the authors employed two design strategies to optimize FPGA resources: quantize network weights to 16-bit fixed-point format and approximate nonlinear activation functions using piecewise linear approximation.

In addition to the compression method proposed in [17], Han *et al.* present an FPGA accelerator designed to operate on sparse LSTM models. The accelerator operates directly on a compressed model by encoding the sparse matrices in memory using CSC format. A control unit fetches this data from memory and schedules computational operations. Operations that do not depend on each other (e.g., the activation function of the input gate and the pre-activation of the forget gate) are scheduled to run in parallel in the accelerator. The accelerator unit is composed of multiple processing elements, a single element-wise unit, and a single activation function unit. Processing elements read from their own dedicated First-in First-out (FiFo) queue, that is fed by the control unit. They contain a sparse matrix read unit, which decodes the CSC-formatted parameter data. Matrix–vector product accumulation is accomplished via a single adder and buffer per processing element. The element-wise unit contains 16 multipliers and an adder tree. The activation function unit is composed of lookup tables for hyperbolic tangent and sigmoid functions, both containing 2,048 samples and quantized to 16-bit format.

Chang *et al.* implement a two-layer LSTM on a Xilinx XC7Z020 in [31]. The FPGA design contains two main computational subsystems: gate modules and element-wise modules. Gate modules perform the matrix–vector multiplication and activation function computation for LSTM cell gates. Element-wise modules combine gate module outputs with element-wise multiplication, addition, and activation functions. All weights and input are quantized to 16-bit fixed-point format. Activation function units use piecewise linear approximation and can be configured at run time to perform either the hyperbolic tangent or sigmoid functions. Input data is fed to gate modules from a direction memory access (DMA) streaming unit, which has independent streams for input and hidden layer data. To synchronize the independent input streams, gate modules have a sync unit that contains a FIFO. Element-wise modules also contain a sync unit to align the data coming from the gate units. Results from the element-wise module are written back to memory through the DMA unit.

Ferreira and Fonseca proposed an FPGA accelerator for LSTM in [32]. This design trades off scalability and flexibility for throughput: network size is fixed at HDL compilation time, but weight and bias parameters are stored in on-chip RAM rather than imported from off-chip memory. Matrix–vector multiplication is tiled using counter and multiplexer logic, which saves resources at the cost of increased computation time (by a factor of the resource sharing ratio). Input and recurrent matrix–vector multiplication are calculated in parallel. Since the size of the input vector is often smaller than the recurrent vector size, the bias-add operation is performed after the input matrix–vector multiply operation is completed, while the recurrent matrix–vector multiply operation is still being completed in parallel. Element-wise operations are also multiplexed: there is one each of a hyperbolic tangent unit, a sigmoid unit, and element-wise multiply and add units. Activation functions are computed using piecewise second-order approximations, evaluated using Horner's rule in order to save multiplier resources. All data is quantized to a signed 18-bit fixed-point representation in order to make full use of Xilinx DSP48E1 slices.

2.3.3   Memory

The memory space demand, which is the physical storage of the neural network parameters, is an important parameter for hardware accelerator design. Many state-of-the-art neural network models contain hundreds of megabytes worth of parameters. This memory demand introduces a unique challenge for FPGA implementation of neural network accelerators, because on-chip memory size and I/O bandwidth are often limited [34]. Moreover, off-chip DRAM access requires an order of magnitude more energy than on-chip memory access [19]. The off-chip parameter access can also be a processing bottleneck because the speed of matrix–vector operations is often limited by memory access time [20]. Indeed, in LSTMs, similar to many other neural network models, the majority of computations is matrix–vector operations and has their parameter in the off-chip memory, so memory bandwidth highly affects system throughput.

Due to the energy and access-time requirements of off-chip memory access, on-chip parameter storage is the optimal design choice, provided that the parameters can fit in the limited on-chip memory capacity. For many models, compression techniques can shrink parameter storage requirements enough to allow the entire model to be stored on-chip. In addition to the efficiency and performance benefits, on-chip parameter storage vastly simplifies the design process by eliminating the need for developing memory interface and buffering schemes. In the case of models compressed using sparsity encoding, extra decoding logic is required, but the implementation of such logic may be simpler than implementing an external memory interface. Many hardware accelerators have been designed to take advantage of on-chip storage [18,32,35].

While on-chip parameter storage is both simple to implement and more efficient than using off-chip memory, it is also less scalable than its counterpart. Many accelerators using on-chip storage have been designed to support a single model;

reconfiguring the design to support another model may be difficult or impossible given resource constraints. Accelerators that utilize off-chip memory, on the other hand, must be designed to support an arbitrary model size and structure. Although off-chip memory access times can be relatively long, various design techniques, such as double buffering, can be used to perform computation during memory downtime [17,36]. Additionally, a hybrid memory approach that utilizes on-chip memory to cache recently used values can be used to reduce the amount of memory access [36,37]. For LSTMs, cell memories are a good candidate for on-chip caching because of the relatively small storage requirement. For example, with an output word size of 32 bits, a cell memory cache size of only 16 kB would support a layer size of up to 4,096 cells. Additional on-chip memory can be used to store a portion of (or, if the model were small enough, all of) the model parameters. While not optimally energy-efficient, many FPGA accelerators that read parameters from off-chip have achieved significant power savings and better or comparable computational speedup compared with CPU and GPU counterparts [36–38]. These designs are more complex than those that rely on on-chip memory, but they provide more utility as general-purpose model accelerators.

Guan *et al.* proposed an FPGA accelerator for LSTM that tries to optimize both memory access and computational performance [36]. To optimize memory access time, the authors proposed to organize the model parameter data in memory in such a way that it can be accessed sequentially for tiled computation. The memory organization is arranged offline prior to the inference. In terms of architectural optimization, the design contains a data dispatch unit, which handles all memory transactions separately from the LSTM accelerator. Additionally, the accelerator uses a ping-pong buffering scheme at its input and output so that new computations can take place while data of the previous and next computations are being transferred to/from memory. To optimize computation performance, the accelerator unit performs tiled matrix–vector multiplication in parallel for each of the LSTM gates. A separate functional unit performs the activation function and element-wise operations. This unit contains an on-chip memory buffer to hold the current state of the cells. To evaluate the accelerator's performance, the authors implement an LSTM model for speech recognition. This model contains three stacked LSTM layers. The base design of the FPGA accelerator uses little memory resources, so the authors also experimented with storing the parameters of the first layer in on-chip memory and found that this approach resulted in an overall speedup of about 1.5×.

In [18], Han *et al.* proposed a general-purpose hardware accelerator for fully connected neural network layers. Implemented in 45 nm CMOS technology, this chip is suitable for accelerating the matrix–vector multiplication of neural networks (including LSTMs). This design utilizes sparsity coding and weight sharing in order to store all network parameters in on-chip SRAM, resulting in significant power savings and speedup. The architecture also takes advantage of the sparsity of the input, dynamically scanning the vectors and broadcasting nonzero elements, along with their row index, to an array of processing elements. Nonzero input vector elements are multiplied by nonzero elements in the corresponding column of the weight matrix and then sent to a row accumulator. In order to balance workload distribution, each processing element has a queue at its input. Input broadcast is halted when any processing element has a full queue.

Nurvitadhi *et al.* studied some techniques for optimization and acceleration of the GRU model in [38]. First, they propose a method for memory access optimization that reduces computation time by an average of 46%. Since the authors targeted NLP applications, the size of the vocabulary, as the GRU input is limited and so, a one-hot encoding approach is used. Therefore, there is a finite number of possible results from the input matrix–vector multiply operation, and these results can be precomputed and cached to avoid expensive computations at run time. Recurrent matrix–vector multiply operations, on the other hand, cannot be precomputed, so the method uses an FPGA for accelerating the remaining calculations. The matrix is divided into column blocks. Each block consists of a floating-point multiply-accumulate unit. Partially accumulated results from the tiled computation are summed in a row reduction unit, and output vector results are sent to a memory write unit. The accelerator only performs matrix–vector operations; the element-wise addition and multiplication as well as activation function computations required by GRU are presumably performed on the host CPU.

2.4   Conclusion

Sequence learning is a broad field of research with many practical applications, from speech recognition to video classification. LSTM networks have been shown to be very effective to handle this special type of problems. However, implementing the inference for such applications can be quite challenging due to the computational complexity of LSTM. A pure CPU software-based implementation will have limited computational throughput and poor energy efficiency. While the performance of a software-based design may be acceptable for some applications, real-time or throughput-oriented applications should rely on GPUs or hardware accelerators in order to get the required power/performance profiles. This chapter reviewed some recent proposals on hardware acceleration of RNNs. Due to the ever-increasing deployment of RNNs in the industry, there is a growing need for more power- and performance-efficient hardware accelerators.

References

[1]   Greff, K., Srivastava, R. K., Koutník, J., Steunebrink, B. R., and Schmidhuber, J. (2017). LSTM: A search space odyssey. *IEEE Transactions on Neural Networks and Learning Systems*, 28(10), 2222–2232.

[2]   Sundermeyer, M., Ney, H., and Schlüter, R. (2015). From feedforward to recurrent LSTM neural networks for language modeling. *IEEE/ACM Transactions on Audio, Speech, and Language Processing*, 23(3), 517–529.

[3]   Yue-Hei Ng, J., Hausknecht, M., Vijayanarasimhan, S., Vinyals, O., Monga, R., and Toderici, G. (2015). Beyond short snippets: Deep networks for video classification. In *Proceedings of the IEEE Conference on Computer Vision and Pattern Recognition*, pp. 4694–4702.

[4]   Xiong, W., Wu, L., Alleva, F., Droppo, J., Huang, X., and Stolcke, A. (2018, April). The Microsoft 2017 conversational speech recognition system. In *2018 IEEE International Conference on Acoustics, Speech and Signal Processing (ICASSP)*, pp. 5934–5938.

[5]   Jiao, Y., Zheng, Y., Jaroniec, M., and Qiao, S. Z. (2015). Design of electrocatalysts for oxygen- and hydrogen-involving energy conversion reactions. *Chemical Society Reviews* 44, no. 8, 2060–2086.

[6]   Chung, J., Ahn, S., and Bengio, Y. (2016). Hierarchical multiscale recurrent neural networks. arXiv preprint arXiv:1609.01704.

[7]   Lei, X., Tu, G. H., Liu, A. X., Li, C. Y., and Xie, T. The insecurity of home digital voice assistants—Amazon Alexa as a case study. [Online]. Available: http://arxiv.org/abs/1712.03327.

[8]   Sadeghian, A., Alexandre, A., and Silvio, S. (2017). Tracking the untrackable: Learning to track multiple cues with long-term dependencies. In *Proceedings of the IEEE International Conference on Computer Vision*, pp. 300–311.

[9]   Donahue, J., Lisa, A., Hendricks, S., *et al.* (2015). Long-term recurrent convolutional networks for visual recognition and description. In *Proceedings of the IEEE Conference on Computer Vision and Pattern Recognition*, pp. 2625–2634.

[10] Schmidhuber, J. (2015). Deep learning in neural networks: An overview. *Neural networks*, *61*, 85–117.

[11] Visin, F., Kastner, K., Cho, K., Matteucci, M., Courville, A., and Bengio, Y. (2015). Renet: A recurrent neural network based alternative to convolutional networks. arXiv preprint arXiv:1505.00393.

[12] Zilly, J. G., Srivastava, R. K., Koutník, J., and Schmidhuber, J. (2017, August). Recurrent highway networks. In *Proceedings of the 34th International Conference on Machine Learning—Volume 70*, pp. 4189–4198. JMLR.org.

[13] Introduction to TensorFlow lite. [Online]. Available: https://www.tensorflow.org/mobile/tflite/

[14] BLAS (basic linear algebra subprograms). [Online]. Available: http://www.netlib.org/blas/

[15] NVIDIA cuDNN. [Online]. Available: https://developer.nvidia.com/cudnn

[16] E. Eshelman. NVIDIA tesla p100 price analysis. [Online]. Available: https://www.microway.com/hpc-tech-tips/nvidia-tesla-p100-price-analysis/

[17] Han, S., Kang, J., Mao, H. *et al.* (2017, February). ESE: Efficient speech recognition engine with sparse LSTM on FPGA. In *Proceedings of the 2017 ACM/SIGDA International Symposium on Field-Programmable Gate Arrays*, pp. 75–84. ACM.

[18] Han, S., Liu, X., Mao, H. *et al.* (2016). EIE: Efficient inference engine on compressed deep neural network. In *2016 ACM/IEEE 43rd Annual International Symposium on Computer Architecture (ISCA)*, pp. 243–254.

[19]   Han, S., Mao, H., and Dally, W. J. Deep compression: Compressing deep neural networks with pruning, trained quantization and huffman coding. [Online]. Available: http://arxiv.org/abs/1510.00149.

[20]   Qiu, J., Wang, J., Yao, S. *et al.* (2016). Going deeper with embedded FPGA platform for convolutional neural network. In *Proceedings of the 2016 ACM/SIGDA International Symposium on Field-Programmable Gate Arrays*, ser. FPGA '16, pp. 26–35. ACM.

[21]   Prabhavalkar, R., Alsharif, O., Bruguier, A., and McGraw, L. (2016). On the compression of recurrent neural networks with an application to LVCSR acoustic modeling for embedded speech recognition. In *2016 IEEE International Conference on Acoustics, Speech and Signal Processing (ICASSP)*, pp. 5970–5974.

[22]   Courbariaux, M., Bengio, Y., and David, J. P. (2015). Binaryconnect: Training deep neural networks with binary weights during propagations. In *Advances in neural information processing systems*, pp. 3123–3131.

[23]   Hubara, I., Courbariaux, M., Soudry, D., El-Yaniv, R., and Bengio, Y. (2017). Quantized neural networks: Training neural networks with low precision weights and activations, *The Journal of Machine Learning Research*, *18*(1), 6869–6898.

[24]   Hou, L., Yao, Q., and Kwok, J. T. Loss-aware binarization of deep networks. [Online]. Available: http://arxiv.org/abs/1611.01600

[25]   Chen, Y., Luo, T., Liu, S. *et al.* (2014, December). Dadiannao: A machine-learning supercomputer. In *Proceedings of the 47th Annual IEEE/ACM International Symposium on Microarchitecture*, pp. 609–622.

[26]   Shin, S., Hwang, K., and Sung, W. (2016, March). Fixed-point performance analysis of recurrent neural networks. In *2016 IEEE International Conference on Acoustics, Speech and Signal Processing (ICASSP)*, pp. 976–980.

[27]   Li, Z., Ding, C., Wang, S. *et al.* (2019). E-RNN: Design optimization for efficient recurrent neural networks in FPGAs. In *2019 IEEE International Symposium on High Performance Computer Architecture (HPCA)*, pp. 69–80.

[28]   Gysel, P., Motamedi, M., and Ghiasi, S. Hardware-oriented approximation of convolutional neural networks. arXiv preprint arXiv:1604.03168, 2016.

[29]   Lin, D., Talathi, S., and Annapureddy, S. (2016). Fixed point quantization of deep convolutional networks. In *International Conference on Machine Learning*, pp. 2849–2858.

[30]   Fu, Y., Wu, E., Sirasao, A. *et al.* Deep learning with INT8 optimization of xilinx devices. [Online]. Available: https://www.xilinx.com/support/documentation/whitepapers/wp486-deep-learning-int8.pdf

[31]   Chang, A. X. M., Martini, B., and Culurciello, E. (2015). Recurrent neural networks hardware implementation on FPGA. arXiv preprint arXiv:1511.05552.

[32]   Ferreira, J. C. and Fonseca, J. (2016). An FPGA implementation of a long short-term memory neural network. In *2016 International Conference on ReConFigurable Computing and FPGAs (ReConFig)*, pp. 1–8.

[33]   Li, S., Wu, C., Li, H. *et al.* (2015). FPGA acceleration of recurrent neural network based language model. In *2015 IEEE 23rd Annual International Symposium on Field-Programmable Custom Computing Machines*, pp. 111–118.

[34] Sharma, H., Park, J., Mahajan, D., *et al.* (2016). From high-level deep neural models to FPGAs. In *2016 49th Annual IEEE/ACM International Symposium on Microarchitecture (MICRO)*, pp. 1–12.

[35] Li, Y., Liu, Z., Xu, K., Yu, H., and Ren, F. (2018). A GPU-outperforming FPGA accelerator architecture for binary convolutional neural networks, *ACM Journal on Emerging Technologies in Computing Systems (JETC)*, *14*(2), 18.

[36] Guan, Y., Yuan, Z., Sun, G., and Cong, J. (2017). FPGA-based accelerator for long short term memory recurrent neural networks. In *2017 22nd Asia and South Pacific Design Automation Conference (ASP-DAC)*, pp. 629–634.

[37] Andri, R., Cavigelli, L., Rossi, D., and Benini, L. (2018). YodaNN: An architecture for ultralow power binary-weight CNN acceleration. *IEEE Transactions on Computer-Aided Design of Integrated Circuits and Systems*, *37*(1), 48–60.

[38] Nurvitadhi, E., Sim, J., Sheffield, D., Mishra, A., Krishnan, S., and Marr, D. (2016). Accelerating recurrent neural networks in analytics servers: Comparison of FPGA, CPU, GPU, and ASIC. In *2016 26th International Conference on Field Programmable Logic and Applications (FPL)*, pp. 1–4.

Chapter 3

Feedforward neural networks on massively parallel architectures

Reza Hojabr[1], Ahmad Khonsari[1,2], Mehdi Modarressi[1,2], and Masoud Daneshtalab[3]

The deployment of neural networks (NN) in modern computing systems has grown increasingly in recent years. The superior performance of NNs in implementing intelligent services has made them an efficient tool in various domains, ranging from pattern recognition in small intelligent handheld devices to big data analysis in large datacenters [1,2]. In addition to their classic applications, several prior work have shown that complex functions can be mimicked and replaced by NNs to speed up the computation at the cost of negligible inaccuracy in results [3].

Due to the complexity and high implementation cost of NNs, proper implementation of these compute-intensive algorithms entails a complete rethink of the neural processing platforms. Recently, customized hardware implementations of NNs have gained considerable attention in the semiconductor industry and this trend has led to the advent of efficient NN accelerators [4–6]. In the domain of smart embedded devices, emerging NN accelerators aim to adjust the area and power consumption subject to the limited area and power budget in embedded systems. On the other side, in large-scale datacenters, NN accelerators are required to run multiple instances of the network, which translates to processing millions of neurons, in parallel. As a result, software implementation of NNs (using GPU or CPU) is being replaced with hardware-based implementations using specialized accelerators.

Motivated by the massive parallelism in the NN computations, hardware accelerators typically consist of multiple processing nodes to fully exploit this inherent parallelism efficiently. However, managing the large amount of data movements between the processing nodes is a major concern in designing such NN hardware accelerators. The large amount of data movement, which results in a high inter-node traffic rate, stems from the computation model of NNs in that the computation units, i.e., neurons, are simple but are replicated in a large-scale structure, with each neuron has many connections to other neurons. To address the need for a parallel architecture

[1]School of Electrical and Computer Engineering, College of Engineering, University of Tehran, Tehran, Iran
[2]School of Computer Science, Institute for Research in Fundamental Sciences (IPM), Tehran, Iran
[3]Division of Intelligent Future Technologies, Mälardalen University, Sweden

and also the high-rate communication, the processing nodes of the accelerators are commonly arranged as a many-core system-on-chip (SoC) connected by a network-on-chip (NoC) [7,8]. Each node contains one or multiple neurons. The deployment of a high-throughput interconnection network helps to reduce the cost of data movements between the neurons, thereby enabling the accelerator nodes to approach their maximum neural information processing throughput. This chapter aims at introducing an efficient interconnection network for NN accelerators.

Some prior work proposed NN accelerators using shared bus topology, since bus provides a simple and low-cost interneuron connection [9,10]. Although being a proper solution for small-scale systems, the non-scalable power consumption and performance of the bus quickly becomes a serious bottleneck, when the size of NN grows. Therefore, recent work proposed replacing bus with more scalable NoC topologies [7,8]. These NoCs showed promising results in handling the heavy traffic load of interneuron communications.

In typical SoCs, the on-chip interconnection network plays a key contribution in the total latency, throughput, power consumption, and hardware cost of the system. The mesh topology, as the most common interconnection network topology, often delivers a fair performance while keeping the implementation cost relatively low. In a 2D mesh, each node is connected to its immediate neighbors in four directions: north, south, east and west. The regular and layout-friendly structure of mesh makes it a proper topology for on-chip implementation in terms of floor planning and circuit-level wiring. However, when the size of the network grows, the average message hop-count of mesh increases proportionally. Particularly, in diagonal routes, when a traffic flow is established from one corner to the opposite corner of the network, packets must travel many intermediate routers. Consequently, for large sizes, the large number of hops translates to a substantial increase in the network latency.

In addition to the hop count problem, the mesh topology suffers from poor collective communication support, when it comes to handling the multicast and broadcast traffic flows. The inherent layer-wise structure of NNs imposes heavy multicast and broadcast traffic flows. These traffic patterns are not naturally suited to the baseline mesh interconnections. This mismatch has been reported in several prior studies. For example, the authors in [11] showed that 10% broadcast traffic reduces the maximum throughput of mesh by $3\times$. To address this problem, several prior work proposed heuristic methods to enable the mesh network to support collective communications (multicast and broadcast) [11,12]. However, there is still a great gap between the multicast/broadcast throughput of mesh with the bandwidth demand of the NN accelerators. This highlights the need for developing and customizing new topologies with inherent multicast/broadcast support for the traffic pattern of NNs.

In this chapter, we present ClosNN [13,14], a specialized NoC for NNs based on the well-known Clos topology. Clos is perhaps the most popular Multistage Interconnection Network (MIN) topology. Clos is used commonly as a base of switching infrastructures in various commercial telecommunication and network routers and switches [15].

MINs, as the most important class of indirect networks, are layer-wise interconnections where each layer is composed of several switches. Packets pass the network layer-by-layer until reaching the output layer, to which the destination nodes are connected. Compared to crossbar switches, MINs have lower implementation cost, so replace the crossbar when a large number of nodes/links should be interconnected.

To design an efficient interconnection network for NN accelerators, the first step is to extract the traffic characteristics of NNs. Our observations show that the traffic pattern of neurons exposes three distinguishing characteristics as follows:

- **Multicast and broadcast:** In feedforward multilayer NNs, multicast and broadcast flows comprise the most part of the traffic, because each neuron sends its output to all neurons in the next layer. According to the fact that multiple neurons are mapped to one processing node, there are several multicast and broadcast flows between the nodes of an accelerator to send the output of a neuron to the nodes where the target neurons are mapped.
- **Predictability:** The design-time predictability of them helps to improve the communication latency and throughput by design-time mapping and scheduling techniques. By considering the structure of the NN (number of layers and number of neurons in each layer), we can predict when a multicast or broadcast flow has to be established.
- **Small-size packets:** Several prior work showed that low-bitwidth number representations (e.g., 16-bit or even lower) are sufficient for neural processing. As a result, the output of each neuron can be easily fitted into a single small flit. The use of short and single-flit packets leads to a significant reduction in the size of switch buffers and also makes the flow control easier.

Based on these observations, we present our novel NoC, ClosNN, which improves both throughput and latency considerably compared to the state-of-the-art NoCs for NN accelerators. In this chapter, we show how the baseline Clos topology can be customized for interneuron communications by leveraging its unique features, i.e., adaptable bisection bandwidth, low diameter, simple routing, and inherent capability of multicast and broadcast communication.

3.1 Related work

From an architectural point of view, the main challenges of designing NN accelerators are 3-fold: complex computation, high memory bandwidth demand, and high-rate communication. A large body of research has been devoted to address these challenges in recent years. Several prior work proposed some heuristic approaches to alleviate the complexity of neural computation [1,5,16]. It is shown that NNs are inherently tolerable to the quantization noise [17–19]. As a result, floating-point arithmetic units can be replaced with the low-cost fixed-point units. Employing low-bitwidth operations during the inference phase of NNs significantly reduces the cost of implementations [20,21], while it keeps the accuracy of results acceptable. For example, Stripes [20] is a novel architecture that relies on bit-serial compute units to parallelize the neural computations with low-bitwidths arithmetic units. In Bit Fusion [21], authors showed that the required bitwidth varies from layer to layer. Motivated by this insight, they proposed a bit-flexible accelerator which is able to dynamically adapt the bitwidth of operations for each layer.

In addition to the inherent error resilience, sparsity is another attractive feature of NNs which aims at reducing the computation cost. For example, sparse convolutional neural network (SCNN) [22] proposes a sparse accelerator for CNNs, which improves energy efficiency by exploiting the zero-valued weights. Specifically, SCNN proposes an architecture to maintain the sparse weights and activations in a compressed encoding to reduce storage requirements. Moreover, exploiting weight repetition, when the same weight occurs multiple times in a weight vector, helps to improve efficiency and save energy in NN accelerators [23,24]. The concepts of NN sparsity and the techniques that leverage it to accelerate NN execution are introduced in Chapter 6 of this book.

A large body of prior work has focused on the emerging memory technologies to overcome the memory bandwidth barrier in NN accelerators. Process-in-memory is a promising solution to tackle this serious challenge [25]. On the other hand, resistive random-access memory (ReRAM) is an emerging nonvolatile memory that is considered the dominant memory architecture in the near future. ReRAM offers a higher density and faster read access compared to traditional DRAM-based memories and early proposals for NN acceleration on ReRAM can be found in the literature [26,27].

Even if the computation and memory challenges are addressed, accelerators can hardly reach their maximum throughput due to the internode bandwidth bottleneck. As mentioned before, on-chip communication for distributing results or raw input data among neurons has a major impact on total energy consumption and performance. In [4], it is shown that data movement among processing elements (PEs) often consumes more energy than computations. Therefore, there is an increasing demand for developing efficient on-chip interconnection networks to decrease the communication latency between PEs in NN accelerators. Some NoC-based hardware accelerators for NNs have been proposed in recent years [10,28,29]. In [10], a comprehensive comparison between various topologies under the neural communication traffic has been presented. The authors showed that the mesh topology has better performance compared to bus, point-to-point links, and tree.

SpiNNaker [7] and EMBRACE [8] are two large-scale spiking neural architectures that use NoC to interconnect cores. In SpiNNaker, the cores are connected by a variant of the torus topology that adds orthogonal links to the baseline torus to reduce diameter. EMBRACE interconnection is arranged as a tree-like hierarchical topology, called H-NoC. NN processing in Embrace relies on special PEs, called neural cell, which can run multiple neurons in parallel. The cells are interconnected in three layers: module, tile, and cluster. In the module layer, up to ten neural cells are connected to a router. The routers themselves are connected to upper layer routers to form a tile. This hierarchy continues by connecting up to four tiles via a switch at the third layer to form a cluster. Up to this layer, a tree-like topology is constructed. If there are more than one clusters in the system, they will be connected by a mesh topology. A concentrated mesh topology has been proposed in [28] to implement NNs. In concentrated mesh, the concentration degree equals to the number of nodes that are connected to each router, with each node hosting several neurons. The routers aggregate the messages of their connected nodes and send them as multicast or broadcast packets to all destination routers. Dragonfly [30] and NoCs with reconfigurable topology [31] are other instances of on-chip interconnection networks that are customized for NNs. These two NoCs aim to increase the scalability of bus by interconnecting multiple small bus-based clusters via a higher level topology. Many prior works have proposed efficient support for collective communication (multicast and broadcast) on NoCs. These architectures aim at reducing the communication latency in on-chip services, such as cache coherency and synchronization [12]. We can classify the existing collective communication approaches into three classes: unicast based, path based, and tree based [32]. In the unicast-based method, a multicast message is converted to several independent unicast ones. Obviously, the main drawback of this scheme is sending several copies of the same data, which leads to an excessive on-chip traffic. Path-based approaches try to find a path that meets all the selected destinations and then send a single packet along the path to deliver data sequentially. Therefore, these methods considerably decrease the traffic load compared to unicast-based ones, but at the cost of latency overhead of serialization. Tree-based approaches form a spanning tree of links that connects the source (as the root node) to all destinations and then send and replicate the packet on the tree. Although both path-based and tree-based approaches alleviate the traffic load compared to the unicast-based approach, they suffer from the routing complexity. Moreover, almost all multicast and broadcast schemes are designed for the mesh topology which is not inherently suitable for collective communication. Our observation in a previous study [33] showed that the Clos topology offers a higher performance than the mesh in handling the multicast traffic of NNs.

Various implementation aspects of Clos topology, such as routing, arbitration, 3D extensions, and floor planning, have been studied in recent years [34–36]. To the best of our knowledge, ClosNN is the first Clos-based architecture that is customized for NNs. In addition to the low diameter and adaptable bisection bandwidth of Clos, its capability of handling multicast and broadcast enables ClosNN to deliver higher performance and throughput, compared to the mesh and tree topologies that are used in the majority of the prior NN accelerators.

3.2   Preliminaries

MINs are composed of two types of nodes: terminal nodes and intermediate nodes. Terminal nodes act as sources and destinations of traffic flows, while intermediate nodes are used to send packets to and from terminal nodes. Crossbar is the simplest indirect topology. A crossbar of size $n \times m$ connects n inputs to m output using $n \times m$ crosspoints. Due to the hardware cost of crossbar switches, some other indirect networks have been proposed to replace a large crossbar with several smaller crossbars in multiple stages. Clos is a well-known MIN that offers a superior performance and efficiency.

A baseline Clos network is composed of three stages of small crossbar switches, called input, middle, and output switches. Generally, a Clos network is parameterized as (m, n, r), where m and r are the numbers of switches at the middle stage and input stage, respectively, and n is the number of input ports of each input-stage switch. In a symmetric Clos, r and n also represent the number of output-stage switches and the number of output ports of each output-stage switch, respectively.

The links are unidirectional and packets are directed forward from input-stage to middle-stage and then to output-stage switches. There is a direct link between every input-stage and middle-stage switch, so each middle-stage switch has a total of r inputs ports. There is also a direct link between every middle-stage and output-stage switch, so a middle-stage switch comes with a total of r output ports. Consequently, in an (m, n, r) Clos, input-stage switches are of size $n \times m$, middle-stage switches are of size $r \times r$, and output-stage switches are of size $m \times n$.

Figure 3.1 shows a three-stage Clos network with $N = n \times r$ input and output ports. Different Clos topologies can be produced by changing the parameters m, n, and r. The number of middle-stage switches (m) plays a key role: as each individual middle-stage switch is connected to all input and output ports, a Clos network with m middle switches provides m distinct routes between every input port to every output port. Increasing the number of middle-stage switches (m) increases the path diversity that directly translates to more routing flexibility and bisection bandwidth. Nonetheless, by increasing the middle switches, the implementation cost grows proportionally.

The Clos topology used in telecommunication and data network infrastructures is typically based on circuit-switching, in which a path between an input–output pair is reserved before the actual transmission. Non-blocking property [32] (any input port can connect to any unique output port, provided that the input and output are not busy themselves) has a critical role in circuit-switched networks. A Clos network benefits from non-blocking property when $m > 2n - 1$. However, in this work, we propose a packet-switched Clos, where each switch is composed of an input-queued crossbar fabric. In packet-switched networks, blocking is not a problem, since all input ports

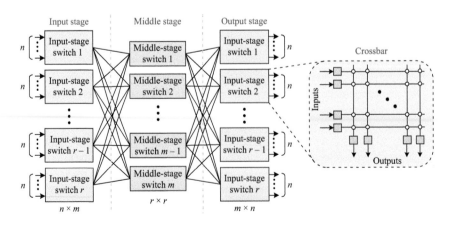

Figure 3.1 A three-stage (m,n,r) Clos network

are equipped with buffers. The capability of buffering and arbitration in all switches enables the network to appropriately share the bandwidth among short interneuron packets.

In packet-switched networks, a flow control is needed to guarantee that there is always available buffering space in the downstream switch before sending a packet. We use the credit-based flow control mechanism [32] in our proposed Clos network.

High-radix networks, such as Clos, have garnered a lot of attention in recent years [34,36,37]. Compared to low-radix networks like mesh, in high-radix networks, routers contain more but narrower links. Since the switches of high-radix networks have more ports (and links), they are able to connect to many other switches, effectively offering lower network diameter. Therefore, low-diameter high-radix networks can potentially offer better latency and throughput. However, the lower diameter of high-radix routers comes at the cost of shorter flits and so, higher packet serialization delays.

However, in NN accelerators, since neurons intrinsically produce short packets, the narrow bitwidth of Clos is not a problem. In the NN accelerators, packets contain the output of a neuron which is often a low-precision fixed-point number plus a few control bits. As a result, leveraging the short packet size, the NN accelerator can benefit from the advantage of low diameter of Clos without suffering from the serialization overhead imposed by narrow links.

3.3 ClosNN: a customized Clos for neural network

Typical NN accelerators are composed of several PEs connected by an on-chip interconnection network. In such accelerators, neurons are mapped and processed on PEs. In this work, we seek an efficient interconnection network as the communication part of these NN processing systems. PEs can be either a specialized hardware or a general-purpose CPU/GPU. In either case, however, the NN generates the same inter-core traffic as long as the neuron-to-core mapping is the same.

Several prior works have shown that the NN computations can be performed by low-bitwidth fixed-point numbers [24,38,39]. As a result, neural information can be transferred using single-flit packets through the interconnection network. In the proposed NoC, packets are composed of neuron outputs (that are 16-bit fixed-point numbers) plus a destination address and a sequence number that specifies by which weight the packet payload should be multiplied. By adopting short and single-flit packets, the complexity of switching and flow control mechanism is reduced and the need for large input buffers is eliminated.

Figure 3.2(a) shows the internal structure of a switch in ClosNN. In this architecture, every input port is equipped with a multiple-entry input buffer to store received packets. The route computation unit handles the routing requests received from the packets at the head of each buffer. For each request, route computation unit returns the output port (or ports) through which the packet should be forwarded. After route computation, the packet (which is still located at the head of buffer) sends a signal to the arbiter unit to request the permission of using the selected output port(s).

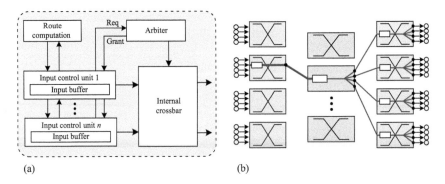

Figure 3.2   (a) The internal architecture of a switch and (b) broadcast on ClosNN

The arbiter allocates output ports to packets in a per-cycle basis and sends back a grant signal (if the desired port is not reserved) and then, the packet can be sent out immediately. If the packet is not allowed to pass (due to arbitration failure), it has to repeat its request in the next cycle. The packet, after receiving the grant signal, is read from the buffer and sent to the output port(s) and from there, to the links toward the downstream switch.

In our design, every switch can easily broadcast its data by leveraging the inherent broadcast capability of Clos networks. Each input link of a switch can be simultaneously connected to any subset of output links of the switch (provided that the output ports are all idle at that time). This capability is implemented in the arbiter unit: if instead of a single output port, the routing function returns a set of output ports to broadcast (or multicast) the packet, the arbiter connects the packet's input port to all or a subset of output ports specified by the routing unit.

3.4   Collective communications on ClosNN

Every input and output port of ClosNN is connected to a PE. We assume that two consecutive layers of an NN, layer n and $n + 1$, are mapped to the PEs at the input and output ports of a ClosNN, respectively. In the feedforward NN model, each neuron in layer n sends its output to all neurons in layer $n + 1$. To implement this data-forwarding scheme, the input ports that are connected to PEs that run neurons of layer n have to communicate with all output ports that are allocated to the neurons of layer $n + 1$. For this purpose, the first step is to packetize the neuron data and deliver it to the input-stage switch. Then, the neuron data are sent to a middle stage and from there, to all or a subset of output-stage switches. Finally, the output-stage switches deliver the data to the PEs at the output side, where the neurons of layer $n + 1$ are mapped. As illustrated in Figure 3.2(b), this procedure is carried out in several steps as follows.

Input-stage routing. Input ports of input-stage switches are connected to PEs at the input side. The generated packets are sent from PEs to the input buffer of the input-stage switches. A controller logic in every input of the switches processes the contents of the input buffers in a first-in-first-served manner. Once a packet reaches to the head of the queue, the route computation unit makes the routing decision to specify the output port to which the packet should be sent.

Many different routing policies have been presented for NoCs. Among them, the routing decision in ClosNN is implemented with the aim of minimizing the queuing time (blocking time) of packets in the middle-stage switches and balancing the network load. To this end, we need a congestion metric: the number of currently free buffer slots of the downstream input ports in the middle-stage switches. When a packet has to be sent from switch x in the input stage to a switch in the middle stage, the routing unit at switch x selects the middle stage with the smallest number of queued packets in its input port that comes from x. By using the credit-based flow control mechanism, the buffer occupancy status of middle-stage switches is available to the route computation unit with no overhead, since this information is already kept and used in each upstream switch. This stage takes one clock cycle.

In ClosNN, only input-stage switches are responsible for the routing decision. After that, packets have a single path toward the destination, so find no routing flexibility in the subsequent stages. The fact that the links are unidirectional makes ClosNN deadlock-free, since there is no cyclic loop in this design.

Input-stage arbitration. The arbitration stage guarantees at most one packet is sent to each output port at each cycle. To request arbitration, the packets that pass the routing stage send a request for the selected output port to the arbiter. The arbitration processes the requests by some arbitration algorithm (e.g., round robin) and for each output port sends back a grant signal to one of the requesting packets. This stage takes one clock cycle. After arbitration, the winner packet passes through the internal crossbar of the switch and then the link to reach the middle-stage switch. In the case of unsuccessful arbitration request, packets will continue to request in the subsequent cycles.

Middle-stage and output-stage broadcast/multicast. To support broadcast, the middle-stage and output-stage switches send the received packets through all downstream paths. Consequently, there is no routing stage in these stages. The arbitration request is also straightforward as each request targets all output ports. Consequently, instead of a separate arbitration for each output port, a single arbiter processes all requests. During this stage, the packet path in the middle-stage and output-stage switches is shown in Figure 3.2(b). Since there is no need for routing in these stages, the only process is the arbitration that is done in a single cycle. Thus, packets can pass these stages in a single cycle at the ideal zero load situation, where there is no blocking penalty. Broadcasting is needed when a packet carries the output of a neuron of layer n and all output ports are connected to PEs that host neurons from layer $n + 1$. In some cases, however, parts of the output ports are allocated to neurons of layer $n + 1$. In this case, there is no need for a broadcast, but the packet should be sent to a subset of outputs. This very likely scenario will happen when two or more NNs are running on a single ClosNN simultaneously and the packets generated by each neuron must be delivered to the neurons of the same NN. Moreover, different layers of the same NN can be mapped onto the PEs and the output of each layer should

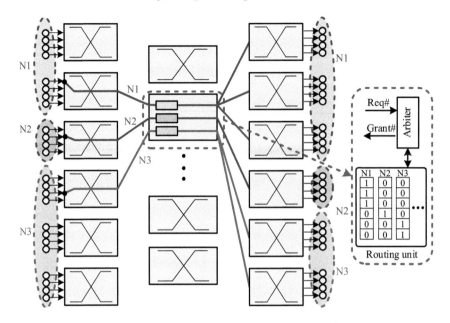

Figure 3.3   Multicast implementation on ClosNN

be delivered to the output ports that are plugged to the neurons of the next layer. To support multicast, a bit vector for each NN is used in the middle-stage and output-stage switches to specify the destination output ports of the neurons of that NN. In this case, an incoming packet must secure all output ports specified by its vector to advance. Packets are matched with their vectors based on an NN identifier in the packet header. For instance, Figure 3.3 shows how the vectors can determine the multicast path of three packets belonging to three different NNs (N1–N3) implemented on a single ClosNN.

3.5   ClosNN customization and area reduction

In the ClosNN topology, the required bandwidth varies from stage to stage. In this section, we analyze the bandwidth of each stage to find the required bandwidth in each stage and remove underutilized network components. Removing the components with unutilized bandwidth leads to a significant reduction in area. We implemented ClosNN in Register-Transfer Level (RTL) using Verilog to calculate the area footprint. The results are extracted by synthesizing the Verilog implementation using a commercial synthesis tool in 45 nm technology.

When using ClosNN to broadcast data, at each cycle, it can send only a single data to all output ports (neurons), while input ports can feed $n \times r$ new data. As depicted in Figure 3.2(b), all delivered packets to the PEs are copies of a single packet, which are replicated in the middle-stage and output-stage switches. As a result, there is an imbalance between the input and output bisection bandwidth demand in ClosNN.

In this case, a single middle-stage switch is used at each cycle to broadcast data, while the others are idle. Therefore, there is a wasted bandwidth between inputs and outputs due to the unused middle-stage switches. In other words, the output-stage switches are the bandwidth bottleneck of the entire system. In a (m, n, r) ClosNN, each output-stage switch can receive up to m packets per cycle, each from one of the middle-stage switches, while it should select only one packet and send multiple copies of that to all of the PEs connected to it (see Figure 3.2). Consequently, the input buffers of output-stage switches will become full quickly and prevent the middle-stage and input-stage switches to work with the maximum bandwidth.

To remove this inefficiency, we propose to employ crossbars with output speedup of 2 or more in the output-stage switches. The output speedup of a switch is the ratio of its output bandwidth to its input bandwidth. A crossbar with output speedup of p has p times as many output ports as input ports. Therefore, in the output stage, by connecting each PE to p output ports of its corresponding switch, each PE can receive p distinct packets at each cycle (Figure 3.4).

In the case of using output-stage switches with output speedup of p, to provide sufficient data for the output layer, ClosNN can now fully use p middle-stage switches, since output-stage switches are able to send p distinct packets to the PEs. As shown in Figure 3.4, the structure of middle-stage switches is intact and there is still one link between each middle-stage and output-stage switch. However, the size of output-stage switches is increased.

As a result, this approach introduces a trade-off between the throughput and area. To explore this trade-off, we compare the area and throughput of a 128×128 ClosNN $(m, 8, 16)$ when m (the speedup of the output-stage switches) changes from 1 to 12 (Figure 3.5(a)). As shown in the figure, area grows more rapidly than throughput when the output speedup increases.

In order to overcome this problem, we can further remove the unused internal bisection width to make input-stage and middle-stage switches simpler. There are

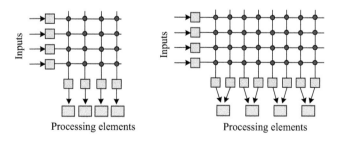

Figure 3.4   A regular 4 × 4 crossbar switch (left) and a crossbar with output speedup of 2 (right)

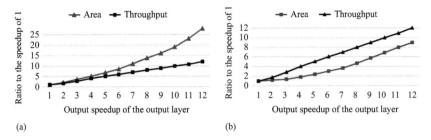

Figure 3.5   *The ratio of area and throughput of an (m,8,16) ClosNN for different output speedup levels to the same network with output speedup of 1 with (a) regular input-stage switches and (b) input-stage switches with reduced output connection (two outgoing connection for input-stage switches). m is set to output speedup of the last-stage switches*

$m \times r$ links between the input-stage and middle-stage switches. These connections are able to carry a maximum of $m \times r$ packets to middle-stage switches, while those switches can send only a maximum of m packets to the output stage. Therefore, we can limit the number of connections that each input-stage switch has (the output degree), to a number less than m. Removing the unused links can reduce the area footprint considerably.

The output degree of the input-stage switches can vary from 1 to m. The output degree of 1 may cause performance loss, since packets have no path diversity. Using the output degree of 2, packets have two options and can be sent to the less-congested middle-stage switch adaptively. Consequently, the average queuing time will be decreased. Although the output degree can be set to any number between 1 and m, our observation shows that there is no considerable performance improvement when output degree increases beyond 2.

This approach decreases the size of input-stage and middle-stage switches considerably. For instance, the crosspoint count of middle-stage switches of a (4, 8, 16) ClosNN before and after applying this area-reduction technique is 16×16 and 16×8, respectively. This shows $2\times$ reduction in the switch size, with no considerable performance loss. Moreover, the size of the 16 input-stage switches is decreased from 8×4 to 8×2.

Figure 3.5(b) explores the trade-off between the throughput and the area when the proposed area-reduction technique is applied. As illustrated by the figure, this technique makes the ClosNN more scalable, since the area grows slower than the throughput. Without loss of generality, we set the output speedup of 4 in this work. As shown in Figure 3.6, a (4, 8, 16) ClosNN with 128 input ports and output speedup of 4 delivers four packets per cycle with the area equals to 2,048 cross-points, while broadcasting on an equivalent crossbar switch delivers one packet per cycle at the cost of 16,384 cross-points.

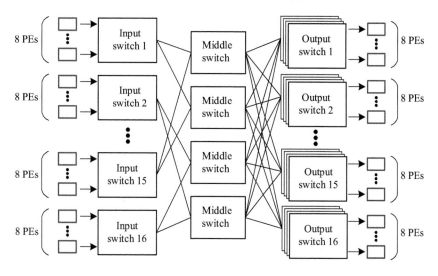

Figure 3.6   A (4,8,16) ClosNN with output speedup of 4

3.6   Folded ClosNN

In multilayer NNs, one ClosNN is placed between any two subsequent layers. As an instance, for a three-layer NN, we need two ClosNN networks; one ClosNN to connect the input layer to the hidden layer and another one to connect the hidden layer to the output layer. In this way, for an NN with n layers, we need $n - 1$ ClosNN networks. In order to make ClosNN scalable, we propose to employ the bidirectional folded Clos architecture.

In a folded Clos, the entire network is folded along the middle stage. In other words, folded Clos is a hierarchical topology in which the first-stage and third-stage switches are combined and the unidirectional links are replaced with bidirectional ones. This architecture benefits from the symmetry of Clos topology, while it further reduces the average hop count.

After folding, as depicted in Figure 3.7, ClosNN's switches are arranged in two layers: leaf and spine. The leaf layer integrates the input-stage and output-stage switches of a conventional Clos: it consists of switches that are connected to both input and output of the network. In the PE side, leaf switches are directly connected to the PEs (neurons) using n bidirectional ports (n inputs and n outputs). In the network side, leaf switches are connected to m spine switches (the network has m middle-stage switches) using m bidirectional ports. Each spine switch has r bidirectional ports, that is, equivalent to the middle-stage switches of the baseline Clos with r unidirectional input and r unidirectional output ports (Figure 3.7).

Several prior works have shown the advantages of the bidirectional folded Clos in terms of floor plan efficiency and circuit-level optimizations [34–36,40]. There is no

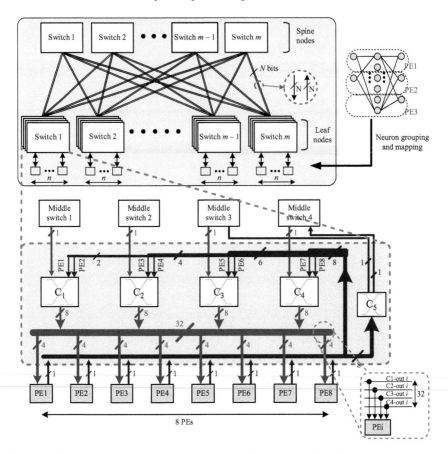

Figure 3.7   The optimized internal structure of a leaf switch with output speedup of 4. The wire unit is 32-bit and the width of links indicates the number of wire units (a connection marked as w has 32 × w wires)

difference in the routing mechanism between the folded Clos and the baseline Clos. In the folded Clos, in much the same way as the baseline, packets first enter a leaf switch and after routing and arbitration cross an upward link to reach a spine switch. Then, the spine switch sends back the packets to leaf switches through downward links and from there, packets are delivered to their destination PEs. If the source and destination of a packet are connected to the same leaf switch, the packet just moves inside it. Therefore, the routing takes less than three hops. This is an advantage of folded Clos compared to the baseline Clos. In Section 3.5, we proposed an area-reduction technique for unidirectional ClosNN. This technique can be applied to fold ClosNN as well. Using the area-reduction technique, the output speedup of the leaf switches increases and the unused upward bandwidth for the broadcast and multicast traffic is removed. The detailed structure of folded ClosNN is outlined in Figure 3.7.

When output speedup is set to 4, each leaf node has n input ports and $4 \times n$ output ports to the PEs.

In the folded ClosNN, we map all NN layers to the same PEs. For example, for a folded ClosNN with N PEs, and a three-layer NN with n_i neurons in layer i ($1 \leq i \leq 3$), each PE can host n_i/N neurons of layer i of the NN. Figure 3.7 also shows this mapping method for a three-layer NN. PEs keep the weight vector and the partial results. Each neuron produces its output when all required data are received. For inter-PE communication, each packet contains two tags: the layer id and the neuron id to specify by which weight the data inside the packet payload should be multiplied. Each PE uses these tags to feed the input data to the right neuron and multiply it by the right weight. Then, the PE adds the result to the partial sum of the neuron.

3.7 Leaf switch optimization

Figure 3.7 shows a ClosNN with output speedup of 4. It consists of four spine switches and eight PEs per switch. The leaf switches have 4 inputs from the spine switches, 8 inputs from the PEs, 2 outputs to spine switches, and 32 outputs to the local PEs (output speedup of 4). As mentioned before, leaf switches can route the packets that have the source and destination node on the same switch internally, effectively offering 1-hop paths for them. However, this benefit comes at the hardware overhead of providing direct connections between the input and output ports of leaf switches. Implementing these connections requires a crossbar switch of size 12×34. This large crossbar will increase the area of ClosNN and may also degrade its clock frequency.

Figure 3.7 shows how ClosNN further trades off the flexibility for smaller area footprint. The full crossbar of each leaf switch is split into five smaller crossbars (C_1–C_5). Crossbar C_5 provides upward data forwarding by multiplexing the eight incoming connections to the two upward connections to the spine switches. The spine-to-leaf and leaf-to-leaf connections are implemented by the crossbars C_1–C_4. The output of these crossbars is connected to all PEs: the output of C_i goes to the ith input port of all PEs. The input of these switches comes from the input ports and the spine switches. Each spine switch is only connected to a single crossbar. Each outgoing link of the PEs is also connected to one of the crossbars C_1–C_4, as shown by Figure 3.7. This design is still capable of connecting any PE to all other PEs on the same switch and also to any spine switch, but with less flexibility and path diversity than a full crossbar of size. Nonetheless, our experiments show that under the broadcast traffic, its negative impact on performance is negligible. Using this connection pattern, the original 12×34 crossbar (with 408 crosspoints) is replaced with four 3×8 and one 8×2 crossbars (with 112 crosspoints in total).

3.8 Scaling to larger NoCs

ClosNN has a modular structure that can be scaled up easily to connect more PEs. The most straightforward way to design a 512-PE system is to increase the number

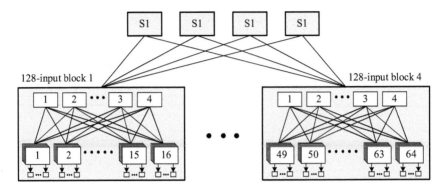

Figure 3.8   The modular structure of 512-node ClosNN

of leaf switches in the baseline two-level topology. However, adding more switches in the input layer increases the size of middle-stage switches. Alternatively, another way to implement a 512-PE system is to extend the 128-PE ClosNN by increasing the depth of the hierarchy. As shown in Figure 3.8, the 512-PE system is a three-layer folded ClosNN which is composed of four 128-PE ClosNN networks, connected by four switches at the third layer.

In this structure, the spine switches of the 128-node units are arranged as 16 switches at the second level. These switches can be considered the leaf for the third layer switches and are connected in the same way as the 16 leaf switches in each 128-node cluster are connected to four spine switches. The connection pattern between the third-layer and second-layer switches is the same as the connection pattern of the leaf and spine switches inside a 128-node cluster. Similarly, up to four 512-node units can be integrated by a forth layer spine switch, comprising up to four switches, to connect 512–2,048 nodes. If implementing a large accelerator requires more than a single chip, we can still use ClosNN to establish both inter-chip and intra-chip connections. In this structure, the PEs of each chip are connected by a ClosNN and the chips themselves are connected by a higher spine layer.

3.9   Evaluation

We compare ClosNN, the concentrated mesh topology of [28] (Cmesh) and the H-NoC topology of EBMRACE [8] in a cycle-accurate NoC simulator [41] under a set of synthetic and realistic workloads. The evaluations are done on 128-PE accelerators with 32-bit links. The links are wide enough to carry a 16-bit fixed point number and routing information in a single flit. The size of the evaluated folded ClosNN is (4,8,16) with the output speedup of 4. In H-NoC, there are eight PEs (each running a single neuron) per neuron router, eight neuron routers per tile router, and two tile routers per cluster router (see Figure 3.9). In the concentrated mesh, the concentration degree is 4 to form an 8 × 4 mesh. We use the multicast routing algorithms

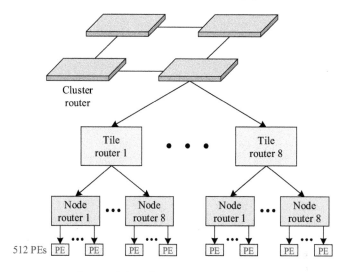

Figure 3.9   The H-NoC topology [8]

developed for H-NoC and concentrated mesh in [8] and [28], respectively. With these NoC sizes, the hop count of ClosNN is 3 hops that is shorter than the maximum hop count of 6 of H-NoC and 12 of Cmesh.

The switches in all considered networks are input-queued with 8-flit deep buffers. The zero-load latency of all switches is three cycles, consisting the route computation, output arbitration, and internal crossbar and link traversal stages. For ClosNN and H-NoC, switch latency is two cycles for downward direction, as there is no need for downward routing. We have also implemented all three NoCs (H-NoC, ClosNN, and Cmesh) in Verilog and synthesized the design in TSMC 45 nm technology point to report power, area, and timing results. The timing results show that all routers can work at 2 GHz. Thus, we consider the same frequency for all of them. We also calculate the latency of links through Spice simulation based on (1) the Clos floor plan presented in [40] and (2) the PE size taken from the CORN accelerator [24]. The results show that the links are fast enough to implement 512 node or larger ClosNN instances with single-cycle link traversal capability.

As mentioned before, the NoCs imposes no restrictions on what type of the PEs are used. To simulate the PE operation, we assume that the PEs perform the multiply and accumulate operation on every received input data in a single cycle.

3.9.1   Performance comparison under synthetic traffic

We first evaluate the NoCs under a uniform broadcast traffic. The comparison metric is the broadcast latency of a packet that is measured from the packet gen- eration time to the time when the packet is delivered to the last target. As Figure 3.10 illustrates, the lower hop count of ClosNN brings about a shorter latency. In addi- tion, the customized design of ClosNN, which tailors its structure to the particular

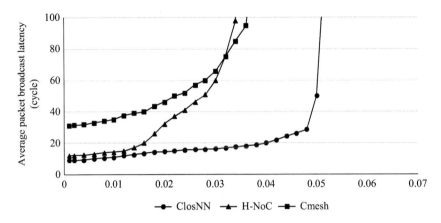

Figure 3.10   Average broadcast latency (from the injection time to the delivery of the last copy of the packet) of concentrated mesh, H-NoC, and ClosNN under uniform traffic

collective traffic of NNs, enables the network to push the saturation point toward higher traffic rates to improve maximum throughput significantly. Note that expanding output speed up will not work for H-NoC, because it features a limited bisection width and upper layers can just broadcast down a single packet to the leaf switches at each cycle. The hardware implementation results show that H-NoC has the smallest area footprint (0.904 mm^2) among the other designs, with 76% smaller area than ClosNN. This superiority of H-NoC's area is due to its minimal interlayer connectivity. However, the performance of ClosNN is still higher than that of H-NoC with the same area. We refer the interested readers to [13] for more detailed results.

3.9.2   Performance evaluation under realistic workloads

To further evaluate the proposed design, we compared the performance offered by ClosNN with that of H-NoC and Cmesh under some realistic workloads. Table 3.1 shows the structure of the NNs selected as the benchmarks. All benchmarks have been implemented and evaluated on the 128-node example of the three considered networks; multiple neurons are mapped onto a similar PE in larger NNs, while smaller NNs occupy just part of the PEs. In the latter case, the broadcast approach is replaced with the multicast scheme depicted in Figure 3.3. A similar neuron to PE mapping is used for all networks. Figure 3.11 shows the NN throughput of the NoCs. To give a better insight into the performance of the NoCs, the results are normalized to Cmesh. Throughput is defined as the maximum NN input arrival rate (input per cycle) that the network can accept to execute (broadcast the data) before reaching to the saturation point. The network saturation point is usually considered the input injection rate at which the packet latency is three times longer than the zero-load

Table 3.1   The structure of realistic workloads

Benchmark	Topology (in:hidden:out)
Digit recognition [42]	784:700:10
Census data analysis [43]	14:64:2
Performance modeling [44]	128:256:128
Image classification [45]	3,072:600:10
ECG analysis [46]	300:300:2

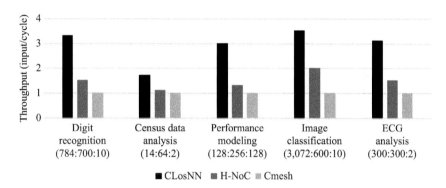

Figure 3.11   Throughput under five practical applications on 128-node networks.
The outcomes are normalized with Cmesh

latency. In these experiments, we set the saturation latency to 50 cycles. As demonstrated in Figure 3.11, ClosNN delivers a higher throughput than H-NoC and Cmesh. The main reason behind this performance improvement is that ClosNN offers a shorter average hop count and better support for collective communication, so it yields higher throughput compared to other two architectures. ClosNN can deliver up to four distinct packets to all PEs per cycle, while H-NoC can deliver only a single packet to all PEs per cycle. Moreover, ClosNN's diameter is three hops, while H-NoC's diameter is five hops. Due to these topological advantages, ClosNN offers up to 2.4× higher throughput (average 1.93×) than H-NoC.

3.9.3   Power comparison

Figure 3.12 shows the power consumption of the three considered NoCs, when they work at the maximum throughput. Different benchmarks inject rather the same traffic rate to the networks at maximum throughput. Therefore, they show close power consumption profile and we just report the power results of *ECG analysis* as a representative benchmark. As expected, because of shorter hop count, ClosNN consumes less power than the other two networks.

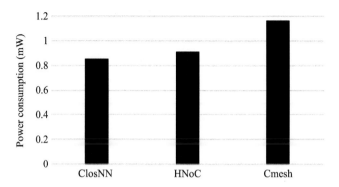

Figure 3.12   Power consumption in 128-node networks under the ECG analysis benchmark

Table 3.2   Throughput under three practical applications on 512-node and 2,048-node networks. The outcomes are normalized to Cmesh

Benchmark	Topology (in:hidden:out)	ClosNN	Normalized throughput (input/cycle)		
			ClosNN	H-NoC	Cmesh
Digit recognition	784:700:10	512	3.8	2.7	1
ECG analysis	300:300:2	512	3.5	2.8	1
Image classification	3,072:600:10	2,048	4.9	3.7	1

3.9.4   Sensitivity to neural network size

As described in Section 3.8, ClosNN can be scaled up to execute larger NNs. To show this capability, we compare 512-node and 2,048-node ClosNNs with the other considered NoCs. The 2,048-node ClosNN uses a four-layer topology in which four 512-node networks are connected by a fourth spine layer. Table 3.2 reports the throughput (as defined in Section 3.9.2) offered by the networks under the three benchmarks of the previous subsection that have more than 512 neurons. The performance numbers are again normalized to Cmesh.

As demonstrated in Table 3.2, the shorter diameter and higher bisection of ClosNN still enables it to outperform the competitor design when the size grows. Cmesh still offers the lower throughput, because when the NN size grows, the average hop count of Cmesh increases proportionally, which directly translated to higher latency and lower throughput. ClosNN has higher network throughput than Cmesh and H-NoC. More detailed evaluation of large-scale ClosNN networks can be found in [13].

3.10 Conclusion

In this work, we demonstrated the predominant performance the Clos-based topologies in dealing with the multicast-based and broadcast-based traffic of NNs. We first showed that the synergy between the multicast-based multilayer communication of NNs and the Clos network makes this topology a proper selection for hardware implementation of NNs. Then, we presented ClosNN, a novel topology for NNs that modifies the baseline-folded Clos. The customizations included expanding its bandwidth and removing its unnecessary connections with respect to the broadcast-based traffic of NNs. In our design, up to 128 cores can be connected by a baseline two-layer-folded ClosNN. For larger structures, ClosNN can be scaled up in a modular fashion by connecting 128-node networks via higher levels of spine switches. The experimental results showed that ClosNN can offer higher throughput and lower latency than the concentrated mesh and the cutting edge Hierarchical topologies and can be considered an adaptable, performance-efficient, and scalable topology to construct large-scale NN accelerators.

References

[1] Du Z, Fasthuber R, Chen T, *et al.* ShiDianNao: Shifting vision processing closer to the sensor. In: ACM SIGARCH Computer Architecture News. vol. 43. ACM; 2015. p. 92–104.

[2] Hauswald J, Kang Y, Laurenzano MA, *et al.* Djinn and tonic: DNN as a service and its implications for future warehouse scale computers. In: ACM SIGARCH Computer Architecture News. vol. 43. ACM; 2015. p. 27–40.

[3] Esmaeilzadeh H, Sampson A, Ceze L, *et al.* Neural acceleration for general-purpose approximate programs. In: Proceedings of the 2012 45th Annual IEEE/ACM International Symposium on Microarchitecture. IEEE Computer Society; 2012. p. 449–460.

[4] Chen YH, Krishna T, Emer J, *et al.* Eyeriss: An energy-efficient reconfigurable accelerator for deep convolutional neural networks. In: IEEE International Solid-State Circuits Conference, ISSCC 2016, Digest of Technical Papers; 2016. p. 262–263.

[5] Zhang S, Du Z, Zhang L, *et al.* Cambricon-X: An accelerator for sparse neural networks. In: Microarchitecture (MICRO), 2016 49th Annual IEEE/ACM International Symposium on. IEEE; 2016. p. 1–12.

[6] Reagen B, Whatmough P, Adolf R, *et al.* Minerva: Enabling low-power, highly-accurate deep neural network accelerators. In: Computer Architecture (ISCA), ACM/IEEE 43rd Annual International Symp. on; 2016.

[7] Painkras E, Plana LA, Garside J, *et al.* SpiNNaker: A 1-W 18-core system-on-chip for massively-parallel neural network simulation. IEEE Journal of Solid-State Circuits. 2013;48(8):1943–1953.

[8] Carrillo S, Harkin J, McDaid LJ, *et al.* Scalable hierarchical network-on-chip architecture for spiking neural network hardware implementations. IEEE Transactions on Parallel and Distributed Systems. 2013;24(12):2451–2461.

[9]   Fakhraie SM, and Smith KC. VLSI—Compatible Implementations for Artifi-
        cial Neural Networks. vol. 382. Berlin, Germany: Springer Science & Business
        Media; 2012.

[10]   Vainbrand D, and Ginosar R. Network-on-chip architectures for neural net-
        works. In: Networks-on-Chip (NOCS), 2010 Fourth ACM/IEEE International
        Symposium on. IEEE; 2010. p. 135–144.

[11]   Jerger NE, Peh LS, and Lipasti M. Virtual circuit tree multicasting: A case
        for on-chip hardware multicast support. In: Computer Architecture, 2008.
        ISCA'08. 35th International Symposium on. IEEE; 2008. p. 229–240.

[12]   Karkar A, Mak T, Tong KF, *et al.* A survey of emerging interconnects for
        on-chip efficient multicast and broadcast in many-cores. IEEE Circuits and
        Systems Magazine. 2016;16(1):58–72.

[13]   Hojabr R, Modarressi M, Daneshtalab M, *et al.* Customizing Clos
        network-on-chip for neural networks. IEEE Transactions on Computers.
        2017;66(11):1865–1877.

[14]   Yasoubi A, Hojabr R, Takshi H, Modarressi M, and Daneshtalab M. CuPAN–
        high throughput on-chip interconnection for neural networks. In: International
        Conference on Neural Information Processing. 2015; pp. 559–566.

[15]   Singh A, Ong J, Agarwal A, *et al.* Jupiter rising: A decade of Clos topolo-
        gies and centralized control in Google's datacenter network. ACM SIGCOMM
        Computer Communication Review. 2015;45(4):183–197.

[16]   Chen T, Du Z, Sun N, *et al.* DianNao: A small-footprint high-throughput
        accelerator for ubiquitous machine-learning. ACM SIGPLAN Notices.
        2014;49(4):269–284.

[17]   Hubara I, Courbariaux M, Soudry D, *et al.* Quantized neural networks: Training
        neural networks with low precision weights and activations. The Journal of
        Machine Learning Research. 2017;18(1):6869–6898.

[18]   Köster U, Webb T, Wang X, *et al.* Flexpoint: An adaptive numerical format for
        efficient training of deep neural networks. In: Advances in Neural Information
        Processing Systems; 2017. p. 1742–1752.

[19]   Zhou S, Wu Y, Ni Z, Zhou X, Wen H, and Zou Y. DoReFa-Net: Training
        low bitwidth convolutional NNs with low bitwidth gradients. arXiv preprint
        arXiv:160606160. 2016.

[20]   Judd P, Albericio J, Hetherington T, *et al.* Stripes: Bit-serial deep neural
        network computing. In: Microarchitecture (MICRO), 2016 49th Annual
        IEEE/ACM International Symposium on. IEEE; 2016. p. 1–12.

[21]   Sharma H, Park J, Suda N, *et al.* Bit Fusion: Bit-level dynamically composable
        architecture for accelerating deep neural network. In: ACM/IEEE 45th Annual
        International Symposium on Computer Architecture (ISCA); 2018.

[22]   Parashar A, Rhu M, Mukkara A, *et al.* SCNN: An accelerator for compressed-
        sparse convolutional neural networks. In: Computer Architecture (ISCA),
        ACM/IEEE 44th Annual International Symposium on; 2017. p. 27–40.

[23]   Hegde K, Yu J, Agrawal R, Yan M, Pellauer M, and Fletcher CW. UCNN:
        Exploiting computational reuse in deep neural networks via weight repetition.
        arXiv preprint arXiv:180406508. 2018.

[24] Yasoubi A, Hojabr R, and Modarressi M. Power-efficient accelerator design for neural networks using computation reuse. IEEE Computer Architecture Letters. 2017;16(1):72–75.

[25] Liu J, Zhao H, Ogleari MA, *et al.* Processing-in-memory for energy-efficient neural network training: A heterogeneous approach. In: 2018 51st Annual IEEE/ACM International Symposium on Microarchitecture (MICRO). IEEE; 2018. p. 655–668.

[26] Song L, Qian X, Li H, *et al.* Pipelayer: A pipelined ReRAM-based accelerator for deep learning. In: 2017 IEEE International Symposium on High Performance Computer Architecture (HPCA). IEEE; 2017. p. 541–552.

[27] Shafiee A, Nag A, Muralimanohar N, *et al.* ISAAC: A convolutional neural network accelerator with in-situ analog arithmetic in crossbars. ACM SIGARCH Computer Architecture News. 2016;44(3):14–26.

[28] Dong Y, Li C, Lin Z, *et al.* Multiple network-on-chip model for high performance neural network. JSTS: Journal of Semiconductor Technology and Science. 2010;10(1):28–36.

[29] Firuzan A, Modarressi M, and Daneshtalab M. Reconfigurable communication fabric for efficient implementation of neural networks. In: Reconfigurable Communication-centric Systems-on-Chip (ReCoSoC), 2015 10th International Symposium on. IEEE; 2015. p. 1–8.

[30] Akbari N, and Modarressi M. A high-performance network-on-chip topology for neuromorphic architectures. In: 2017 IEEE International Conference on Computational Science and Engineering (CSE) and IEEE International Conference on Embedded and Ubiquitous Computing (EUC). vol. 2. IEEE; 2017. p. 9–16.

[31] Firuzan A, Modarressi M, Daneshtalab M, *et al.* Reconfigurable network-on-chip for 3D neural network accelerators. In: Proceedings of the Twelfth IEEE/ACM International Symposium on Networks-on-Chip. IEEE Press; 2018. p. 18.

[32] Dally WJ, and Towles BP. Principles and Practices of Interconnection Networks. San Francisco, USA: Elsevier; 2004.

[33] Yasoubi A, Hojabr R, Takshi H, *et al.* CuPAN—High throughput on-chip interconnection for neural networks. In: International Conference on Neural Information Processing. Springer; 2015. p. 559–566.

[34] Kao YH, Yang M, Artan NS, *et al.* CNoC: High-radix Clos network-on-chip. IEEE Transactions on Computer-Aided Design of Integrated Circuits and Systems. 2011;30(12):1897–1910.

[35] Chen L, Zhao L, Wang R, *et al.* MP3: Minimizing performance penalty for power-gating of Clos network-on-chip. In: 2014 IEEE 20th International Symposium on High Performance Computer Architecture (HPCA). IEEE; 2014. p. 296–307.

[36] Kao YH, Alfaraj N, Yang M, *et al.* Design of high-radix Clos network-on-chip. In: Networks-on-Chip (NOCS), 2010 Fourth ACM/IEEE International Symposium on. IEEE; 2010. p. 181–188.

[37]   Jain A, Parikh R, and Bertacco V. High-radix on-chip networks with low-radix routers. In: Proceedings of the 2014 IEEE/ACM International Conference on Computer-Aided Design. IEEE Press; 2014. p. 289–294.

[38]   Zhang Q, Wang T, Tian Y, *et al.* ApproxANN: An approximate computing framework for artificial neural network. In: Proceedings of the 2015 Design, Automation & Test in Europe Conference & Exhibition. EDA Consortium; 2015. p. 701–706.

[39]   Venkataramani S, Ranjan A, Roy K, *et al.* AxNN: Energy-efficient neuromorphic systems using approximate computing. In: Proceedings of International Symposium on Low Power Electronics and Design. ACM; 2014. p. 27–32.

[40]   Zia A, Kannan S, Rose G, *et al.* Highly-scalable 3D Clos NOC for many-core CMPs. In: NEWCAS Conference (NEWCAS), 2010 8th IEEE International. IEEE; 2010. p. 229–232.

[41]   Jiang N, Becker DU, Michelogiannakis G, *et al.* A detailed and flexible cycle-accurate network-on-chip simulator. In: 2013 IEEE International Symposium on Performance Analysis of Systems and Software (ISPASS); 2013. p. 86–96.

[42]   LeCun Y, Bottou L, Bengio Y, *et al.* Gradient-based learning applied to document recognition. Proceedings of the IEEE. 1998;86(11):2278–2324.

[43]   Asuncion A, and Newman D. UCI machine learning repository; 2007. http://www.ics.uci.edu/~mlearn/MLRepository.html.

[44]   Esmaeilzadeh H, Saeedi P, Araabi BN, Lucas C, and Fakhraie SM. Neural network stream processing core (NnSP) for embedded systems. In: 2006 IEEE International Symposium on Circuits and Systems. IEEE; 2006. p. 4.

[45]   Krizhevsky A, and Hinton G. Learning multiple layers of features from tiny images. Technical report, University of Toronto. 2009;1(4):7.

[46]   Moody GB, and Mark RG. The impact of the MIT-BIH arrhythmia database. IEEE Engineering in Medicine and Biology Magazine. 2001;20(3):45–50.

Part II

Deep learning and approximate data representation

Chapter 4

Stochastic-binary convolutional neural networks with deterministic bit-streams

*M. Hassan Najafi[1], S. Rasoul Faraji[2], Bingzhe Li[2],
David J. Lilja[2], and Kia Bazargan[2]*

4.1 Overview

Stochastic computing (SC), an unconventional paradigm processing random bit-stream, has been used for low-cost and low-power implementation of neural networks (NNs). Inaccuracy of computations and long processing time have made prior SC-based designs of NNs inefficient compared to conventional fixed-point binary radix-based designs. Long random or pseudorandom bit-streams often need to be generated and processed to produce acceptable results. The long processing time further leads to a significantly higher energy consumption than the energy of binary design counterparts.

Low-discrepancy (LD) bit-streams have been recently used for fast-converging and deterministic computation with SC circuits. In this chapter, we propose a low-cost, low-latency, and energy-efficient design of convolutional NNs (CNNs) based on LD deterministic bit-streams. Experimental results show a significant reduction in the energy consumption compared to previous random bit-stream-based implementations and to the optimized fixed-point design with no quality degradation.

The remainder of this chapter is organized as follows: Section 4.2 introduces the current challenges in implementing SC-based NNs. Section 4.3 presents necessary information on SC and discusses the recently developed deterministic methods of processing LD bit-streams. In Section 4.5, we describe our proposed method for high-quality energy-efficient design of CNNs. In Section 4.6, we evaluate the performance and hardware efficiency of the proposed design by hardware implementation of a LeNet5 NN architecture. Finally, Section 4.7 summarizes this chapter.

4.2 Introduction

Large-scale NNs mainly operate on high-performance server or GPU clusters. The speed of these clusters, however, is not enough to keep up with current high processing

[1]School of Computing and Informatics, University of Louisiana at Lafayette, Lafayette, LA, USA
[2]Department of Electrical and Computer Engineering, University of Minnesota, Twin Cities, MN, USA

speed demands. The computing requirement at a server or GPU cluster further implies high power and energy consumption. A promising method to overcome these short-comings is designing specific hardware-based NNs to exploit the maximum degree of parallelism and achieve a significant reduction in processing time, power, and energy consumption.

High computational complexity of large-scale NNs makes the conventional fixed-point hardware implementations expensive, energy inefficient, and in many cases impractical with limited hardware resources. SC [1–3] has been recently used for low-area and low-power implementation of CNNs [4–17]. This unconventional computing paradigm has the potential to enable fully parallel and scalable hardware design of CNNs. Multiplication, as an essential and costly operation in conventional fixed-point hardware designs of CNNs, can be implemented with simple standard AND gates in SC. Low-cost design of multiplication operations results in significant savings in hardware design of NNs. Redundant representation of data with long bit-streams further makes SC-based implementations of NNs tolerant to noise (i.e., bit-flips).

Quality degradation, long processing time, and high energy consumption, how-ever, are still the main barriers in efficient design of SC-based NNs. Random fluctuations in generating bit-streams and correlation between bit-streams result in approximate computations and hence quality loss in different layers of NNs. A long processing time is often inevitable to produce acceptable results. This long processing time leads to high energy consumption, which in most cases is higher than that of the corresponding conventional fixed-point binary design. Designing high accuracy energy-efficient SC-based NNs is still an open problem.

Deterministic computations with stochastic bit-streams [18–20] have been recently introduced as an evolution in the SC paradigm. By properly structuring bit-streams, computation with SC logic can be performed deterministically. The results are completely accurate and the same as the results from the conventional binary designs. The operations must run for an exact number of cycles (i.e., the product of the length of input bit-streams) to guarantee producing accurate results. These meth-ods were initially developed based on unary bit-streams (streams with first all 1s and then all 0s). The nature of unary bit-streams, however, leads to a long processing time and so a high energy consumption to produce acceptable results. These weaknesses made the early unary bit-stream-based deterministic methods inefficient for applica-tions that can tolerate some degrees of inaccuracy (e.g., image processing and NN designs). We developed a hybrid binary-unary method in [21] to mitigate the energy consumption issue of unary bit-stream-based designs. However, the method of [21] is not applicable to multivariate functions such as the multiplication operation.

The early deterministic methods were revised in [22] by bringing random-ization back into bit-stream representation and replacing unary bit-streams with pseudorandom bit-streams. For a fixed accuracy level, by generating deterministic pseudorandom bit-streams, a lower processing time and a lower energy consump-tion were achieved compared to the unary stream-based deterministic methods. More recently, LD deterministic methods are proposed in [23] for fast-converging and energy-efficient processing of bit-streams with SC circuits.

In this chapter, we propose a hybrid bit-stream-binary design for energy-efficient, low-cost, and yet accurate implementation of CNNs. We use LD deterministic bit-streams to implement the first convolutional layer of the NN, as convolutional layers account for more than 90% of the overall hardware cost in some CNNs [7]. We explore the impact of using different combinations of LD sequences in generating deterministic bit-streams for the proposed design. Experimental results show a significant reduction in the energy consumption and hardware cost compared to the conventional fixed-point design. In contrast to prior SC and hybrid stochastic-binary designs, the proposed design gives the same classification rate as the fixed-point design.

4.3 Background

4.3.1 Stochastic computing

SC is a reemerging computing paradigm operating on random bit-streams. Indepen-dent of the length (and interleaving of 0s and 1s), the ratio of the number of the ones to the length of the bit-stream determines the value in the [0,1] interval. For example, 1011110010 is a representation of 0.6 in the stochastic domain. Computation accuracy increases with the length of the bit-stream. In contrast to conventional binary radix representation, all digits of a bit-stream have the same weight. In a noisy environment, faults in the high-order bits of a binary radix representation can produce large errors. With a stochastic representation, however, a single bit-flip results in a small error. This error tolerance scales to high error rates so that multiple bit flips produce only small and uniform deviations from the nominal value.

Beside the ability of tolerating high rates of noise, implementing complex oper-ations with simple hardware is another primary advantage of SC. Multiplication, as a costly and common operation in CNNs, can be implemented with a single standard AND gate in stochastic domain. As shown in Figure 4.1, an AND gate works as a stochastic multiplier if independent (uncorrelated) bit-streams are connected to its inputs.

To convert data from binary radix format to bit-stream representation, an unbiased random number from a random or pseudorandom source is compared to a constant number (based on the target input data). The output of the comparison produces one bit of the stochastic bit-stream in each cycle. A "1" is generated at the output of the comparator if the random number is less than the constant number. A "0" is gen-erated otherwise. Figure 4.2 shows the structure of a binary-to-bit-stream converter

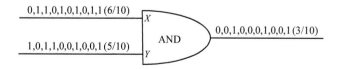

Figure 4.1   Example of stochastic multiplication using AND gate

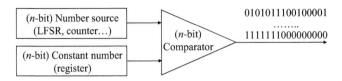

Figure 4.2   Structure of a stochastic bit-stream generator

Sobol Seq 1	0	1/2	1/4	3/4	1/8	5/8	3/8	7/8	1/16	9/16	5/16	13/16	3/16	11/16	7/16	15/16
Sobol Seq 2	0	1/2	3/4	1/4	5/8	1/8	3/8	7/8	15/16	7/16	3/16	11/16	5/16	13/16	9/16	1/16
Sobol Seq 3	0	1/2	1/4	3/4	7/8	3/8	5/8	1/8	11/16	3/16	15/16	7/16	5/16	13/16	1/16	9/16
Sobol Seq 4	0	1/2	3/4	1/4	7/8	3/8	1/8	5/8	7/16	15/16	11/16	3/16	9/16	1/16	5/16	13/16

Figure 4.3   MATLAB® built-in first four Sobol sequences

responsible for generating stochastic bit-streams. The generated bit-streams are processed using SC circuits and an output bit-stream is produced. The output bit-stream
can be converted back to binary format by simply counting the number of ones in the
bit-stream using a binary counter.

4.3.2   Deterministic low-discrepancy bit-streams

LD sequences such as Halton and Sobol sequences have been previously used to
improve the speed of computation on stochastic bit-streams [24–26]. The 1s and 0s
in the LD bit-streams are uniformly spaced and so the streams do not suffer from
random fluctuations. The output converges faster to the correct value and as a result
a lower processing time is expected for a fixed accuracy level.

We showed in [23] that Sobol sequences can be used for fast-converging deterministic multiplication of stochastic bit-streams. A different Sobol sequence is used
to convert each independent input data to a bit-stream representation. When multiplying two N-bit precision numbers, each number is converted to a 2^{2N}-bit bit-stream
by comparing it to the first 2^{2N} numbers of a different Sobol sequence. Alternatively,
the inputs can first be converted to bit-streams of 2^N-bit length by comparing each
to the first 2^N numbers of a different Sobol sequence. The bit-stream corresponding
to the first input is then repeated until it becomes a stream of 2^{2N}-bit length. The
bit-stream corresponding to the second input is stalled after every 2^N clock cycles
and repeated until it similarly becomes a stream of 2^{2N} bits. Both of these methods
produce correct (completely accurate) results when executing the operation for 2^{2N}
clock cycles. They also produce a similar output and have the same truncation error
when processing short bit-streams ($\leq 2^N$ bits).

Figure 4.3 shows the first 16 numbers of the first four Sobol sequences
from the MATLAB built-in Sobol sequence generator. An important property of
Sobol sequences, including these four sequences, is that the first 2^N numbers of
any Sobol sequence can precisely present all possible N-bit precision numbers in

the [0,1] interval. Hence, the only error in converting input data to 2^N bits length Sobol-based bit-streams is the quantization error (there is no random fluctuations error). In the following, we see an example of multiplying two 2-bit precision numbers, 2/4 and 3/4, by converting them to bit-streams of 16 bits by comparing them to the first 16 numbers of Sobol Sequence 1 and Sobol Sequence 2, respectively, and ANDing the generated bit-streams. Note that a "1" is generated in the bit-stream if the Sobol number from the Sobol sequence is less than the target input data.

$$
\begin{array}{rl}
2/4 = & 1100\ 1100\ 1100\ 1100 \\
3/4 = & 1101\ 1110\ 0111\ 1011 \\
\hline
6/16 = & 1100\ 1100\ 0100\ 1000
\end{array}
$$

As can be seen, the deterministic and exact output of multiplying the two 2-bit precision input data is produced by ANDing the two generated 16 bits long bit-streams. With the conventional random stream-based SC, we need to run the multiplication operation multiple times (each time generating and ANDing a different pair of bit-streams) and then find the mean of the outputs to produce statistically significant results. Since the input data is converted to deterministic bit-streams, the output of processing Sobol-based bit-streams has a standard deviation of zero. Once processing the bit-streams is therefore sufficient to have an output free of variation.

We evaluated the impact of using four different combinations of Sobol sequences in generating bit-streams for all possible cases of multiplying two 8-bit precision input data in the [0,1] interval. The results are reported in Table 4.1. We compare the performance using the mean absolute error (MAE) metric. The computed MAEs are multiplied by 100 and reported as a percentage. As shown in Table 4.1, all the four selected combinations of Sobol sequences give exact results after 2^{16} cycles (processing 2^{16}-bit streams). When processing for a smaller number of cycles, the outputs include some truncation error due to inaccurate representation of data. As reported, the rate of this error changes for different combinations of Sobol sequences. The change

Table 4.1 *Mean absolute error (%) comparison of using different combinations of Sobol sequences in LD bit-stream-based multiplication of 8-bit precision input data*

Operation cycles	Sobol 1 and 2	Sobol 1 and 4	Sobol 2 and 3	Sobol 3 and 4
4	15.8	15.8	15.8	15.8
5	14.7	11.1	10.0	9.5
6	13.5	9.5	12.1	9.3
7	13.2	11.2	10.6	9.3
8	8.9	7.8	7.8	8.9
9	6.3	10.4	5.7	7.9
10	6.1	7.9	5.7	6.7
16	3.7	4.3	3.9	4.4
32	1.8	2.4	1.9	2.3
2^{16}	0.0	0.0	0.0	0.0

in the order of numbers in the Sobol sequences leads to different interactions between bit-streams and therefore producing different outputs. In this chapter, we convert the input data to LD deterministic Sobol-based bit-streams for accurate processing of data in CNNs. We experimentally show that processing these bit-streams for only a few cycles is sufficient to achieve the same results as the results from the conventional fixed-point binary counterpart.

4.3.3   Convolutional neural networks

CNNs are an important and common class of NNs that have proven to be very effective in areas such as image recognition and classification. A general CNN consists of convolutional layers followed by some pooling and fully-connected layers. A convolutional layer extracts a feature map from its input by applying a set of kernels (filters) and by activating them when specific types of features are found in the inputs. Each pixel in a feature map is a convolution neuron which is obtained by convolving a filter-sized moving window and the inputs in the moving window. The activation functions are nonlinear transformation functions such as rectified linear units (ReLUs), sigmoid, and hyperbolic tangent (tanh) function which are used to extract specific types of features from the convolution neurons. Choosing each of these functions has a trade-off between performance and computational complexity. To reduce the dimensions of feature maps and hence mitigating the over-fitting issues, a pooling layer subsamples the data. There are various pooling layers such as average pooling, max pooling, and L2-norm pooling. The fully-connected layer fully connects its input to all activated neurons of its previous layer. Each neuron in the fully-connected layer finds dot-product (inner-product) of its inputs and corresponding weights. Finally, a loss function is also necessary to specify the deviation between the predicted and real labels in the network-training process. The loss function can be softmax loss, cross-entropy loss, sigmoid, or Euclidean loss in a loss layer.

In this chapter, we focus on the dot-product operation as the basic and essential operation in the convolutional and fully-connected layers. We implement the *first* convolutional layer of CNN using a hybrid deterministic bit-stream-binary dot-product design. We do not use bit-stream processing in the subsequent layers, since accuracy losses from processing bit-streams would compound and require long bit-streams to achieve accurate results.

4.4   Related work

SC has been used in recent years for low-area and low-power implementations of NNs. We point to [27] as one of the first work applying SC to NNs. SC has been also applied to deep belief networks [28], radial basis function NNs [29], and the restricted Boltzmann machine—a type of artificial NNs [30]. An efficient implementation of deep NNs (DNNs) based on integral SC is proposed in [11] resulting in up to 33% reduction in energy consumption with respect to the conventional binary radix implementation. SC has been also adopted for efficient implementation of DNNs in [5] by removing near-zero weights, applying weight scaling, and integrating the activation function with the accumulator. Authors in [17] propose a new representation for stochastic numbers improving the accuracy of SC multiplication in DNNs. They report $4\times$–$9.5\times$ accuracy improvement at the cost of a negligible hardware overhead. A dynamic precision scaling is proposed in [16] for efficient design of SC-based CNNs. The precision of input/output data can be arbitrary changed at run-time with the developed methodology. The result is more than 50% in operations-per-area while losing less than 1% in recognition accuracy.

Authors in [8] introduced a new SC multiplication algorithm, called BISC-MVM, for matrix–vector multiplication. The proposed method of [8] significantly reduces the number of clock cycles taken in the stochastic multiplication resulting in a significant energy consumption reduction compared to the conventional SC-based designs of CNNs. Authors in [12] extend the work of [8] and develop an architecture, called SkippyNN, that further reduces the computation time of SC-based multiplications in the convolutional layers of NNs. On average, SkippyNN offers $1.2\times$ speedup and $2.2\times$ energy saving compared to the conventional binary implementations. A spin-CMOS-based stochastic NN architecture is proposed in [31] achieving a significant area, power, and energy consumption saving. The stochastic multiplications are performed by CMOS AND gates, while the sum of products is accumulated by spintronic compressor gates. We also refer to [6,7,9,10,14] as some other recent related works in the literature.

Hybrid stochastic-binary designs of NNs have been also developed to reduce the energy consumption and to improve the accuracy of bit-stream-based NNs. Lee *et al.* [4] used SC to implement the first convolutional layer of the NN. The remaining layers were all implemented in the binary radix domain. The result was a significant improvement in the energy-consumption compared to conventional all-binary design and a better accuracy compared to prior SC designs. Hybrid stochastic-binary designs proposed in [5–7] also use approximate parallel counter, accumulative parallel counter, and binary arithmetic to improve the accuracy and energy-efficiency of NN designs. However, none of these prior designs is able to guarantee achieving the same classification rate as the conventional fixed-point binary design. All the prior SC-based implementations also have some variations in producing the results (nonzero standard variation) and so none of them is deterministic.

4.5 Proposed hybrid binary-bit-stream design

Convolutional layers, including the first layer, account for the most hardware area and power cost in a class of CNNs [7]. Dot-product is the basic operation in these layers, multiplying and accumulating the input data and the kernel's weights (obtained from the training step), followed by an activation function. In this chapter, we use the LD bit-stream processing method of [23] for energy-efficient and low-cost design of the first convolutional layer. To avoid the issue of compounding errors over multiple layers, we limit our work to the first layer of NN.

4.5.1   Multiplications and accumulation

We perform the multiplication operations in the bit-stream domain. We convert the two inputs of each multiplication operation to corresponding bit-stream representation using two different Sobol sequences. Instead of costly fixed-point binary multipliers, multiplications are implemented using simple standard AND gates. The deterministic method discussed in Section 4.3.2 guarantees generating independence bit-streams and processing bit-streams accurately. Deterministic computation is performed on the generated bit-streams and the output bit-streams are converted back to binary radix format implicitly by accumulating them in the binary domain using conventional binary adders.

Note that the correlation between the produced multiplication output bit-streams does not affect the accuracy of the accumulation as the accumulation step is performed in the binary domain. Therefore, only two different Sobol sequences are sufficient to convert all input data to bit-stream representation. The generated LD bit-streams will be reused by a large number of dot-product units, minimizing the overhead of Sobol sequence-based bit-stream generators in the overall cost of the NN design.

4.5.2   Handling negative weights

The weight inputs of the dot-product units involve both positive and negative data. The common approach to support representation of negative data and performing signed multiplication in the stochastic domain is through extending the range of numbers from $[0,1]$ in the unipolar to $[-1,1]$ in the bipolar stochastic domain [2]. The bipolar processing of bit-streams, however, requires a longer processing time than the unipolar processing for a fixed accuracy. To avoid a longer latency, we first divide the weights into positive and negative subsets. We then convert the data in each subset to bit-stream representation assuming that they are all positive (taking the absolute value of the negative values). In the accumulation step (APC units in Figure 4.4), the multiplication outputs of the "positive" and the "negative" subsets are first summed separately and then subtracted from each other to produce the final output value.

As we discussed, when multiplying two N-bit precision numbers, producing exact (completely accurate) results with the deterministic methods of processing bit-streams requires running the operation for 2^{2N} cycles. As we showed in Table 4.1, performing the operation for fewer cycles than 2^{2N} introduces inaccuracy in the produced results due to truncation error. However, we will show in Section 4.6 that due to the inaccuracy tolerance of NNs, the same or even in some cases a lower misclassification rate than the rate of the fixed-point design can be achieved using the proposed design.

Figure 4.4 shows our proposed bit-stream-binary hybrid design for the first convolutional layer of the NN. We use this design to implement the first layer of the LeNet-5 NN topology [32] as a well-studied and common CNN. We implement a 784-11520-2880-1280-320-800-500-10 configuration of this topology as illustrated in Figure 4.5. The selected CNN consists of two convolutional layers, two max-pooling layers, two fully-connected layers, and one softmax layer. The first convolutional layer

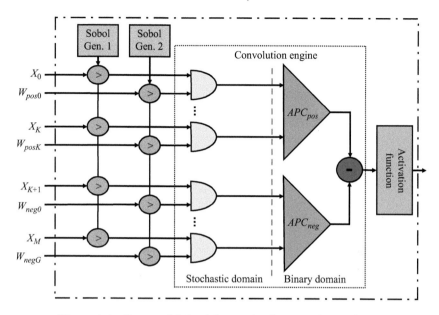

Figure 4.4   Proposed hybrid design for the convolutional layer

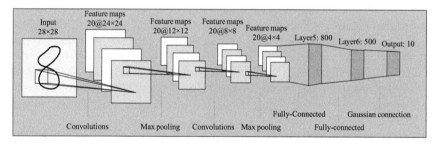

Figure 4.5   Configuration of the implemented NN based on LeNet5 topology

processes each pixel of the input image with 20 filters of 5 × 5 size. We perform the
multiplication operations in the bit-stream domain. The output bit-streams are accumulated in each cycle using binary adders, implicitly converting from bit-stream to
binary radix representation. The produced output in binary format is passed to a
ReLU activation function. The remaining layers of the NN are all implemented in
the binary domain. Parallel processing of all input pixels in the first layer requires
24 × 24 × 5 × 5 parallel multiplication operations for each filter. Therefore, exploiting bit-stream-based computing can significantly decrease the hardware footprint and
power cost compared to the cost of the corresponding conventional fixed-point binary
counterpart.

4.6 Experimental results

We use MNIST, a standard image database for handwritten digit recognition, to train and test the NN. The database includes 10,000 testing and 60,000 training 28×28 gray-scale images. We evaluated the efficiency of the proposed design by comparing it to a baseline 8-bit fixed-point implementation of the NN. Accuracy evaluation of both the proposed hybrid and also the fixed-point baseline design was performed in MATLAB. Misclassification rate (one minus the classification accuracy) was measured for each design and multiplied by 100 to report the accuracy in percentage. We also implemented both designs using Verilog hardware description language for hardware cost comparisons. The Synopsys Design Compiler vH2013.12 is used to synthesize the implemented designs in 45 nm technology. We train the NN over the 60,000 training images using the 8-bit fixed-point binary design. In the inference step, we evaluate the performance of the NN with the 10,000 test images with both the fixed-point binary and the proposed hybrid bit-stream-binary designs.

For the hybrid approach, we implemented five design structures: (1) the conventional random bit-stream-based design, (2–5) the proposed deterministic LD bit-stream-based designs with different pairs of Sobol sequences as the required number source in converting input data to bit-stream representation. The implemented structures only differ in the bit-stream generation part (converting input pixel intensities and kernel's weights from binary to bit-stream representation) and the core logic to perform the multiplications and accumulations is the same in all structures.

For the random bit-stream-based design, we use the MATLAB built-in random number generator to generate the required random numbers for the bit-stream generation process. For the proposed deterministic LD bit-stream-based designs, we use four different combinations of the first four Sobol sequences from the MATLAB built-in Sobol sequence generator (Figure 4.3). Input test images and kernel's weights are converted to their corresponding bit-stream representation by comparing them to the Sobol numbers from these four Sobol sequences.

4.6.1 Performance comparison

Classification of the 10,000 input test images of the MNIST dataset with the 8-bit fixed-point binary design showed a misclassification rate of 0.80%. Table 4.2 compares the misclassification rates of the implemented bit-stream-based designs for different numbers of operation cycles. For the conventional random stream-based approach, we report the average of 20 trials running the simulation for statistical significance. As reported, the proposed deterministic bit-stream-based designs achieve a higher classification rate than the conventional random stream-based one for all different operation cycles (bit-stream lengths).

As shown in Table 4.2, the optimum number of processing cycles to produce high-quality outputs with the proposed hybrid design is *only* eight cycles. Choosing Sobol Sequence 1 and Sobol Sequence 4, for example, as the two required sources of numbers in the bit-streams generation process gives a misclassification rate of 0.81% after eight cycles. A percentage of 0.81 means only one additional error (out

Table 4.2 Misclassification rates (number of incorrect recognitions/10,000 × 100) of the implemented bit-stream-based designs for different number of operation cycles

Design approach\operation cycles	2^{16}	2^8	2^6	2^5	2^4	9	8	7	6	5	4
Conventional random SC	0.80%	0.81%	0.88%	0.93%	1.08%	1.33%	1.41%	1.48%	1.70%	1.91%	2.46%
Proposed design—Sobol 1 and 2	0.80%	0.79%	0.79%	0.82%	0.84%	0.86%	**0.84%**	0.87%	0.92%	1.15%	1.12%
Proposed design—Sobol 3 and 4	0.80%	0.79%	0.77%	0.85%	0.86%	0.89%	**0.84%**	0.91%	1.05%	1.12%	1.12%
Proposed design—Sobol 1 and 4	0.80%	0.79%	0.79%	0.83%	0.83%	0.95%	**0.81%**	0.87%	0.98%	1.12%	1.12%
Proposed design—Sobol 2 and 3	0.80%	0.79%	0.80%	0.78%	0.85%	0.89%	**0.88%**	1.12%	1.17%	1.12%	1.12%

The bold values highlight the miss-classification rates of the implemented design for the optimum processing time of 8 cycles.

of 10,000 test images) compared to the number of errors with the 8-bit fixed-point binary design. With other combinations of Sobol sequences (e.g., 3 and 4, 1 and 4, and 2 and 3) also a similar level of error rate is achieved.

As reported, increasing the number of processing cycles to nine cycles has raised the misclassification rates in the proposed hybrid design. The main reason is imprecise representation of input data with 9-bit streams compared to the 8-bit bit-stream representation. The general trend, however, is a decreasing behavior in the error rate when increasing the number of processing cycles. After 2^6 cycles, the same or even a lower misclassification rate than the 8-bit fixed-point design is achieved. The reason behind achieving a better rate compared to the baseline fixed-point design is that computation on truncated bit-streams has turned a couple of misclassifications into correct classification. Comparing the misclassification rates of the eight cycle case with the 2^6 or longer cases, only a few misclassifications (out of 10,000 test images) can be corrected with longer bit-streams. Considering the fact that energy is directly proportional to processing time, eight is the optimum number of processing cycles for the proposed design. If the application accepts higher misclassification rates, even four cycles might satisfy the quality expectations (with a misclassification rate of around 1.1%) and become an efficient termination point for the processing.

An advantage of using the proposed design compared to prior random bit-stream-based designs is that the results are deterministic. The produced outputs depend on the selected combination of Sobol sequences for the bit-stream generation step and therefore have a standard deviation of zero and are reproducible. We can guarantee achieving the same classification rate every time processing the same set of inputs. Due to their inherent randomness, the conventional random bit-stream-based designs have higher standard deviations and also higher worst misclassification errors for different bit-stream lengths.

4.6.2   Cost comparison

The synthesis results of a 5×5 convolution engine are reported in Table 4.3. A total of $20 \times 24 \times 24$ convolution units is required to perform all the convolutions of the first layer in parallel. Table 4.4 shows the synthesis results of the first convolutional layer for the case of parallel processing all pixels of an input image with one filter (implementing 24×24 convolution units in parallel). For the proposed design, we used the Sobol sequence generator of [25] to convert input data from binary format to deterministic bit-stream representation. We do not consider the cost of the bit-stream

Table 4.3   *Area (μm^2), critical path latency (ns), power consumption (mW) (at maximum working frequency), and energy consumption (pJ) of the convolution engine (5×5 filter)*

Design approach	Area (μm^2)	CP (ns)	Power (mW)	Energy/cycle (pJ)
Fixed-point binary (non-pipelined)	19,902	1.60	15.15	24.24
Fixed-point binary (fully pipelined)	31,736	0.95	26.52	25.19
Proposed LD bit-stream-binary	851	0.88	1.28	1.13

generators in the numbers reported in Table 4.3 as the two Sobol sequence generators are shared in converting all the input image and weight data. The effective cost of the comparators used in the bit-stream generators is also insignificant considering the fact that each generated bit-stream is being used by a large number of convolution units. We include the overhead cost of bit-stream generators in the numbers reported in Table 4.4.

For the fixed-point binary design, we report the synthesis results for two cases of non-pipelined and fully pipelined implementations. Due to replacing costly 8-bit fixed-point multipliers with simple AND gates, more than $23\times$ ($37\times$) hardware area saving is achieved from the non-pipelined (fully pipelined) fixed-point design to the proposed hybrid design for implementation of a 5×5 convolution engine. The critical path latency and power consumption are also significantly decreased with the proposed design. As reported in Table 4.4, for the entire convolutional layer (including the overhead cost of bit-stream generators), the hardware area cost is reduced around $19\times$ ($30\times$).

The important metric to evaluate the efficiency of the proposed design is still energy consumption. Energy is evaluated as the product of processing time and power consumption. The output of the convolution unit in the non-pipelined fixed-point design is ready in only one clock cycle. This results in a total energy consumption of 24.2 pJ for the convolution unit (Table 4.3) and 14.5 nJ for the entire convolutional layer (Table 4.4). The fully pipelined design is faster but costs significantly higher area and power and consumes 16 nJ energy per cycle for the entire convolutional layer.

The energy consumption of the proposed hybrid design depends on the number of cycles generating and processing bit-streams. Multiplying the number of cycles by the energy per cycle from Table 4.4 gives an energy consumption of 4.1 nJ when processing for eight cycles (8×0.52 nJ). The proposed design therefore achieves more than 70% energy saving compared to the non-pipelined fixed-point design while preserving the quality of the results. Although pipelining the fixed-point design increases the maximum working frequency (reduces the critical path latency) and the throughput, it costs higher hardware area and power consumption, longer total end-to-end latency, and higher energy consumption for processing each input data.

With the conventional random stream-based design, a significantly longer processing time (e.g., 64–256 cycles) is required to achieve the same classification rate as the fixed-point design. This longer processing time makes the prior bit-stream-based designs energy inefficient compared to the fixed-point and to the proposed hybrid design.

Table 4.4 Synthesis results of the convolutional layer (24 × 24 convolution engines + bit-stream generators)

Design approach	Area (μm^2)	CP (ns)	Power (W)	Energy/cycle (nJ)
Fixed-point binary (non-pipelined)	10,966,339	1.94	7.47	14.50
Fixed-point binary (fully pipelined)	17,212,059	1.28	12.56	16.07
Proposed LD bit-stream-binary	581,752	1.12	0.46	0.52

Note that we implemented 24 × 24 parallel 5 × 5 convolution engines to parallel process a 28 × 28 input test image with one filter. To parallel process this input image with 20 filters, we need to implement 20 copies of the implemented design. The bit-stream generators responsible for converting data and also the two Sobol number generators will be shared between more convolution engines and therefore the overhead cost of bit-stream generation will be further reduced.

4.7 Summary

In this chapter, we proposed a low-cost and energy-efficient design for hardware implementation of CNNs. LD deterministic bit-streams and simple standard AND gates are used to perform fast and accurate multiplication operations in the first layer of the NN. Compared to prior random bit-stream-based designs, the proposed design achieves a lower misclassification rate for the same processing time. Evaluating LeNet5 NN with MINIST dataset as the input, the proposed design achieved the same classification rate as the conventional fixed-point binary design with 70% saving in the energy consumption of the first convolutional layer. If accepting slight inaccuracies, higher energy savings are also feasible by processing shorter bit-streams.

Acknowledgment

This work was supported in part by National Science Foundation grant no. CCF-1438286. Any opinions, findings, and conclusions or recommendations expressed in this material are those of the authors and do not necessarily reflect the views of the NSF.

References

[1] B. R. Gaines. Stochastic computing systems. In *Advances in Information Systems Science*, pages 37–172. Boston, MA: Springer, US, 1969.

[2] A. Alaghi and J. P. Hayes. Survey of stochastic computing. *ACM Transactions on Embedded Computing Systems*, 12(2s):92:1–92:19, 2013.

[3] W. Qian, X. Li, M. D. Riedel, K. Bazargan, and D. J. Lilja. An architecture for fault-tolerant computation with stochastic logic. *IEEE Transactions on Computers*, 60(1):93–105, 2011.

[4] V. T. Lee, A. Alaghi, J. P. Hayes, V. Sathe, and L. Ceze. Energy-Efficient Hybrid Stochastic-Binary Neural Networks for Near-Sensor Computing. In *Design, Automation Test in Europe Conference Exhibition (DATE), 2017*, pages 13–18, March 2017.

[5] K. Kim, J. Kim, J. Yu, J. Seo, J. Lee, and K. Choi. Dynamic Energy-Accuracy Trade-off Using Stochastic Computing in Deep Neural Networks. In *DAC'16*, New York, NY, USA, 2016. ACM.

[6] J. Li, A. Ren, Z. Li, *et al*. Towards Acceleration of Deep Convolutional Neural Networks using Stochastic Computing. In *2017 22nd ASP-DAC*, pages 115–120, January 2017.

[7] H. Sim, D. Nguyen, J. Lee, and K. Choi. Scalable Stochastic Computing Accelerator for Convolutional Neural Networks. In *2017 22nd Asia and South Pacific Design Automation Conference (ASP-DAC)*, January 2017.

[8] H. Sim and J. Lee. A New Stochastic Computing Multiplier with Application to Deep Convolutional Neural Networks. In *2017 54th ACM/EDAC/IEEE Design Automation Conference (DAC)*, June 2017.

[9] Z. Li, A. Ren, J. Li, *et al*. Structural Design Optimization for Deep Convolutional Neural Networks using Stochastic Computing. In *Design, Automation Test in Europe Conference Exhibition (DATE), 2017*, pages 250–253, March 2017.

[10] A. Ren, Z. Li, C. Ding, *et al*. SC-DCNN: Highly-Scalable Deep Convolutional Neural Network Using Stochastic Computing. In *ASPLOS'17*, New York, USA, 2017.

[11] A. Ardakani, F. Leduc-Primeau, N. Onizawa, T. Hanyu, and W. J. Gross. VLSI implementation of deep neural network using integral stochastic computing. *IEEE Transactions on VLSI Systems*, 25(10):2688–2699, 2017.

[12] R. Hojabr, K. Givaki, S. M. Reza Tayaranian, *et al*. SkippyNN: An Embedded Stochastic-Computing Accelerator for Convolutional Neural Networks. In *Design Automation Conference (DAC)*, 2019.

[13] B. Li, Y. Qin, B. Yuan, and D. Lilja. Neural network classifiers using a hardware-based approximate activation function with a hybrid stochastic multiplier. *ACM Journal on Emerging Technologies in Computing Systems*, 15(1):12:1–12:21, 2019.

[14] B. Li, M. H. Najafi, and D. Lilja. Low-Cost Stochastic Hybrid Multiplier for Quantized Neural Networks. *ACM Journal on Emerging Technologies in Computing Systems*, 15(2):18:1–18:19, 2019.

[15] B. Li, M. H. Najafi, B. Yuan, and D. J. Lilja. Quantized Neural Networks With New Stochastic Multipliers. In *2018 19th International Symposium on Quality Electronic Design (ISQED)*, pages 376–382, March 2018.

[16] H. Sim, S. Kenzhegulov, and J. Lee. DPS: Dynamic Precision Scaling for Stochastic Computing-based Deep Neural Networks. In *Proceedings of the 55th Annual Design Automation Conference*, DAC'18, pages 13:1–13:6, New York, NY, USA, 2018. ACM.

[17] A. Zhakatayev, S. Lee, H. Sim, and J. Lee. Sign-Magnitude SC: Getting $10\times$ Accuracy for Free in Stochastic Computing for Deep Neural Networks. In *Proceedings of the 55th Annual Design Automation Conference*, DAC'18, pages 158:1–158:6, New York, NY, USA, 2018. ACM.

[18] D. Jenson and M. Riedel. A Deterministic Approach to Stochastic Computation. In *Proceedings of the 35th International Conference on Computer-Aided Design*, ICCAD'16, New York, NY, USA, 2016.

[19] M. H. Najafi, S. Jamali-Zavareh, D. J. Lilja, M. D. Riedel, K. Bazargan, and R. Harjani. Time-encoded values for highly efficient stochastic circuits. *IEEE*

Transactions on Very Large Scale Integration (VLSI) Systems, 25(5):1644–1657, 2017.

[20] M. H. Najafi, S. Jamali-Zavareh, D. J. Lilja, M. D. Riedel, K. Bazargan, and R. Harjani. An overview of time-based computing with stochastic constructs. *IEEE Micro*, 37(6):62–71, 2017.

[21] S. R. Faraji and K. Bazargan. Hybrid Binary-Unary Hardware Accelerators. In *2019 24th Asia and South Pacific Design Automation Conference (ASP-DAC)*, January 2019.

[22] M. H. Najafi and D. Lilja. High quality down-sampling for deterministic approaches to stochastic computing. *IEEE Transactions on Emerging Topics in Computing*, 1, 2018.

[23] M. H. Najafi, D. J. Lilja, and M. Riedel. Deterministic Methods for Stochastic Computing Using Low-discrepancy Sequences. In *Proceedings of the International Conference on Computer-Aided Design*, ICCAD'18, pages 51:1–51:8, New York, NY, USA, 2018. ACM.

[24] A. Alaghi and J. P. Hayes. Fast and Accurate Computation Using Stochastic Circuits. In *Proceedings of the Conference on Design, Automation & Test in Europe*, DATE'14, Belgium, 2014.

[25] S. Liu and J. Han. Energy Efficient Stochastic Computing with Sobol Sequences. In *Design, Automation Test in Europe Conference Exhibition (DATE), 2017*, pages 650–653, March 2017.

[26] S. Liu and J. Han. Toward energy-efficient stochastic circuits using parallel Sobol sequences. *IEEE Transactions on Very Large Scale Integration (VLSI) Systems*, 26(7):1326–1339, 2018.

[27] B. D. Brown and H. C. Card. Stochastic neural computation. I. Computational elements. *IEEE Transactions on Computers*, 50(9):891–905, 2001.

[28] K. Sanni, G. Garreau, J. L. Molin, and A. G. Andreou. FPGA Implementation of a Deep Belief Network Architecture for Character Recognition Using Stochastic Computation. In *2015 49th Annual Conference on Information Sciences and Systems (CISS)*, pages 1–5, March 2015.

[29] Y. Ji, F. Ran, C. Ma, and D. J. Lilja. A Hardware Implementation of a Radial Basis Function Neural Network Using Stochastic Logic. In *Proceedings of the 2015 Design, Automation & Test in Europe Conference & Exhibition*, DATE'15, pages 880–883, San Jose, CA, USA, 2015. EDA Consortium.

[30] B. Li, M. H. Najafi, and D. J. Lilja. Using Stochastic Computing to Reduce the Hardware Requirements for a Restricted Boltzmann Machine Classifier. In *Proceedings of the 2016 ACM/SIGDA International Symposium on Field-Programmable Gate Arrays*, FPGA'16, pages 36–41, New York, NY, USA, 2016. ACM.

[31] B. Li, J. Hu, M. H. Najafi, S. Koester, and D. Lilja. Low Cost Hybrid Spin-CMOS Compressor for Stochastic Neural Networks. In *2019 International Great Lakes Symposium on VLSI (GLSVLSI)*, May 2019.

[32] Y. Lecun, L. Bottou, Y. Bengio, and P. Haffner. Gradient-based learning applied to document recognition. *Proceedings of the IEEE*, 86(11):2278–2324, 1998.

Chapter 5

Binary neural networks

Najmeh Nazari and Mostafa E. Salehi[1]

Convolutional neural networks (CNNs) are used in a spread spectrum of machine learning applications, such as computer vision and speech recognition. Computation and memory accesses are the major challenges for the deployment of CNNs in resource-limited and low-power embedded systems. The recently proposed binary neural networks (BNNs) use just 1 bit for weights and/or activations instead of full-precision values, hence substitute complex multiply-accumulation operations with bitwise logic operations to reduce the computation and memory footprint drastically. However, most BNN models come with some accuracy loss, especially in big datasets. Improving the accuracy of BNNs and designing efficient hardware accelerator for them are two important research directions that have attracted many attentions in recent years. In this chapter, we conduct a survey on the state-of-the-art researches on the design and hardware implementation of the BNN models.

5.1 Introduction

Due to the promotion of high-performance computer architectures, deep learning has rapidly grown to an extent that exceeds the human accuracy level [1]. A particular model of deep neural networks (DNNs) is the convolutional neural network (CNN) model that attained noticeable results in several computer vision tasks, such as image classification [2], and object localization and detection [3].

CNN models were primarily designed with the aim of increasing accuracy. In fact, CNN models are continuously becoming more and more complicated and deeper to achieve more accuracy. For instance, the ResNet network exploits 50 layers and uses 25.5M of parameters and performs 3.9G multiply-and-accumulate (MAC) operations [4] for achieving 94.7% top-5 classification accuracy on the ImageNet dataset. According to the state-of-the-art researches, as CNNs go deeper and larger, they give higher accuracy, but at the cost of higher complexity. For instance, in [1], He *et al.* have explored the deep model of ResNet with 1,202 layers to give very high accuracy, but obviously, the model suffers from high computation and memory bandwidth demand. Almost in all other CNN models, the massive computations and the huge amount of memory accesses are the major challenges of deep CNNs.

[1]School of Electrical and Computer Engineering, College of Engineering, University of Tehran, Tehran, Iran

The life cycle of CNN consists of two training and inference phases. The parameters of a CNN are learned through examining an enormous number of training datasets during the training phase. Afterward in the inference phase, the trained CNN is employed to classify data which were never seen by the trained CNN during training phase. The training phase usually needs tremendous computational resources for calculating multiple weight-update iterations on a large dataset. Commonly, training a DNN model is done on a powerful computer platform and may take several hours/days to complete, depending on the size of the datasets. The inference phase takes aggressively less time compared with the training phase, but many acceleration methods target the inference phase, because it should be carried online on a probably edge device with limited resources.

Many prior researchers have proposed CNN accelerators for reducing the volume of computations and memory accesses with minor accuracy loss [5,6]. Most of these accelerators could not still meet the tight power and resource constraints of embedded devices. Consequently, the development of efficient models is essential due to the increasing demands of running high-quality CNNs on power-limited embedded devices [7,8]. As an effective approach, several methods have employed compact CNN architectures and also different pruning techniques to reduce the number of operations and the model size [9–11]. These methods are comprehensively studied in Chapter 6.

Many researchers have employed fixed point operands instead of floating-point ones to reduce computation complexity [7,12]. Further, some researchers reduce the precision beyond fixed-point operands and use very few bits for representing data to get the so-called BNNs. In fact, they apply just 1 or 2 bits to represent operands to aggressively reduce computation [13,14]. Due to their low power consumption and low complexity, BNNs are extremely appropriate for battery-operated embedded systems, Internet of Things (IoT) platforms, and wearable devices. Despite its good power/latency profile, applying the BNN model to large datasets, such as ImageNet, leads to significant accuracy loss. Several works have attempted to address the issue of accuracy loss [15,16] and also efficient hardware implementation of BNNs [17,18]. This chapter aims at introducing the BNN modes, studying its challenges, and presenting the main solutions for these challenges.

The rest of this chapter is organized as follows. In Section 5.2, we present the basic concepts of the BNN model. Some major BNN optimization techniques are discussed in Section 5.3. Open source frameworks for BNNs are presented in Section 5.4. Moreover, Section 5.4 discusses the existing customized hardware implementation of BNNs. Finally, we conclude this chapter in Section 5.5.

5.2   Binary neural networks

CNNs have attained state-of-the-art performance especially in lots of computer vision tasks. Deep CNNs require massive amount of memory accesses and intensive computations in the form of fixed/floating-point MAC operations. More recently, by implementing a wide range of services based on computer vision in embedded devices, exploiting CNNs on the smartphones and other handheld devices is gaining more and more attention. Some important services include object detection and localization, image classification, image to text conversion, and face recognition. Moreover, the CNNs are also commonly used in the IoT edge devises that commonly have limited memory and power budgets. Thus, decreasing the CNN computations has become an essential challenge.

Generally, BNN have been proposed to eliminate MAC operations via binarizing weights and/or activations. In this model, only two values are deployed for weights and/or activations (not definitely 0 and 1). Although this approach significantly lessens the amount of computations, it leads to growing accuracy loss, especially for large data sets. Since the achieved accuracy is not desirable for large datasets, ternary neural networks (TNN) are also proposed with the purpose of reducing accuracy loss through adding an extra state to weights or/and activations over the BNNs.

In the following parts, first, we comprehensively discuss binary and ternary weight neural (TWN) networks with binarized and ternarized weights, respectively. Afterward, we review binarized and ternarized neural networks which have outstripped previous approaches by applying binary and ternary activations, respectively.

5.2.1 Binary and ternary weights for neural networks

Three separate steps can be considered for stochastic gradient descent (SGD) training process, which is one of the major training methods for neural networks. Step 1: Forward propagation that computes the unit activations in a layer-by-layer manner and finally obtains the output of DNN by taking DNN input. Step 2: Backward propagation that computes the training objective's gradient regarding activations of each layer by taking the DNN target. Backward propagation act contrarily compared with forward propagation and starts from the top layer and goes down to the first layer. Step 3: Parameter update that computes the gradient with regard to each layer's parameters and then updates the parameters using obtained gradients and previous values.

The method proposed in [19] introduces an approach called BinaryConnect that constraints the weights to take just $+1$ or -1 values during the forward (step 1) and backward (step 2) propagations. Generally, -1 and 1 values are encoded to 0 and 1 binary values, respectively. Therefore, MAC operations are substituted with simple additions or subtractions. It should be mentioned that since parameter changes are tiny, maintaining full-precision weights during the parameter updates (step 3) is essential. Besides, right after weight update, the real value weights must be clipped within the $[-1,1]$ interval to prevent growing weights.

Selecting an efficient binarization method is one of the most critical issues in designing a binary network. As mentioned earlier, in the BinaryConnect, the real-valued weights (w) are replaced by -1 or $+1$. Mostly, for binarizing weights, deterministic and stochastic binarization functions are used which are demonstrated in (5.1) and (5.2), respectively:

$$wb = \begin{cases} +1 & \text{if } w \geq 0, \\ -1 & \text{otherwise} \end{cases} \tag{5.1}$$

$$wb = \begin{cases} +1 & \text{with probability } p = \sigma(w), \\ -1 & \text{with probability } 1 - p \end{cases} \tag{5.2}$$

where σ, as a hard sigmoid function, determines the probability distribution as

$$\sigma(x) = clip\left(\frac{x+1}{2}, 0, 1\right) = max\left(0, min\left(1, \frac{x+1}{2}\right)\right) \tag{5.3}$$

Although binarization weight with stochastic binarization function works better than deterministic binarization function [20], the sign function is more popular due to its simple hardware implementation compared with stochastic functions. BinaryConnect has used stochastic binarization function during the training phase and deterministic function throughout test time inference.

As mentioned earlier, BinaryConnect removes 2/3 of multiplications during the training process and leads to 3× speedup for the training process. The impact of deterministic BinaryConnect during test time is noticeable compared with conventional CNNs with real value weights (from 32 bits floating point to 1 bit). Actually, BinaryConnect decreases all multiplication operations, memory to computation bandwidth, and memory storage by a factor of about 32. BinaryConnect has achieved near state-of-the-art results on MNIST, CIFAR10, and SVHN datasets.

The method presented in [21] has tried to remove most of the multiplication operations during the training of neural networks. In comparison with BinaryConnect, this method also deals with backward weight update (step 3) in addition to forward propagation (step 2) and backward propagation (step 2). Since many learned weights generally have converged to zero or near zero, ternary connect approach adds an extra 0 state for weights as well. In the same way as the binary models, the ternary model replaces all MAC operation with simple addition or subtraction in the forward propagation. Besides, compared with binary connect, 0 values reduce computations.

To omit more multiplications, [21] proposes a method which consist of two components. First, for forward propagation, weights are stochastically binarized by using binary connect or ternary connect functions according to (5.4) and (5.5), respectively:

$$Wt = \begin{cases} P(Wt = 1) = \dfrac{W+1}{2} \\ P(Wt = -1) = 1 - P(Wt = 1) \end{cases} \tag{5.4}$$

$$Wt = \begin{cases} P(Wt = 1) = W; P(Wt = 0) = 1 - W & \text{if } W \geq 0 \\ P(Wt = -1) = -W; P(Wt = 0) = 1 + W & \text{if } W < 0 \end{cases} \tag{5.5}$$

where P, W, and Wt are the probability, real value weight, and ternarized weight, respectively.

Second, an approach called "quantized back propagation" is introduced to substitute most multiplications in the backward pass with bit-shifts. To obtain this goal, inputs are rounded to the closest power of 2 values to replace multiplications with binary shifts. They also explore the number of appropriate bits for input quantization and find that 3–4 bits is sufficient to achieve good performance.

Therefore, this method succeeds to decrease multiplications drastically with negligible performance loss and achieves near state-of-the-art results on MNIST, CIFAR10, and SVHN datasets. It is worth noting that noisy weights that are obtained by binarization or ternarization can be a form of regularization which can improve the model generalization. Therefore, it improves the accuracy similar to Dropout [22] and DropConnect [23].

TWN networks with weights constrained to -1, 0, and $+1$ are proposed to achieve high accuracy compared with BinaryConnect while standing good model compression rate [19]. It should be mentioned that 2-bit storage is required for a weight, hence TWN achieves a model compression rates of $16\times$ and $0.5\times$, compared with the conventional CNNs (32-bit floating point precision) and the BinaryConnect model, respectively. Although TWN increases memory storage, it reduces the amount of computation that arises from 0 values in weights. To put it simply, 0 values increase sparsity in the neural network model and lead to eliminating corresponding computational operations.

Similar to BinaryConnect, TWN removes all multiplications in the forward pass and substitutes MAC operations with additions and subtractions. Mostly, deterministic and stochastic ternarization functions are also used for ternarizing weights which are demonstrated in (5.5) and (5.6), respectively:

$$Wt = \begin{cases} +1 & \text{if } W > \Delta, \\ 0 & \text{if } |W| \leq \Delta, \\ -1 & \text{if } W < -\Delta. \end{cases} \tag{5.6}$$

$$\Delta = \frac{0.7}{n} \sum_{i=1}^{n} |W_i| \tag{5.7}$$

where W is the real value weight, Wt is ternarized weight, n is the total number of weights in a kernel, and Δ is the threshold parameter which adjusts the amount of sparsity. TWN uses the deterministic function for ternarizing weights and obtains appropriate threshold parameters according to (5.7). However, [24] has considered $\Delta = 1/3$ for simple hardware implementation.

It is worth bearing in mind that using scaling factors for the weights plays a crucial role in attaining proper accuracy for image classification, particularly for large datasets [13]. Therefore, TWNs mostly use scaling factors for weights. In order to do that, TWNs just consider $|W| > \Delta$ and remove $|W| < \Delta$ for computing scaling factor. Therefore, the appropriate scaling factor is the average of absolute $|W| > \Delta$ values which is calculated as:

$$\gamma = \frac{1}{|n_\Delta|} \sum_{i \in n_\Delta} |X_i| \tag{5.8}$$

where γ is a scaling factor and $|n_\Delta|$ denotes the amount of $|X|$, which is greater than Δ. TWN has achieved near state-of-the-art results on MNIST, CIFAR10, and large-scale ImageNet datasets, in that the amount of accuracy loss is negligible compared with full-precision CNNs.

The amount of sparsity is not determined in TWN, hence the area would be the same as BinaryConnect. Actually, TWN networks do not inherently reduce area and just prune the computations which are related to zero weights. The worst case is when all weights are nonzero, where all computation resources are similar to BinaryConnect. Sparse ternary connect (STC) [24] has introduced the ρ parameter ($0 \leq \rho \leq 1$) to adjust the amount of sparsity in zero values. In this model, $N = |W| \times \rho$ is the number of weights in a kernel that must be zero. Therefore, STC proposes an architecture that is more resource-efficient compared with the previous works.

STC has explored the design space of ρ parameter on CIFAR10 to find the appropriate accuracy. It has shown that the accuracy degradation is pretty negligible when $\rho = 0.5$, hence they can drop half of the elements of the weight matrix. STC has deployed (5.5) and (5.6) to ternarize weights during the training and test phase, respectively. It should be mentioned that Δ is considered 1/3 to ensure simple implementations of the inference phase in hardware. Although the STC method leads to slight accuracy degradation, its impact in increasing the network sparsity reduces the computation resource from 20.07% to 44.78%.

According to many reports, the latency of the access to different levels of the memory hierarchy is about $4\times$ to $400\times$ greater than latency of an integer operation. Memory access also consumes more energy than computation. NullaNet [14] has introduced a method to eliminate the memory accesses required for reading the model parameters (weights) during the test stage. In this method, activations are binarized while the neural network is trained with binary activations and full-precision weights. Since both the inputs and outputs of all layers are binary, the output of a neuron can be implemented by a Boolean function. In other words, the dot product of neuron's inputs and weights is replaced with logic gates via synthesizing Boolean expression. Thus, there is no need to read weight parameters from memory during inference phase. For better understanding, an efficient realization of a neuron by logic gates is demonstrated in Figure 5.1.

NullaNet is evaluated on the MNIST dataset with two different neural networks including multilayer perceptron (MLP) and CNN. NullaNet has obtained classification accuracy near the full-precision CNNs while reducing the amount of energy, implementation resources, and memory accesses considerably.

5.2.2   *Binarized and ternarized neural networks*

As mentioned in the previous section, binary and TWN networks replace MAC operations with simple additions and subtractions. Binarized neural networks (BNNs) [20] surpassed BinaryConnect by using both binary activations and weights during inference and gradient computation in training. They present an approach to train BNNs at run time, as well as during the parameter gradient calculation at train time. They have demonstrated that convolution can be approximated by XNOR and bitcount operations, as shown in Figure 5.2, where x, w, and y are activation, weight, and their multiplication result, respectively. Bitcount counts the number of 1 values, hence the output of bitcount (Y in Figure 5.2) is a fixed-point number which is generally considered as a 24-bit fixed point. It should be mentioned that this approach is not applied to the first layer. However, this is not a major issue since compared with

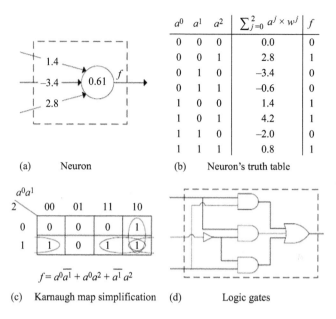

a^0	a^1	a^2	$\sum_{j=0}^{2} a^j \times w^j$	f
0	0	0	0.0	0
0	0	1	2.8	1
0	1	0	−3.4	0
0	1	1	−0.6	0
1	0	0	1.4	1
1	0	1	4.2	1
1	1	0	−2.0	0
1	1	1	0.8	1

(a)   Neuron   (b)   Neuron's truth table

$a^0 a^1$

2	00	01	11	10
0	0	0	0	1
1	1	0	1	1

$f = a^0 \overline{a^1} + a^0 a^2 + \overline{a^1}\, a^2$

(c)   Karnaugh map simplification   (d)   Logic gates

Figure 5.1   Efficient realization of a neuron in NullaNet [14]

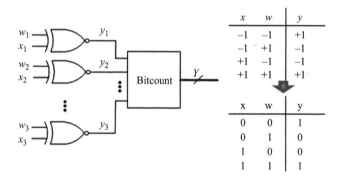

x	w	y
−1	−1	+1
−1	+1	−1
+1	−1	−1
+1	+1	+1

x	w	y
0	0	1
0	1	0
1	0	0
1	1	1

Figure 5.2   Binary CNN operation

other layers, the first layer involves fewer computations that arise from much fewer channels (e.g., Red, Green, and Blue channels).

Since batch normalization (BN) layer and the ADAM optimizer [25] algorithms require many multiplications, BNN suggests applying shift-based BN and AdaMax. By replacing computation-intensive MAC operations with XNOR and bit-count, computations would be reduced intensely. Furthermore, memory footprint is considerably reduced in comparison with full-precision computations. BNN has obtained accuracy levels compared with the conventional models on MNIST, CIFAR10, and SVHN datasets. In [13], the authors proposed two interesting BNN models: binary weight networks (BWN) and XNOR network (XNOR-Net), which are two efficient and accurate binary approximation for CNNs. BWN and XNOR-Net have attempted to increase the image classification accuracy compared with BinaryConnect and BNNs. To achieve this goal, scaling factors are applied to weights for BWN and to both activations and weights for XNOR-Net. Figure 5.3 illustrates the approximation of convolution in XNOR-Net.

In [13], as shown in Figure 5.3, the average of absolute weight values (α) is the optimal scaling factor for weights. The paper also proposes appropriate scaling factors for activations (K) that are calculated through a full-precision convolution. As shown in the middle of Figure 5.3, first, the average of the absolute values of the elements (A) is calculated across the channel. Second, a full-precision convolution operation is performed on matrix A and the 2D filter (as mentioned by k in [13]). This way, a 2D convolution is required for obtaining scaling factors of activation (K).

As shown in Figure 5.4(a), a typical block in CNNs is generally comprised four layers: (1) convolution, (2) BN, (3) activation, and (4) pooling. BN normalizes the values with their average and variance. A block diagram of binary CNN is illustrated in Figure 5.4(b). XNOR-Net carried out the normalization step before binarization to reduce the dynamic range of the activations and lessen information loss that may arise as a result of binarization.

The binary activation layer (BinActiv) calculates the scaling factor and sign function of the activations and then, BinConv computes binary. Afterward, non-binary activation such as ReLU is done and finally pooling operation is deployed. It should be noted that the operations of the first and last layers are done on full-precision numbers in XNOR-Net. XNOR-Net has achieved noticeable performance on the ImageNet dataset and outperforms other BNNs.

Similar to BinaryConnect and BNN, real type weights are deployed for updating parameters due to the tiny changes of the parameters in gradient descent. Once the training phase is completed, real value weights are removed and binary weights are used during the inference phase (test time).

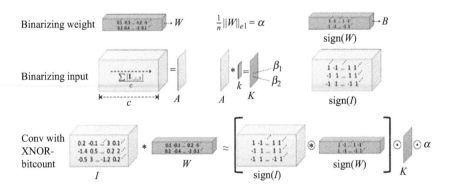

Figure 5.3   Approximating convolution in XNOR-Net [13]

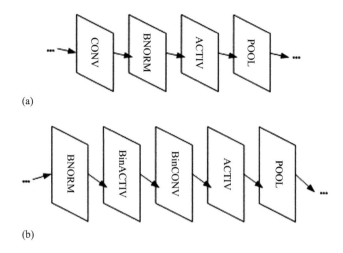

(a)

(b)

Figure 5.4   Block structure of (a) conventional CNN and (b) XNOR-Net

Table 5.1   A single neuron i definition in TNNs [26]

	Teacher network	Student network
Weights	$W_i = [w_j], w_j \in R$	$W_i = [w_j], w_j \in \{-1, 0, 1\}$
Bias	$b_i \in R$	$b_i^{\text{lower}} \in Z, b_i^{\text{higher}} \in Z$
Transfer function	$y_i = W_i^T X + b_i$	$y_i = W_i^T X$
Activation function	$n_i^t = \begin{cases} -1 \text{ with probability } -\alpha \text{ if } \alpha < 0 \\ 1 \text{ with probability } \alpha \text{ if } \alpha > 0 \\ 0 \quad\quad\quad\quad\quad\quad\quad \text{ otherwise} \end{cases}$ where $\alpha = \tanh(y_i), \alpha \in (-1, 1)$	$n_i^s = \begin{cases} -1 \text{ if } y_i < b_i^{\text{lower}} \\ 1 \quad \text{ if } y_i > b_i^{\text{higher}} \\ 0 \quad \text{ otherwise} \end{cases}$

A recent method in [26] proposes a TNN and restricts both activations and weights to $\{-1,0,1\}$. It uses teacher–student methods to train TNNs. In this method, the teacher and student networks have the same architecture, with each neuron acting according to Table 5.1. In fact, each neuron of student network imitates the equivalent neuron's behavior in the teacher network without any multiplications.

The TNNs make the model sparse by approximating small weights to zero. Therefore, these networks would be more energy-efficient. Sparsity in TNNs is illustrated in Figure 5.5, where X and Y denote inputs and outputs, respectively. In this figure, weights and activations are demonstrated by lines and circles, respectively. The forward computation is done when both weight and activation are nonzero, which are shown by lines in Figure 5.5. In other words, the ternarized neural network is a sparse BNN that performs computations, only when both activation and weight are nonzero.

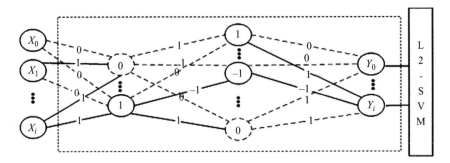

Figure 5.5   Neurons and their synaptic weights in TNNs (sparse binary networks)

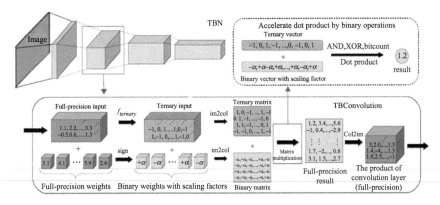

Figure 5.6   TBN with ternary inputs and binary weights (with scaling factor α) [28]

Some recent papers provide hardware for these TNN models on both FPGA and ASIC platforms. In [27], implementing TNN on FPGAs shows 3.1× more energy efficiency than the software-based designs under the MNIST, CIFAR10, SVHN, and CIFAR100 datasets.

A new low-precision neural network model, called ternary–binary network (TBN), is presented in [28]. As shown in Figure 5.6, TBN restricts the inputs and weights to take values from the {−1,0,1} and {−1,1} sets, respectively. They have shown that an optimal trade-off among memory, performance, and efficiency are provided by incorporating binary weights and ternary inputs. It should be mentioned that a scaling factor is used for binary weights similar to XNOR-Net. They have deployed *XOR* and *AND* gates to perform multiplication. They have obtained ∼32× memory saving and 40× speedup compared with a full-precision CNN design. Not only TBN reduces implementation cost, but also achieves remarkable accuracy on MNIST, CIFAR10, SVHN, and ImageNet datasets by deploying TBN.

All of the aforementioned designs need to store full-precision weights to update parameters during the training phase. Therefore, full-precision memory access is required to store weights during backpropagation. GXNOR-Net [27] has tried to address this issue by introducing a discretization framework. The contributions of GXNOR-Net are twofold. First, it presents a multi-discretization function (e.g., ternary discretization) for neuronal activations. It also presents derivatives and approximation method for non-differential activation function to implement backpropagation, as shown in Figure 5.7.

Second, GXNOR-Net introduces a discrete state transition (DST) methodology to eliminate the full-precision weights in the training phase to reduce the memory/computation demand significantly. Weights are constrained in a discrete space by using the DST methodology, and thus there is no need to store full-precision hidden weights during the entire training phase. Figure 5.8 shows the difference between

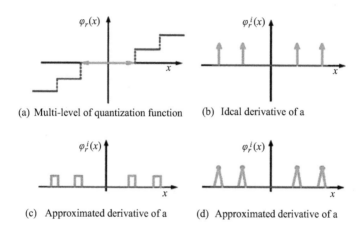

(a) Multi-level of quantization function   (b) Ideal derivative of a

(c) Approximated derivative of a   (d) Approximated derivative of a

Figure 5.7   *Multilevel neuronal activations discretization and derivative approximation methods [27]*

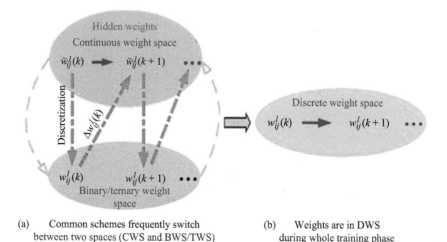

(a)   Common schemes frequently switch between two spaces (CWS and BWS/TWS)   (b)   Weights are in DWS during whole training phase

Figure 5.8   *Discretization of weights illustration [27]*

DST and the approach employed in previous designs (such as BWN, TWN, BNN, and XNOR-Net).

Figure 5.8(a) outlines the deployed methodology in most of the previous works: it switches between two spaces in each iteration (continuous weight space (CWS) and ternary weight space (TWS)/binary weight space (BWS)). Figure 5.8(b) displays the GXNOR-Net's method, called discrete weight space (DWS), which uses discrete weights during the whole training phase. Both weights and inputs are ternarized ($\{-1,0,1\}$) in GXNOR-Net, hence they can also benefit from sparsity and be more energy efficient. GXNOR-Net uses (5.6) as a ternarization function for activations and finds the proper Δ by experimental explorations. In this method, the amount of sparsity can be controlled by Δ.

In fact, GXNOR-Net is a gated version of XNOR-Net which makes the network sparser. Both GXNOR-Net and XNOR-Net use *XNOR* gates for multiplication, so $2\times$ *XNOR* gates are required for 2-bit weights and activations. Although GXNOR-Net has achieved noticeable accuracy on MNIST, CIFAR10, and SVHN datasets, there are not any results reported on large datasets, such as ImageNet and CIFAR100 datasets.

The authors in [29] introduced TOT-Net, a ternarized neural network with $\{-1,0,1\}$ values for both weights and activation functions and showed that it can achieve a higher level of accuracy with lower computational load over the competitors. In fact, TOT-Net introduces a simple bitwise logic (*XOR* gate and *AND* gate) for convolution computations to reduce the cost of multiply operations. In comparison with GXNOR-Net, as shown in Figure 5.9, TOT-Net requires fewer gates for generating the output enable signal. TOT-Net has ternarized both activations and weights based on TWN approach [30]. TOT-Net also proposes a novel piecewise activation function, and optimized learning rate for different datasets to improve accuracy. This way, by using an evolutionary optimization approach, novel piecewise activation functions customized for TOT-Net are explored. As an example, {Elish, Sigmoid} and {Sigmoid, Leaky_Relu} exhibited the best performance as piecewise activation functions for CIFAR-10 and CIFAR-100, respectively.

Figure 5.10 demonstrates the corresponding hardware architectures for the networks studied in this section. For the sake of readability, we present one neuron with three synaptic weights. Figure 5.10(a) shows the baseline hardware architecture for a

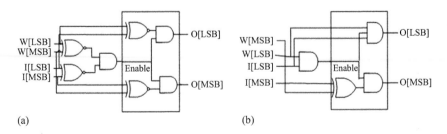

(a)   (b)

Figure 5.9   Multiplication operation in (a) GXNOR-Net and (b) TOT-Net

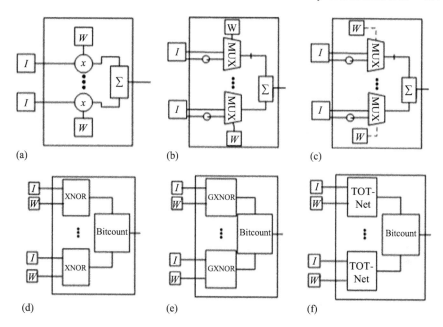

Figure 5.10 Comparison of computation logic in different architectures: (a) conventional neural networks, (b) BWN, (c) ternary weight network, (d) XNOR-Net, (e) GXNOR-Net, and (f) TOT_Net

full-precision CNN which is implemented by a MAC unit. BinaryConnect architecture, shown in Figure 5.10(b), considers binary weight and substitutes multiply with multiplexer. As illustrated in Figure 5.10(c), TWN adds an extra 0 state to weights, hence sparsity has been increased and weights also act as an enable signal. XNOR-Net which is shown in Figure 5.10(d) replaces MAC unit with XNOR-bitcount. Figure 5.10(e) displays GXNOR-Net. The architecture is similar to sparse XNOR-Net, but it uses the control gate to determine the enable signal. Finally, TOT-Net is shown in Figure 5.10(f) and introduces a more efficient architecture than GXNOR-Net.

For more clarifications, the structure of weights, activations and inputs in the mentioned works and also in a fullprecision CNN are all outlined in Table 5.2. Furthermore, for better comparison, the accuracy achieved by each of these designs on various datasets is listed in Table 5.3. In this table, the ImageNet and CIFAR10 datasets are tested with different CNN models. As shown in Table 5.3, BNNs and TNNs have achieved high accuracy, sometimes close to the fullprecision accuracy on small datasets that are MNIST, CIFAR10, and SVHN. However, these networks suffer from accuracy loss on large datasets including CIFAR100 and Image-Net. Therefore, recent researches have attempted to decrease the gap between the accuracy of the fullprecision CNNs and BNNs which are overviewed in the next section.

Table 5.2 Comparison of mentioned methods in term of activation and input domain

Method	Training			Deployment		
	Inputs	Weights	Activations	Inputs	Weights	Activations
Full precision [13]	R	R	R	R	R	R
BinaryConnect [19]	R	$\{-1,1\}$	R	R	$\{-1,1\}$	R
BWN [13]	R	$\{-1,1\}$ with α	R	R	$\{-1,1\}$ with α	R
TWN [30]	R	$\{-1,0,1\}$ with α	R	R	$\{-1,0,1\}$ with α	R
BNN [20]	R	$\{-1,1\}$	$\{-1,1\}$	R	$\{-1,1\}$	$\{-1,1\}$
XNOR-Net [13]	R	$\{-1,1\}$ with α	$\{-1,1\}$ with K	R	$\{-1,1\}$ with α	$\{-1,1\}$ with K
TNN [26]	$\{-1,0,1\}$	R	$\{-1,0,1\}$	$\{-1,0,1\}$	$\{-1,0,1\}$	$\{-1,0,1\}$
TBN [28]	Both R or $\{-1,0,1\}$	$\{-1,1\}$ with α	$\{-1,0,1\}$	Both R or $\{-1,0,1\}$	$\{-1,1\}$ with α	$\{-1,0,1\}$
GXNOR-Net [27]	Not reported	$\{-1,0,1\}$	$\{-1,0,1\}$	Not reported	$\{-1,0,1\}$	$\{-1,0,1\}$
TOT-Net [29]	R	$\{-1,0,1\}$ with α	$\{-1,0,1\}$ with β	R	$\{-1,0,1\}$ with α	$\{-1,0,1\}$ with β

R stands for real value, K and α stand for activations scaling factor and weights scaling factor, respectively.

Table 5.3   Classification accuracies of mentioned methods

Method	Datasets						
	MNIST (LeNet-5)	**CIFAR10**		**SVHN (VGG-7)**	**CIFAR100**	**ImageNet[+]**	
		VGG7	**NIN**			**AlexNet**	**ResNet-18**
Full precision [13]	99.48	92.88	89.67	97.68	64.32	57.2/80.2	69.3/89.2
BinaryConnect [19]	99.05	91.73	NA	97.85	NA	35.5/61	NA
BWN [13]	99.38	92.58	NA	97.46	NA	56.8/79.4	60.8/83
TWN [30]	33.38	92.56	NA	NA	NA	54.5/76.8	65.3/86.2
BNN [20]	98.60	89.85	NA	97.47	NA	27.9/50.42	NA
XNOR-Net [13]	99.21	90.02	85.74	96.96	54.10	44.2/69.2	51.2/73.2
TNN [26]	99.33	87.89*	NA	97.27*	51.6	NA	NA
TBN [28]	99.38	90.85	NA	97.27	NA	49.7/74.2	55.6/79.0
GXNOR-Net [27]	99.32	92.50	NA	97.37	NA	NA	NA
TOT-Net [29]	99.34	NA	87.53	NA	61.61, NIN	42.99/68.2 (20epoch)	NA

[+] Presenting both top-1 and top-5 accuracies, respectively.
*TNN uses VGG-like architecture which is proposed by [31].

5.3   BNN optimization techniques

Various BNNs and TNNs were introduced in the previous section. The main concerns of these methods are to reduce the computations and memory storage demand to make them appropriate for power- and resource-limited devices. However, accuracy loss, especially in large datasets, is a major challenge in this way. Therefore, many works have attempted to address this issue and reduce accuracy loss. In this section, we introduce two major innovations in this line.

The method proposed in [14] is one of the most noticeable promising approaches that targets reducing the accuracy loss in BNNs on large datasets. The authors demonstrated that the common training methods are not suitable for BNNs due to some of their inherent properties. Instead, they proposed to train BNNs with both high compression rate and high accuracy on large datasets via the following techniques.

- **The learning rate.** Generally, the learning rate is initialized to 0.01 for full-precision CNNs which is shown not to be appropriate for BNNs. Actually, many weights of the BNNs are frequently changed and their sign changes are about three orders of magnitude more frequently than the full-precision CNNs. They have explored and found that for lower learning rates (say 0.0001), the changes in the sign in BNNs become closer to full-precision CNNs. Therefore, accuracy is significantly increased compared with other BNNs, especially for ImageNet dataset.

- **The scaling factor.** As mentioned in Section 5.2, XNOR-Net has deployed a scaling factor for both weights and activations to enhance accuracy compared with BNN. Since scaling factor computations are complex, [14] have proposed a method to binarize both weights and activations without scaling factor. Actually, they substitute ReLU layer with PReLU layer to compensate accuracy loss that may arise by the elimination of the scaling factor. Thus, the convolutional layer can only be performed by XNOR-Popcount.
- **The regularizer.** CNNs have deployed regularizer to obtain model generalization and prevent overfitting. The full-precision CNNs often use the L2 regularization to drive weights close to zero [14]. In the BNNs, driving weights to values near $+1$ or -1 is desirable in order to achieve minor binarization error. In [16], a new regularization method is proposed that is appropriate for BNNs and makes the weights closer to $+1$ and -1.
- **Multiple binarization.** BNNs have just considered $\{-1,1\}$ values that are encoded to 1-bit values (0 and 1) during the binarization process. The technique presented in [16] proposes to use multiple binarizations for activations to save accuracy. Although m-level binarization leads to m$\times$ grow in computation, they have shown that with $m = 2$ for activations (two levels of binarization), the top-5 accuracy of ImageNet dataset grows by 5.8%.
- **Binarizing the last layer and improving the overall compression rate.** The studied designs, such as XNOR-Net and BNN, only binarize the inner layers, hence both first and last layers are still full precision. Binarizing the last layer leads to remarkable accuracy loss and difficulties in the training process [32]. A technique in [16] introduces a scale layer which is inserted between the last binarized layer and the softmax function. The scalar parameter is learnable during the training phase and is initialized to 0.001. By adding the scale layer, the compression rate of BNNs increases, while the accuracy loss is kept negligible.

The method presented in [16] has increased compression rate about 3$\times$ and also improves the classification accuracy about 2% on ImageNet datasets in comparison with XNOR-Net.

Accurate-binary-convolution network (ABC-Net) is a two-step method that tries to reduce accuracy loss of binarization [15]. First, the real values of weights are approximated by a linear combination of multiple binary bases, as shown in Figure 5.11 (left). This way, binary weights can keep values close to their full-precision values. Second, multiple binary activations are used for inputs to reduce information loss, as shown in Figure 5.11 (right).

As mentioned earlier, ABC-Net estimates full-precision weights (W) by deploying a linear combination of M binary filters $B_i = 0:M$ which are constrained to the $\{-1,+1\}$ set, as

$$W \approx \alpha_1 B_1 + \alpha_2 B_2 + \ldots + \alpha_M B_M \tag{5.9}$$

For binarizing activations, ABC-Net first passes inputs to activation function h, outlined in (5.10), to ensure $h(x)$ is restricted to take values from [0,1]. It should be mentioned that v is a shift parameter:

$$h_v(x) = \text{clip}(x + v, 0, 1) \tag{5.10}$$

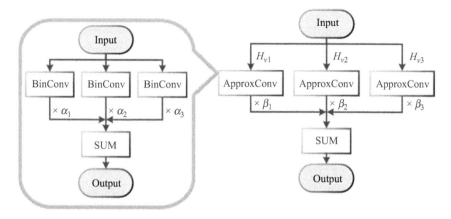

Figure 5.11   A block structure of convolution in ABC-Net [15]

Similar to estimating weights, ABC-Net estimates real value activations (R) by deploying a linear combination of N binary activations $A_i = 0{:}N$ as shown in (5.11):

$$W \approx \beta_1 A_1 + \beta_2 A_2 + \ldots + \beta_N A_N \qquad (5.11)$$

where $A = H_v(R)$. Therefore, convolution can be calculated by (5.12), as

$$\text{Conv}\,(W, R) \approx \sum_{m=1}^{M} \sum_{n=1}^{N} \propto_m \beta_n \text{Conv}\,(B_m, A_n) \qquad (5.12)$$

$M \times N$ bitwise convolution can be calculated in parallel. Figure 5.11 shows ABC-Net with $M = N{=}3$ that consists of 9 BinConvs which are calculated concurrently.

Similar to XNOR-Net, ABC-Net has changed the layer's order in the CNN block but it locates pooling layers after convolutions. Therefore, the original activity chain of (1) convolution, (2) BN, (3) activations, and (4) pooling has been reordered as to (1) convolution, (2) pooling, (3) BN, and (4) activations. Furthermore, ABC-Net has deployed a full-precision pretrained model in order to have a perfect initialization.

By using these techniques, they have achieved the classification accuracy very close to a full-precision CNN counterpart. The results on ImageNet show that the classification accuracy is within 4% of the full-precision model for $M = N = 5$.

5.4   Hardware implementation of BNNs

As mentioned earlier, BNNs keep the weights and/or activations by 1 bit. Thus, memory storage and accesses are reduced considerably. The fact that XNOR-bitcount and MUX-addition are used instead of MAC operations in BNNs results in the advent of many hardware accelerators for embedded BNNs. In particular, in [33], it has shown that due to bit-level logic operations, custom hardware is a more appropriate option than GPUs and CPUs to implement BNN.

YodaNN [34], as one of the first architecture prototypes, presents a flexible, energy-efficient and performance-scalable accelerator design for BWTs. In this accelerator, weights and activations are binary and 12-bit numbers, respectively. By implementing and deploying latch-based standard cell memory which provides more energy efficiency and voltage scalability compared with SRAM, they have obtained energy efficiency of 61.2 tera operations per second per watt.

In [35], an optimized FPGA-based hardware accelerator for a nine-layer binary convolutional neural networks (BCNN) is presented. Since the input image is fixed point, the first layer processing elements are also fixed point. The design utilizes Lookup Tables (LUTs) instead of DSP48 slides to implement bitwise operations and uses bitcount to accumulate LUT outputs. The proposed FPGA-based architecture is $8.3\times$ faster and $75\times$ more energy efficient than Titan X GPU in small batch sizes. In large batch sizes, the proposed architecture achieves near Titan X GPU throughput and $9.5\times$ energy efficiency.

The authors in [17] presented a fully synthesizable ultra-efficient hardware accelerator, XNOR Neural Engine (XNE), for BNNs. It is designed in the form an IP core which can be integrated into a microcontroller for low-power embedded devices.

Note that in all BNNs, the BN layer is deployed after the convolution and fully connected layers. Afterward, the sign function is performed. However, hardware accelerators typically combine the sign function and normalization together for simple implementation.

For conventional deep CNNs, there are some methods and tool for automatic FPGA implementation. A well-known example is DNNWeaver [36] which generates a synthesizable code for FPGA and a scheduler software code based on the Caffe model of a CNN. There are also some similar tools for BNNs. The first framework for BNN (either CNN or MLP), called FINN [37], generates fast and flexible BNN FPGA accelerators by deploying a flexible heterogeneous streaming architecture. Both weights and activations are in the form of binary numbers in FINN framework. ReBNet [38] has introduced a new framework based on FINN that overcomes the accuracy loss of BNNs by multiple levels of residual binarization for activations. The number of binarization levels is determined based on a given accuracy threshold. The explorations of ReBNet reveals that 2 and 3 levels of binarization is often enough to get reasonable accuracy.

5.5   Conclusion

Due to the ever-increasing deployment of CNNs in embedded and handheld devices, neural network models with binarized and ternarized weights and/or activations have attracted considerable attention in recent years. These approaches substitute massive computation-intensive MAC operations with simple bitwise operations. Furthermore, memory storage/bandwidth demand is significantly reduced due to the low bit-width of the parameters. In this chapter, we presented a survey on the state-of-the-art BNNs and TNNs which are suitable for low-power and resource-limited embedded systems. We further reviewed some recent works that aim at tackling the main challenge of low-precision neural networks, i.e., accuracy loss. With current advances, BNNs and TNNs are becoming a promising candidate to implement future low-power embedded systems.

References

[1] K. He, X. Zhang, S. Ren, and J. Sun, "Deep residual learning for image recognition," In *Proceedings of the IEEE Conference on Computer Vision and Pattern Recognition*, pp. 770–778, 2016.

[2] A. Krizhevsky, I. Sutskever, and G. E. Hinton, "ImageNet classification with deep convolutional neural networks," *Advances in Neural Information Processing Systems*, pp. 1097–1105, 2012.

[3] R. Girshick, J. Donahue, T. Darrell, and J. Malik, "Rich feature hierarchies for accurate object detection and semantic segmentation," In *Proceedings of the IEEE Conference on Computer Vision and Pattern Recognition*, pp. 580–587, 2014.

[4] V. Sze, Y. H. Chen, T. J. Yang, and J. S. Emer, "Efficient processing of deep neural networks: a tutorial and survey," *Proceedings of the IEEE*, vol. 105, no. 12, pp. 2295–2329, 2017.

[5] S. Han, J. Pool, J. Tran, and W. J. Dally, "Learning both weights and connections for efficient neural networks," *Advances in Neural Information Processing Systems*, pp. 1135–1143. 2015.

[6] Y.-H. Chen, J. Emer, and V. Sze, "Eyeriss: a spatial architecture for energy-efficient dataflow for convolutional neural networks," *ACM SIGARCH Computer Architecture News*, vol. 44, no. 3, pp. 367–379, 2016.

[7] P. Gysel, J. Pimentel, M. Motamedi, and S. Ghiasi, "Ristretto: A framework for empirical study of resource-efficient inference in convolutional neural networks," *IEEE Transactions on Neural Networks and Learning Systems*, vol. 29, pp. 1–6, 2018.

[8] Y. Ma, N. Suda, Y. Cao, J.-S. Seo, and S. Vrudhula, "Scalable and modularized RTL compilation of convolutional neural networks onto FPGA." In *2016 26th International Conference on Field Programmable Logic and Applications (FPL)*, pp. 1–8. IEEE, 2016.

[9] T. J. Yang, Y. H. Chen, and V. Sze, "Designing energy-efficient convolutional neural networks using energy-aware pruning," In *Proceeding of the 30th IEEE Conference Computer Vision Pattern Recognition, CVPR 2017*, pp. 6071–6079, 2017.

[10] A. G. Howard, M. Zhu, B. Chen, *et al.*, "MobileNets: efficient convolutional neural networks for mobile vision applications," ArXiv Preprint ArXiv:1704.04861, 2017.

[11] F. N. Iandola, S. Han, M. W. Moskewicz, K. Ashraf, W. J. Dally, and K. Keutzer, "SqueezeNet: AlexNet-level accuracy with $50\times$ fewer parameters and <0.5 MB model size," In *International Conference on Learning Representations*, 2017.

[12]   A. Zhou, A. Yao, Y. Guo, L. Xu, and Y. Chen, "Incremental network quantization: towards lossless CNNs with low-precision weights," ArXiv Preprint ArXiv:1702.03044, 2017.

[13]   M. Rastegari, V. Ordonez, J. Redmon, and A. Farhadi, "XNOR-Net?: ImageNet classification using binary," In *European Conference on Computer Vision*, pp. 525–542. Springer, Cham, 2016.

[14]   M. Nazemi, G. Pasandi, and M. Pedram. "NullaNet: training deep neural networks for reduced-memory-access inference." ArXiv Preprint arXiv:1807.08716, 2018.

[15]   X. Lin, "Towards accurate binary convolutional neural network," In *Advances in Neural Information Processing Systems*, pp. 345–353, 2017.

[16]   W. Tang, G. Hua, and L. Wang, "How to train a compact binary neural network with high accuracy?" In *AAAI Conference on Association for the Advancement of Artificial Intelligence*, pp. 2625–2631, 2017.

[17]   F. Conti, P. D. Schiavone, S. Member, and L. Benini, "XNOR neural engine: a hardware accelerator IP for 21.6 fJ/op binary neural network inference," ArXiv Preprint arXiv:1807.03010, 2018.

[18]   A. Al Bahou, G. Karunaratne, R. Andri, L. Cavigelli, and L. Benini, "XNORBIN?: A 95 TOp/s/W hardware accelerator for binary convolutional neural networks," In *2018 IEEE Symposium in Low-Power and High-Speed Chips (COOL CHIPS)*, pp. 1–3, IEEE, 2018.

[19]   M. Courbariaux and J. David, "BinaryConnect?: training deep neural networks with binary weights during propagations," *Advances in Neural Information Processing Systems*, pp. 3123–3131, 2015.

[20]   I. Hubara, "Binarized neural networks," *Advances in Neural Information Processing Systems*, pp. 4107–4115, 2016.

[21]   Z. Lin, R. Memisevic, and M. Courbariaux, "Neural networks with few multiplications," In *International Conference on Learning Representations*, pp. 1–9, 2017.

[22]   N. Srivastava, G. Hinton, A. Krizhevsky, I. Sutskever, and R. Salakhutdinov, "Dropout: a simple way to prevent neural networks from overfitting," *The Journal of Machine Learning Research*, vol. 15, no. 1, pp. 1929–1958, 2014.

[23]   L. Wan, M. Zeiler, S. Zhang, Y. LeCun, and R. Fergus, "Regularization of neural networks using DropConnect," *Proceedings of 30th International Conference on Machine Learning*, no. 1, pp. 109–111, 2013.

[24]   C. Jin, H. Sun, and S. Kimura, "Sparse ternary connect: Convolutional neural networks using ternarized weights with enhanced sparsity," In *Design Automation Conference (ASP-DAC), 2018 23rd Asia and South Pacific*, pp. 190–195. IEEE, 2018.

[25]   D. P. Kingma and J. Ba, Adam: a method for stochastic optimization. ArXiv Preprint arXiv:1412.6980, 2014.

[26]   H. Alemdar, V. Leroy, A. Prost-Boucle, and F. Pétrot, "Ternary neural networks for resource-efficient AI applications," In *2017 International Joint Conference on Neural Networks (IJCNN)*, pp. 2547–2554. IEEE, 2017.

[27] L. Deng, P. Jiao, J. Pei, Z. Wu, and G. Li, "GXNOR-Net: training deep neural networks with ternary weights and activations without full-precision memory under a unified discretization framework," *Neural Networks*, vol. 100, no. 4, pp. 49–58, 2018.

[28] D. Wan, F. Shen, L. Liu, *et al.*, "TBN: convolutional neural network with ternary inputs and binary weights," In *Proceedings of the European Conference on Computer Vision (ECCV)*, pp. 315–332, 2018.

[29] N. Nazari, M. Loni, M. E. Salehi, M. Daneshtalab, and M. Sjödin. "TOT-Net: an endeavor toward optimizing ternary neural networks," In *2019 22st Euromicro Conference on Digital System Design (DSD)*, IEEE, 2019.

[30] B. Liu, "Ternary weight networks," ArXiv Preprint arXiv:1605.04711, 2016.

[31] M. Courbariaux, Y. Bengio, and J. David, "BinaryConnect: training deep neural networks with binary weights during propagations," In *Advances in Neural Information Processing Systems (NIPS)*, pp. 3105–3113, 2015.

[32] G. Radients, "Dorefa-net: training low bitwidth convolutional neural networks with low bitwidth gradients," ArXiv Preprint arXiv:1606.06160, 2016.

[33] E. Nurvitadhi, D. Sheffield, J. Sim, A. Mishra, G. Venkatesh, and D. Marr, "Accelerating binarized neural networks: comparison of FPGA, CPU, GPU, and ASIC," In *2016 International Conference on Field-Programmable Technology (FPT)*, pp. 77–84. IEEE, 2016.

[34] R. Andri, L. Cavigelli, D. Rossi, and L. Benini, "YodaNN: an architecture for ultra-low power binary-weight CNN acceleration," *IEEE Transactions on Computer-Aided Design of Integrated Circuits and Systems*, vol. 37, no. 1, pp. 48–60, 2018.

[35] L. Zichuan, K. Xu, H. Yu, and F. Ren, "A 7.663-TOPS 8.2-W energy-efficient FPGA accelerator for binary convolutional neural networks," In *International Symposium on Field-Programmable Gate Array*, pp. 290–291, 2017.

[36] H. Sharma, J. Park, D. Mahajan, *et al.*, "From high-level deep neural models to FPGAS," In *The 49th Annual IEEE/ACM International Symposium on Microarchitecture*, p. 17. IEEE Press, 2016.

[37] Y. Umuroglu, N. J. Fraser, G. Gambardella, and M. Blott, "FINN: a framework for fast, scalable binarized neural network inference," In *Proceedings of the 2017 ACM/SIGDA International Symposium on Field-Programmable Gate Arrays*, pp. 65–74. ACM, 2017.

[38] M. Ghasemzadeh, M. Samragh, and F. Koushanfar, "ReBNet: residual binarized neural network," In *The 26th IEEE International Symposium on Field-Programmable Custom Computing Machines*, 2017.

Part III

Deep learning and model sparsity

Chapter 6

Hardware and software techniques for sparse deep neural networks

Ali Shafiee[1], Liu Liu[1], Lei Wang[1], and Joseph Hassoun[1]

6.1 Introduction

Over the past four decades, every generation of processors has delivered $2\times$ performance boost, as predicted by Moore's law [1]. Ironically, the end of Moore's law occurred at almost the same time as computationally intensive deep learning algorithms were emerging. Deep neural networks (DNNs) offer state-of-the-art solutions for many applications, including computer vision, speech recognition, and natural language processing. However, this is just the tip of the iceberg. Deep learning is taking over many classic machine-learning applications and also creating new markets, such as autonomous vehicles, which will tremendously amplify the demand for even more computational power.

Hardware specialization was an effective response to meet the computational demands by devising efficient hardware architectures rather than relying on transistors' characteristics improvement. In the last decade, many startups have emerged to make specialized hardware accelerators only for running DNNs efficiently [2]. The market also welcomes these changes, e.g., the sale of Application Specific Integrated Circuits, ASICs, and Fields Programmable Gate Arrays, FPGAs, in the global data centers for deep learning computation increased from almost 0% in 2016 to 25% in 2018 [3]. However, there is still a need to further accelerate the hardware for two main reasons. First, in the next decade, the rise of internet of things will significantly increase the number of smart devices and sensors on the edge and the service requirements in the cloud, and DNN algorithms are expected to be heavily employed in both. Second, the main incentive for hardware buyers is the minimum of $2\times$ improvement, in terms of performance and power efficiency, and if the hardware designers cannot deliver $2\times$ performance improvements, the demand for new hardware might gradually diminish. Thus, there is a compelling need for computer architects to devise architectures that can boost the performance of dense DNN accelerators, since very soon they will become the de facto standard of DNN hardware accelerator.

Another form of hardware optimization leverages the property of DNNs that most of operations for DNN are over-parameterized. In fact, a huge network is needed only

[1]Samsung Semiconductor Inc., San Jose, CA, USA

for the initial model training to reach the best results in order to avoid getting stuck into local minima. Once the network is fully trained, it can be compressed using one or more well-studied techniques, such as model compression, quantization, or pruning (sparsity), before being used for inference.

Researchers have shown that dense neural networks can be pruned to a sparse one without losing accuracy.* Moreover, rectified linear unit (ReLU)-based DNNs generate sparse input tensors, making many of the computations in a convolutional layer ineffectual. Exploiting such input and parameter sparsity dramatically improves the hardware performance, and it has already found its way into commercial products. For example, recently, Cambricon announced that its server accelerators can achieve 80 TFLOPS (FP16 operations) with only 110 W when the sparse mode is enabled, and companies like Facebook and Google are considering adding sparsity to their accelerators' requirements [5,6].

In this chapter, we review some of the software and hardware techniques to make the dense networks sparse and to use it for performance boost. First, we review different types of sparsity methods and how they can be achieved. Then, we discuss various software techniques to prune a network. Finally, we review some of the hardware architectures that support sparsity.

In this chapter, the input to a convolutional and fully connected layer would be called input channel, input feature map, input tensor, input activation, and input neurons, interchangeably. Similar style of notations is also used for outputs. Additionally, kernel, parameters, weights, and synopses refer to the parameters used in a convolutional or fully connected layer.

6.2   Different types of sparsity methods

In general, there are four types of sparsity methods, as described next.

1. **Activation sparsity**: Activation sparsity is a result of employing ReLU as a nonlinear activation function [7]. ReLU zeros out all of the negative outputs in a tensor, both in the inference mode and during the forward pass of model training. Moreover, in the backward pass of model training, ReLU avoids propagating the error values from neurons that had negative outcomes in the forward pass (see Figure 6.1). Therefore, activation sparsity exists in ReLU-based DNNs in both inference and training modes, and it appears in the dense DNNs as well.

   While the abovementioned feature of ReLU is an advantage for hardware optimization, it is essentially a weakness from the software perspective. More precisely, in ReLU, weights do not get updated if their corresponding outcome is negative, which prevents updating almost half of the weights in the model. As a result, numerous solutions have been proposed to use a nonzero value for neurons with negative outcomes while applying a linear function to the positive

---

*Pruning DNNs sometimes even helps improve the accuracy [4].

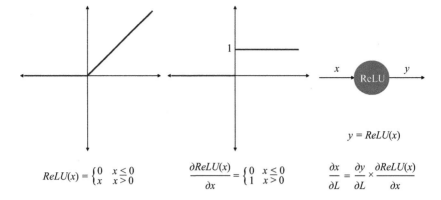

$$ReLU(x) = \begin{cases} 0 & x \leq 0 \\ x & x > 0 \end{cases} \qquad \frac{\partial ReLU(x)}{\partial x} = \begin{cases} 0 & x \leq 0 \\ 1 & x > 0 \end{cases} \qquad \frac{\partial x}{\partial L} = \frac{\partial y}{\partial L} \times \frac{\partial ReLU(x)}{\partial x}$$

Figure 6.1   ReLU (left), its derivation (middle), and the chain rule for ReLU

neurons, similar to ReLU [8]. These approaches have shown a marginal boost in model accuracy at the cost of having dense activation tensors, thus preventing their widespread adoption.

In addition, it is worth noting that most sequence models such as recurrent neural networks (RNNs) and long short-term memory still heavily rely on sigmoid and tanh nonlinearity, which severely reduces the number of zeros in the activation tensors. However, the trends show that ReLU (or clipped ReLU) is still the most dominant nonlinear activation function in convolutional neural networks (CNNs).

2. **Weight sparsity**: In the 1990s, LeCun *et al.* showed that it is possible to eliminate many unimportant weights from multilayer perceptrons and expect better generalization [9]. Later, Han *et al.* reevaluated this idea for DNNs to achieve much smaller networks with almost no loss in accuracy, but at the cost of longer training times [10]. Unlike activation sparsity, which changes from one input to another, weight sparsity is known before deploying the trained model. As a result, in the accelerators that are based on weight sparsity, the software layer can help to simplify the hardware complexity. However, this sparsity is not available during most of the training time. In Section 6.2, we cover software approaches to prune DNNs, efficiently.

3. **Output sparsity**: CNN and Fully Connected (FC) layers' outcomes are calculated by adding products of many pairs of activations and weights. In ReLU-based DNNs, an outcome will be useless if the sum of products ends up to be negative. Therefore, it could be avoided if it is predicted or speculated that the final result will likely be a negative number. This is called output sparsity.

4. **Value sparsity**: Most of the activations and weights values are distributed around zero making most of the bit positions in the activations and weights zero. We called the sparsity of 1s in a value, value sparsity. Value sparsity covers both weight and activation sparsity. An architecture based on such sparsity uses very low precision arithmetic units to capture only the effectual bit positions.

6.3   Software approach for pruning

6.3.1   Hard pruning

Usually, it is believed that in neural networks, weights with small magnitude contribute less comparing to the ones with large magnitude. Thus, most pruning approaches attempt to remove the small weights. Reference [11] addresses this process via the introduction of (hard) binary masks on top of weight tensors in the neural networks. By injecting the masking ops into the computational graph (during training), it sorts the weights in a layer by their absolute values and mask to zero the smallest magnitude weights until some desired sparsity level is reached. The back-propagated gradient will not flow through the weights where they are masked out in the forward pass. The final sparsity is achieved by carefully designed incremental sparsity training and is automated.

Following the similar paradigm, Changpinyo *et al.* [12] apply binary masks on the weight tensors as well. However, such masks are channel-wise random instead of arbitrary locations, and the mask is predefined and remains unchanged during training.

6.3.2   Soft pruning, structural sparsity, and hardware concern

Comparing to hard pruning, soft pruning does not remove connections (weights). Instead, it prunes the weight tensors via regularization, usually $\ell1$ regularization, which is a smooth approximation of $\ell0$ regularization. Han *et al.* [10] and [13] further pointed out that $\ell2$ regularization provides better sparse network using prune-retrain-prune scheme, despite that $\ell1$ regularization provides better train-prune accuracy. Meanwhile, structural concern is addressed by group sparsity. According to Wen *et al.* [14], sparsity regularization and connection pruning approaches, however, often produce nonstructured random connectivity in DNN and thus, irregular memory access that adversely impacts practical acceleration in hardware platforms. And group lasso can provide preferred group sparsity for more efficient data access because group lasso can effectively zero out all weights in some groups [14]. This is also successfully used in the RNNs [15].

With the emergence of dedicated DNN processing platform, it is desired to propose sparsity that is compatible to specific hardware platform. Kang [16] proposed a new pruning scheme reflecting the accelerator architectures, to achieve the same number of weights remain for each weight group (WG) corresponding to activation fetched simultaneously. Yu *et al.* [17] share the similar idea of customizing pruning to the underlying hardware by matching the pruned network to the data-parallel hardware organization, i.e., SIMD-aware weight pruning and node pruning.

6.3.3   Questioning pruning

Despite the merits of pruning in regards to its straightforward approach and performance guarantee (from the pretrained model), some works show that pruning is not an effective way to find efficient network structure. In more details, Liu *et al.* [18] made the following statements:

1. Training a large, over-parameterized model is not necessary to obtain an efficient final model.
2. Learned "important" weights of the large model are not necessarily useful for the small pruned model.
3. The pruned architecture itself, rather than a set of inherited "important" weights, is what leads to the efficiency benefit in the final model, which suggests that some pruning algorithms could be seen as performing network architecture search.

6.4 Hardware support for sparsity

An efficient DNN accelerator design should deliver low latency and high throughput for both dense and optimized DNNs (both sparse and low precision). In addition, the accelerator's performance should increase as the DNN gets more compressed (e.g., becomes more sparse). With these requirements in mind, we list some of the challenges and overheads in the design of a sparse DNN accelerator:

- *Support for sparsity increases the control logic overhead.* In dense DNN accelerators, many processing elements (PEs) can share the same control signals as the operations are embarrassingly parallel. However, sparsity leads to variability in PEs' execution time. Therefore, each PE requires some private control logic, since the PEs are independent to each other to some extent. In addition, in order to synchronize memory accesses and correctly reduce the results of PEs, some registers might be needed to store PEs' output.
- *Support for sparsity requires metadata overhead.* To distinguish between zero and nonzero values, some additional metadata are required. The format of such metadata differs from one architecture to another. However, in some architectures, the metadata space is separate from the data space. Hence, the metadata space would be wasted during the execution of dense DNNs or even for low-precision DNNs.
- *Support for sparsity makes the data path more complicated.* In order to increase computation sparsity, we need to introduce some multiplexers to send the nonzero inputs to idle PEs, or the result of a PE to the correct partial register. Furthermore, sparsity requires more registers in order to increase the efficiency. These overheads might be acceptable for floating point-based or 16-bit fixed point PEs. However, this might translate to a much higher area overhead for a low-precision PEs. Therefore, adopting sparsity seems less challenging for DNN accelerators for training than for inference, as training PE supports large floating-point units.

In addition to the challenges, we should also look into the opportunities of sparsity methods. Figure 6.2 depicts the potential benefits of different types of sparsity for different layers of AlexNet [19]. As it is shown, on average half of the activations

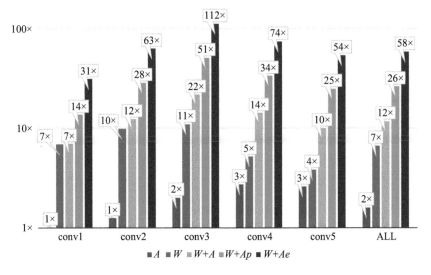

*Figure 6.2   Potential benefits of activation sparsity (A), weight sparsity (W), both
activation and weight sparsity (W+A), weight sparsity with dynamic
precision activation (W+Ap), and weight sparsity with value sparsity
for activations [19]*

are sparse, which implies an upper bound for activation and output sparsity improvements. With weight sparsity, it is possible to shrink computation by $7\times$. When both activation and weight sparsity are considered, the potential performance boost goes up to $12\times$. Figure 6.2 also shows that considering dynamic precision is better than considering sparsity for activation and eliminate $26\times$ of ineffectual computations. Dynamic precision is a type of value sparsity that considers variable precision for a group of activations. Finally, if zero weights are skipped and only effectual bits of the activations are computed, then the number of computations shrink by $58\times$, on average.

While Figure 6.2 shows a huge potential for performance and power efficiency improvement, the overheads to achieve these potentials are not trivial and can impose significant area overhead. In the rest of the section, we review the hardware techniques that take advantage of various types of sparsity methods.

6.4.1   Advantages of sparsity for dense accelerator

Even dense architectures can take advantage of sparsity in two ways.

- Clock gating: Eyeriss skips an Multiply and Accumulate (MAC) operation if any of the operands to a multiplier is zero [20]. Figure 6.2 shows that it is possible to clock $12\times$ of operations, in AlexNet. However, this does not translate to $12\times$ power reduction as even the original nonzero operations do not consume MAC's peak power.
- Compression: Sparse tensors can be compressed to save the bandwidth, power [20, 21], and, potentially, capacity [22]. Eyeriss uses run-length encoding to compress the data sent from its global buffer to each PE. Run-length encoding keeps a stream of pairs of numbers: a nonzero value and its distance to the next nonzero

value. This approach works well when the tensor is very sparse [23]. Alternatively, one can use the zero-value compression scheme, where a bitmap of bit flags is maintained, one per each value to indicate whether it is zero or not, followed by all the nonzero values. This approach is used by Nvidia [21,24] and some other works [25].

6.4.2   Supporting activation sparsity

Cnvlutin optimized DaDianNao architecture by enabling skipping zero activation [23]. In every cycle, DaDianNao computes multiplication of a 16×16 matrix (of synapses) and a 16×1 vector (of neurons), in each tile. DaDianNao showed that such operations suffice to support both CNN and FC layers. In this architecture, 16×16 synaptic values are loaded from a wide eDRAM bank (also called synapse buffer or SB) to an array of 16×16 multipliers, while the other operands come from broadcasting 16 neuron values from the input neuron buffer or NBin (see Figure 6.3(a)). Hence, if a neuron value is zero, it causes 16 multiply-by-zero operations. In order to avoid underutilizing the multipliers, Cnvlutin decomposes the multiplier array to sixteen 16×1 multiplier vectors (or subunits). Thus, all the multipliers in a subunit share the same neuron values. In addition, Cnvlutin breaks 1 eDRAM bank to 16 banks, one for each subunit. This way, different subunits do not need to be synchronized in every cycle (however, they cannot be fully independent as they should still contribute to the appropriate output neurons). Due to the loose independence, each subunit can now skip zeros (see Figure 6.3(b)). To this end, Cnvlutin stores only nonzero input neurons with their offset. The index is used to fetch the appropriate weights from SB. Cnvlutin also relies on a dispatcher to send the pairs of values and offsets from the central buffer. In the central buffer, data are stored using zero-free neuron array format (ZFNAf). In this format, data are decomposed into bricks, that is 16 same indexed neurons in 16 consecutive input feature maps. Each brick is compressed, separately, by storing only its nonzero values. For each brick, Cnvlutin stores the offsets in a different storage unit next to the central unit. Cnvlutin does not leverage ZFNAf to save capacity in order to simplify locating the bricks. Hence, each brick of data occupies 16 positions whether it is compressible or not. Dispatcher reads the required bricks from the central buffer in ZFNAf format and distributes them to the tiles. The result of the computation is also encoded to ZFNAf once it is passed through ReLU, right before storing it in the central buffer. Cnvlutin reported $1.37 \times$ improvement in the throughput with only 4.5% area overhead (measured for 65 nm technology). This low area overhead is due to two main reasons. First, it works with 16-bit values, so the metadata overhead and control is marginal, and second, most of the area is occupied by large eDRAM banks.

6.4.3   Supporting weight sparsity

In this section, we review three approaches that take advantage of weight sparsity: (1) Cambricon-X [26] and (2) Bit-Tactical (TCL) [19] which add weight sparsity to their inner-product-based architectures, and (3) Samsung's neural processing unit (NPU) that relies on accumulation [27].

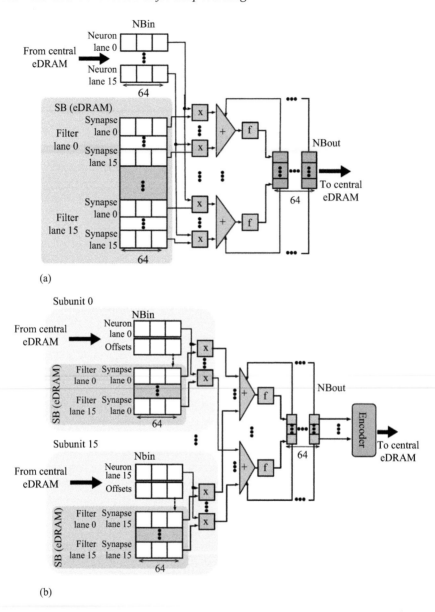

Figure 6.3   The tile structure of (a) baseline vs. (b) Cnvlutin [23]

6.4.3.1   Cambricon-X

Cambricon-X [26] optimizes DianNao [28] architecture to support weight sparsity. DianNao consists of multiple PEs, each of which performing an inner product operation for one output neuron, in every cycle. Each PE has an SB, to store the weights of some number of neurons, locally. Besides PEs, DianNao has the following components in its data path. (1) A NBin that holds the current activation that needs to be broadcast to PEs. (2) A output neuron buffer or NBout to hold the outcomes of PEs. (3) A buffer controller (BC) and (4) an interconnection to send appropriate input neurons to each PEs and collect the results (see Figure 6.4).

To support weight sparsity, Cambricon-X relies on two approaches:

- On the software level, the nonzero weights are packed and sent to SBs. This is feasible because zero weights are already known before deploying. Figure 6.5 shows the weight arrangement in SB for one small PE. As depicted, each neuron's weights are stored next to each other. Note that the number of SB rows allocated to the two output neurons in the figure is different and depends on their level of weight sparsity. Therefore, the number of computation cycles per output neuron and per PE is variable.
- In the control buffer, Cambricon-X keeps some metadata for each PE indicating which of its weights are zero and which of them are nonzero. This information is available to the indexing module in BC. Per PE there is one such module that uses the metadata to select and pack only those input neurons for which their corresponding weight in the PE is nonzero. As a result, Cambricon-X can avoid zero weight multiplication in PE to improve power efficiency. This approach also boosts the throughput, as calculating one output neuron takes fewer cycles compared to DianNao.

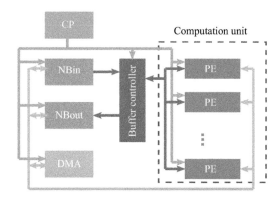

Figure 6.4   High-level organization of Cambricon-X [26]

Figure 6.5   The nonzero synopses for two neurons (left) and their organization in SB (right) [26]

According to the synthesis result [26], the overhead of Cambricon-X is nontrivial and sparsity support increases the area and power by $2.11\times$ and $1.96\times$, respectively. The overhead seems justifiable for FC layers, as Cambricon-X improves the FC-layer throughput by $4.84\times$ compared to DianNao. However, the improvement for CNN layer is approximately $2.5\times$, on average, compared to DaDianNao. Therefore, Cambricon-X seems to be more appropriate for workloads where FC layers' execution dominates the total runtime.

6.4.3.2   Bit-Tactical

TCL is another proposal that targets weight sparsity for inner-product-based architecture. TCL is built on top of a dense architecture that performs a matrix-by-vector multiplication (MVM) operation using multiple inner product unit (IPU), in each tile (see Figure 6.6). A CNN layer output can be computed as series of such MVM operations. Moreover, multiple MVMs are needed to calculate one output neuron, hence MVM results are accumulated for multiple cycles. Figure 6.6 shows how each IPU computes one output in four cycles. As it is shown, many of the multipliers are idle if weight and activation tensors are sparse. TCL offers two solutions to keep multipliers busy, thus, improving efficiency. In the first solution, if the current weight is zero, TCL will fetch the next nonzero weights from later cycles that contribute to the same output. This approach is called weight lookahead of N, if looking ahead up to N cycles is permitted. Figure 6.6 (top) shows how weight lookahead of 1 can increase throughput. Note that fetching a weight from later cycles requires fetching its corresponding activations as well. Hence, lookahead of N increases activation fetch bandwidth by a factor of N. In addition, an N-to-1 multiplexer (MUX) is introduced per multiplier to pick the right activations. Since weight sparsity is known before deploying, the select signals for these MUXs are computed off-line. In the second solution, TLC allows a lane to borrow weight from its above neighbors. This approach is called lookaside M, if up to M above neighboring lanes can lend weight to a lane. With lookahead h and lookaside d, an $(h+d+1)$-to-1 MUX is required per milliliter. Figure 6.7 (bottom) shows how lookahead of 1 combined with lookaside of 1 improve utilization.

According to [19], weight lookahead of 1 and lookaside of 6 can improve utilization by more than 60%.

6.4.3.3   Neural processing unit

Recently, researchers from Samsung proposed a hierarchical NPU that supports weight sparsity. NPU leverages multiple dimensions of parallelism: (1) it computes multiple output feature maps (OFMs); (2) in each OFM, it computes a 4×4 region; and (3) it divides input feature maps (IFMs) between multiple units and reduces their result together, at the end.

NPU is hierarchical. On the highest level, NPU has two cores each of which is responsible for half of the input channels. Inside each core, there are two data storage units (DSUs) that store one quarter of IFMs and their corresponding weights. Each core also has 16 dual MAC Arrays (dual-MAAs) with 32 multipliers and 16 partial sum registers. The 16 partial sum registers hold the partial sum for a 4×4 cell of one OFM. Each dual-MAA receives two 4×4 cells and their corresponding weights.

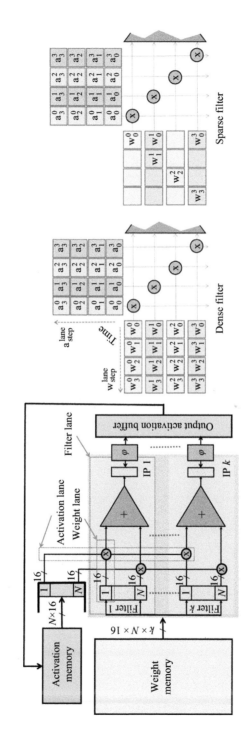

Figure 6.6   *Dense baseline architecture for TCL (left) and IPU computations inputs for one output (right)* [19]

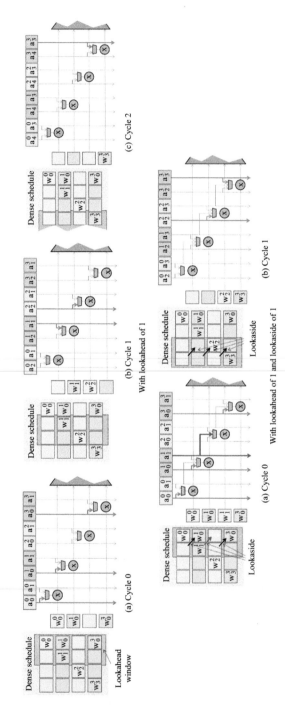

Figure 6.7 Lookahead of 1 (top) and lookahead and lookaside of 1 inputs for one IPU (bottom) [19]

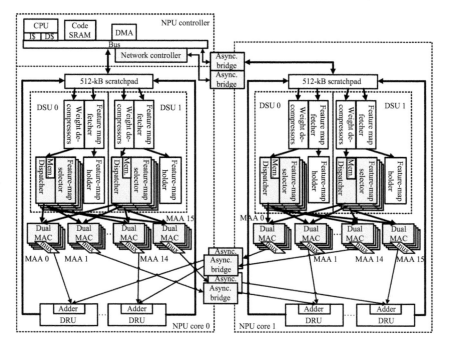

Figure 6.8   Overall architecture of NPU [27]

Each of the 16 activations in an input cell share is multiplied with the same weight, however, the product results are accumulated for 16 different output positions of an output cell. Per DSU, there is a dispatcher unit that sends input cells and their weights to dual-MAAs, iteratively (see Figure 6.8). Since all the inputs in a cell share the same weight, NPU can skip zero weight. This is mainly done with the help of the software layer that passes only the nonzero weights. For every dual-MAAs in a core, each dispatcher unit frames one input cell and its nonzero weights in every cycle. Any dual-MAA receives two cells, for the dispatcher of each DSU, and their weights and updates the output partial sum cells. Once all the cells for all the IFMs are done, the results of the partial sums from two cores will be added together to make the final results.

According to [27], with 75% sparsity, NPU can achieve 6.9 TOPs/W and 3.5 TOPs/W for 5 × 5 and 3 × 3 kernels, respectively.

6.4.4 Supporting both weight and activation sparsity

In this section, we review three methods that enable both activation and weight sparsity in their designs: efficient inference engine (EIE) [29], ZeNA [30], and sparse CNN (SCNN) [22]. EIE targets sparsity in FC layer, while ZeNA and SCNN are more effective for CNN layers.

6.4.4.1   Efficient inference engine

Energy EIE is designed based on the observation that, on average, 90% of the computations in FC layers are ineffectual. FC layer can be considered a large MVM. EIE consists of multiple PEs, say N, each of them performing an MVM for some of the matrix rows. The rows are interleaved between PEs to achieve more balanced load work distribution. Due to this way of work distribution, each PE computes $1/N$th of the resulting vector. Each PE stores its sub-matrix in a modified compressed sparse column format that keeps two vectors for each column of the sub-matrix: (1) a vector of nonzero elements and (2) a vector of the distances between the elements in the first vector (up to 15). EIE compacts these two vectors for all the columns and put them together to make a larger vector containing pairs of nonzero values and distances. Since different columns have different numbers of nonzero elements, EIE stores another vector that points to the beginning of each column in the larger ensemble. If p_j represents the beginning of column j, then $p_{j+1} - p_j$ implies the number of nonzero elements in this column.

Using this format, EIE devised an architecture to perform just the effectual computations. This architecture has two main units. The central control unit, CCU, that formats the input vector, and PEs that perform the computations (see Figure 6.9). CCU broadcasts nonzero input elements and their indices to each of the PEs. Each PE backlogs them in their activation queue. If an element in the activation queue is indexed j, it means that it should be multiplied to all the nonzero elements of column j. Every PE has an 8B wide sparse matrix static random access memory (SRAM) that stores pairs of values and distances, as well as two pointer SRAM banks that keep the pointers to the beginning and the end of each column's pairs in the sparse matrix SRAM. Using these SRAMs, EIE performs its computations, as follows:

1. It first fetches the front element from the activation queue and its index, say j.
2. It uses j to access pointer SRAM banks to retrieve the pointer to the beginning and the end of the elements of column j in the sparse matrix SRAM.
3. Using these pointers, it then fetches one pair at the time, from sparse matrix SRAM, and multiplies the value with the activation fetched in the first step.
4. Using the distance value in the fetched pair, EIE finds the appropriate accumulator and accumulates the multiplication result to it.
5. Once all the computations are done, the accumulator values are sent to ReLU.

EIE also improves efficiency by relying on low-precision quantization and weight sharing. When all of these optimizations are applied, EIE achieves 102 GOPs computation power for sparse FC layers, in 45 nm. This translates to three TOPs computation power for uncompressed matrices.

6.4.4.2   ZeNA

ZeNA is a multi-cluster architecture with each cluster consisting of weight and activation SRAMs, multiple PEs, and an interconnect that connects the SRAMs and PEs together [30]. Each PE has its own local weight, activation, and partial sum buffer making ZeNa similar to Eyeriss in the data path for dense DNNs. However, ZeNA adds a few more items to enable zero skipping. To this end, each PE in ZeNA has

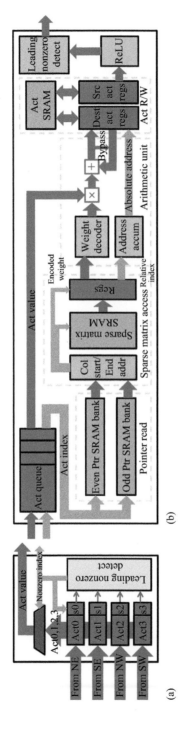

Figure 6.9   EIE's main components [29]. (a) logic to detect nonzero nodes. (b) processing element unit

a local fetch controller that has activation and weight zero bit-vectors to find which activations or weights are zero. The fetch controller calculates all the nonzero pairs of activation and weight and forwards them to nonzero index unit. PE data path picks one index per cycle and performs the corresponding MAC for the elements pointed by the selected index. As a result, PE performs only the nonzero MAC operations (see Figure 6.10).

In each ZeNA's cluster, PEs are divided into multiple WGs. In a WG, each PE works on a different OFMs. The same PEs in different WGs receive the same kernels, hence working on the same OFM. However, they contribute to different output positions (see Figure 6.11). Note that the number of PEs might not be enough to cover all of the OFMs. Therefore, ZeNA divides the OFMs into subgroups (sub-WG) and executes them iteratively. This way of work distribution, combined with imbalanced sparsity in both activation and weight tensors, can cause inefficiency. ZeNA devises two approaches to mitigate PE underutilization: (1) intra-WG load balancing and (2) inter-WG load balancing. In intra-WG load balancing, ZeNA first sorts the OFMs based on the number of nonzero weights they have. As a result, the sub-WG of OFMs deploying together has an almost similar number of multiplications to perform. In inter-WG load balancing, ZeNA allows different WGs to steal work from each other. Since all of the WGs share the same weights, it only needs to redirect the activations from one WG to another.

In comparison with Eyeriss [20], ZeNA boosts the performance by 4.4× and 5.6× for AlexNet and VGG-16, respectively. Although Eyeriss takes advantage of sparsity by clock gating the multiply-by-zero operations, ZeNA is still 25% more power efficient mostly because it finishes its task sooner and is able to save static power.

6.4.4.3   Sparse convolutional neural network

SCNN is another architecture that targets both weight and activation sparsity. SCNN comprises of 64 PEs, a layer sequencer that manages the activation and weight

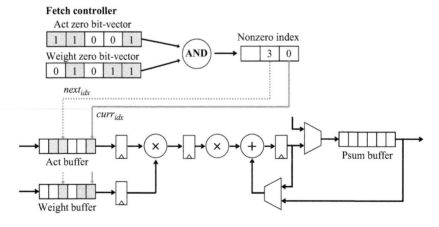

Figure 6.10   ZeNA's PE organization [30]

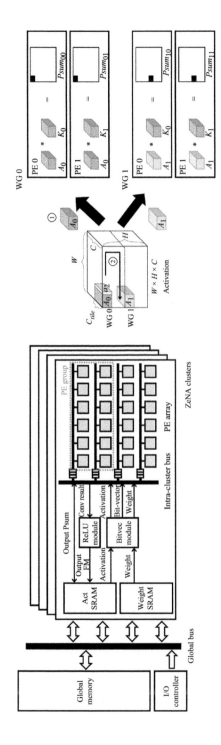

Figure 6.11 High-level organization of ZeNA (left) and its work distribution [30]

transfers between DRAM and PEs, and the interconnect between PEs. SCNN has three main features, as follows:

- Planar tiled: SCNN distributes the work between its 64 PEs in the planar dimension. More specifically, each PE receives and holds 1/64 of each input channel.
- Input stationary: Unless IFM is too large, each PE keeps one portion of the input during the entire execution of the CNN layer. In multiple iterations, the layer sequencer broadcasts kernel values for a few OFMs to all the PEs. Each PE independently computes some pixels of those OFMs. Finally, the OFM results are passed through ReLU and written back to the PE's SRAM output region (ORAM).
- Cartesian product: At every cycle, a vector of I nonzero input values and a vector of F nonzero filter values are fetched from SRAM into each PE, and the $I \times F$ outer product is computed. These $I \times F$ numbers contribute to different output positions (see Figure 6.12). In the dense case, finding the output position for the product results is trivial. To find the output position for the sparse case, SCNN loads corresponding to the input and filter values, in parallel with loading their value. The indices are sent to the coordinate computation units that find the appropriate output position for each product. The products are then routed to the output partial sum banks using a crossbar.

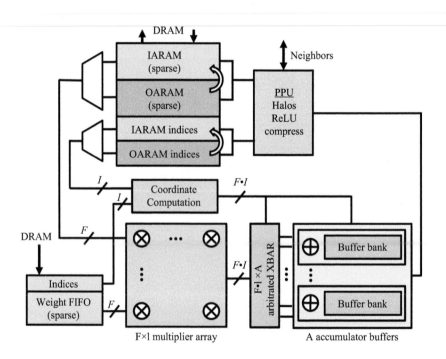

Figure 6.12   Structure of a SCNN's PE [22]

This way, SCNN almost always makes the multiplier busy with effectual computations at the cost of more complicated output units. In addition, SCNN keeps the compressed version of both activation and input, and hence it needs only half the capacity needed by dense architectures.

SCNN is implemented in 16 nm with 1,024 16-bit fixed-point multipliers. On average, it can improve the performance by 2.7× with respect to an optimized dense model. This improvement requires more area to implement the accumulation buffer and the crossbar in each PE (40% overhead). Last but not least, SCNN improves the energy by 2.3× compared to the optimized dense architecture.

6.4.5 Supporting output sparsity

In modern DNNs and CNNs, a large fraction of activation outputs are zero due to the unique property of ReLU. In this section, we discuss four architectures that leverage output sparsity.

6.4.5.1 SnaPEA

SnaPEA [31] takes advantage of this important stats to cut computations further. One technique involves statically reordering the weights based on their signs so that during the convolution operation, positive weights are always processed before negative weights. There is an additional index buffer added to each PE to hold the original weight indexes to associate the right input activation for each reordered weight. Since activations are nonnegative, when the partial sum becomes zero or negative during the computation, the computation can be stopped, since the ReLU'ed output will definitely be zero. This technique terminates unnecessary computations without altering the true results, hence referred to as the "exact mode." Built on top of exact mode, another mode is to aggressively predict whether a particular convolution window will end up with negative or zero result. To do this, a set of MAC operation step (n) and threshold (th) pairs are generated off-line by a greedy algorithm and stored. The predictive activation unit compares thresholds against the actual partial sums at each MAC operation step during run time to perform output sparsity speculation. These speculation parameters are also knobs to trade-off accuracy for desired speedup. In determining the parameters, a greedy algorithm iteratively searches through the design space with a cost function of minimizing operations while maintaining certain accuracy. In SnaPEA architecture, PE's are organized in a 2D array as shown in Figure 6.13 to facilitate hardware parallelism. The same input activation is broadcast along the horizontal direction, whereas the same weights are broadcast in the vertical direction. Similar to other sparsity schemes, parallelism slows down performance boost obtained by one PE due to the portioning. Faster PE's have to wait for the slower ones in the same horizontal group. In this case, idle PE's are power gated to save power. Note that in both modes, computation reduction is also accompanied by skipped input/weight buffer reads. This chapter reported on average 1.3× speedup and 1.16× energy reduction over Eyeriss in exact mode. With 3% accuracy loss in the predictive mode, the average speedup and energy saving are 2.02× and 1.89×, respectively.

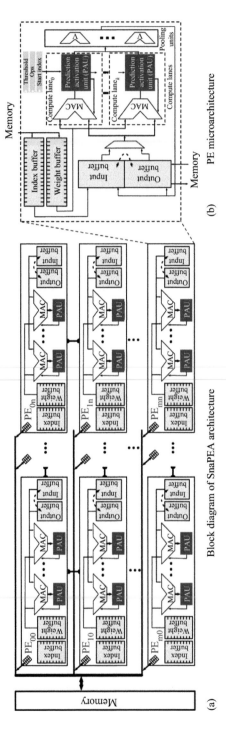

Block diagram of SnaPEA architecture

(a)

(b)   PE microarchitecture

Figure 6.13   (a) High-level organization of SnaPEA and (b) its PE structure [31]

6.4.5.2 Uniform Serial Processing Element

While zero and negative inputs to the ReLU activations capture a significant amount of unnecessary operations, there are other computation reduction opportunities. Authors in [32] extend the definition of ineffectual output neurons (iEON) to be output activations that have no influence on the subsequent layers that are "removed" by ReLU as well as max pooling operations. Skipping all iEON operations brings even more performance speedup. Their proposed prediction-based scheme first computes higher bits of input activations and/or weights in the prediction stage in the rational that activation outputs are mainly dominated by the multiplication of the highest bits whether the outputs go to ReLU or max pooling. The prediction results are written into two tables (ReLUTable and MAXTable). Minimum numbers of the highest bits required to perform predictions can be different for different layers and are determined offline. To be able to reuse the computation results as well as the hardware incurred in the prediction stage, serial multiplier architecture is used. So, regardless of the number of the highest bits computed in the first stage, the unified hardware as shown in Figure 6.14 will carry on the rest of the computation if it is deemed effectual.

Serial multiplier takes multiple cycles to finish multiplication of all bits. This chapter introduces other dimensions of parallelism by deploying PE's to simultaneously process multiple OFMs and multiple pixels in each OFM to scale out the architecture. If activations and weights are broadcast to two dimensions of the PE array, PE idle cycles will be unavoidably introduced due to uneven and random distribution of EONs in OFMs. Completely breaking data sharing dependency makes memory bandwidth a bottleneck. To overcome this synchronization issue brought by input and weight sharing, the authors use only one type of data sharing in the execution stage. Weight (or kernel) sharing is employed when computing a convolutional layer followed by max pooling due to the fact that the number of EONs in different OFMs is almost the same. On the other hand, for convolutional layers followed by ReLU activations where the number of EON's in each OFM varies, input sharing is employed because the total number of EONs at the same pixel locations is nearly the same across different OFMs. In either case, data loading and assignment time should be able to overlap with data processing time, proportional to the number of least significant bits in the execution stage to keep all PE's fully used.

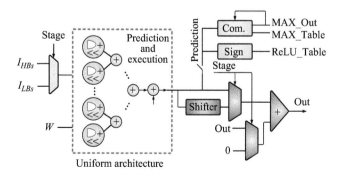

Figure 6.14   Unified serial PE structure [32]

For fully connected layers where there is no filter reuse, this prediction-based optimization means that not all weight bits are loaded from off-chip memory, improving energy efficiency.

The lossless prediction-based architecture showed an average 1.8× and 1.6× speedup over zero-activation skipping scheme Cnvlutin and precision reduction scheme stripes, respectively, without the need of retaining the network.

6.4.5.3 SparseNN

There are other works using prediction to exploit output sparsity. SparseNN [33] deploys a lightweight run-time predictor for the output activation sparsity on the fly. The predictor is based on truncated singular value decomposition (SVD) to decompose weight matrix into two low-rank matrices. The computation complexity is smaller as compared to the original feedforward, also insignificant to the bypassed computations.

6.4.5.4 ComPEND

ComPEND [34] re-encodes the weights with inverted two's complement so that MSB has a positive weight and all others have negative weight. The input and output activations are encoded normally. Multiplications are processed serially. MSBs are computed first, as the computation progresses, the bit serial sum goes toward negative as shown in Figure 6.15. By checking the sign inversion in the intermediate results of the bit serial sum, this scheme can detect negative results before finishing the calculation of all bits. The advantage is that the off-line weight encoding removes the need of weight reordering as used in SnaPEA.

6.4.6 *Supporting value sparsity*

6.4.6.1 Bit-pragmatic

Realizing multiplication as a sequence of shift and add operations allows skipping zero bit positions. Bit-pragmatic [35] showed that this approach reduces the effectual computation demand, dramatically. It also devises a modified version of DaDianNao tile architecture, Pragmatic tile, to take advantage of this observation. The high-level organization of baseline and the modified tiles are shown in Figure 6.16. The baseline consists of multiple IPUs that perform inner product operations. As the operands, all the IPs share the same vector of activations from NBin but receive their own

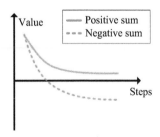

Figure 6.15   The trend of the sum of bit-serial products with inverted two's complement weight encoding [34]

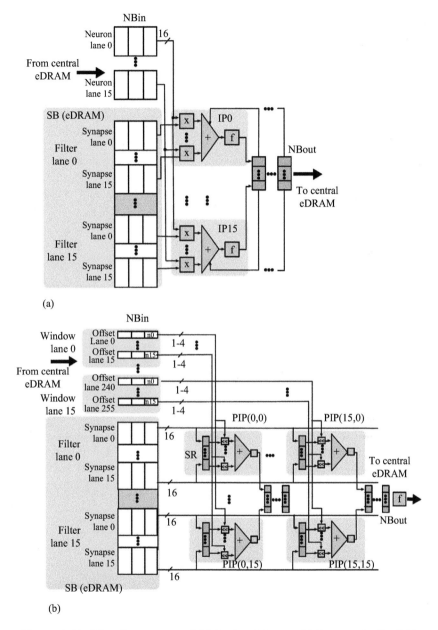

Figure 6.16   The tile structure of (a) DaDainNao vs. (b) Pragmatic tile [35]

vector of weights from SB. The results are accumulated to the appropriate output neurons in the NBout. Bit-pragmatic modifies this tile as follows. (1) It represents input value received from NBin into a series of 4-bit nonzero bit positions. Every cycle it broadcasts one of such offset values to the IPs. (2) It replaces the multiplier in the IP with shift units. Every such unit left shift the weight values according to its corresponding offset value. (3) Since shift logic is smaller than a multiplier, more shift-based IPs are accommodated into one tile. However, naively replicating the number of causes linearly increases in SB bandwidth requirements. This is because in the naive approach, more IPs are added for more output channels and each output channel has its own set of weight. Pragmatic tile mitigates the bandwidth requirement by adding more IPs for different neuron of the same output channels. As a result, multiple IPs can now share the same weight vector. Thus, there is no need for more weight bandwidth. However, the IPs sharing the same weights require different input vectors. Therefore, Pragmatic tile linearly increases NBin bandwidth to deliver appropriate inputs to every IPs in each cycle. Notice that since NBin bandwidth is much smaller than SB bandwidth in the baseline tile, due to input sharing, it makes a better candidate for bandwidth expansion.

According to [35], Pragmatic tile can outperform DaDianNao [36] by 2.6× at the cost of 35% area overhead.

6.4.6.2   Laconic architecture

Sharify *et al.* leverage value sparsity and propose laconic tile that improves Bit-pragmatic with two proposals [37].

- Instead of using the offset in the 2′s complement presentation, they use modified booth encoding to reduce the number of effectual bit position.
- Based on the observation that weight values are distributes around zero, they apply values sparsity to weight as well.

A laconic tile is comprised of multiple laconic PEs, each of which perform-ing as an inner product using low-precision units, sequentially. Figure 6.17 shows the structure of a laconic PE. There is one low-precision unit per vector position that inde-pendently computes the multiplication of a pair of an activation and its corresponding weight. Since both activations and weights are represented in modified booth format, the low-precision units only perform exponents addition along with determining the

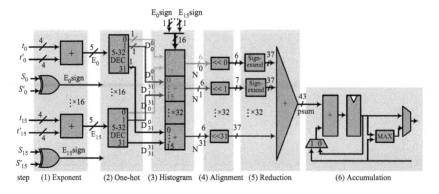

Figure 6.17   Laconic PE's pipeline [37]

sing, iteratively. For any possible results of exponent addition, laconic PE keeps a counter that gets updated if any of the low-precision unit output matches its value. Once all the low-precision operations are done, the counters are shifted and added to find the final result.

Laconic tile can outperform a dense tile by $2.3\times$ in terms of performance and $2.13\times$ in terms of energy efficiency, on average.

6.5 Conclusion

In this chapter, we have reviewed the potential of sparsity to boost the performance and energy efficiency of DNN accelerators. We first identified four sparse methods: (1) activation, (2) weight, (3) output and (4) value sparsity. Then we reviewed software techniques to prune a DNN network. Finally, we went over some of the prior works that leverage different methods of sparsity.

References

[1] Hennessy JL, and Patterson DA. A new golden age for computer architecture. Communications of the ACM. 2019;62(2):48–60.

[2] Shan Tang. List of AI Chips; 2019. Available from: https://github.com/basicmi/AI-Chip.

[3] Deliotte. Hitting the Accelerator: The Next Generation of Machine-Learning Chips; 2018. Available from: https://www2.deloitte.com/content/dam/Deloitte/global/Images/infographics/technologymediatelecommunications/gx-deloitte-tmt-2018-nextgen-machine-learning-report.pdf.

[4] Han S, Pool J, Narang S, *et al.* DSD: Dense-sparse-dense training for deep neural networks. arXiv preprint arXiv:1607.04381. 2016.

[5] Jouppi NP, Young C, Patil N, *et al.* In-datacenter performance analysis of a tensor processing unit. In: 2017 ACM/IEEE 44th Annual International Symposium on Computer Architecture (ISCA). IEEE; 2017. p. 1–12.

[6] Hemsoth N. Facebook Sounds Opening Bell for AI Inference Hardware Makers; 2018. Available from: https://www.nextplatform.com/2018/09/13/facebook-sounds-opening-bell-for-ai-inference-hardware-makers/.

[7] Krizhevsky A, Sutskever I, and Hinton GE. ImageNet classification with deep convolutional neural networks. In: Advances in Neural Information Processing Systems; 2012. p. 1097–1105. Available from: http://www.proceedings.com/17576.html

[8] Xu B, Wang N, Chen T, and Li, M. Empirical evaluation of rectified activations in convolutional network. arXiv preprint arXiv:1505.00853. 2015.

[9] LeCun Y, Denker JS, and Solla SA. Optimal brain damage. In: Advances in Neural Information Processing Systems; 1990. p. 598–605. Available from: https://dl.acm.org/citation.cfm?id=109230.109298

[10]   Han S, Mao H, and Dally WJ. Deep compression: Compressing deep neural network with pruning, trained quantization and Huffman coding. arXiv preprint arXiv:1510.00149. 2015.

[11]   Zhu, MH, and Gupta S. To Prune, or Not to Prune: Exploring the Efficacy of Pruning for Model Compression. arXiv preprint arXiv:1710.01878. 2017.

[12]   Changpinyo S, Sandler M, and Zhmoginov A. The Power of Sparsity in Convolutional Neural Networks. ICLR. 2017. Available from: https://arxiv.org/abs/1702.06257.

[13]   Han S, Pool J, Tran J, *et al.* Learning both Weights and Connections for Efficient Neural Network. In: Cortes C, Lawrence ND, Lee DD, *et al.*, editors. Advances in Neural Information Processing Systems 28; 2015. p. 1135–1143. Available from: https://dl.acm.org/citation.cfm?id=2969366

[14]   Wen W, Wu C, Wang Y, *et al.* Learning Structured Sparsity in Deep Neural Networks. In: Lee DD, Sugiyama M, Luxburg UV, *et al.*, editors. Advances in Neural Information Processing Systems 29; 2016. p. 2074–2082. Available from: https://dl.acm.org/citation.cfm?id=3157329

[15]   Narang S, Undersander E, and Diamos G. Block-sparse recurrent neural networks. arXiv preprint arXiv:1711.02782. 2017.

[16]   Kang H. Accelerator-aware pruning for convolutional neural networks. In *IEEE Transactions on Circuits and Systems for Video Technology*. IEEE; 2019.

[17]   Yu J, Lukefahr A, Palframan D, *et al.* Scalpel: Customizing DNN pruning to the underlying hardware parallelism. In: Proceedings of the 44th Annual International Symposium on Computer Architecture. ISCA'17; 2017.

[18]   Liu Z, Sun M, Zhou T, *et al.* Rethinking the value of network pruning. In: International Conference on Learning Representations; 2019. Available from: https://openreview.net/forum?id=rJlnB3C5Ym.

[19]   Delmas A, Judd P, Stuart DM, *et al.* Bit-tactical: Exploiting ineffectual computations in convolutional neural networks: Which, why, and how. arXiv preprint arXiv:180303688. 2018.

[20]   Chen YH, Emer J, and Sze V. Eyeriss: A spatial architecture for energy-efficient dataflow for convolutional neural networks. In: ACM SIGARCH Computer Architecture News. vol. 44. IEEE Press; 2016. p. 367–379.

[21]   Rhu M, O'Connor M, Chatterjee N, *et al.* Compressing DMA engine: Leveraging activation sparsity for training deep neural networks. In: 2018 IEEE International Symposium on High Performance Computer Architecture (HPCA). IEEE; 2018. p. 78–91.

[22]   Parashar A, Rhu M, Mukkara A, *et al.* SCNN: An accelerator for compressed-sparse convolutional neural networks. In: 2017 ACM/IEEE 44th Annual International Symposium on Computer Architecture (ISCA). IEEE; 2017. p. 27–40.

[23]   Albericio J, Judd P, Hetherington T, *et al.* Cnvlutin: Ineffectual-neuron-free deep neural network computing. ACM SIGARCH Computer Architecture News. 2016;44(3):1–13.

[24]   Nvidia. 2018. NVIDIA Deep Learning Accelerator. Available from: http://nvdla.org/primer.html

[25] Aimar A, Mostafa H, Calabrese E, *et al.* Nullhop: A flexible convolutional neural network accelerator based on sparse representations of feature maps. IEEE Transactions on Neural Networks and Learning Systems. 2018;(99):1–13.

[26] Zhang S, Du Z, Zhang L, *et al.* Cambricon-x: An accelerator for sparse neural networks. In: The 49th Annual IEEE/ACM International Symposium on Microarchitecture. IEEE Press; 2016. p. 20.

[27] Song J, Cho Y, Park J-S, *et al.* 7.1 An 11.5 TOPS/W 1024-MAC butterfly structure dual-core sparsity-aware neural processing unit in 8nm flagship mobile SoC. In *2019 IEEE International Solid-State Circuits Conference* (ISSCC). IEEE; 2019. p. 130–132.

[28] Chen T, Du Z, Sun N, *et al.* Diannao: A small-footprint high-throughput accelerator for ubiquitous machine-learning. In: ACM Sigplan Notices. vol. 49. ACM; 2014. p. 269–284.

[29] Han S, Liu X, Mao H, *et al.* EIE: Efficient inference engine on compressed deep neural network. In: 2016 ACM/IEEE 43rd Annual International Symposium on Computer Architecture (ISCA). IEEE; 2016. p. 243–254.

[30] Kim D, Ahn J, and Yoo S. A novel zero weight/activation-aware hardware architecture of convolutional neural network. In: Design, Automation & Test in Europe Conference & Exhibition (DATE), 2017. IEEE; 2017. p. 1462–1467.

[31] Akhlaghi V, Yazdanbakhsh A, Samadi K, *et al.* SnaPEA: Predictive early activation for reducing computation in deep convolutional neural networks. In: 2018 ACM/IEEE 45th Annual International Symposium on Computer Architecture (ISCA). IEEE; 2018. p. 662–673.

[32] Song M, Zhao J, Hu Y, *et al.* Prediction based execution on deep neural networks. In: 2018 ACM/IEEE 45th Annual International Symposium on Computer Architecture (ISCA). IEEE; 2018. p. 752–763.

[33] Zhu J, Jiang J, Chen X, *et al.* SparseNN: An energy-efficient neural network accelerator exploiting input and output sparsity. In: 2018 Design, Automation & Test in Europe Conference & Exhibition (DATE). IEEE; 2018. p. 241–244.

[34] Lee D, Kang S, and Choi K. ComPEND: Computation pruning through early negative detection for ReLU in a deep neural network accelerator. In: Proceedings of the 2018 International Conference on Supercomputing. ACM; 2018. p. 139–148.

[35] Albericio J, Delmás A, Judd P, *et al.* Bit-pragmatic deep neural network computing. In: Proceedings of the 50th Annual IEEE/ACM International Symposium on Microarchitecture. ACM; 2017. p. 382–394.

[36] Chen Y, Luo T, Liu S, *et al.* Dadiannao: A machine-learning supercomputer. In: Proceedings of the 47th Annual IEEE/ACM International Symposium on Microarchitecture. IEEE Computer Society; 2014. p. 609–622.

[37] Sharify S, Mahmoud M, Lascorz AD, *et al.* Laconic deep learning computing. arXiv preprint arXiv:180504513. 2018.

Chapter 7

Computation reuse-aware accelerator for neural networks

*Hoda Mahdiani[1], Alireza Khadem[2], Ali Yasoubi[1],
Azam Ghanbari[1], Mehdi Modarressi[1,3], and
Masoud Daneshtalab[4]*

The ever-increasing demand for power efficiency in current deep submicron and nano semiconductor technologies along with rapid growth of embedded/server applications based on deep learning has brought about a renaissance in the hardware implementation of neural networks. Fast execution of neural networks using special-purpose hardware accelerators is an old course of research. However, neural network acceleration has recently regained attention, mainly due to the growing need for deep learning algorithms in a broad scope of applications, ranging from smart sensors to embedded systems and further to data analysis services in servers. Neural networks are the most efficient and straightforward way to implement classification and pattern recognition algorithms which serve as the basis of these machine learning systems. In addition to these traditional application domains, prior research shows that equipping Central Processing Units (CPUs) and Graphics Processing Units (GPUs) with a neural network unit as a universal, trainable, and approximate accelerator in order to implement complex functions leads to considerable power/performance benefits [1].

The large size of neural networks in many recent application domains, such as computer vision and data analytics, poses both throughput and energy-efficiency challenges to the underlying processing hardware. In this chapter, we show how the high computation redundancy in neural information processing, coupled with the inherent approximate nature of neural networks, can be exploited by an approximate computation-reuse mechanism to implement power-efficient neural network accelerators.

State-of-the-art neural networks in many applications, such as computer vision and data analytics, are orders of magnitude larger than conventional simple networks that have long been used since the 1990s, requiring up to millions of arithmetic operations per input [2]. Consequently, designing neural network accelerators with

[1] School of Electrical and Computer Engineering, College of Engineering, University of Tehran, Tehran, Iran
[2] Department of Electrical Engineering and Computer Science, University of Michigan, Ann Arbor, USA
[3] School of Computer Science, Institute for Research in Fundamental Sciences (IPM), Tehran, Iran
[4] Division of Intelligent Future Technologies, Mälardalen University, Sweden

low power, high throughput, and efficient memory bandwidth usage is critical to support large neural networks [2–7].

In recent years, approximate computing has been considered as the primary means of achieving such power efficiency/throughput improvement [5–7]. These methods take advantage of the fact that neural network is an approximate model in nature: the main idea is that when neural networks approximate the target algorithm rather than producing an exact result, arithmetic operations can relax the constraint of producing (and paying the latency and power costs of) exact full-precision results.

In addition to approximation, a high degree of redundancy in arithmetic operations is another attractive property of neural networks which makes them amenable to computation reuse. This redundancy stems from the fact that in each round of neural network execution, a fixed set of input data and neuron weights are shared across many arithmetic operations. This feature increases the probability of finding repetitive arithmetic operations (which execute on the same operands) because many operations have already one operand in common. The number of repeated operations can increase drastically if we consider two operations repetitive not only when two sets of operands exactly match, but also when they are close enough to be considered identical under a given degree of approximation.

In this chapter, we show the power of computation reuse in reducing the power consumption of neural networks.

Although computation reuse has been used in several previous low-power designs, our early study showed that the particular computation pattern of neural networks provides a unique opportunity for computation reuse to increase power efficiency considerably [8].

To exploit the computation redundancy for reducing power consumption, CORN, the computation reuse-aware neural network accelerator is proposed. CORN eliminates computation redundancy by reusing the output of an arithmetic operation for subsequent operations with repetitive operands.

Experimental results show that CORN can exploit the inherent computation redundancy and approximate nature of neural networks to reduce power consumption by 61% on average, compared with state-of-the-art low-power neural network accelerators.

7.1 Motivation

The most common form of neural networks is the multi-layer perceptron (MLP) model; an n-layer MLP consists of one input layer, $n-2$ hidden layers, and one output layer. All neurons in any given layer i receive the same set of inputs from layer $i-1$. Each neuron computes the dot product of the input and weight vectors and passes the result to an activation function (AF) to produce the final output.

Multiplication operations account for the majority of the power consumption and latency of neural information processing. In an n-layer neural network with N_i neurons in layer i, the output of the xth neuron of layer i is sent to layer $i+1$ and multiplied to the xth weight of all N_{i+1} neurons at that layer, thereby is reused in N_{i+1}

different multiplications. If the xth weight of a neuron is equal or close to the xth weight of two or multiple (say r) other neurons in that layer, one of them can perform the multiplication and share the result with the other r neurons.

In this case, just one operand should be matched to allow computation reuse. This is the primary reason for higher computation reuse opportunity in neural networks, compared with other computational models, where two operands should be matched for computation reuse.

A typical computation reuse mechanism is cache-based, in that it stores the operands and results in a cache and uses the operands of a new operation as the tag and index to look up the cache. CORN, however, do not rely on such a caching mechanism; instead, it relies the offline information about the neural network structure to extract computation reuse form the MAC operations that are executing at the same cycle. In a prior work, we showed that most DSP applications can benefit from their coefficient-based computation pattern, in which one multiplication operand comes from a set of predefined coefficients, to reduce the cache size and lookup complexity [9].

Also, since quantization and reducing the precision of numbers are some commonly used techniques to degrade the cost of computations, using these methods can increase the chance of having repetitive weights. For instance, if the weights are displayed in K bits, the number of unique and non-repetitive weights is smaller than or equal to 2^K, which enhances the efficiency of computation reuse approaches [10].

The neural network characteristics of some applications are listed in Table 7.1. As a quantitative motivation on the potential impact of computation reuse on power reduction, Table 7.2 shows the number of repetitive multiplications in several applications that are widely used as neural network benchmarks. The table also shows the impact of approximation on the amount of redundant computation.

For evaluation of computation reduction and accuracy, the 16-bit fixed-point values are considered as baseline. The approximation is applied by reducing the bit width of the fractional part of the numbers. As can be seen, the rate of redundant computation is considerable for these applications, and as expected, it increases with precision reduction. Due to the approximation property of neural networks, an acceptable accuracy level is preserved under most of these reduced precisions. Accuracy is

Table 7.1   Benchmarks and input data

Applications	Dataset	Topology
Digit recognition	MNIST [11]	784:500:500:500:10
Census data analysis	Adult [12]	14:48:02
Data analysis	Wine [12]	13:8:12:10:3
Object classification	IRIS [12]	4:6:10:8:3
Image classification	CIFAR [8]	3072:500:10
FFT	Mibench [8]	8:140:1
ECG analysis	MIT-BIH Database [13]	300:200:2

Table 7.2   Redundant multiplication rate due to repetitive weights when reducing the precision from 16 to 4 bits

	Multiplication reduction				Accuracy			
	4 bits (%)	6 bits (%)	8 bits (%)	16 bits (%)	4 bits (%)	6 bits (%)	8 bits (%)	16 bits (%)
MNIST	88	67	38	13	91	97	99	100
Adult	47	33	9	3	98	99	99	100
Wine	34	13	3	1	98	99	100	100
IRIS	23	7	2	1	96	98	99	100
CIFAR	95	83	62	30	21	72	98	100
FFT	26	19	13	9	95	98	98	100
ECG	83	58	29	9	99	99	100	100

defined as the difference between the output and the reference output generated by a full-precision neural network.

The second source of redundancy in computations is the neural network input data, particularly when processing a continuous data stream. This input stream in case of several application domains, such as online image, speech, and pattern recognition, features gradual changes. An example is the consecutive frames of a video that have many pixels in common. In this case, the computation related to identical (or nearly identical) pixels can be eliminated to save power.

7.2   Baseline architecture

The CORN architecture exploits the computation redundancy of neural networks to reduce power consumption. An array of multipliers and adders that are connected by a programmable crossbar comprise the main processing components of a CORN core (Figure 7.1). The core also has four memory elements that keep the input data, neuron weights, and reusability information.

The first table, weight table (WT), keeps the weights of neurons. An $N \times K$ table has N rows, each of which can be allocated to the neurons of a neural network layer with K weights ($WT(i,j)$ keeps the jth weight of the ith neuron).

Input vector (InpV) keeps the input data of the core: it stores the K-element input received from the previous layer (InpV(i) is the output of the ith neuron of the previous layer).

In this architecture, once InpV is filled with valid data, a controller unit starts processing the input data by multiplying the input vector to weight table elements in K consecutive cycles. At each cycle i, the ith element of input vector and the ith weight of all neurons ($WT(x,i)$, $1 \leq x \leq N$) are multiplied in parallel. $WT(x,i)$ and InpV(i) are sent to the xth multiplier and the result is forwarded to the xth adder to accumulate. Finally, after K cycles, the accumulator values are passed to AF to generate the final output of each neuron.

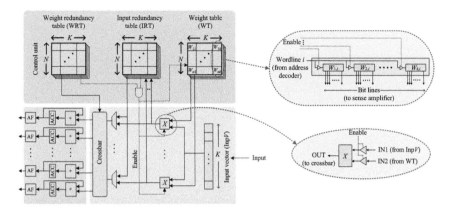

Figure 7.1   The architecture of a CORN core

Each CORN core can be allocated to a single neural network layer. To allow multiple groups of neurons (e.g., multiple layers) share a single CORN core, the three tables in Figure 7.1 are duplicated. CORN allocates to each group of neurons its own set of tables, but shares the multiply-and-accumulate datapath in time. Only one table is active at a time: a shadow table is not activated until the processing of the current table completes.

If the neural network size is larger than the total storage capacity of CORN cores, neural network data (weights plus reuse data) should be stored in off-chip memory. Using multiple tables, processing the active table can be overlapped with loading shadow tables, effectively hiding memory latency. This work focuses on the computation reuse capability of CORN and memory-aware scheduling is left for future work.

7.2.1   Computation reuse support for weight redundancy

The computation reuse in the proposed architecture is enforced by two components: weight redundancy table (WRT) and a programmable crossbar.

WRT keeps the reuse information. This table is filled offline: once the training phase is completed, the elements of each weight table column, which will be multiplied to the same input, are examined to find repetitive weights under a given approximation level (precision). Then, for each cycle, WRT keeps a K-bit mask vector to determine enabled multipliers and another K-element vector to determine which crossbar input should be connected to each crossbar output to pass right multiplication result to the adders corresponding to inactivated multipliers. Unlike a conventional crossbar, this crossbar is capable of connecting an input to multiple outputs.

Figure 7.2(a) illustrates a simple example. In the hidden layer, the first weights of neurons $N1$, $N2$, and $N3$, which will be multiplied to $x1$ at the first cycle of the hidden layer calculations, are equal. In this case, just one neuron, say $N1$, carries out the multiplication and the result is reused for neurons $N2$ and $N3$. To enforce such computation reuse, WRT should disable the multipliers of $N2$ and $N3$ and configures

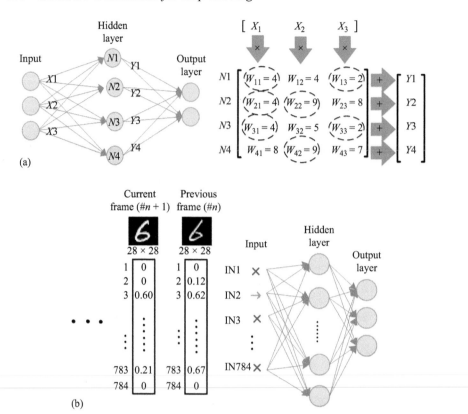

Figure 7.2   Computation reuse sources: (a) a sample neural network and equivalent weight table for the hidden layer. Repetitive weights in each column are shown as circled numbers and (b) removing (nearly) repetitive input elements (denoted by x) in raw input

the crossbar to connect the $N1$'s input port (the input port connected to the multiplier of $N1$) to the output ports of $N1$, $N2$, and $N3$.

To allow fast switching between enabling and disable states, multiplier circuit is not power/clock-gated, but its input lines are gated. The enable signal is also applied to weight table to prevent reading bit lines related to repetitive weights to save power further (Figure 7.1).

7.2.2   Computation reuse support for input redundancy

As the input data cannot be pre-characterized at design time, we use a simple online redundancy detection logic. It involves using another table, called input redundancy table (IRT), to store the previous input vector of the layer and their multiplication results. This way, the current and previous input vectors are compared element-wise, and if the ith elements of the two vectors match, there is no need to multiply the ith input to the *i*th weight of all *N* neurons. In this case the enable signals of all multipliers are disabled by IRT, and the results will be provided by the table that stores the previous calculations (see the multiplexers in front of the crossbar in Figure 7.1).

Since exploiting input redundancy is costly (previous input and multiplication result must be stored), it is only applied to the raw input data. Input data may benefit from the gradual change, so it is more likely to find repetitive elements in raw input. Once the data is processed by the input layer, the possibility of finding repetitive input for hidden and output layers reduces significantly, and thereby the obtained power saving may not be too significant to compensate for the power and area overhead of input redundancy extraction circuit.

7.3 Multicore neural network implementation

A single CORN core can host *N* neurons with *K* weights. As the internal structure of CORN indicates, all neurons must be from the same layer.

In two cases, the storage and processing requirement of a neural network layer exceeds the capacity of a single core. First, when the number of weights of a neuron (denoted as *W*) is greater than *K* and second, when the layer has more than *N* neurons.

7.3.1 More than K weights per neuron

This case does not need any extra processing component because the weights of a neurons are sent serially to the same multiplier. However, they need the depth of every weight table row to be as large as *W*. This problem can be solved by distributing the weights and reuse information across shadow tables (which was originally proposed to allow multiple layers share a single core's datapath). In this case, the tables are activated one by one in the order that the weights are stored. This configuration involves duplicating input vector, as it should accommodate a longer input array. Assuming each core has *S* duplicate tables, if *W* is still greater than the total depth of the tables ($S \times K$), a second CORN core must be used to host the rest $W - S \times K$ weights. Two cores process their own part independently and finally, one of them should sum up two partial accumulated values to generate final neuron output.

7.3.2 More than N neurons per layer

Layers with more than *N* neurons should either be distributed across multiple tables in the same core or across multiple cores, with each core processing at most *N* neurons from the layer.

In either case, the layer should be grouped into *N*-neuron clusters first. To increase computation reuse, CORN groups neurons based on the similarity between their weights. The key point is that the neurons of a layer can be arranged and processed in any order. Taking advantage of this flexibility, clustering can be done in such a way that neurons with more repetitive weights are grouped together. For example, consider the hidden layer of the neural network in Figure 7.2(a) and suppose that each CORN core can be allocated to at most two neurons. In this case, by mapping neurons, $N1$ and $N3$ to one core and $N2$ and $N4$ to another core, the number of repetitive weights on each core is maximized.

Grouping the neurons of each layer with maximized computation reuse is an instance of the well-known clustering problem in graph theory [14]. The clustering problem is defined as grouping a set of objects into C clusters in such a way that objects that belong to the same cluster are more similar to each other than to those in other clusters.

We consider neurons as objects and the vector of weights of each neuron as its attribute that is used as the similarity metric. The vector of weights of two neurons are compared element-wise to calculate their similarity. The algorithm maximizes similarity in each group by placing neurons that have the greatest number of common weights to the same group. Thus, each cluster contains neurons with the most possible similarity and hence, computation reuse.

We solve this problem by the k-means clustering algorithm. The k-means is one of the fastest and simplest iterative algorithms to solve the clustering problem. Compared with simple greedy algorithms that can hardly find optimal solutions, the k-means algorithm explores many combinations of neurons in a disciplined and fast manner to approach (or ideally reach) to the optimal clustering. The details of the k-means algorithm can be found elsewhere [14]. The baseline k-means algorithm puts no restriction on cluster size, but we slightly modified it to return clusters with a given size.

When this offline procedure forms the clusters, neurons of each cluster are mapped to the same core and are ready to process input data.

7.4   Experimental results

The benchmarks listed in Table 7.1 are used to evaluate CORN in terms of power consumption and output error (accuracy loss).

We implement two state-of-the-art neural network accelerators for the comparison purpose. The first method, referred to as ApproxNN [6], uses approximate multiplier units to trade off accuracy for power reduction. The second method, referred to as AxNN [7], uses some sophisticated offline processing to detect the sensitivity of the output to each neuron and sets less precision for those neurons to which the final output is less sensitive.

All considered neural networks are implemented on the baseline CORN architecture, but the logic related to computation reuse is disabled for AxNN and ApproxNN. Each CORN core can keep 16 neurons each with 16 weights ($N = 16$, $K = 16$), and each table has one replica (two copies).

More extensive neural networks use multiple CORN cores, connected by a network-on-chip. We modeled the inter-core communication power consumption based on a simple mesh topology.

We have implemented a simulator for CORN in C++. The training phase of the neural networks is carried out by MATLAB®. We have also implemented CORN in RTL Verilog and used a commercial synthesis and power analysis tool to calculate its area and power consumption in 45 nm.

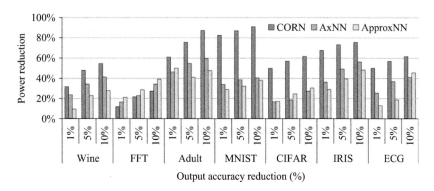

Figure 7.3 Power reduction under three accuracy loss constraints

Figure 7.3 shows the power saving of the considered neural network accelerators for three given output accuracy constraint levels. The bars represent power reduction over the baseline architecture. We selected this iso-accuracy representation because more insight into the relative performance of the methods can be gained when they all give the same output accuracy.

Different accuracies are obtained by changing the numerical precision of neural networks. We use 16-bit fixed-point numbers and the precision is reduced by truncating the fractional bits. In CORN, operations are done on full 16-bit fixed point numbers, but the reduced bit widths are used during the offline repetitive weight and input detection procedures only. The other methods use reduced precision for the main calculation by making data values (for AxNN) or operations (for ApproxNN) approximate.

As the figure indicates, CORN can reach 61% power reduction, on average, whereas AxNN and ApproxNN reduce power by 38% and 32%, respectively. The main source of this superior performance is the considerable amount of computation redundancy in neural networks that are effectively exploited by CORN to save power. Although the amount of power reduction is application-dependent, as a general trend, it increases for lower precisions and larger neural network sizes. Whereas the former trend seems obvious, the latter is mainly due to the fact that large networks provide a larger pool to search for repetitive weights. Hence more repetitive weights can be extracted potentially.

CORN uses both weight and input redundancy extraction. We measured the effect of each method on power saving and observed that 12% of the 61% average power reduction is due to the input redundancy elimination (up to 27% in adult workload). In some datasets, like FFT, two consecutive inputs are not correlated. Thus, while paying the overhead of comparing and storing multiplication results (that neutralize a portion of potential power reduction), they do not benefit from input-induced computation reuse. Therefore, we can disable the input redundancy extraction circuit for such applications to eliminate its unnecessary activity.

Input redundancy extraction is particularly beneficial for workloads that are inherently repetitive and periodic. In a prior work, we have shown the effectiveness of input-induced computation reuse for low-power electrocardiogram (ECG) monitoring in healthcare devices [15].

Synthesis results show that CORN increases the baseline architecture's area by 13%. The programmable crossbar and the tables that keep the computation reuse information are the main sources of this area overhead. These components also have some power overhead that is by far less than power reduction obtained by computation reuse. For example, in the data analysis benchmark with 1% accuracy reduction, CORN increases the power consumption of the control unit and internal connections by 0.29 mW (from 0.10 mW of the baseline to 0.39 mW of CORN) that is by far less than the 0.83 mW power saving of multiplication and weight memory read operations (from 1.69 mW of the baseline to 0.87 mW of CORN).

7.5   Conclusion and future work

Power consumption has long been a significant concern in neural networks. In particular, large neural networks that implement novel machine learning techniques require much more computation, and hence power, than ever before.

In this chapter, we showed that computation reuse could exploit the inherent redundancy in the arithmetic operations of the neural network to save power. Experimental results showed that computation reuse, when coupled with the approximation property of neural networks, can eliminate up to 90% of multiplication, effectively reducing power consumption by 61%, on average in the presented architecture.

The proposed computation reuse-aware design can be extended in several ways. First, it can be integrated into several state-of-the-art customized architectures for LSTM [16], spiking [17], and convolutional neural network models to further reduce power consumption. Second, we can couple computation reuse with existing mapping [18, 19] and scheduling [20] algorithms toward developing reusable scheduling and mapping methods for neural network. Computation reuse can also boost the performance of the methods that eliminate ineffectual computations in deep learning neural networks [21]. Evaluating the impact of CORN on reliability [22] and customizing the CORN architecture for FPGA-based neural network implementation [23, 24] are the other future works in this line.

References

[1]   A. Yazdanbakhsh, J. Park, H. Sharma, *et al.*, "Neural acceleration for GPU throughput processors," in *Proceedings of MICRO*, pp. 482–493, 2015.

[2]   Y. Chen, J. Emer, V. Sze, *et al.*, "Eyeriss: A spatial architecture for energy-efficient dataflow for convolutional neural networks," in *Proceedings of ISSCC*, pp. 262–263, 2016.

[3]   T. Chen, Z. Du, N. Sun, *et al.*, "DianNao: a small-footprint high-throughput accelerator for ubiquitous machine-learning," in *Proceedings of ASPLOS*, pp. 269–284, 2014.

[4] S. Sarwar, S. Venkataramani, A. Raghunathan, *et al.*, "Multiplier-less artificial neurons exploiting error resiliency for energy-efficient neural computing," in *Proceedings of DATE*, pp. 145–150, 2016.

[5] B. Reagen, P. Whatmough, R. Adolf, *et al.*, "Minerva: enabling low-power, highly-accurate deep neural network accelerators," in *Proceedings of ISCA*, 2016.

[6] Q. Zhang, T. Wang, Y. Tian, *et al.*, "ApproxANN: an approximate computing framework for artificial neural network," in *Proceedings of DATE*, pp. 701–706, 2015.

[7] S. Venkataramani, A. Ranjan, K. Roy, *et al.*, "AxNN: energy-efficient neuromorphic systems by approximate computing," in *Proceedings of ISLPED*, pp. 27–32, 2014.

[8] A. Yasoubi, R. Hojabr, M. Modarressi, *et al.*, "Power-efficient accelerator design for neural networks using computation reuse," in *IEEE Computer Architecture Letters*, 2016.

[9] M. Modarressi, H. Nikounia, A.H. Jahangir, *et al.*, "Low-power arithmetic unit for DSP applications," in *Proceedings of SoC*, pp. 68–71, 2011.

[10] K. Hegde, J. Yu, R. Agrawal, *et al.*, "UCNN: exploiting computational reuse in deep neural networks via weight repetition," in *Proceedings of ISCA*, 2018.

[11] Y. Lecun, L. Bottou, Y. Bengio, *et al.*, "Gradient-based learning applied to document recognition," in *Proceedings IEEE*, vol. 86, no. 11, pp. 2278–2324, 1998.

[12] M. Lichman, "Machine learning repository," Technical Report, University of California-Irvine, 2013.

[13] MIT-BIH Database, ecg.mit.edu, 2016.

[14] D. MacKay, *Information Theory, Inference, and Learning Algorithms*, Cambridge, UK: Cambridge University Press, 2003.

[15] M. Modarressi and A. Yasoubi, "Low-power online ECG analysis using neural networks," in *Proceedings of Euromicro DSD*, pp. 547–552, 2016.

[16] Z. Que, T. Nugent, S. Liu, *et al.*, "Efficient weight reuse for large LSTMs," in *Proceedings of the IEEE 30th International Conference on Application-specific Systems, Architectures and Processors (ASAP)*, pp. 17–24, 2019.

[17] H. Vu and A. Ben Abdallah, "A low-latency *K*-means based multicast routing algorithm and architecture for three dimensional spiking neuromorphic chips," in *Proceedings of IEEE International Conference on Big Data and Smart Computing*, 2019.

[18] M. F. Reza and P. Ampadu, "Energy-efficient and high-performance NoC architecture and mapping solution for deep neural networks," in *Proceedings of the 13th IEEE/ACM International Symposium on Networks-on-Chip*, 2019.

[19] Y. Hosseini Mirmahaleh, M. Reshadi, H. Shabani, *et al.*, "Flow mapping and data distribution on mesh-based deep learning accelerator," in *Proceedings of the 13th IEEE/ACM International Symposium on Networks-on-Chip*, 2019.

[20] L. Waeijen, S. Sioutas, Y. He, *et al.*, "Automatic memory-efficient scheduling of CNNs," in *Proceedings of the 19th International Conference on Embedded Computer Systems: Architectures, Modeling, and Simulation*, pp. 387–400, 2019.

[21] M. Nikolic, M. Mahmoud, A. Moshovos, *et al.*, "Characterizing sources of ineffectual computations in deep learning networks," in *Proceedings of International Symposium on Performance Analysis of Systems and Software*, pp. 165–176, 2019.

[22] M. A. Neggaz, I. Alouani, P. R. Lorenzo, *et al.*, "A reliability study on CNNs for critical embedded systems," in *Proceedings of the IEEE 36th International Conference on Computer Design*, pp. 476–479, 2018.

[23] Y. Shen, T. Ji, M. Ferdman, and P. Milder, "Argus: an end-to-end framework for accelerating CNNs on FPGAs," *IEEE Micro*, vol. 39, no. 5, pp. 17–25, 1 Sept.–Oct. 2019.

[24] P. Meloni, A. Capotondi, G. Deriu, *et al.*, "NEURAghe: exploiting CPU-FPGA synergies for efficient and flexible CNN inference acceleration on Zynq SoCs," *ACM Transactions on Reconfigurable Technology and Systems*, vol. 11, no. 3, pp. 1–23, Dec. 2018.

Part IV

Convolutional neural networks for embedded systems

Chapter 8

CNN agnostic accelerator design for low latency inference on FPGAs

Sachin Kumawat[1], Mohammad Motamedi[1], and Soheil Ghiasi[1]

8.1 Introduction

Convolutional neural networks (CNNs) have been widely used in various machine-learning tasks such as image classification. With the growing capabilities of parallel and distributed computing, CNNs with billions of computations per inference can now be trained and deployed to solve complex image classification, object detection and segmentation tasks. Due to the availability of specialized computation units and their energy efficiency, field-programmable gate arrays (FPGAs) are well suited for CNNs. CNN processing is compute intensive and can become bounded by the underlying memory system implementation. Performance of FPGAs depends upon efficient usage of both on-chip digital signal processors (DSPs) and block random access memory (BRAMs) while keeping the logic resource usage in check. This creates challenges in designing highly parallel circuits and their efficient mapping of FPGAs, which needs to be thoroughly investigated.

In this chapter, we study the factors impacting CNN accelerator designs on FPGAs, show how on-chip memory configuration affects the usage of off-chip bandwidth, and present a uniform memory model that effectively uses both memory systems. A majority of the work in the area of FPGA-based acceleration of CNNs has focused on maximizing the throughput [1–3]. Such implementations use batch processing for throughput improvement [4–6] and are mainly tailored for cloud deployment. However, they fall short in latency-critical applications such as autonomous driving, drone surveillance and interactive speech recognition. Therefore, we avoid batching of any kind and focus on reducing the latency for each input image. In addition, we avoid the use of Winograd Transformations as used in [4,7] to retain flexible support for various filter sizes and different CNN architectures, both [4,7] are optimized only for 3 × 3 filter layers and lack flexibility. Furthermore, we provide complete end-to-end automation, including data quantization exploration with Ristretto [8]. The efficiency of the proposed architecture is shown by studying

[1]Department of Electrical and Computer Engineering, University of California, Davis, Davis, CA, USA

its performance on AlexNet [9], VGG [10], SqueezeNet [11] and GoogLeNet [12]. The novel ideas that will be discussed in this chapter are mentioned in what follows:

1. We present a highly reconfigurable OpenCL accelerator architecture that supports all convolution filter sizes and fully connected layers (FCLs). This is achieved by exploring data reuse strategies combined with optimal loop coalescing. As a result, if synthesized with enough resources, different CNNs can be run even without reprogramming the FPGA. We call this cross-network support.
2. We propose a unified memory model which is used to derive a precise analytical model of total execution cycles. Experimental results show that our policy is highly accurate for both compute-bound and memory-bound layers with a maximum of 3.99% difference with onboard tests.
3. We achieve a near theoretical performance efficiency of 95.8% on VGG which outperforms all other implementations, including hand-tailored designs for specific CNNs. We also achieve more than $2\times$ latency improvement over the state-of-the-art results on Intel's Stratix V GXA7 FPGA.
4. Finally, we present FICaffe, an end-to-end automated synthesizer that requires minimal user intervention.

8.2   Brief review of efforts on FPGA-based acceleration of CNNs

In recent years, the research community has put forth a number of efforts toward CNN acceleration using FPGAs. Zhang *et al.* [3] introduced tiling schemes and architecture optimization based on a roofline model. They concluded off-chip memory bandwidth to be the primary performance bottleneck, ignoring impacts of the on-chip bandwidth. Suda *et al.* [13] built regression models to predict resource usage and genetic algorithm to optimize runtime. They ran global optimizations to directly minimize the runtime. Since then, researchers have also realized the importance of on-chip bandwidth and sequential accesses for taking full advantage of the off-chip memory as wider access requests in continuous bursts reduce off-chip DRAM latency. Consequently, works like [2] explored on-chip bandwidth by considering data requirements of parallel computation units, while authors in [4,6] studied the impact of streaming burst accesses as well. Further in [14], authors considered bandwidth balancing by presenting a code balance term, which is similar to computation-to-communication ratio used in [3], and a machine balance term, defined as the ratio of available on-chip or off-chip bandwidth to maximum required accelerator bandwidth. They compare different ratios of these terms for both memory types to determine computation bottlenecks. While this allows looking at potential performance impacts due to unmatched available bandwidths, they do not consider optimizations based on imbalance as the terms are fixed for an FPGA platform and CNN type. Therefore, an optimization scheme that examines the complete impact of the implemented memory hierarchy and parallel computation units still needs to be explored.

Another important problem that needs consideration is processing element (PE) architecture. Almost all proposed architectures can be categorized in three classes: (1) matrix multiplication [5,6,13–15], (2) systolic array [16,17] and (3) parallel vector [1,3,4,7,18]. As can be seen, matrix-multiplication-based schemes overwhelmingly dominate the spectrum. It is a well-explored area where stock algorithms for multi-threaded CPUs and GPUs can be repurposed for the task. Implementing systolic arrays, on the other hand, requires careful data transfer and register sharing, which can absorb high amount of logic resources with OpenCL. Consequently, both [16,17] are RTL-based designs. Finally, simultaneous parallel multiplication is an SIMD-based approach which is well suited for OpenCL as it reduces complexity in control plane and only requires replication of data plane. Moreover, there is no intercommunication between PEs, which eases FPGA routing. This is important for scalability as interconnect complexity can quickly rise with higher number of PEs for matrix multiplier and systolic arrays. Thus, we adopt parallel vector multiplications and design highly efficient PEs in this work.

8.3 Network structures and operations

CNNs have dramatically improved computer vision tasks such as object recognition, surveillance, image restoration and reconstruction [19]. Classification on the comprehensive ImageNet dataset is one such task on which recent modular networks such as SqueezeNet, GoogLeNet and ResNet have outperformed regular feed-forward CNNs, including AlexNet and VGG. These complex networks have repeated structures with regular convolutional layers as shown in Figure 8.1. Therefore, by accelerating convolutional layer and FCL, along with low overhead feature concatenation, we can achieve low-latency, high-throughput inference for a large variety of Networks. We briefly discuss major CNN layers and introduce the notations and abbreviations summarized in Table 8.1.

8.3.1 Convolution

Convolution layers (CLs) are one of the most compute intensive layers in a CNN. For a given 3D input image (2D image with channel depths), called input feature maps (IFMs), a 3D weighted filter is applied by point-wise multiplication with IFMs, which are then accumulated to compute a single pixel in output feature maps (OFMs). A single feature map is also referred to as a channel. Weights are shared within an OFM channel, i.e., each pixel of an OFM is computed using the same set of filter parameters, while they slide across IFMs. Figure 8.2 shows all dimensional variables involved in a CL. CLs consist of a lot of data reuse and have ample independent computations, providing opportunities and trade-offs for parallelism which are explored in Section 8.4. Weight filters are sometimes also referred to as kernels but in this chapter, we use kernels only to denote OpenCL kernels.

8.3.2 Inner product

Inner product layers, also known as FCLs, are weighted the sum of 1D input features. Inner product computations are simple in nature but are data intensive and

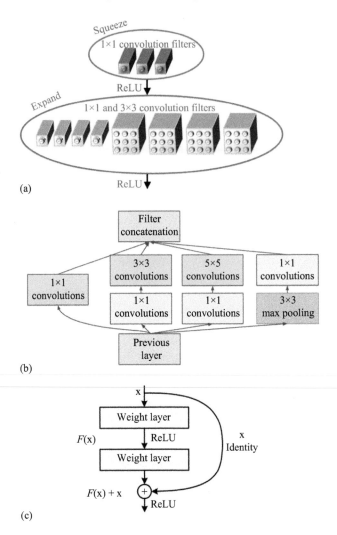

(a)

(b)

(c)

Figure 8.1   Next-generation CNNs use repeated modules which use concatenation of regular layer outputs: (a) SqueezeNet, fire-module [11]; (b) GoogLeNet, inception-module [12]; (c) ResNet, residual-network [11]

have no weight reuse. Therefore, the computation time of FCLs is bounded by the available memory bandwidth. In Figure 8.2, if we set $N_C=N_R=M_C=M_R=1$, the layer will be reduced to an FCL. Consequently, the filter dimensions will also become 1. As we can see, FCLs are just a special case of CLs. We exploit this to restructure FCL computation while using the same convolution data flow as discussed in Section 8.7.

Table 8.1 *Frequently used abbreviations*

Full name	Abbreviation
Input feature maps	IFMs
Output feature maps	OFMs
Convolution layer	CL
Fully connected layer	FCL
Pooling layer	PL
Digital signal processor	DSP
Processing element	PE
Convolution engine	CE
Operations	OPs

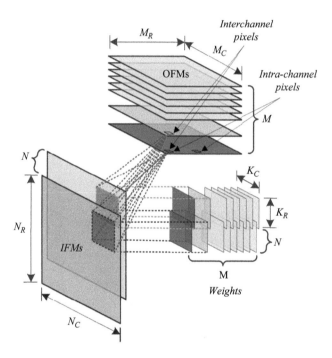

Figure 8.2 *A typical CNN layer showing feature map and filter dimensions*

8.3.3 Pooling

Pooling is also similar in structure to convolution with the main difference being that it is usually applied to each IFM channel separately. As a result, pooling output has the same number of channels as input and is generally applied to reduce OFM size. Two types of pooling filters are commonly used, maximum and average. PLs have relatively low computation latency than CLs and FCLs but can result in complex data path as we discuss in Section 8.7.

8.3.4   Other operations

Other operations in CNNs include using nonlinear activation on top of feature map, normalization, scaling, element-wise arithmetic and filter concatenation. Rectified Linear Unit (ReLU) function is a popular nonlinearity in CNNs for its effectiveness and simplicity. Krizhevsky *et al.* [9] proposed local response normalization (LRN), used along with ReLU, which has helped in training by alleviating diminishing gradient problem. But since then, LRNs have fallen out of use and batch normalization is being adopted with the next-generation of CNN architectures [20,21]. Therefore, we do not implement LRN and present results for AlexNet and GoogLeNet by skipping normalization operations. Apart from that, in recent architectures, filter concatenation has been used where OFMs resulting from different branches of the network are concatenated to form IFM channels for the next layer. Finally, utility layers like element-wise addition and scaling are used to implement batch normalization and residual modules of ResNet.

8.4   Optimizing parallelism sources

The two main factors that affect performance in FPGA designs are computation density and memory bandwidth. In OpenCL, this is exhibited by fully pipelined stall-free operation and translated into (1) number of multiply-accumulates (MACs) performed per cycle and (2) memory access stall cycles. The aim is to maximize the number of MAC operations performed every clock cycle without ever encountering memory stalls. We first introduce different independent computations involved in convolution and explore specific techniques that have been studied in published literature. We derive conclusions and present our acceleration strategy in further sections.

8.4.1   Identifying independent computations

Same colored filters in Figure 8.2 (red and blue shades) represent one 3D convolution filter. All multiplications in such a 3D filter, which produces one OFM pixel, are independent and can be done in parallel. This is often referred to as intra-filter parallelism. Figure 8.3 shows all the loops involved in convolution where S denotes the filter stride. Intra-filter parallelism refers to simultaneous execution of iterations in Loops 4 and 5. Apart from that intra-channel OFM pixels can be computed independently by reusing the same weight parameters, multiplied and accumulated with different parts of IFMs. This is represented by simultaneous execution of iterations in Loops 2 and 3. Furthermore, interchannel OFM pixels can also be computed independently. IFM data can be potentially shared with the same pixel of a different OFM channel. This can be done by executing multiple iterations of Loop 1 in the same cycles. It is also possible to compute multiple layers in pipelined parallel fashion but has a huge resource overhead and is generally not implemented. Therefore, the number of MACs/cycle depends on how many such independent computations are done in parallel, while stall cycles depend upon input and weight data reuse along with consequences of memory system hierarchy used.

```
1:  for ( m = 0, m < M, m + = 1) do                                    ▷ :Loop 1
2:    for ( r = 0, r < M_R, r + = 1) do                                ▷ :Loop 2
3:      for ( c = 0, c < M_C, c + = 1) do                              ▷ :Loop 3
4:        out[r][c][m] = bias [m]
5:        for ( kr = 0, kr < K_R, kr + = 1) do                         ▷ :Loop 4
6:          for ( kc = 0, kc < K_C, kc + = 1) do                       ▷ :Loop 5
7:            for ( n = 0, n < N, n + = 1) do                          ▷ :Loop 6
8:              out[r][c][m] + =
9:                in[r × S + kr][c × S + kc][n] × wt [kr][kc][n]
```

Figure 8.3   Loops involved in a convolution layer

8.4.2   Acceleration strategies

The collective research efforts for CNN acceleration using FPGAs have proposed many approaches and present various trade-offs. Some solutions are not particularly effective for the next generation of deep networks and many are inefficient for latency-driven designs. In the following discussion, we explain common design techniques and analyze which strategies are better suited for the latency-sensitive applications. We also propose novel techniques and explain how they improve the performance.

1. **Reduce weight buffer bandwidth**: Filter dimensions for any layer are mostly restricted to not more than 7–11, which is small enough to fit in on-chip BRAMs. The trend is, in fact, to move toward even smaller sizes of 1×1 and 3×3 filters across entire networks as it reduces total model weight size. This results in a very small overhead of weight data communication with off-chip memory. On the other hand, IFM/OFM data traffic can result in large number of memory stalls and requires overlapping of computation with data transfer, often done using dual-buffering. Unlike IFMs/OFMs, we do not use dual-buffering for weight data, which also eases the on-chip bandwidth requirements and saves BRAM resources.

2. **Inefficient intra-filter parallelism**: For high flexibility targeted in FICaffe, we process filters in sequential manner. Concurrent computations within filters either make it challenging or inefficient to support wide variety of filter sizes and can result in idle PEs. For example, Zhang *et al.* [6] fixed filter size to 5×5 and incurred significant penalty for 3×3 filter layers. Similarly, authors in [4,7,14] fixed their filter sizes to 3×3 which does not maps well to networks with variety of filter sizes such as AlexNet and GoogLeNet. Therefore, we do not incorporate intra-filter parallelism in FICaffe. This further reduces the bandwidth requirement of weight buffers.

3. **Avoid intra-channel parallelism**: Certain parallelization opportunities are inherently more inefficient than others. The optimizer presented in [16] for an RTL accelerator results in inter and intra-channel parallelization. This requires multiple input pixels from the same IFM channel every cycle. Since filter strides over IFM channels tend to overlap, to support arbitrary filter size and stride values,

this requires carefully designed data access from on-chip buffers. Data must also be shifted within registers to avoid data duplication in IFM buffers. Such fine-tuned data flow control in OpenCL either results in high logic consumption or requires higher on-chip IFM buffer size and bandwidth. Therefore, intra-channel parallelization is unattractive for FICaffe.

4. **Improve bandwidth for FCLs**: Even though newer networks like SqueezeNet, GoogLeNet and ResNet have shown that FCLs can be eliminated without losing accuracy, FCLs can form a significant part of runtime in networks such as AlexNet. Hence, it is important to optimize FCL computation as well. To improve the weight reuse in FCLs, batching of multiple input vectors is adopted but is not possible for latency-sensitive applications. Therefore, input reuse should be maximized to reduce the off-chip bandwidth requirements for FCLs. Both CLs with 1×1 filters and FCLs have poor weight reuse and are memory bound. As a result, we optimize the architecture for CLs and provide acceleration for FCLs by data reconfiguration.

8.5   Computation optimization and reuse

In this section, we present novel, efficient structuring of computation loops while avoiding fixed filter sizes. We then analyze data reuse and propose loop coalescing for high-efficiency execution.

8.5.1   Design control variables

To use inter OFM parallelism, we first choose to compute a subset of OFM channels in parallel, denoted by Tm. We also process a subset of IFM channels every cycle, denoted as Tn. Modern FPGAs can have up to 50 Mb of BRAMs. However, this is not enough to store entire IFMs, OFMs and weight data of common CNN layers. Dual-buffering makes this even worse. For this reason, majority of the layer data is stored in the off-chip DRAMs with limited bandwidth of up to 20–30 GBps on typical modern FPGA boards. Therefore, the feature maps are carefully broken into smaller channel tiles of working data in on-chip memory which is discarded only when no longer required.

Usually, subsets of Tr rows and Tc columns of IFMs and OFMs are considered [3,6,16] resulting in a total of $Tr \times Tc$ elements transferred from DRAMs at once. Since depth of the local memory system depends only on the total elements in a tile, we instead choose to break only the rows into subsets of Tr. For a given CNN, if max_c is the maximum number of columns for any layer in the network, then the OFM buffer depth is determined by $Tr \times max_c$. Tiling only one dimension simplifies interconnect and IFM's random data access pattern without incurring any performance trade-off. In later sections, we show that Tr also has a significant impact on performance as it represents the burst length for off-chip memory accesses.

In summary, Tn and Tm control parallel computation and on-chip bandwidth, while Tr controls depth of the on-chip buffer banks and burst length in FICaffe.

8.5.2   *Partial sums and data reuse*

Once data is transferred to on-chip memories, it should be ideally reused as many times as required. But the amount of achievable reuse largely depends upon the order in which computation is done. Based on the design variables introduced in previous sections, three different iteration variables are introduced:

$$N\_itr = \left\lceil \frac{N}{Tn} \right\rceil, \qquad M\_itr = \left\lceil \frac{M}{Tm} \right\rceil, \qquad R\_itr = \left\lceil \frac{M_R}{Tr} \right\rceil \qquad (8.1)$$

N_itr is the number of iterations taken to use all IFM channels once, completing all computations for an output pixel. M_itr and R_itr are the numbers of iterations to compute partial sums along all channels and all rows, respectively. The number of times that OFM partial sums are moved in and out of off-chip memory depends on these variables and should be minimized. On top of that poor on-chip data and weight reuse also contribute toward higher off-chip bandwidth requirements.

Two main strategies and six different cases emerge for data reuse based on these variables. These are summarized in Figure 8.4.

8.5.2.1   IFMs first strategy

In the first strategy, N_itr iterations over IFM channels are completed first, continuously accumulating Tm OFM channels till completion. Execution order of the iteration loops for this strategy are shown in Figure 8.4 as cases C_{11}, C_{12}, C_{13}. For every iteration of M_itr loop, all N_itr iterations are run again and the same IFMs are reloaded from DRAMs M_itr times, resulting in poor reuse. The cases also have different weight usage shown in Table 8.2. Since weight traffic is relatively small,

for j < M_iter	for j < M_iter	for r < R_iter
for i < N_iter	for r < R_iter	for j < M_iter
for r < R_iter	for i < N_iter	for i < N_iter
(C_{11})	(C_{12})	(C_{13})
for i < N_iter	for i < N_iter	for r < R_iter
for j < M_iter	for r < R_iter	for i < N_iter
for r < R_iter	for j < M_iter	for j < M_iter
(C_{21})	(C_{22})	(C_{23})

Figure 8.4   Loop ordering cases for tiling and data reuse

Table 8.2   Data reuse and partial sum behavior in different cases

Case	IFMs first strategy			OFMs first strategy		
	C_{11}	C_{12}	C_{13}	C_{21}	C_{22}	C_{23}
IFM reuse	Partial ✗	Partial ✗	Partial ✗	Partial ✗	Full ✓	Full ✓
Weight reuse	Full ✓	Partial ✗	Partial ✗	Full ✓	Partial ✗	Partial ✗
OFM partial sum	Yes ✗	No ✓	No ✓	Yes ✗	Yes ✗	Yes ✗

partial instead of full reuse does not have significant performance impact. On the other hand, partial IFMs reuse and partial OFMs sum generation incur significant penalties. It can be seen that this strategy works well when OFM sizes are similar to IFM dimensions. Since typical IFM dimensions for CLs are larger than OFMs, the absence of partial sums in cases C_{12} and C_{13} does not compensate for the higher IFM data bandwidth requirement, so we do not discuss this strategy further.

8.5.2.2 OFMs first strategy

In another strategy, all OFM channels are partially computed by completing *M_itr* loop first. This provides us with three more cases C_{21}, C_{22}, C_{23}. For C_{21}, weights are completely used, while both IFMs and OFMs do multiple off-chip trips. A partially computed OFM tile is swapped with a next row tile which results in reloading of new IFM tile as well. For C_{22} and C_{22}, however, IFMs are loaded once and completely used before moving to the next OFM row tile. Both cases present similar advantages but for C_{23}, in particular, OFMs are effectively computed as independent segments, which look like different layers of *Tr* rows. We use the case C_{23} as it has the lowest bandwidth requirement.

8.5.3 Proposed loop coalescing for flexibility with high efficiency

We unroll loops to vectorize on *Tm* and *Tn* channels of OFMs and IFMs, respectively. We coalesce the loop structure in Figure 8.3 and also use dual buffering to hide off-chip data access latency. Coalescing nested loops into the same level reduces register and logic requirements for fully pipelined loops in OpenCL. Coalescing also avoids the pipeline launch overhead introduced by each nested loop. Loops for the three iteration variables of (8.1) are coalesced into one *tiling loop* as shown in Figure 8.5 and processed in the order described for case C_{23}. A second loop consists of Loops 3, 4, 5 and the tilled version of Loop 2 in Figure 8.3. These are coalesced into a single *compute loop* at line 2 of Figure 8.5.

The resulting loops are synthesized in deeply pipelined fashion resulting in pipelined parallelism of intra-filter and intra-channel computations. Due to the loop

```
1:  for (x = 0, x < R_itr × M_itr × N_iter, x += 1) do¹        ▷ :Not Fully Pipelined with II of 2
2:    for (w = 0, w < K_R × K_C × M_C × m_R, w += 1) do²        ▷ :Fully Pipelined with II of 1
3:      #pragma unroll
4:      for (m = 0, m < Tm, m += 1) do
5:        #pragma unroll
6:        for (n = 0, n < Tn, n += 1) do
7:          out [m] += in[n] × wt[m][n]
```

$$^1\text{tiling Loop}$$

$$^2\text{compute Loop}, m_R = \begin{cases} min\ (Tr, M_R), & \text{if } r < R\_itr - 1 \\ M_R - (R\_itr - 1) \times Tr, & \text{otherwise} \end{cases}$$

Figure 8.5   Proposed loop coalescing and unrolling

structure, it is possible to synthesize FICaffe compute loop with an initiation interval (II) of 1 (i.e., new iteration is launched every cycle). The complex nature of computing loop restricts II of tiling loop to be at least 2 (new iteration launched every two cycle) and is not fully pipelined. Therefore, we structure FICaffe's architecture design in a way to keep large number of iterations in the fully pipelined compute loop and fewer in tiling loop. This has the following implications:

- Number of iterations in tilling loop can be reduced by increasing Tn, Tm and Tr as seen from (8.1). If more resources are available on FPGA, wider SIMD vector can be supported, resulting in lower N_itr and M_itr iterations. While an even more number of available BRAMs can ensure deeper buffers, i.e., larger Tr tiles possible, it also results in longer pre- and post-processing overheads. This diminishes the gain from improved off-chip burst access behavior for large Tr. Its cumulative effect is studied in Section 8.6.3.
- The filter dimensions $K_R \times K_C$ appear in compute loop. Therefore, FICaffe can process all filter sizes in fully pipelined fashion resulting in high efficiency if the number of stalls encountered in the compute loop is low.
- Filter reuse for $M_C \times m_R$ output pixels also appears in the compute loop ensuring that FICaffe can process any layer dimension in fully pipelined fashion as well.

8.6 Bandwidth matching and compute model

8.6.1 Resource utilization

Before developing the runtime model for the proposed architecture, we first look at the resource usage estimation. The three design variables Tn, Tm and Tr control the amount of FPGA resources consumed by a particular architecture. Total number of PEs required can simply be written as

$$\#PE = Tn \times Tm \tag{8.2}$$

FPGAs provide various configurable DSP architectures. For example, Intel's DSPs for Stratix devices can handle one single-precision floating-point multiplication, one 32-bit fixed-point multiplication and two 16-bit fixed-point multiplications. Therefore, the exact number of DSPs required can be calculated by determining DSP's operating mode (computation type and precision):

$$\#DSP = \frac{\#PE}{PEs\_per\_DSP} \tag{8.3}$$

We can also estimate the number of on-chip BRAMs required to implement the local memory system. BRAMs are static RAM blocks of BR_size bits each. They can be reconfigured into a set of *data_width* × *depth* configurations with restrictions on at least one of them. If *max_BR_width* is the maximum allowed width for the BRAMs, we can estimate the number of BRAMs as

$$\#BRAM = \left\lceil \frac{vector\_size \times DW}{max\_BR\_width} \right\rceil \times \left\lceil \frac{buffer\_depth}{BR\_depth} \right\rceil \tag{8.4}$$

$$BR\_depth = \frac{BR\_size}{min(vector\_size \times DW, \ max\_BR\_width)} \tag{8.5}$$

where *DW* is the number of data quantization bits and *buffer_depth* is the required depth of the particular buffer, adjusted up to the next power of two. Also, *vector_size* denotes the number of elements accessed every cycle in parallel:

$$vector\_size = \begin{cases} Tn, & \text{for IFM buffers} \\ Tm, & \text{for OFM buffers} \\ Tn \times Tm, & \text{for Weight buffers} \end{cases} \tag{8.6}$$

To estimate register and logic usage, regression and interpolation techniques such as in [13] are proposed but since FPGA logic is grouped into modules or slices containing 2–8 registers and 2–6 look up tables, such modeling has limited use as choosing a different device will require learning the estimates again. Instead, we use accurate pre-synthesis logic estimates already provided by OpenCL compilers to obtain logic usage estimates.

8.6.2   Unifying off-chip and on-chip memory

FICaffe takes advantage of on-chip, off-chip bandwidth matching. We allow the unmatched bandwidth impact to factor into the predicted performance which gives us better runtime estimates and independence from the underlying FPGA platform used.

8.6.2.1   Impact of unmatched system

To determine access latency for a memory system, suppose the accelerator runs at *freq* frequency. If number of data elements loaded/stored from/to the memory are *num_data_elem* and *DW* is the data width in number of bits, then the number of cycles spent in memory access is given by

$$num\_cycles = mem\_latency \times freq \tag{8.7}$$

$$mem\_latency = \frac{data\_size}{mem\_bw} \tag{8.8}$$

$$data\_size = num\_data\_elem \times DW \tag{8.9}$$

where *mem_bw* is the bandwidth of the memory system. The effective bandwidth *mem_bw* can be determined in the following way.

Let us denote *off_chip_bw* as the theoretical bandwidth specification of DRAMs and *on_chip_bw* as the total bandwidth provided by BRAM buffers as defined later.

It is often not possible to fully use the DRAM device bandwidth without wide data requests and sequential accesses for burst transfer [6]. As a result, the number of independent parallel on-chip buffer ports affects off-chip bandwidth usage. For example, IFM buffer banks have *Tn* independent ports to supply parallel pixels every cycle. Accordingly, IFM tiles are loaded with *Tn* elements every cycle, even though off-chip memory might be able to provide more.

Figure 8.6 shows achieved bandwidth with DDR3 DRAMs operating at 800 MHz for different on-chip buffer widths with small burst lengths of 128. Maximum capable performance of the memory used is 25 GB/s and the memory controller provides a 1,024 bit wide interface. As we can see, to cache data in a 64 bit wide on-chip buffer, the requests have to be 64 bits per cycle which achieved only 1.32 GB/s, a fraction of the available off-chip memory performance. By increasing the on-chip memory bandwidth, per cycle requests can also be widened correspondingly and gives better off-chip bandwidth usage. It is not just enough to make request widths equal to interface width of 1,024, as even more wider requests can also improve the burst behavior. Further improvement requires longer burst access of sequential data. For feature map buffers, the burst length is represented by depth of the buffer. For example, for OFM buffers maximum possible burst is $Tr \times max_c$. The burst access effects of on-chip memory are incorporated in the runtime model presented in the next section by assuming that all burst accesses within maximum off-chip bandwidth limits do not encounter any stalls.

8.6.2.2   Effective bandwidth latency

We need to consider both the maximum bandwidth *off_chip_bw* and the request bandwidth *on_chip_bw*, to study memory latency. Hence, (8.10) yields the effective bandwidth *mem_bw*, visible to the accelerator as

$$mem\_bw = min(off\_chip\_bw,\ on\_chip\_bw) \qquad (8.10)$$

$$on\_chip\_bw = vector\_size \times DW \times freq \qquad (8.11)$$

where *vector_size* is the number of data elements accessed every cycle as shown in (8.6). For stall-free operation, we want the *on_chip_bw* to be as close to *off_chip_bw* as possible.

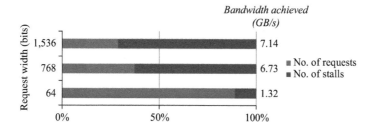

Figure 8.6   Impact of data request width on achieved off_chip_bw. DRAM interface is 1,024 bits wide and burst accesses are 128 long

Lower *on_chip_bw* would mean that *off_chip_bw* is under used and there is room for memory performance improvement. On the other hand, higher *on_chip_bw* would mean that performance is memory bound and is restricted by *off_chip_bw*. As the architecture scales, *on_chip_bw* requirement subsequently surpasses *off_chip_bw* and the DRAM bandwidth becomes the bottleneck. FICaffe's architecture optimizer considers impacts of this unmatched *off_chip_bw* and *on_chip_bw* and tries to adjust the design parameters accordingly. We express (8.7)–(8.10) into a single expression as follows:

$$num\_cycles = \frac{num\_data\_elem \times DW}{min(off\_chip\_bw,\ on\_chip\_bw)} \times freq$$

$$= num\_data\_elem \times avg\_cycles\_per\_elem \tag{8.12}$$

where we represent the factor *avg_cycles_per_elem* as *ACPE* for brevity. This term is calculated accordingly with *on_chip_bw* of the buffers it is used for, represented as $ACPE_i$, $ACPE_o$ and $ACPE_w$ for IFM, OFM and weight buffers, respectively.

8.6.3   Analyzing runtime

We categorize total runtime cycles, *total_cycles*, into the following five stages:

1. *ifm_pl_cycles*: number of cycles to preload the very first IFM tile
2. *wt_ld_cycles*: total weight load latency cycles
3. *conv_cycles*: total number of cycles taken by convolution
4. *mem_ldst_cycles*: total number of load/store cycles required to transfer subsequent IFM tiles and OFM partial sums
5. *ofm_ps_cycles*: number of cycles required to store the last OFM tile after computation

Cycles contributed by stages 1, 2, 4 and 5 are memory stall overheads that need to be minimized. The rest of this section is dedicated to model these variables in terms of layer parameters.

Before computation starts, the first IFM tile and the weight filters are loaded. All IFM columns N_C and IFM rows, determined by the weight filter dimension and Tr as shown next, are loaded:

$$ifm\_pl\_cycles = N_C \times (K_R + S \times (min(Tr,\ M\_R) - 1))$$

$$\times Tn \times ACPE_i \tag{8.13}$$

Weight filters are completely loaded onto on-chip buffers and discarded before a new tile processing begins. But weights are reloaded to process a different row tile in the same Tm set of OFMs due to partial reuse in case C_{23}. Thus, we see a factor of R_itr in total weight data traffic:

$$wt\_ld\_cycles = K_C \times K_R \times (N\_itr \times Tn) \times (M\_itr \times Tm)$$

$$\times R\_itr \times ACPE_w + bias\_cycles \tag{8.14}$$

$$bias\_cycles = M\_itr \times Tm \times ACPE_o \tag{8.15}$$

If iterations of the compute loop in Figure 8.5 are launched every cycle and do not incur any stalls, then the total number of cycles taken for convolution can be expressed as

$$conv\_cycles = K_C \times K_R \times M_C \times M_R \times N\_itr \times M\_itr$$
$$+ R\_itr \times N\_itr \times M\_itr \qquad (8.16)$$

where the second term is added to include initiation interval cycles of the tiling loop as it is not coalesced with compute loop.

It is possible to potentially hide IFM loads and OFM partial sum load/stores inside the convolution cycles. All but the first IFM tile load, all partial OFM loads and all but the last OFM tile store constitutes the intermediate traffic:

$$mem\_ldst\_cycles = ifm\_ld\_cycles + ofm\_ld\_cycles$$
$$+ ofm\_st\_cycles \qquad (8.17)$$

Details of each of these terms follows next. Since convolution filters can have strides less than the filter dimensions, IFM row tiles tend to slightly overlap over the edges. This results in some of the required data being discarded from IFM buffers and brought back from global memory. This overlap is not significant for CLs with large IFM dimensions. For smaller IFMs in deeper layers of CNNs, IFM sizes do become smaller but then do not require row tiling if Tr is large enough. This presents another trade-off in optimizing Tr. As IFM traffic computation is complex, we instead calculate number of IFM elements required by every OFM row tile:

$$rows1 = \begin{cases} 0, & \text{if } R\_itr = 1 \\ (K_R + S \times (Tr - 1)) \times (R\_itr - 2), & \text{otherwise} \end{cases} \qquad (8.18)$$

$$rows2 = K_R + S \times (M_R - (R\_itr - 1) \times Tr) \qquad (8.19)$$
$$ifm\_ld\_cycles = N\_itr \times N_C \times (rows1 + rows2)$$
$$\times Tn \times ACPE_i \qquad (8.20)$$

where (8.18) is the number of elements in all but the first and last row tiles as they are counted separately in (8.13) and (8.19), respectively. For OFMs, partial sums are loaded in all but the first N_itr iteration of the tiling loop as the sums are initialized by bias terms. On the other hand, partial sums are stored to global memory at the end of every tiling loop iteration. But since *ofm_st_cycles* only considers hidden cycles, for accurate estimates, we remove the last *ofm_ps_cycles* which are never hidden:

$$ofm\_ld\_cycles = M_C \times M_R \times M\_itr \times (N\_itr - 1)$$
$$\times Tm \times ACPE_o \qquad (8.21)$$
$$ofm\_st\_cycles = M_C \times M_R \times M\_itr \times N\_itr \times Tm \times ACPE_o$$
$$- ofm\_ps\_cycles \qquad (8.22)$$

Finally, size of the last OFM tile is equal to $M_R - (R\_itr - 1) \cdot Tr$ which can also be Tr if Tr is a factor of M_R:

$$ofm\_ps\_cycles = M_C \times (M_R - (R\_itr - 1) \times Tr) \times ACPE_o \qquad (8.23)$$

The total number of execution cycles can then be computed by combining the five stages as shown:

$$
\begin{aligned}
total\_cycles = \ & ifm\_pl\_cycles + wt\_ld\_cycles \\
& + max(conv\_cycles,\ mem\_ldst\_cycles) \\
& + ofm\_ps\_cycles
\end{aligned}
\qquad (8.24)
$$

8.6.3.1 Estimating required off-chip bandwidth

If *mem_ldst_cycles* cannot be overlapped within *conv_cycles*, off-chip memory bandwidth affects the performance. This is represented by the third term in (8.24). If we set the denominator in (8.12) as equals to *off_chip_bw*, then by setting *mem_ldst_cycles = conv_cycles*, we can solve for the minimum *off_chip_bw* required for a particular configuration for complete stall-free operation.

8.7 Library design and architecture implementation

HLS frameworks like OpenCL provide fast design cycles, however they require more on-chip resources. Consequently, hybrid implementations like RTL-OpenCL [5] and System Verilog-OpenCL [14] have emerged in literature. We design modular OpenCL kernels motivated by RTL style distribution of functionality. This gives us several advantages. First, each OpenCL kernel runs independently which gives us both full concurrency and pipelined parallelism. This is helpful in effective use of dual buffering and also helps in reducing any inter-kernel communication stalls. Second, modularity helps us with easy plugging of different layers implemented as separate OpenCL kernels. A complete OpenCL kernel can be removed before synthesis if that function is not required for a particular CNN. Finally, it also allows us to easily launch a subset of kernels. This is required for cases such as when a PL is not stitched directly on top of CL and needs to be computed separately, which is common in GoogLeNet.

8.7.1 Concurrent architecture

Figure 8.7 shows an overview of the designed architecture. Input, weight and output loads/stores are done by their respective kernels named *Load IFM*, *Load Weights* and *Load/Store OFM* which interface to the off-chip memory controller. Buffered IFM random data access and flow control is provided by *IFM0 Reuse* and *IFM1 Reuse* kernels which implement dual-buffering. Weight data is loaded from off-chip memory which is simultaneously provided to computation and cached into on-chip buffers for reuse. Partial OFM sums are always produced and accessed in sequence, which allows us to structure OFM buffers as FIFOs. This reduces address-generation complexity. FIFO input access and output data redirection are provided by individual low

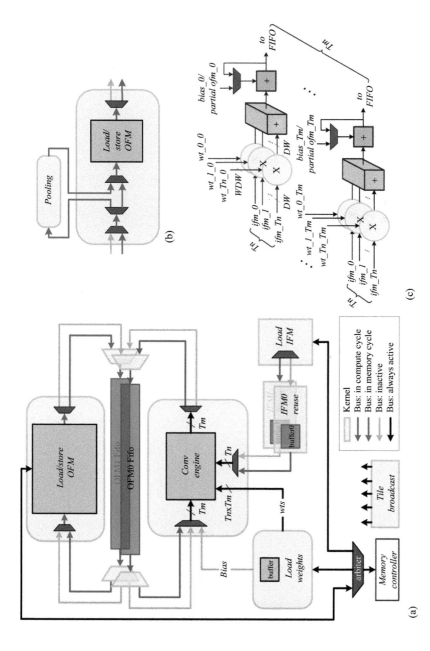

Figure 8.7 *Modular accelerator architecture: (a) architecture overview; (b) plugging new layers; (c) convolution engine with parallel PEs*

complexity kernels shown as MUXes and De-MUXes in Figure 8.7(a). They receive control from *Load/Store OFM*. *Tile Broadcast* kernel connects to every other kernel. It interfaces with the host and is responsible for communicating interlayer config-uration parameters, intra-layer tile sizes and launch commands to other kernels. A network's per layer configuration values are once transferred to DRAMs along with the model data and are distributed by *Tile Broadcast*. We design all kernels except *Tile Broadcast* as *autorun* kernels and do not require any host intervention once the computation starts.

8.7.2   Convolution engine

ConvEngine (CE) performs the main convolution computations. It receives weights, input pixels and either the bias terms if it is the first *N_itr* iteration or the partial sums otherwise and pushes the new partial or complete sums into OFM buffers. Figure 8.7(c) shows the internal structure of CE. It continuously accumulates the multiplied weights and pixels in every cycle, while the accelerator steps through the entire filter size in sequence. It computes *Tm* independent output pixels in parallel while reducing *Tn* input channel pixels with an adder tree every cycle. Figure 8.7(c) shows the multipliers, adder tree and the accumulator at the end.

8.7.2.1   Optimal DRAM access

Left side of Figure 8.8(a) shows how IFMs for an example CL are stored inside the off-chip memory. Different colors (including shades) represent different channels and different shades (within the same color) represent data belonging to the same channel tile *Tn* or *Tm*. We roll the 2D channels into a single dimension in row major order. *Tn* different IFM channels are interleaved to provide parallel access. Figure 8.8(b) and (c) also shows weight and OFM interleaving patterns with respective wide *vector_size*

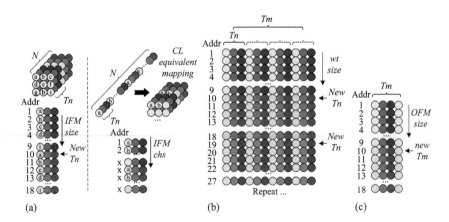

Figure 8.8   *Data-arrangement patterns for data and weights in CLs and FCLs: (a) IFM access for CL (left) and FCL (right), (b) weight access, (c) OFM access*

accesses. Since case C_{23} is used in tiling loop, all weights along M OFM channels are stored contiguously before weights for next IFM channel tile as shown in Figure 8.8(b).

8.7.3 Restructuring fully connected layers

FCLs are a special case of CLs where all input, weight and output channels are reduced to single-pixel channels. Due to lack of weight sharing, they demand high memory bandwidth. It is possible to process FCLs in the same way as CLs but the tiling and compute loops are not coalesced together. Since all input and output data are along the channels, majority of iterations are in tiling loop and the compute loop incurs heavy initiation interval stalls. This results in more partial sums and higher data traffic. To address this, we restructure the input features as shown in the right side of Figure 8.8(a). Input features are mapped as pixels of the same channel in *Tn*-interleaved pattern. We map up to IFM's *buffer_depth* features as the same channel pixels. If $N >$ IFM's *buffer_depth*, remaining features are grouped into a new *Tn* tile. For FCLs, we set $K_C \times K_R$ equals to the number of elements in the newly mapped IFM tile. Since no weight data is reused in FCLs, we do not buffer the filters and continuously load weights from off-chip and directly provide to CE, hence removing any restriction due to limited weight buffer depths. This modifies our model for FCLs as

$$N\_itr = \left\lceil \frac{N}{buffer\_depth} \right\rceil \tag{8.25}$$

$$K_R \times K_C = buffer\_depth \tag{8.26}$$

which drastically reduces total iterations in tiling loop and simultaneously transfers them to the compute loop.

8.7.4 Zero overhead pooling

We propose a shift-register-based pooling engine in Figure 8.9, which results in zero overhead when stitched on top of a CL. OFM pixels enter the shift register in row major

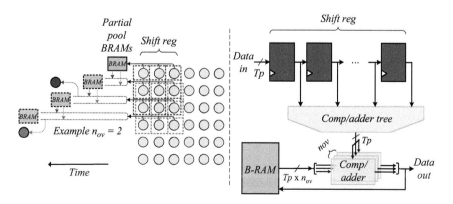

Figure 8.9   Pooling processing sequence (left) and architecture (right)

fashion. The shift register collects pooling filter width number of pixels and computes partial pools using a comparator or adder tree. Partial pooled values are stored into on-chip memory in row major sequence and read back when next set of partial pools is generated for that pooling filter, until the complete filter is processed. Figure 8.9 also shows the computation sequence for pooling. Just as convolution filters, pooling filters can also overlap, which means partial pools are shared between multiple pooled pixels. To process the incoming OFM pixels without stalls, we simultaneously compute all n_{OV} overlapping filters. Partial pool computed in current cycle along with previous n_{OV} partial pools read from BRAMs are used to compute new partial pools and stored back to BRAMs in parallel. Therefore, processing Tm pixels can result in high on-chip bandwidth and logic resource requirements for pooling. Hence, we process a factor of Tp pixels every cycle. Since OFM pixels are produced every $K_R \times K_C$ convolution cycles, as long as Tm/Tp is lower than that, there will be no pooling overhead. If convolution is 1×1, we compute pooling as a separate layer as it is not possible to hide pooling latency.

8.7.5   Other layers

We plug the pooling layer from *Load/Store OFM* kernel to use the already present data redirection logic as shown in Figure 8.7(b). Other layers like normalization, scaling or element-wise layers are plugged in a similar way. Apart from that we concatenate filters for free by setting interleaving size of OFMs in DRAMs to be the total width of concatenated channels. For each new concatenated layer, an offset is incremented by number of channels of the previous layer. This allows us to implement any level of nested branched networks creating support for even more network architectures.

8.8   Caffe integration

FICaffe is an extension to the widely used deep learning framework Caffe. The fully automated acceleration flow is shown in Figure 8.10. FICaffe's flow includes

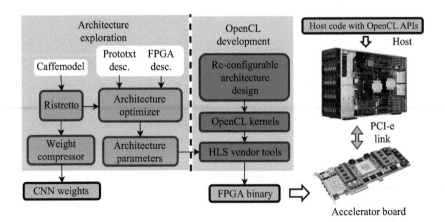

Figure 8.10   FICaffe end-to-end acceleration flow

Ristretto [8], which is an automated CNN-approximation tool that explores different quantization schemes and can be used to compress and fine-tune learned models. FICaffe's tool-set is written in python with pycaffe interfacing and only requires Caffe's prototxt and caffemodel files as inputs. First, Ristretto is used to analyze and generate static or dynamic fixed-point quantization schemes for each layer. The quantization results are used to generate modified CNN weights which are transferred once to FPGA board DRAMs. A parser extracts layer attributes from the prototxt file, which are used by architecture optimizer along with the quantization results from Ristretto. It generates optimized hardware and software configuration, tiling factors and the required host and device library files. Following this, the OpenCL compiler takes over and generates the FPGA binary. Finally, the same binary can be used to accelerate specific or multiple networks accordingly.

8.9   Performance evaluation

To verify the computation model, we implement FICaffe on a DE5-Net board with a Stratix V GXA7 FPGA, 4 GB DDR3 DRAM @ 800 MHz and PCI-E Gen3 ×8 interface with the host PC. Our host is a 6-Core Intel's Xeon CPU E5-2603 v3 @ 1.60 GHz, with 16 GB RAM. Intel's OpenCL SDK v16.0 is used to synthesize the libraries. The board uses the PCI-E port along with an external power supply.

8.9.1   Optimizer results

8.9.1.1   Latency estimation model

Table 8.3 shows result of the total estimated cycles and its distribution for each stage along with actual number of cycles measured by Intel's OpenCL SDK Profiler for different layers of GoogLeNet.* It can be observed that filters of size 3×3 and more have enough computation to avoid any intermediate memory stalls with a small overhead. FCL and CLs with 1×1 filter, in contrast, are memory bound as the *total_cycles* is dominated by *mem_ldst_cycles* of stage 4. Due to our restructuring of FCLs, all memory stalls appear only in weight cycles and N_itr becomes 1 for FCLs

Table 8.3   Estimated vs measured execution cycles for chosen GoogLeNet layers ($<Tn, Tm, Tr, Tp> = 4, 48, 13, 8$)

Filter, stride	OFM size	Stage 1	Stage 2	Stage 3	Stage 4	Stage 5	Total (8.24)	Measured	% Error
CL ($7 \times 7 \times 3$, 2)	$56 \times 56 \times 64$	8,050	1,123	1,229,312	78,214	784	1,239,269	1,240,217	0.08
CL ($5 \times 5 \times 32$, 1)	$28 \times 28 \times 96$	608	1,146	313,600	28,128	364	315,718	324,026	2.56
CL ($3 \times 3 \times 96$, 1)	$28 \times 28 \times 128$	510	1,856	508,032	122,062	364	510,762	526,101	2.92
CL ($1 \times 1 \times 192$, 1)	$28 \times 28 \times 16$	420	138	37,632	93,294	364	94,216	98,136	3.99
FCL ($1,024 \times 1,000$)		1	10,731	5,376	–	1	16,109	16,085	0.15

*We have separate versions of library files with the same structure but synthesized as *task parallel* instead of *autorun* to instantiate profiling counters.

with input that can entirely fit in IFM buffers, removing the need for *mem_ldst_cycles*. While 1 × 1 convolution is bounded by data traffic due to IFMs and OFM partial sums (*mem_ldst_cycles*, stage 4), dense inner product computation in FCL is limited by weight data traffic (*wt_ld_cycles*, stage 2).

8.9.1.2   Exploration strategy

To choose optimum values of design variables, we perform design space exploration to estimate resource usage and runtime latency. We allow *Tn* to vary as powers of two, while *Tm* takes intermediate values as well to improve DSP usage. Performance usually scales linearly with DSPs up to some power of two due to the nature of feature map channel dimensions used in most CNNs, after which the gain is nominal. Designs that do not satisfy DSP and BRAM requirements of the FPGA board are rejected. We then check for logic usage of designs in descending order of the highest performance and select the first one that satisfies the logic resource thresholds. This reduces the total exploration time.

8.9.1.3   Design variable optimization

The runtime and resource optimization strategies for VGG and GoogLeNet are shown in Figure 8.11. Figure 8.11(a) and (d) shows how the runtime latency varies with the sweep of *Tn* and *Tm* for valid designs that satisfy resource constrains of the FPGA. Optimal pairs of these tiling factors are obtained for the design with the least latency. Furthermore, *Tr* also has an impact on performance along with BRAM usage. For a network with large layers like VGG, i.e., with large max_c, *Tr* can only be increased to a relatively lower extent as the buffer depth quickly saturated BRAM resources. This can be seen in Figure 8.11(b) as *Tr* has a maximum sweep of up to 18. On the other hand, GoogLeNet layer dimensions are relatively smaller and *Tr* tile can be made as large as 68 but buffer initialization overheads start dominating for deeper on-chip buffers and best performance occurs at 13 itself, visible in Figure 8.11(e). To provide higher on-chip bandwidth, buffer depths, i.e., the burst length needs to be sacrificed, leading to poor off-chip memory performance. To keep the CE from stalling, we give higher preference to the on-chip bandwidth by instantiating as wide on-chip buffers as needed and then further optimize the performance by exploring the *Tr* values. Figure 8.11(c) and (f) shows how BRAM resources saturate with different *Tr* values for VGG and GoogLeNet, respectively. We can see that used BRAMs change in incremental steps. If the value of *Tr* at a step in Figure 8.11(f) falls inside the monotonous region in Figure 8.11(e), BRAM requirement can be reduced by reducing *Tr* by 1 with marginal to no reduction in performance. This can result in simplified routing leading to higher operating frequency.

8.9.2   Onboard runs

8.9.2.1   Network-specific runs

We run the optimizer for four different CNNs to minimize total cycles taken in all layers of a particular CNN. The resulting architecture configurations <*Tn, Tm, Tr, Tp*>

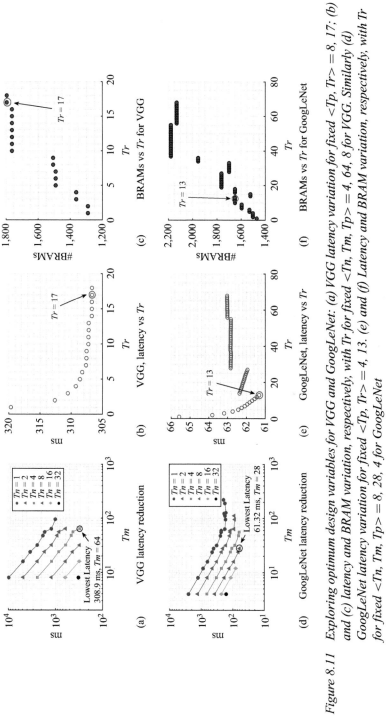

Figure 8.11 *Exploring optimum design variables for VGG and GoogLeNet: (a) VGG latency variation for fixed <Tp, Tr> = 8, 17; (b) and (c) latency and BRAM variation, respectively, with Tr for fixed <Tn, Tm, Tp> = 4, 64, 8 for VGG. Similarly (d) GoogLeNet latency variation for fixed <Tp, Tr> = 4, 13. (e) and (f) Latency and BRAM variation, respectively, with Tr for fixed <Tn, Tm, Tp> = 8, 28, 4 for GoogLeNet*

and performance are shown in Table 8.4.[†] For latency estimates, 200 MHz operation is assumed, which when scaled by the synthesized frequency, closely models the measured onboard latency. The DSP usage for SqueezeNet and GoogLeNet is lower as we use a number of DSPs for average pooling. This is because pooling filter size is allowed to be set from host side just like convolution filter size for maximum flexibility. Since both of these networks only have one such layer, DSP usage and performance can both be improved just by fixing the average pool filter size in hardware.

8.9.2.2   Cross-network run

Due to the highly flexible nature of FICaffe's PEs, the same architecture can be used across multiple networks without the need to reprogram the FPGA with a different binary. This is useful when deploying systems that combine outputs from multiple CNNs. Such ensemble of networks can achieve higher accuracy and more robustness. Table 8.5 shows the achieved performance for each CNN and device usage when a common cross-network library is optimized for all four CNNs considered together. Note that the resulting library configuration is dominated by optimizations for SqueezeNet and GoogLeNet as their performances are very close to fully optimized runtime in Table 8.4. Performance of AlexNet and VGG suffers mainly because of suboptimal tile configuration.

Table 8.4   Network-specific synthesis performance

CNN	No. of operations (GOPs)	Tiles $<Tn,Tm,Tr,Tp>$	Frequency (MHz)	Estimated, scaled latency (ms)	Measured latency (ms)	Difference (%)
AlexNet	1.45	4,64,14,8	195	18.56, 19.04	20.59	7.53
VGG	30.76	4,64,17,8	185	306.68, 331.57	339	2.19
SqueezeNet	1.66	4,56,26,4	195	33.24, 34.13	37.73	9.54
GoogLeNet	3.16	8,28,13,4	209	61.33, 58.69	62.88	6.66

Table 8.5   Cross-network synthesis device utilization and performance for $<Tn,Tm,Tr,Tp> = <8, 28, 26, 4>$

Resource	Available	Estimated	Synthesized	CNN	Time (ms)
DSPs	256	256	252 (98%)	AlexNet	27.12
BRAMs	2,700	2,370	2,253 (88%)	VGG	399.90
ALMs	234,720	–	166,652 (71%)	SqueezeNet	39.08
Freq (MHz)	–	200	197.47	GoogLeNet	64.74

[†]FPGA resources are not reported for every Network due to space constraints, see Table 8.7 for some results.

8.9.3   Architecture comparison

We compare FICaffe's performance with state-of-the-art work on AlexNet and VGG. Most of the previous works in related literature are throughput oriented and use batching to improve raw throughput numbers. In contrast, FICaffe optimizes the architecture for latency-sensitive applications and does not consider batching. While batching improves the throughput, it increases the latency/image. Therefore, for fairness, we also compare processing efficiency of PEs. Efficiency represents the percentage of total runtime that a PE spends in performing arithmetic computations. It also normalizes the effects of underlying FPGA platform used and the chip technology node and helps compare the architecture on a level field. PE Efficiency is calculated as

$$PE\ efficiency = \frac{Ops\ achieved/s/PE}{MaxOps/PE/s} = \frac{Throughput/\#PEs}{2 \times freq} \tag{8.27}$$

Note that latency cannot be directly calculated from throughout. Only a lower bound on latency can be inferred from raw throughput numbers. Further, we intentionally do not compare performance density which is the number of operations done per DSP per cycle, because FICaffe does not yet take advantage of two 18×18 multiplications on a single Stratix V DSP. This is because Intel's SDK version 16.0 (restrictions from Vendor BSP at that time) is not very effective at analyzing complex OpenCL code to use all multipliers per DSP.

8.9.3.1   Raw performance improvement

Stratix V GXA7 is a small-to-medium-sized FPGA with only 256 DSPs. Directly comparing the raw latency numbers with bigger chips does not give a clear idea of effectiveness of the FICaffe architecture. Therefore, in Table 8.6, we compare the latest published results for full AlexNet and VGG acceleration on this chip in [13]. We can see that FICaffe achieves more than $2\times$ better runtime on AlexNet and almost twice on VGG as well.

8.9.3.2   Comparison with state-of-the-art

From Table 8.7, we can see that FICaffe is the only design that does not take advantage of CNN-specific optimizations and input batching and is completely OpenCL based. With high flexibility, FICaffe has the best PE efficiency when compared to all recent works for VGG. Works presented in [14,16] are optimized specifically to VGG and [4]

Table 8.6   *Comparison of inference time/image on Stratix V GXA7*

CNN	FPGA2016 [13]	FICaffe	Speedup
AlexNet	45.7 ms	20.59 ms	2.22×
VGG	651.2 ms	339 ms	1.92×

Table 8.7 FICaffe compared with other designs

	ICCAD'16 [6]		FPGA'17 [16]	FCCM'17 [5]	FPGA'17 [4]	FPGA'17 [14]	FICaffe	
Framework	Xilinx HLS		RTL	OpenCL+RTL	OpenCL	OpenCL+Sys V.	OpenCL	
Precision	fixed, 16		fixed, 8-16	fixed, 16	float, 16	fixed, 8-16	fixed, 8-16	
Platform	Virtex 690t	Kintex KU060	Arria-10 GX1150	Stratix-V GSMD5	Arria-10 GX1150	Arria-10 GX1150	Stratix V GXA7	
CNN (GOPs)	VGG (30.76)		VGG (30.76)	VGG (30.76)	AlexNet (1.45)	VGG (30.76)	AlexNet (1.45)	VGG (30.76)
Freq. (MHz)	150	200	150	150	303	385	195	185
#PEs*, #DSPs	2,833, 2,833/36,00	1,058, 1,058/2,760	3,136, 1,518/1,518	2,048, 1,036/1,590	2,504, 1,476/1,518	2,432, 2,756/3,036	256, 256/256	
#BRAMs	1,248/2,940	782/2,160	19,00/2,713	919/2,014	2,487/2,713	1,450/2,713	1,539/2,560	1,780/2,560
Throughput (GOPs/s)	354	266	645.25	364.4	1,382	1,790	70.42	90.74
CNN specific	No		Yes	No	Yes	Yes	No	
Input batching	CL 1, FCL 32		No	Yes	CL 1, FCL 96	No	No	
Latency/Img. (ms)	2,084.16	3,236.8	>47.67	–	>94.12	>17.18	20.59	339
PE eff (%)	41.6	62.8	68.6	59.3	91.1	84.3	70.5	**95.8**

* Number of PEs mentioned are our best effort for fair comparison as some articles do not explicitly report them.

for AlexNet. Authors in [14] achieve very high throughput for VGG as they optimize their architecture only for 3×3 filters. Additionally, they achieve good processing efficiency without any batching in FCLs, because VGG is highly compute bound. VGG has $20\times$ more computation than ALexNet, whereas both have similar amount of FCL computations. Effect of this fact is also visible in FICaffe's efficiency for VGG, but unlike [3], we achieve high efficiency without synthesizing RTL IPs.

Authors in [4] propose to reduce bandwidth requirement for both CL and FCLs. These improvements can be attributed to the use of Winograd Transformations for convolution, batching in FCLs and the assumption that all IFMs/OFMs for a layer can be transferred to on-chip memories before processing. Their approach is neither automated nor arbitrarily scalable like FICaffe, as they manually fix intra-filter parallelism and perform Winograd for only 3×3 filters. Also Gflop/s reported in [4] is no IEEE 754 compliant.

Like FICaffe, authors in [6] also consider integration with Caffe but only report on ALexNet and VGG. Their main contribution is systematic analysis of input-major and weight-major schemes for FCLs and is based on empirical modification to roofline model. Unfortunately, their PE efficiency is poor even with batching and has very high latency/image. They leave a large gap between achievable performance as they too use intra-filter parallelism by unrolling fixed filter size to 5×5. Finally, while the work presented in [5] does support smaller filters of 1×1, they do not report actual number of PEs and to the best of our knowledge do not achieve high PE efficiency either. Notice that choice of FPGA impacts the final latency values. A larger FPGA with a rich plethora of resource always yields a better performance. To compare different architectures, one may normalize the achieved latency by the available resource.

References

[1] Mohammad Motamedi, Philipp Gysel, Venkatesh Akella, and Soheil Ghiasi. 2016. Design Space Exploration of FPGA-Based Deep Convolutional Neural Networks. In *Design Automation Conference (ASP-DAC), 2016 21st Asia and South Pacific*. IEEE, 575–580.

[2] Mohammad Motamedi, Philipp Gysel, and Soheil Ghiasi. 2017. PLACID: A Platform for FPGA-Based Accelerator Creation for DCNNs. *ACM Transactions on Multimedia Computing, Communications, and Applications (TOMM)* 13, 4 (2017), 62.

[3] Chen Zhang, Peng Li, Guangyu Sun, Yijin Guan, Bingjun Xiao, and Jason Cong. 2015. Optimizing FPGA-Based Accelerator Design for Deep Convolutional Neural Networks. In *Proceedings of the 2015 ACM/SIGDA International Symposium on Field-Programmable Gate Arrays*. ACM, 161–170.

[4] Utku Aydonat, Shane O'Connell, Davor Capalija, Andrew C. Ling, and Gordon R. Chiu. 2017. An OpenCL™ Deep Learning Accelerator on Arria 10. In *Proceedings of the 2017 ACM/SIGDA International Symposium on Field-Programmable Gate Arrays (FPGA'17)*. ACM, New York, NY, USA, 55–64. DOI: http://dx.doi.org/10.1145/3020078.3021738

[5]   Yijin Guan, Hao Liang, Ningyi Xu, *et al.* 2017. FP-DNN: An Auto-mated Framework for Mapping Deep Neural Networks onto FPGAs With RTL-HLS Hybrid Templates. In *Field-Programmable Custom Computing Machines (FCCM), 2017 IEEE 25th Annual International Symposium on.* IEEE, 152–159.

[6]   Chen Zhang, Zhenman Fang, Peipei Zhou, Peichen Pan, and Jason Cong. 2016. Caffeine: Towards Uniformed Representation and Acceleration for Deep Convolutional Neural Networks. In *Computer-Aided Design (ICCAD), 2016 IEEE/ACM International Conference on.* IEEE, 1–8.

[7]   Roberto DiCecco, Griffin Lacey, Jasmina Vasiljevic, Paul Chow, Graham Tay-lor, and Shawki Areibi. 2016. Caffeinated FPGAs: FPGA Framework For Convolutional Neural Networks. In *Field-Programmable Technology (FPT), 2016 International Conference on.* IEEE, 265–268.

[8]   Philipp Gysel, Mohammad Motamedi, and Soheil Ghiasi. 2016. Ristretto: Hardware-oriented approximation of convolutional neural networks. *arXiv preprint arXiv:1605.06402* (2016).

[9]   Alex Krizhevsky, Ilya Sutskever, and Geoffrey E Hinton. 2012. Ima-geNet Classification with Deep Convolutional Neural Networks. In *Advances in Neural Information Processing Systems 25*, F. Pereira, C. J. C. Burges, L. Bottou, and K. Q. Weinberger (Eds.). Curran Associates, Inc., 1097–1105.   http://papers.nips.cc/paper/4824-imagenet-classification-with-deep-convolutional-neural-networks.pdf

[10] Karen Simonyan and Andrew Zisserman. 2014. Very deep convolutional networks for large-scale image recognition. *arXiv preprint arXiv:1409.1556* (2014).

[11] Forrest N Iandola, Song Han, Matthew W Moskewicz, Khalid Ashraf, William J Dally, and Kurt Keutzer. 2016. SqueezeNet: AlexNet-level accu-racy with 50x fewer parameters and <0.5 MB model size. *arXiv preprint arXiv:1602.07360* (2016).

[12] Christian Szegedy, Wei Liu, Yangqing Jia, *et al.* 2015. Going Deeper with Convolutions. In *Proceedings of the IEEE Conference on Computer Vision and Pattern Recognition.* 1–9.

[13] Naveen Suda, Vikas Chandra, Ganesh Dasika, *et al.* 2016. Throughput-Optimized OpenCL-Based FPGA Accelerator for Large-Scale Convolutional Neural Networks. In *Proceedings of the 2016 ACM/SIGDA International Symposium on Field-Programmable Gate Arrays.* ACM, 16–25.

[14] Jialiang Zhang and Jing Li. 2017. Improving the Performance of OpenCL-Based FPGA Accelerator for Convolutional Neural Network. In *Proceedings of the 2017 ACM/SIGDA International Symposium on Field-Programmable Gate Arrays FPGA'17).* ACM, New York, NY, USA, 25–34. DOI: http://dx.doi.org/10.1145/3020078.3021698.

[15] Jiantao Qiu, Jie Wang, Song Yao, *et al.* 2016. Going Deeper with Embedded FPGA Platform for Convolutional Neural Network. In *Proceedings of the 2016 ACM/SIGDA International Symposium on Field-Programmable Gate Arrays.* ACM, 26–35.

[16] Yufei Ma, Yu Cao, Sarma Vrudhula, and Jae-sun Seo. 2017. Optimizing Loop Operation and Dataflow in FPGA Acceleration of Deep Convolutional Neural Networks. In *Proceedings of the 2017 ACM/SIGDA International Symposium on Field-Programmable Gate Arrays*. ACM, 45–54.

[17] Atul Rahman, Jongeun Lee, and Kiyoung Choi. 2016. Efficient FPGA Acceleration of Convolutional Neural Networks Using Logical-3D Compute Array. In *Design, Automation & Test in Europe Conference & Exhibition (DATE), 2016*. IEEE, 1393–1398.

[18] Ying Wang, Jie Xu, Yinhe Han, Huawei Li, and Xiaowei Li. 2016. Deep-Burning: Automatic Generation of FPGA-Based Learning Accelerators for the Neural Network Family. In *Design Automation Conference (DAC), 2016 53nd ACM/EDAC/IEEE*. IEEE, 1–6.

[19] Yann LeCun, Koray Kavukcuoglu, and Clément Farabet. 2010. Convolutional Networks and Applications in Vision. In *Circuits and Systems (ISCAS), Proceedings of 2010 IEEE International Symposium on*. IEEE, 253–256.

[20] Kaiming He, Xiangyu Zhang, Shaoqing Ren, and Jian Sun. 2016. Deep Residual Learning for Image Recognition. In *Proceedings of the IEEE Conference on Computer Vision and Pattern Recognition*. 770–778.

[21] Sergey Ioffe and Christian Szegedy. 2015. Batch Normalization: Accelerating Deep Network Training by Reducing Internal Covariate Shift. In *International Conference on Machine Learning*. 448–456.

Chapter 9

Iterative convolutional neural network (ICNN): an iterative CNN solution for low power and real-time systems

Katayoun Neshatpour[1], Houman Homayoun[1], and Avesta Sasan[1]

With convolutional neural networks (CNN) becoming more of a commodity in the computer vision field, many have attempted to improve CNN in a bid to achieve better accuracy to a point that CNN accuracies have surpassed that of human's capabilities. However, with deeper networks, the number of computations and consequently the energy needed per classification has grown considerably. In this chapter, an iterative approach is introduced, which transforms the CNN from a single feed-forward network that processes a large image into a sequence of smaller networks, each processing a subsample of each image. Each smaller network combines the features extracted from all the earlier networks, to produce classification results. Such a multistage approach allows the CNN function to be dynamically approximated by creating the possibility of early termination and performing the classification with far fewer operations compared to a conventional CNN.

9.1 Motivation

Powerful models have been trained using machine learning methods on large data sets to increase the performance of object recognition. Image recognition on a realistic variety of images is only possible by training on large datasets. However, only recently has a large set of labeled datasets become available. ImageNet [1] is an example of such datasets. ImageNet is an image database organized according to the WordNet [2] hierarchy (currently only the nouns), in which each node of the hierarchy is depicted by hundreds and thousands of images. ImageNet includes average of over 500 images per node.

While neural networks have become ubiquitous in applications, including vision, speech recognition and natural language processing, CNNs are designed to make mostly correct assumptions about the nature of images, with much fewer connections

[1]Department of Electrical and Computer Engineering, George Mason University, Fairfax, VA, USA

and parameters than similarly size layers, with slightly accuracies that are theoretically only slightly worse.

However, many neural network algorithms and especially CNN as a part of this family, due to their deep networks and dense connectivity, are computationally intensive. For example, AlexNet [3], a CNN learning algorithm that won the 2012 ImageNet visual recognition challenge, contains 650K neurons and 60M parameters which demands computational performance in the order of hundreds of Mega Operations per Second (MOPS) per classification. Next generations of vision-based CNN algorithms, as illustrated in Figure 9.1, have further improved their prediction accuracy; however, this is achieved via even deeper networks. VGG [4], GoogleNet [5] and ResNet [6] have improved the prediction accuracy via increasing the CNN depth from 8 in AlexNet to 19, 22 and 152 layers, respectively. As a result, the floating point operations (FLOPs) have increased from 729 MOPS to up to 19.6 GOPS. Table 9.1 shows how the complexity of these CNNs in terms of FLOP count has dramatically increased over time to enhance their classification accuracy.

Thus, most recent CNN algorithms are composed of multiple computational layers involving standard structure-stacked convolutional layers, interleaved with contrast normalization and max pooling followed by one or more fully connected (FC) layers. These sophisticated solutions have improved accuracy to a point that

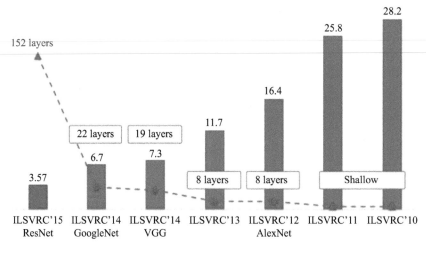

Figure 9.1   *Top 5 accuracy of the state of the art CNNs [6]*

Table 9.1   *Specification of the existing CNN architectures*

	AlexNet [3]	ZFNet [7]	VGG [4]	GoogLeNet [5]	Resnet [6]
Top-5 accuracy (%)	80.2	88.8	89.6	89.9	96.3
Layers	8	8	19	22	152
FLOPs	729M	663M	19.6G	1.5G	11.3G

classification accuracies have surpassed that of human's capabilities. However, with deeper networks and added sophistication, the number of computations needed per classification has grown considerably, making CNN an extremely computational intensive and power hungry solution.

As a result, besides higher performance requirements, there is a need to aggressively reduce the power consumption of these platforms as many desired platforms for vision-based applications are energy constrained. Adopting complex vision algorithms in many of mobile and handheld, embedded systems and IoT applications will not be feasible if energy consumption barrier is not addressed. At the same time, many of desired applications require real-time and short-latency response. The good news is that learning by nature is approximate. Neural networks are trained and proven to be tolerant against input noise. If learning is approximate in nature, why should its underlying structure be designed to be a 100% accurate? What if a little approximation in hardware, with little or no degradation on output, could save us significant power, performance and/or area? Can we recover from additional inaccuracy of approximate hardware through learning? How do we identify the error-tolerant computations that can benefit from approximate hardware? Can we reformulate learning to provide more approximation opportunities for the hardware? The goal here is to answer these questions.

CNN is a computational and power hungry solution. However, most interesting applications of computer vision are in Robotics, CPS and IoT domains which on average are resource constrained. In addition, such applications demand real time and fast turnaround time (low latency). Therefore, the optimization space involves accuracy, latency, power and area. With this in mind, we reformulate the learning from a single feed-forward network to a series of smaller networks that could be traversed iteratively. Figure 9.2 illustrates a high-level abstraction of the approximate CNN. In iterative learning, each iteration works on small set of subsampled input features and enhances the accuracy of classification. Upon reaching an acceptable classification Ct, further iterations are ignored. This creates the possibility of performing the classification with far less operations compared to a conventional learning algorithm. In addition, first iteration(s) could provide useful feedback to the underlying hardware, managing the HW approximation intents. This is especially true, if in addition to classification, we are interested in localization. This could provide us with many opportunities for approximation.

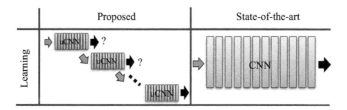

Figure 9.2   Reformulating the CNN into an iterative solution

9.2 Background on CNN

CNNs are constructed from multiple computational layers formed as directed acyclic graph (DAG) [8,9]. Each layer extracts an abstraction of data provided in the previous layer, called a feature map (fmap). Most common layers are pooling (*POOL*), convolution (*CONV*) and *FC*.

In CONV layers, as illustrated in Figure 9.3, two-dimensional (2-D) filters slide over the input images/feature-maps (*Ifmaps*) performing convolution operation to extract feature characteristics from local regions and generating output images/feature-maps (*Ofmaps*).

Equation (9.1) illustrates how the CONV layer is being computed.

$$Of[z][u][x][y] = Bias[u] + \sum_{(k=0)}^{(C-1)} \sum_{(i=0)}^{(R-1)} \sum_{(j=0)}^{(R-1)} If[z][k][Ux+i][Uy+j]W[u][k][i][j],$$

$$0 \le z \le N; \ 0 \le u \le M; 0 \le x,y \le E; \ E = \frac{(H-R+U)}{U},$$

$$(9.1)$$

where *Of* is the *Ofmap*, *If* is the *Ifmap*, *W* is the filter weight vector and *Bias* is a 1-D bias that is added to the results.

Computation of CONV layer in popular CNNs accounts for more than 90% of the overall operations and requires a large amount of data movement and memory operations [10]. In addition, the large size of *Ifmaps*, *Ofmaps* and partial results, which are generated during the CONV processing, increases the memory requirements for these architectures and requires large portion of the accelerator hardware

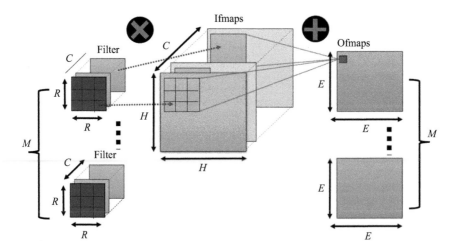

Figure 9.3   Computing one CONV layer using input Ifmap/image and filters to produce the output (Ofmaps)

area to be dedicated to various forms of memory structures, including global buffers, various First in First out (FIFO) and local register files. Depending on the type of data flow, the proportion of memory requirement in different levels of memory hierarchy changes [11].

After every CONV layer, a nonlinear operation is applied to each *Ofmap* pixel to introduce nonlinearity in the network. An example of such nonlinear operator is the rectified linear unit that replaces all negative pixel values by zero. Other nonlinear functions include *Tanh* and *Sigmoid* operators.

Some other CNN architectures also require the normalization (NORM) layer; however, usage of NORM layer has been reduced in recent CNNs [4].

POOL layers perform down-sampling along the spatial dimensions of *Ifmaps* by partitioning them into a set of subregions and combining the values in each subregion into a single value. Max-pooling and average-pooling are examples of POOL operators which use the maximum and the average values for each subregion, respectively.

The outputs from the CONV and POOL layers represent high-level features of the input image. Each CNN includes multiple CONV, nonlinear and POOL layers with their outputs fed to FC layers. FC layers combine all the neurons in the previous layer and connect them to every single neuron in the next layer. FC layers fuse the features extracted in the CONV layers to generate a relational representation of these features with respect to each class in the classifier detection set. In the last layer, a softmax classifier uses the outputs of the last FC layer to produce normalized class probabilities for various classes. Softmax classifier is a multi-class version of the binary logistic regression classifier, which produces un-normalized log probabilities for each class using cross-entropy loss.

9.3 Optimization of CNN

In the literature, various optimization approaches have been proposed to reduce the computational complexity and to enhance the energy-efficiency of the CNN architectures, including Tensor decomposition and low-rank optimization [12,13], parameter compression and exploitation of sparsity [14], binarized neural networks [15–19], and precision reduction of weights and/or neurons by fixed-point tuning and quantization [20–24].

Other works have focus on deploying a dynamically configured structure that allows the complexity of CNN to be adjusted in the run-time. All of the aforementioned approaches are orthogonal to the dynamically configured CNN discussed in this chapter, which modifies the structure of the network and could be applied to iterative CNN (ICNN) as well. A summary of these approaches is described in the sequel.

In [25], a dynamic approach is proposed that breaks the CNN into partial networks. In this approach, based on classification confidence of partial networks, the number of active channels per layer is adjusted. This allows the CNN to be partially or fully deployed. While this approach reduces the computation for classification of a large number of images, the memory footprint required to keep all the intermediate features in the case of non-satisfactory confidence results from partial networks is quite large. In ICNN, this is solved by only keeping the feature-maps of the last CONV layer.

A conditional deep learning network (CDLN) is proposed in which [26], FC layers are added to the intermediate layers to produce early classification results. The forward pass of CDLN starts with the first layer and monitors the confidence to decide whether a sample can be classified early, skipping the computation in the proceeding layers.

While CDLN uses only FC layers at each exit point, BranchyNet [27] proposes using additional CONV layers at each exit point (branch) to enhance the performance.

References [26,27] are tested for ten-class data sets (MNIST [28], CIFAR-10) for up to four stages. On the other hand, in [29], ICNN is proposed for the 1,000-class ImageNet for seven stages, and input images are sampled into its sub-bands using discrete wavelet transform (DWT); thus, the computation load is reduced by processing sub-bands with reduced dimensions in each subnetwork.

The solutions in [25–27,29] create a multistage (iterative) classification strategy in which early termination is practiced when classification confidence reaches a desired threshold in a given stage, skipping all future stages. Reference [30] shows that besides early termination, the classification outcome of each iteration of ICNN can be used to reduce the computational complexity and number of required parameters in the subsequent iterations.

In this chapter, we provide a detailed description of the ICNN architecture. We introduce various policies to reduce the computational complexity of CNN through the iterative approach. We illustrate how the policies construct a dynamic architecture suitable for a wide range of applications with varied accuracy requirements, resources and time-budget, without further need for network retraining. Furthermore, we carry out a visualization of the detected features in each iteration through deconvolution network to gain more insight into the successive traversal of the ICNN. Moreover, we formulate the probability of miss-classification (MC) to find the number of parameters that if pruned will have no or little impact on the resulting classification accuracy.

9.4   Iterative learning

State-of-the-art DAG-based CNN networks are composed of a single feed-forward computational network, where the prediction is given and its confidence is determined after performing all necessary computations. The reformulation is driven by the needs of resource-constrained vision applications for reducing the energy consumption and the classification latency when deploying CNN solutions. In ICNN, a large CNN block is decomposed into many smaller networks (uCNN in Figure 9.2), allowing iterative refinement and greater control over the execution of algorithm. Thus, not all images pass through all the uCNNs; by monitoring the successive execution of uCNN networks, a thresholding mechanism decides when to terminate the forward uCNN traversal based on the current classification confidence of the images. In addition, the ability to change the required confidence threshold from classification to classification allows the system to trade off the accuracy of prediction vs. energy consumed per iteration.

Using ICNN requires a methodology for subsampling the input image for the use of each iteration. Preferably, each subsample is obtained using a different sampling method to push each smaller network (uCNN) to learn new features that are not extracted in the previous iterations. For this reason, *discrete wavelet* sampling could be applied to input images to decompose them into various input sets (subbands). The classification is then initiated by digesting the first subsampled as input in the first iteration. Upon completion of first computational round (first uCNN), the classification confidence is tested. If the confidence is unsatisfactory, it could be progressively increased by working on additional input samples (chosen from remaining sub-bands). DWT provides the learning algorithm with an attractive start point because in addition to frequency information, it also preserves temporal information of an image [31]. However, note that other sampling mechanisms could also be used for ICNN.

The DWT of an image is calculated by passing it through a series of high- and low-pass filters. Consider $h[n]$ as the impulse response of the high-pass filter, and $g[n]$ as the impulse response of low-pass filter. Then, each row of the image is considered a signal $x[n]$. To obtain the first order DWT transformation of the image, for each row of the image, the low-pass and high-pass filters are first convolved with the image values in each row. Note that since half the frequencies of the signal (row of pixels) is removed by each filter, the low-pass and high-pass filters subsample the input signal by half the frequency.

$$y_{low}[n] = (x \times g)[n] = \sum_{n=0}^{Width} x[k]g[2n-k] \tag{9.2}$$

$$y_{high}[n] = (x \times h)[n] = \sum_{n=0}^{Height} x[k]h[2n-k] \tag{9.3}$$

As illustrated in Figure 9.4(a), application of the DWT to each row results in generation of two subsampled images. Each image has the same height as the original image, but half the width. By placing these two images next to one another, the resulting image is equal to the size of the original image. The same sampling mechanism could now be applied in vertical direction, considering each column of pixel values as discrete signal x. This results in generation of four sub-bands. Each sub-band is a subsample of the original input and is obtained using a different filtering mechanism. If more subsamples are required, we could apply the DWT to any of the sub-bands hierarchically. In this work, we have used seven iterations, hence, we have applied a second transformation to the LL sub-band to generate four level-2 sub-bands. Figure 9.4(b) shows the two resulting sub-bands by applying 2-level DWT to a dog image.

A high-level representation of envisioned iterative learning algorithm fed by DWT is illustrated in Figure 9.5. Each iteration is a uCNN, which takes a new DWT sub-band as its input and refines the confidence of learning network. DWT, being a convolutional filter, could be readily computed using processing elements in CNN processing engine of interest or could be provided directly to each uCNN.

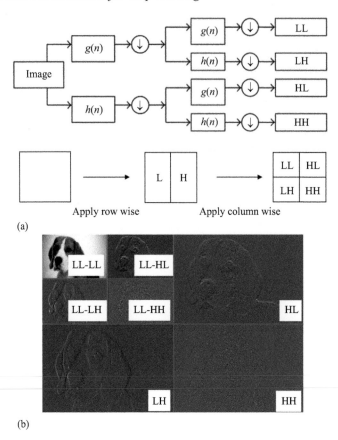

(a)

(b)

Figure 9.4   (a) DWT filter structure (b) sub-bands generated from a 2-level 2-dimensional Haar discrete wavelet transformation (DWT) of an input image

The iterative transformation of learning algorithm has many advantages: it could be terminated as soon as a uCNN produces the desired confidence level. Furthermore, iterations could be avoided if the first uCNN detection confidence is below a certain threshold signifying no contextually significant input. And confidence could be improved by moving to the next iteration, if the current measure of confidence remains between demarcated thresholds, aiding the rise or decline of classification confidence.

Figure 9.6 shows the decomposition of the *i*th uCNN. The Concat layer in Figure 9.6 fuses the *Ofmaps* of the last CONV layer in the current iteration with the *Ofmaps* of the last CONV layers from previous iterations. Note that the number of *Ofmaps* which are processed at any given CONV layer in each uCNN is considerably smaller than that of original network. Hence, the computational complexity of each uCNN is considerably smaller than that of AlexNet.

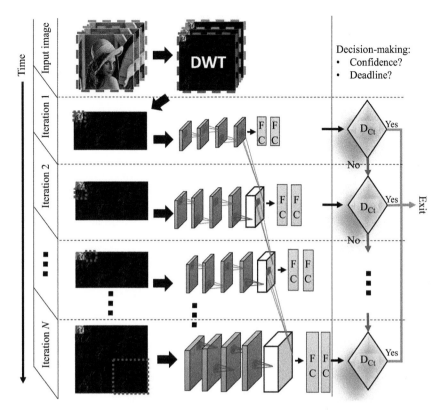

Figure 9.5   Iterative CNN (ICNN) general architecture where each uCNN is fed by features extracted from its previous uCNN, and a DW sub-band generated from DWT transformation of the input image

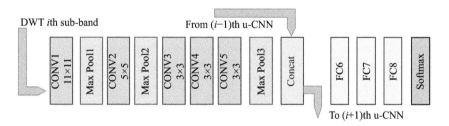

Figure 9.6   The architecture of the ith uCNN for the iterative AlexNet. Note that the first uCNN receives no data from the previous iteration and the last passes no data to the next iteration

9.4.1   Case study: iterative AlexNet

ICNN was implemented to generate an iterative version of AlexNet. Note that the size of the convolutions remains the same for all the layers of each iteration and they are identical to the size of the convolutions in the original AlexNet. However, the number of channels has been changed. Moreover, the size of the images has changed, as the input is being fed by the reduced size DWT transforms rather than the original images.

The significant difference between the iterative version of AlexNet and the original AlexNet is that the number of output channels is significantly lower in each uCNN.

9.5   ICNN training schemes

Training of the ICNN was completed in multiple steps. In each training step, the weights were initialized from a Gaussian distribution with zero mean and a standard deviation of 0.01. Each training step is started with a learning rate of 0.01. The learning rate is then reduced by $2\times$ every 20-epoch until the learning rate was as low as 10^{-6}. By one-epoch, we refer to one pass of all the 1.2 million images in ImageNet; however, for data augmentation purposes, every few epochs in the order of the images were modified, the image crops were altered and horizontal mirror of the images was used. To train the network, Tesla K80 GPUs were deployed.

When training the ICNN, two different training policies could be adopted. In the first method, the iterations are trained in sequence and in the second method, all iterations are trained in parallel. Each training process, the implications of each training approach, and the trade-offs for adopting one training approach vs. other are discussed next.

9.5.1   Sequential training

The first training method introduced is a multistep training process carried out sequentially. In this approach, the first uCNN network is separated and its weights are trained as described in Section 9.10.1. Starting from second iteration and moving up, each uCNN is then trained without changing the filter weights in the previous iterations. When training the ith uCNN (uCNN[i]), this training constraint is enforced by keeping the learning rate of convolutional layers in uCNN[1]-uCNN[$i-1$] equal to zero. Hence, the weights in the previous iterations are only used during forward propagation of error during the training process, without affecting the back propagation's update process.

9.5.2   Parallel training

The second training method is a two-step training process. In the first step, the FC layers of the intermediate iterations are removed, and only the FC layers of the last iteration which combine the features from the last CONV layer of all iterations are kept. The resulting network, which is the last iteration of ICNN, is trained first using the training process described earlier, yielding the weights for the FC layer of the last iterations, and CONV layers of *all* the iterations (Figure 9.7).

In the second step, the FC layers in all other iterations are added to construct parallel networks for the rest of the iterations. Subsequently, the weights in all the CONV layers are kept constant by setting their learning rate to zero, and the

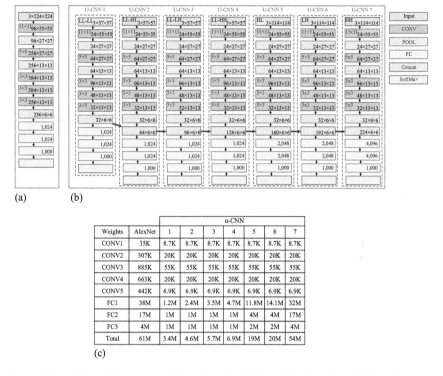

(a)   (b)

		u-CNN						
Weights	AlexNet	1	2	3	4	5	6	7
CONV1	35K	8.7K	8.7K	8.7K	8.7K	8.7K	8.7K	8.7K
CONV2	307K	20K	20K	20K	20K	20K	20K	20K
CONV3	885K	55K	55K	55K	55K	55K	55K	55K
CONV4	663K	20K	20K	20K	20K	20K	20K	20K
CONV5	442K	6.9K	6.9K	6.9K	6.9K	6.9K	6.9K	6.9K
FC1	38M	1.2M	2.4M	3.5M	4.7M	11.8M	14.1M	32M
FC2	17M	1M	1M	1M	1M	4M	4M	17M
FC3	4M	1M	1M	1M	1M	2M	2M	4M
Total	61M	3.4M	4.6M	5.7M	6.9M	19M	20M	54M

(c)

Figure 9.7   The architecture of (a) original CNN and (b) iterative CNN with seven iterations. (The numbers in the boxes on left show the filter sizes for CONV layers and the numbers on right show the number and size of Ofmaps.) (c) Comparing the number of required parameters for executing each CONV and FC layer in ICNN and AlexNet

weights in the FC layers of the intermediate iterations are trained in parallel. Note that back-propagation at this step does not update the filter values in the CONV layers and only the weights in FC layers are updated.

In terms of training time, the parallel training is considerably faster. Using a single Tesla K-80 GPU, the parallel training was concluded in 7 days, while the sequential training took about 3 weeks to conclude.

In terms of prediction accuracy, the parallel and sequential training introduce an interesting trade-off. Figure 9.8 shows the top-5 and top-1 accuracy of both sequential and parallel training. Figure 9.8(a) and (c) captures the results for only one crop. It should be noted that to increase the prediction accuracy during the inference phase, rather than feeding only one image to the network, various works [3–6] extract five crops from images (four corner crops and one center crop), along with their horizontal mirrors (ten image crops in total), calculate the average of the output of softmax layer from all ten crops and conclude the classification. To make a fair comparison with related work, in Figure 9.8(b) and (d), the results for the average of ten crops are depicted.

As illustrated in Figure 9.8, sequential training provides higher accuracy in early iterations and has a front-loaded accuracy gain, which is advantageous for low-power and real-time systems that could benefit from improved accuracy with low delay.

On the other hand, the parallel training suffers from lower classification accuracy in earlier iterations while gaining a higher accuracy in the last iteration(s). Based on Figure 9.8, the difference between the accuracy of the two approaches is more significant in both the early iterations and the latter ones. To get a better insight on the difference between the two training scheme, Figure 9.9 shows the growth of the top-5 accuracy in percentage. Since the parallel approach incurs lower and higher accuracy

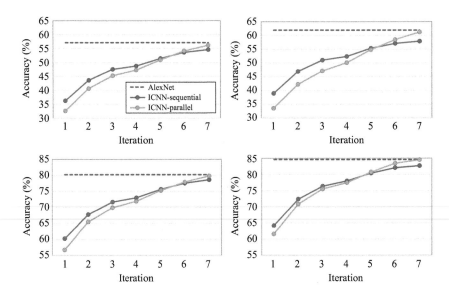

Figure 9.8 *AlexNet vs. iterative AlexNet using (a) top-1 accuracy with one crop,*
           (b) top-1 accuracy with average of ten crops, (c) top-5 accuracy with
           one crop and (d) top-5 accuracy with average of ten crops

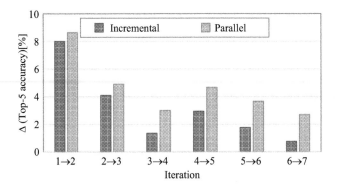

Figure 9.9 *Increase in the top-5 accuracy of ICNN (a) sequential and (b) parallel*

in the first and last iterations, respectively, parallel training covers a larger range of accuracy values, and each iteration contributes more significantly to the accuracy.

Depending on accuracy, latency and power requirements of the hosting hardware (or application) when working on a batch or stream of images, one training process may become more appealing than the other.

9.6 Complexity analysis

As mentioned in the previous section, the number of *Ofmaps* in each u-CNN is considerably reduced with respect to the original CNN. Figure 9.10 shows the number of FLOPs for a forward pass of the iterative AlexNet per image at each iteration.

It should be noted that after the first convolution, all the CONV and FC layers in AlexNet are grouped (group=2), where the first half of the filters are only connected to the first half of the input channels and the second half only connected to the second half. This reduces the number of multiplications by a factor of 2. The grouping convention of AlexNet has been taken into account for the calculations of FLOP count in Figure 9.7. The figure shows that even if executed to the last iteration, ICNN still has a lower computational complexity (needing 30% fewer FLOPs) than the original AlexNet. On top of this, many images are detected at earlier iterations, removing the need to process subsequent uCNNs. This further reduces the total FLOP count for a large number of images. More specifically, images detected in iterations 1, 2, 3, 4, 5 and 6, respectively, require $12.2\times, 6.1\times, 4\times, 3\times, 2.3\times$ and $1.8\times$ fewer FLOPs when compared to the original AlexNet.

As stated previously, the computation intensive layers in AlexNet are CONV layers, and ICNN considerably reduces the required FLOP count. However, when it comes to the parameter count, in AlexNet, the largest number of parameters is associated with FC layers. This problem, as illustrated in Figure 9.7(c), is exacerbated for the Iterative AlexNet, where FC layers are repeated for each uCNN. Although the input *Ifmaps* to the FC layers in each uCNN is smaller than that of AlexNet, repetition

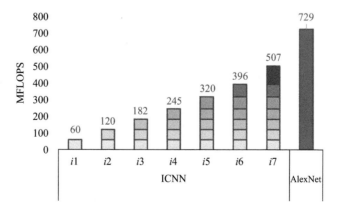

Figure 9.10   The FLOP count comparison of iterative-AlexNet (ICNN representation) vs. AlexNet

of FC layers increases the number of parameters for the iterative representation of AlexNet. To remedy this, the size of FC layers in uCNNs could be reduced to smaller sizes (e.g., 1,024 or 2,048) at the expense of lower classification accuracy in these iterations. In addition, the size of parameters in these layers could be reduced to have a fewer number of bits. Note that this is an AlexNet model-specific problem and ICNN representation of other popular networks could experience significant reduction in both parameter and FLOP counts. For example, ICNN model of ResNet will require far fewer parameters for the final classification as it only has a single FC layer.

Additionally, for resource-contained applications not all the parameters of the network are kept in the memory. Assuming that the processing unit only keeps the parameters needed for the current CONV or FC layer in the memory, the maximum memory footprint for keeping network parameters in iterative-AlexNet is reduced by 12%. It should be noted that while this analysis is carried out for AlexNet, the same trend is expected with iterative version of other CNN architectures.

9.7   Visualization

The rate of improvement in the prediction accuracy in each iteration of ICNN depends on the network being able to learn distinct features in each iteration and leverage all features learned in the previous iterations. To illustrate how ICNN learns distinct features in each iteration, visualization techniques are used to present the features learned in different iterations.

9.7.1   Background on CNN visualization

With the increasing deployment of CNN for classification, various works have focused on visualizing these networks to understand how they produce such accurate results. More specifically, it is most beneficial to visualize which features trigger each neuron. Understanding what each neuron is responsible for helps enhancing the performance of the overall network.

The easiest way to visualize a neuron's function is by searching for input image samples in the dataset that triggers the strongest response in a given neuron [32]. Another approach is to use deconvolutional networks to project the feature activations back to the input pixel [33]. For this purpose, deconvolutional networks construct layers from the image upward in an unsupervised fashion. A deconvolution simply reverses the forward and backward passes of convolution [34]. In [7], deconvolutional networks were used to develop a technique that reveals the input stimuli that excite individual feature maps at various layers in the model. Since then, various works have used the deconvolution networks for semantic segmentation [35], flow estimation [36] and generative modeling [37].

9.7.2   Visualizing features learned by ICNN

In this work, we use the deconvolutional networks to demonstrate how hidden convolution layers of each iteration extract features distinct from other iterations. In each iteration, as illustrated in Figure 9.6, CONV1 consists of 24 feature maps. Figure 9.11 captures the top 9 activations for the 24 feature maps of each iterations. As illustrated,

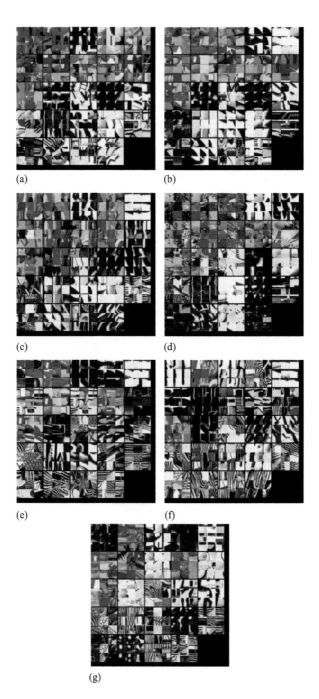

(a)   (b)

(c)   (d)

(e)   (f)

(g)

Figure 9.11   Visualization of features in a fully trained model for layers CONV1 for
iterations (a) 1, (b) 2, (c) 3, (d) 4, (e) 5, (f) 6 and (g) 7. The figure
shows the top 9 activations for all 24 feature maps across the
validation data. For each feature map, we illustrate the image patches
that cause high activations. Note that while some filters in each
iteration are activated with the same features as previous iterations,
still many of the feature maps are activated by new features in
each iteration

while some feature maps from different iterations are triggered by somewhat similar image patches, most of them differ substantially. This observation is more significant for the next CONV layers (CONV2).

Figures 9.12 and 9.13 depict the top 9 activations for all 64 feature maps of CONV2 and 96 feature maps of CONV3 layers, respectively, in all iterations. Each figure shows the reconstructed patterns from the training set that triggers the

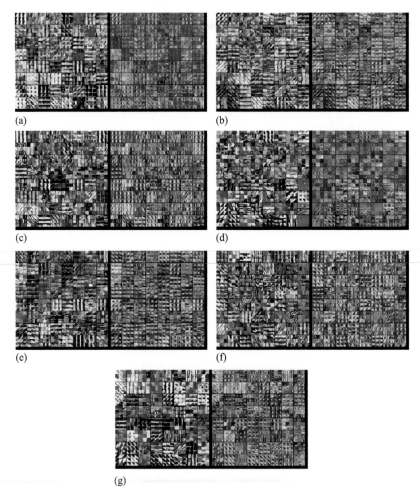

(a)   (b)

(c)   (d)

(e)   (f)

(g)

Figure 9.12   Visualization of features in a fully trained model for layers CONV2 of for iterations (a) 1, (b) 2, (c) 3, (d) 4, (e) 5, (f) 6 and (g) 7. The figure shows the top 9 activations for all 64 feature maps of CONV2 layer across the validation data, projected down to pixel space using deconvolutional network approach. The reconstructed patterns from the validation set which cause high activations in a given feature map are depicted on the right, and the corresponding image patches are depicted on the left

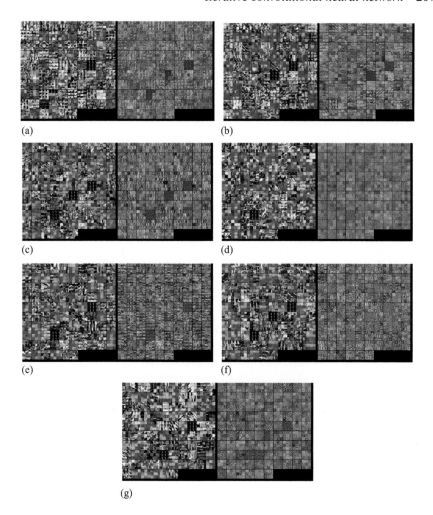

(a)

(b)

(c)

(d)

(e)

(f)

(g)

Figure 9.13   *Visualization of features in a fully trained model for layers CONV3 of for iterations (a) 1, (b) 2, (c) 3, (d) 4, (e) 5, (f) 6 and (g) 7. The figure shows the top 9 activations for all 96 feature maps of CONV3 layer across the validation data, projected down to pixel space using deconvolutional network approach. The reconstructed patterns from the validation set which cause high activations in a given feature map are depicted on the right, and the corresponding image patches are depicted on the left*

highest filter response in a given feature map on the left, and the corresponding image patch that triggered the response on the right.

The extracted features are drastically different in the same CONV layer in different iterations. The ability to extract different features in different iterations, and ability of the ICNN to combine these features after last CONV layer of each iteration are the reasons why the accuracy of each iteration increases.

We use the deconvolutional networks to demonstrate how hidden convolution layers of each iteration extract features distinct from other iterations. In each iteration, as illustrated in Figure 9.6, CONV1 consists of 24 feature maps. Figure 9.11 captures the top 9 activations for the 24 feature maps of each iteration. As illustrated, while some feature maps from different iterations are triggered by somewhat similar image patches, most of them differ substantially. This observation is more significant for the next CONV layers (CONV2).

Figures 9.12 and 9.13 depict the top 9 activations for all 64 feature maps of CONV2 and 96 feature maps of CONV3 layers, respectively, in all iterations. Each figure shows the reconstructed patterns from the training set that trigger the highest filter response in a given feature map on the left, and the corresponding image patch that triggered the response on the right.

The extracted features are drastically different in the same CONV layer in different iterations. The ability to extract different features in different iterations, and ability of the ICNN to combine these features after last CONV layer of each iteration are the reasons why the accuracy of each iteration increases.

It should be noted that the networks in Figures 9.11 and 9.12 are trained with the sequential approach. To allow faster training, instead of initiating the weights from Gaussian distribution, we initiated the weights in the CONV layer of each iteration to the values in the corresponding CONV layer of the previous iteration (for the first iteration, the weights were initiated with Gaussian distribution). As a result, the patterns identified in each iteration for some feature maps are somewhat correlated albeit, different. See the first feature map in Figure 9.12 (top left 3×3 image). This feature map is triggered for image patches with vertical, diagonal and blurrier vertical lines in iteration 1, 2 and 3, respectively. After the 4th iteration, the same feature map index starts identifying completely different patterns, which is indicative of the evolving nature of ICNN.

9.8   Contextual awareness in ICNN

Real-time application of deep learning algorithms is often hindered by high computational complexity and frequent memory accesses. Network pruning is a promising technique to solve this problem [38]. The network can be pruned by learning only the important connections. That is, if the weight of a connection is less than a threshold, the connection is dropped [39,40]. This approach is previously deployed in the training phase of CNN by discarding negligible weight values. However, ICNN enables us to apply the pruning at run-time. This capability is the result of having an early classification that provides ICNN with a hint to avoid computation related to classes that are least probable.

Upon completion of the first uCNN, ICNN develops a form of contextual awareness as its first FC classifier outputs the probability of various classes with respect to an input image. We explore how this feature may be used to reduce the computational complexity of CONV or FC layers in the next iterations based on the class probabilities. To this end, we compare the class probabilities from various iterations to understand how the predictions and class probabilities derived in each iteration relate to the ones in the next iterations.

For example, in ICNN, as illustrated in Figure 9.14, after executing each uCNN (each iteration) the class probabilities area biased, dividing the classes into two sets of probable and improbable classes. Note that with each iteration, the set of probable classes reduces, as classification becomes more accurate. Hence, the probability of classes could be used as an effective measure to reduce computation in the future iterations by avoiding computation related to improbable classes altogether.

9.8.1 Prediction rank

We introduce *prediction rank* (PR) as an indicator of prediction accuracy of a model for each image. Consider an image with class label α. After executing a uCNN, all the class probabilities are sorted in descending order. The location of the class α in the sorted array of class probabilities is called PR. Needless to mention, PR can be any value from 1 to 1k, with 1 and 1k indicating the highest and the lowest image detection accuracy, respectively. If statistical analysis of the dataset for class α shows that PR is always smaller than L in all iterations, where ($1 \leq L \leq 1k$), limiting the number of computed class probabilities in the ICNN to L instead of 1k will have no impact on the probability of detection of class α. On the other hand, if the number of computed classes (i.e., L) is chosen smaller than PR variation for class α, then by pruning the computation for class α we will end up with MC. Expanding this to all classes, the probability of MC conditioned on pruning the classes to those with $PR \leq L$ is given by

$$P(MC|P_{th} = L) = \sum_{i=1}^{1,000} P(C[i])P(PR(C[i]) > L) \tag{9.4}$$

In the previous equation, the P_{th} is the pruning threshold, $C[i]$ is the ith class, $PR(c[i])$ is the PR for $C[i]$ and L is the chosen limit for pruning. For obtaining the probability $P(PR(C[i]) > L)$, we define the decision function D as

$$D(\alpha^{C[i]}(j), L) = \begin{cases} 1, & \text{if } PR(\alpha^{C[i]}(j)) > L \\ 0, & \text{else} \end{cases} \tag{9.5}$$

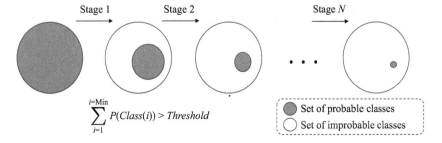

Figure 9.14   Reduction in size of probable classes in each iteration

In the previous equation, $\alpha^{C[i]}(j)$ is the jth image member of class $C[i]$. If we define $S[i]$ as the number/size of images in the dataset (or expected number of images in the batch) that belongs to class $C[i]$, $P(PR(C[i]) > L)$ is computed as follows:

$$P(PR(C(i)) > L) = \frac{\sum_{i=1}^{S[i]} D(\alpha^{C[i]}(j), L)}{S[i]} \tag{9.6}$$

By using (9.4), the pruning threshold L could be chosen to set the probability of MC due to pruning to a desired value. The higher the value of L, the higher the classification accuracy, but at the cost of higher computational complexity. The value L could reduce from iteration to next iteration, making the pruning more aggressive as the accuracy of classification increases.

In order to get a sense on the impact of choosing a value for L, for each class we find the mean (μ) and variation (σ) of PR based on all the data in validation set.

Figure 9.15 shows the mean (PR_μ) and variation (PR_σ) of PR for all 1k classes sorted in descending order of PR_μ at the first iteration. Assuming a normal distribution, 95% of images of each class will have a PR below $PR_\mu + 2 \times PR_\sigma$. In Figure 9.15, $PR_\mu + 2 \times PR_\sigma$ of none of the classes exceeds 500, suggesting that by removing 50% of classes ($P_{th} = 500$) the prediction accuracy does not drop beyond 5% for any of the classes.

Figure 9.16(a) and (b) shows the maximum of PR_μ and $PR_\mu + 2 \times PR_\sigma$ among all classes for all the iterations. The maximum of $PR_\mu + 2 \times PR_\sigma$ is reduced as ICNN moves to the next iteration, indicating that in subsequent iterations, the pruning policy could be more aggressive. Note that based on the eliminated classes, the computational complexity of the next iterations is reduced by pruning the neurons in the FC layers and/or the filters in the CONV layers, which are highly correlated to classes with close to zero probabilities.

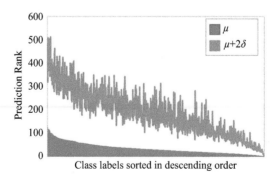

Figure 9.15   *Prediction rank (PR_μ and $PR_\mu + 2 \times PR_\sigma$) for various classes at iteration 1*

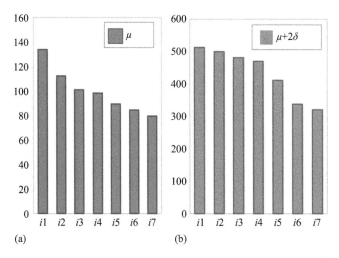

Figure 9.16   Prediction rank (PR$_\mu$ and PR$_\mu$ + 2 × PR$_\sigma$ for various classes at iteration 1): (a) maximum PR$_\mu$ among all classes in each iteration and (b) maximum PR$_\mu$ + 2 × PR$_\sigma$ among all classes in each iteration

9.8.2   Pruning neurons in FC layers

Let us sort the classes probabilities for each image in descending order. The rank of a class is the location of the class in the sorted array. When we set the pruning threshold (P_{th}) to value L in a given iteration, all classes with ranks greater than L are eliminated in the next iteration. Hence, computation of FC layer for these classes could be skipped. This results in significant reduction in required FC computation, and elimination of memory transfer of parameters related to the classification of eliminated classes.

For example, let us consider the input image to be classified as a tabby cat image. The first iteration of ICNN yields high probability values for tabby cat, Egyptian cat, Persian cat and possibly other animals, while the probability values associated with other categories (e.g., various types of vehicles) are close to zero. Hence, in the FC layer of next uCNN, the neurons for other low probability categories are disabled and those classes are eliminated.

9.8.3   Pruning filters in CONV layers

In addition to eliminating neurons in the FC layers, CONV filters in final layer(s) can also be eliminated. To this end, for each class, we carry out a statistical analysis on the 1.2 million images in the training set. In this study, we identify the classes that are least affected by elimination of each CONV filters at each iteration. When we set the pruning threshold (P_{th}) to value L in a given iteration, all classes with ranks greater than L are eliminated in the subsequent iteration. Hence, the required CONV filters are only those needed by remaining classes, and the computation of other filters could be skipped.

It should be noted that while filter pruning has been a well-known approach for reducing the computational complexity of CNN [38–40], ICNN allows the pruning to be carried out based on the feedback from previous iterations. An ignorant pruning approach removes a number of filters that least affect the overall accuracy; however, context-aware pruning allows us to remove the filters that least affect the top-P_{th} classes of the previous iteration, promising an increased accuracy.

9.9   Policies for exploiting energy-accuracy trade-off in ICNN

The iterative transformation of learning algorithm can be exploited to yield the highest accuracy while meeting hard deadlines or create an efficient trade-off between computational complexity and accuracy. To this end, we investigate the following policies to explore the benefits of ICNN and its trade-offs in terms of computational complexity (thus energy consumption) and accuracy.

9.9.1   Dynamic deadline (DD) policy for real-time applications

Many real-time applications require fast and deadline-driven computations to operate safely and correctly. To speed up the CNN-based classifier, one could adapt more powerful resources and benefit from higher parallelism. However, such solutions are extremely expensive in terms of hardware cost and energy requirements. ICNN, on the other hand, provides a cost and energy-effective solution for real-time applications. Each uCNN in ICNN is able to produce a classification allowing early exit upon reaching a scheduled deadline. For the deadline-driven applications, the ICNN classifier processes the input image up until the uCNN iteration, in which the scheduled deadline is reached, and subsequently a classification are made. Consequently, the accuracy of the detection and computational complexity is dependent on the time-budget and the number of iterations that can be completed within the scheduled deadline. Note that in this mode of operation, only FC layer(s) in the last processed uCNN iteration are required to make a classification decision, and the FC layers in the previous iterations for availability of computation-time-budget are skipped. This is due to the fact that for the deadline-driven applications, we rely solely on the classification results from the last processed iteration.

Algorithm 1 captures the implementation of DD policy. In this algorithm, N marks the number of ICNN iterations. $uCNN_{CONV}(i, img)$ invokes the convolution layers in the ith uCNN with img as input, returning *Ofmaps* from the last CONV layer (Of_μ) and the elapsed time (t_{CONV}). The *Ofmaps* are concatenated with the *Ofmaps* from the previous iterations. Subsequently, t_{CONV} is compared to the deadline, t_D, and if lower with a t_{mrg} margin, the next uCNN is invoked. The $t_{mrg}[i + 1]$ accounts for the projected time of the next iteration of uCNN. Upon reaching the deadline, $uCNN_{FC}(i, Of)$ invokes the FC layers of the ith uCNN producing a vector of probabilities P_r, one for each of 1k labels.

Algorithm 1: Dynamic deadline (DD)

$Of \leftarrow []$;
$t_{mrg}[i] \leftarrow iteration\_time\_budget$;
for $i = 1$ to $N - 1$ **do**
    $t_{CONV}, Of_\mu \leftarrow uCNN_{CONV}(i, img)$;
    $Of \leftarrow Of_\mu + Of$;
    if $(t_{CONV} + t_{mrg}[i + 1]) < t_D$ **then**
        exit;
    end if
end for
$\bar{P}_r \leftarrow uCNN_{FC}(i, Of)$;

9.9.2 Thresholding policy (TP) for dynamic complexity reduction

Using this policy, the ICNN terminates as soon as a uCNN produces the desired classification confidence. The classification confidence is calculated by summing the probabilities of top-C (e.g., $C = 5$) suggested classes. Note that, in this approach, the FC layers of the previous uCNNs are not skipped, as the calculations for classification confidence rely on the output of the FC layers. When processing a batch of images, while the first iteration in ICNN may yield a high confidence for a test image, it might yield a lower confidence for another test image. The ICNN, in this case, terminates the classification after the first iteration for the first image but proceeds to the next iteration for the second image. This decision is made dynamically based on a predefined detection confidence-threshold (D_{Ct}).

Algorithm 2 implements the thresholding policy (TP). The $uCNN(i, \bar{C}_L, img)$ function invokes the ith uCNN with img as input, requesting classification result for all class labels in the $\bar{C}_L$ vector, and produces a vector of probabilities $\bar{P}_r$, one for each label in $\bar{C}_L$ which contains all 1,000 labels. After each uCNN, the sum of top-5 probabilities ($\sum_{k=1}^{5} \bar{P}_r[k]$) is compared with detection confidence threshold ($\bar{D}_{Ct}[i]$), and if greater, the image is classified. Note that some of the images never reach a

---

Algorithm 2: Thresholding policy (TP)

1: **for** $i = 1$ to $N - 1$ **do**
2:     $\bar{P}_r \leftarrow uCNN(i, \bar{C}_L, img)$;
3:     Sort_descending($\bar{P}_r$);
4:     **if** $((\sum_{k=1}^{5} \bar{P}_r[k]) > \bar{D}_{Ct}[i])$ **then**
5:         exit;
6:     **end if**
7: **end for**
8: $\bar{P}_r \leftarrow uCNN(N, C_L, img)$;

---

classification confidence above D_{Ct}. For these images, the results of the classification in the last iteration are used.

In this approach, classification for various images is terminated in different uCNN iterations. Thus, the total complexity of classification dynamically varies for each image. Moreover, the number of parameters required for images classified in early iterations significantly drops, which directly results in reduction in the number of memory accesses, required memory footprint and energy consumption. Note that the D_{Ct} values could be different for each iteration of the ICNN allowing ICNN to exercise complicated TPs. We explore variants of TP as explained next.

9.9.2.1   Fixed thresholding policy

In the fixed TP, a fixed value for D_{Ct} is used across all uCNNs.

9.9.2.2   Variable thresholding policy

In variable TP, the confidence threshold value for different iterations is varied.

9.9.3   Context-aware pruning policy

Based on the contextual awareness obtained upon completion of the initial uCNNs, CONV and FC pruning policies are beneficial.

9.9.3.1   Context-aware pruning policy for FC layer

Context-aware pruning policy (CAPP) for FC layer modifies the FC layer in the next uCNN classifier to skip the computation and memory transfer of parameters related to the classification of classes with very low probabilities.

Based on the discussion in Section 9.8.2, Algorithm 3 introduces the implementation of CAPP for FC neurons. In the first uCNN, C_L contains all 1,000 labels. The $uCNN(i, \bar{C}_L, img)$ function invokes the ith uCNN for an input img returning a vector of probabilities $\bar{P}_r$ that store one probability for each label in $\bar{C}_L$. Subsequently, the less-probable classes are pruned based on pruning threshold stored in pruning policy vector $\bar{P}_{th}$. For instance, $P_{th}[i] = 100$ results in only choosing the 100 labels and disables all other neurons in the FC layer of the $uCNN(i + 1)$ associated with the eliminated labels.

Algorithm 3: Context aware pruning policy for FC layer ($CAPP_{FC}$)

1: **for** $i = 1$ to $N - 1$ **do**
2:      $\bar{P}_r \leftarrow uCNN(i, \bar{C}_L, img)$;
3:      Sort_descending($\bar{P}_r$);
4:      $\bar{C}_L \leftarrow \bar{C}_L[1 : \bar{P}_{th}[i]]$;
5: **end for**
6: $\bar{P}_r \leftarrow uCNN(N, \bar{C}_L, img)$;

Since the compute-intensive parts of the CNN architectures are the CONV layers, the pruning slightly reduces the computational complexity as it only affects the FC layers. However, it considerably reduces the number of weights needed to be moved to the memory. CAPP is yielding a dynamic trade-off between accuracy, the required memory footprint and computational complexity. Pruning a larger number of classes results in higher complexity and memory footprint reduction while negatively affecting the accuracy. It should be noted that, unlike the thresholding scheme, the pruning scheme yields the same computational complexity for all the images.

9.9.3.2 Context-aware pruning policy for CONV layer

Visualization of the ICNN filters by using deconvolution networks as described in [7] makes it possible to identify and remove trained CONV filters that are closely associated with the classification of low-probability classes, extending the pruning feature into CONV layers. The pruning feature based on filter visualization is explored in Algorithm 4.

Algorithm 4: Context-aware pruning policy for CONV layer ($CAPP_{CONV}$)

1: Pre-Process:Obtain $\bar{Pre}(i, cnv, c)$
2: **for** $i = 1$ to $N - 1$ **do**
3:      $\bar{P}_r \leftarrow uCNN(i, \bar{C}_L, img)$;
4:      Sort_descending($\bar{P}_r$);
5:      **for** $cnv=1$ in $CONV_{lst}$ **do**
6:          $Fltr_{rem} = \{\}$
7:          **for** $c = 1$ to $P_{th}[i]$ **do**
8:              $Fltr_{rem}+ = \bar{Pre}(i, cnv, c)[1 : rm]$
9:          **end for**
10:          $Fltr_{rem} \leftarrow Maj(Fltrrem, rm)$
11:          Update($uCNN, i, $ cnv, $Fltr_{rem}$)
12:      **end for**
13: **end for**
14: $\bar{P}_r \leftarrow uCNN(N, \bar{C}_L, img)$;

Algorithm 4 requires a statistical analysis by preprocessing a large dataset (i.e., 1.2 images in the training set). Based on this analysis, for each iteration, target CONV layer and class, a vector is calculated, in which filters are arranged based on accuracy loss due to their removal from the network in an ascending order. $\bar{Pre}(i, cnv, c)$ shows the preprocessing vector for the ith iteration, where cnv refers to the target CONV layer and c refers to class label. Thus, the removal of the filter associated with the first argument in $\bar{Pre}(i, cnv, c)$ has the least effect on overall accuracy of class c. $CONV_{lst}$ is the list of CONV layers targeted for filter pruning. The variable rm is the number of filters to be removed from each CONV layer.

In the ith iteration, the filters least affecting the top-P_{th} classes are gathered in $Fltr_{rem}$ determining the candidate filters for removal. Subsequently, the majority function *Maj(Fltrrem, rm)* returns *rm* most repeated arguments in $Fltr_{rem}$. This allows us to find the union of filters that least affect the top-$P_{th}[i]$ classes in the *i*th iteration. Subsequently, *Update(uCNNi, cnv, Fltr_{rem})* updates the *i*th uCNN by removing the *rm* filters in $FLtr_{rem}$ from *cnv*th CONV.

9.9.4 Pruning and thresholding hybrid policy

The pruning and thresholding hybrid policy (PTHP) scheme takes advantage of both early termination in the thresholding scheme and the pruning of the FC layers in CAPP. Two variants of PTHP are studied.

9.9.4.1 Fixed percentage PTHP

Algorithm 5 shows the first studied hybrid policy. *uCNN(i, C_L, img)* invokes the *top-*5 uCNN with *img* as input, requesting classification result for all class labels in the C_L vector, and produces a vector of probabilities P_r, one for each label in C_L. In the first uCNN, $\bar{C}_L$ contains all 1,000 labels. After each uCNN, the top-5 confidence ($\sum_{k=1}^{5} \bar{P}_r[k]$) is compared with $D_{Ct}[i]$. If confidence is greater, the image is classified. Otherwise, a number of classes are pruned based on pruning policy $P_{th}[i]$ defined for each iteration. For example, *Prune[i]* = 100 results in choosing only the top 100 labels and disables all other neurons in the FC layer of next uCNN related to eliminated labels.

Algorithm 5: Fixed-percentage pruning and thresholding ($PTHP_{FP}$) policy

---

1: **for** $i = 1$ to $N - 1$ **do**
2:     $\bar{P}_r \leftarrow uCNN(1, \bar{C}_L, img)$;
3:     Sort_descending($\bar{P}_r$);
4:     **if** $((\sum_{k=1}^{5} \bar{P}_r[k]) > D_{Ct}[i])$ **then**
5:         exit;
6:     **else**
7:         $\bar{C}_L \leftarrow \bar{C}_L[1 : \bar{P}_{th}[i]]$;
8:         $\bar{P}_r \leftarrow uCNN(i, \bar{C}_L, img)$;
9:     **end if**
10: **end for**
11: $\bar{P}_r \leftarrow uCNN(N, \bar{C}_L, img)$;

9.9.4.2 Confidence-tracking PTHP

Algorithm 6 illustrates the confidence-tracking pruning and thresholding hybrid policy ($PTHP_{CT}$) policy. In the first uCNN, the probability for all classes (all labels) is computed. In the while loop, if top-5 confidence is above the detection threshold $D_{Ct}[i]$, the classification is terminated. Otherwise, based on the value of a *saturation threshold* $S_{th}[i]$, a number of labels are selected for further processing in the next layer. The selected classes are the minimum number of labels with an accumulated probability of no less than $S_{th}[i]$. In this algorithm, $\bar{CC}_L$ is the shrunk version of $\bar{C}_L$ that only contains the labels of interest.

Algorithm 6: Confidence-tracking pruning and thresholding (PTHP$_{CT}$) policy

---

> $\bar{P}_r \leftarrow uCNN(1, \bar{C}_L, img);$
> **for** $i = 1$ to $N - 1$ **do**
> > Sort_descending($\bar{P}_r$);
> > **if** $((\sum_{k=1}^{5} \bar{P}_r[k]) > D_{\bar{C}t}[i])$ **then**
> > > exit;
> >
> > **else**
> > > $Sum = 0,\ \bar{CC}_L = [],\ \text{label}=1;$
> > > **while** $Sum < S_{th}[i]$ **do**
> > > > $Sum+ = \bar{P}_r[label];$
> > > > $\bar{CC}_L[label] = \bar{C}_L[label];$
> > > > label++;
> > >
> > > **end while**
> > > $\bar{P}_r \leftarrow uCNN(i + 1, \bar{CC}_L, img);$
> >
> > **end if**
>
> **end for**

9.9.5   *Variable and dynamic bit-length selection*

There are two general approaches to convert a neural network to fixed point. One is to train a network with fixed-point constraints [22,23]. While this approach yields high accuracy, it requires tight integration between the network design, training and implementation, which is not always feasible. The other approach is to convert a trained network into a fixed point model. This approach is more suited for applications where a pretrained network is used with no access to the original training data [15].

Moreover, while the first approach focuses to finding an optimal solution, the goal of ICNN is to be a dynamic solution, which can both yield high-confidence results at expense of higher run-time and energy consumption or yield faster fairly lower-confidence results with low-energy consumption. Moreover, the fixed-point conversion of ICNN is a solution to the large number of parameters requires by these types of networks.

In [24], a thorough exploration of optimal fixed point bit-width allocation across CNN layer shows without further training, a minimum of 16 bit-length is required for the parameters of the CNN to yield results with an accuracy comparable to single-precision floating point. Similar story applies to the MS-CNN; however, in the early iterations of MS-CNN, the network is less sensitive to quantization errors induced by fixed-point transformation. In addition, in the case of loss in accuracy, it could recover in the future iterations. This allows the quantization to be applied more aggressively in early iterations.

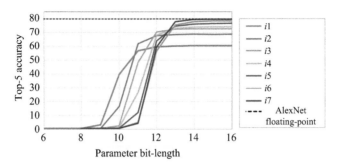

Figure 9.17   Sensitivity of top-5 accuracy in iterative AlexNet

Table 9.2   *Parameter size of variable bit-length conversion of iterative AlexNet vs. single precision AlexNet*

Iteration	i1	i2	i3	i4	i5	i6	i7	AlexNet
Parameter bit-length	11	11	12	13	14	15	16	32
Original parameter size (MB)	13.4	18.2	22.9	27.6	72.6	82	216	244
Updated parameter size (MB)	4.6	6.2	8.6	11.2	31.8	38.4	108	–

Figure 9.17 shows the sensitivity of accuracy of MS-CNN to the bit-length of the parameters at each iteration. At each iteration, the optimal bit-length is derived from a saturation point, after which increased bit-length does not enhance the accuracy. As shown in Figure 9.17, this saturation point is pushed to lower bit-lengths for earlier iterations. Hence, for MS-CNN, rather than selecting an optimal bit-length for the entire network, various subnetworks deploy different bit-lengths allowing further reduction in the number of parameters. Table 9.2 shows the size of parameters for various iterations of iterative AlexNet and a single-precision AlexNet. While the number of parameters required for iterative AlexNet is 80% higher than original AlexNet, variable bit-length selection for iterative AlexNet reduces its parameter size by more than 15%.

In addition to per-iteration variable bit-length adjustment, the contextual knowledge from early iterations allows the precision of parameters corresponding for classification of less probable classes to be reduced *dynamically*, allowing further flexibility in tuning MS-CNN to meet the requirements of larger set of applications.

9.10   ICNN implementation results

9.10.1   *Implementation framework*

An iterative version of AlexNet was designed to build a 1,000-class image classifier for the ImageNet dataset [29]. The iterative AlexNet was implemented in Caffe [41], a deep learning framework developed by Berkeley AI Research.

Following the methodology in [5] to solve the over-fitting problem, the training set was augmented by reshaping images to $3 \times 256 \times 256$ and extracting $3 \times 228 \times 228$ crops from each image (resulting in $(228 - 256 + 1)^2 = 841$ crops). Moreover, the horizontal mirrors of each crop were added to the dataset (a total of 1,682 crops per image).

To prepare the sub-band for the ICNN, a 2-level 2-D DWT was captured through the Haar filter [42] for each channel (i.e., R, G and B) of the images. The resulting sub-bands are four RGB images of size $3 \times 57 \times 57$ in smaller sub-bands (corresponding to LL-LL, LL-LH, LL-HL and LL-HH) and three RGB images of $3 \times 114 \times 114$ in larger sub-bands (corresponding to HL, LH and HH). The seven resulting sub-bands allow sampling of the input image by $7\times$, and as a result building the ICNN with seven iterations. To increase the number of iterations, the DWT depth can be increased or alternatively, DWT can be applied to the other sub-bands (LH, HL and HH).

The sub-bands are stored in a lightning memory-mapped database (LMDB) format [43], which is the database of choice when using large datasets. For the preprocessing and storage of images, several python package libraries, including LMDB, PyWavelets [44] and OpenCV, were used. Moreover, a mean image was calculated for each sub-band based on the training data to achieve normalization [45]. The mean images are subtracted from each image for all the sub-bands to ensure a zero mean for every feature pixel.

For training the ICNN, we initialize the weights from a Gaussian distribution with zero mean and a standard deviation of 0.01. We start each training step with a learning rate of 0.01.

For reporting the accuracy values, we evaluated the 50K images in the validation set of ImageNet repository. We use the FLOP count as an indicator of computational complexity (MFLOP is equivalent to Mega FLOP). The results for the implementation of policies introduced in this section is summarized next.

9.10.2 *Dynamic deadline policy for real-time applications*

Figure 9.18 shows the overall accuracy and FLOP count of each iteration when using DD policy. Each bar representing the FLOP count of an iteration accumulates the total FLOP count of its previous iteration with that of CONV and FC layer of current iteration. The figure shows that assuming a large time-budget, continuing the ICNN to the last iteration still results in lower computational complexity (38% lower than original AlexNet) with only a 1% reduction in the top-5 accuracy. Note that the reduction in FLOPs in last iterations of ICCN with *DD* policy is more significant that what was shown in Figure 9.10 for computational complexity. This is mainly a result of skipping the intermediate FC layers. On the other hand, assuming limited timing budget, a reliable classification decision could still be made in the early iterations with much lower computational cost. Thus, ICNN is no longer limited to a one-fits-all architecture and is allowed to make an efficient use of the resources to make the best prediction, based on the requirements of each application.

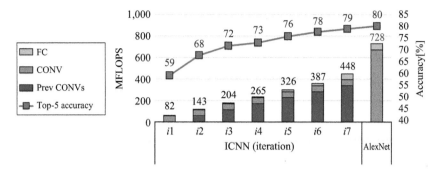

Figure 9.18   The FLOP count and accuracy for dynamic deadline policy

9.10.3   Thresholding policy for dynamic complexity reduction

9.10.3.1   Fixed thresholding policy

Figure 9.19 shows the total number of images classified up to each iteration and their top-5 score for various fixed D_{Ct} values. Each blue bar represents the number of classified images, and each green bar represents the number of correctly classified images. Hence, the difference between the height of blue and green bar is the number of incurred MCs. Each bar is divided into two segments. The first segment is accumulated number of classified images up to that iteration, and the second segment is the classifications being concluded in that iteration. The final bars on iteration 7 have an additional segment for *remaining* images that have not passed the classification threshold, however, are classified for lack of further iterations. For the *remaining* images, the top-5 classification accuracy is significantly lower than those with confidence values higher than the threshold. With increasing values of D_{Ct}, the number of these *remaining* images increases, pushing the classifier toward the last iteration and thus increasing the total FLOP count.

Figure 9.20 sums up the results for various D_{Ct} values, which shows that with each new iteration, the ICNN detects more images with high classification confidence. This is to be expected, as the last iterations combine a larger number of features in more complex architectures with a larger number of parameters, allowing a more accurate prediction model and thus classifying more images.

Moreover, by increasing the value of D_{Ct}, the number of images classified in early iterations decreases; however, the classification accuracy (correct label within top-5) increases. In Figure 9.19, this is illustrated by comparing the difference in the heights of *top-5* and *detected* bars at each iteration, where a larger delta means larger MC. More specifically, higher values of D_{Ct} enhance the accuracy at the expense of larger computation complexity.

Thus, an intelligent selection of D_{Ct} maintains a trade-off between accuracy and computational complexity. Note that training is oblivious to value of D_{Ct}, hence, the value of D_{Ct} could be tuned at run-time to dynamically control the trade-off between accuracy and computational complexity. Figure 9.20 illustrates this trade-off where

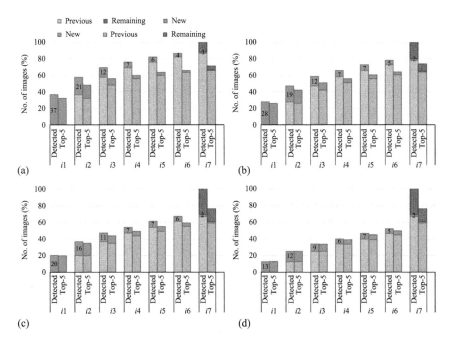

(a)

(b)

(c)

(d)

*Figure 9.19   Number of classified images and the number of classified images with
a correct label in the top-5 probabilities for various confidence
threshold (Dc$_t$): (a) Dc$_t$ = 0.6, (b) Dc$_t$ = 0.7, (c) Dc$_t$ = 0.8,
(d) Dc$_t$ = 0.9*

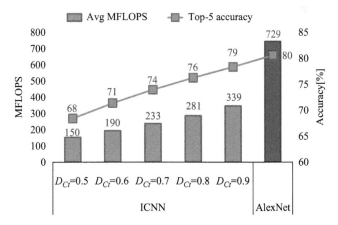

*Figure 9.20   The avg FLOP count for setting fix D$_{Ct}$ for all iterations and detecting
remaining images with original AlexNet*

the overall accuracy of ICNN, as well as the average number of FLOPs required to process the 50K images in the validation-set changes with the selection of D_{Ct} values (D_{Ct} is fixed across all uCNN layers). Interestingly, with a fixed confidence threshold of 0.9, the overall accuracy is the same as using the data from all the iterations to process all images (see Figure 9.8) while requiring only half the FLOPs.

9.10.3.2 Variable thresholding policy

Figure 9.21(a) shows the overall accuracy and average FLOP count for variable TP. It should be noted that since not all images go through all the iterations of ICNN, the FLOP count varies for each image. Thus, in Figure 9.21, the average parameter and FLOP counts are reported over 50K images in the validation set. Moreover, to better highlight how the TP contributes to reducing computational complexity, the FLOP and parameter counts are devised relative to the last iteration of ICNN. Figure 9.21(b) shows the $\bar{D}_{Ct}$ values for each iteration of the studied TPs. T1–T10 are sorted based on FLOP counts, with T1 corresponding to the policy with the lowest FLOP count and T10 the highest.

Figure 9.21 shows that even with a mild TP as in T10, the FLOP and parameter counts are reduced by up to 25% and 80%, respectively, with negligible accuracy loss. It should be noted that the number of parameters in early iterations of ICNN is significantly lower than the latter iterations. For instance, the first and the last iteration account for less than 3% and more than 50% of the total parameter count, respectively. This is due the fact that FC layers require 99× more parameters compared

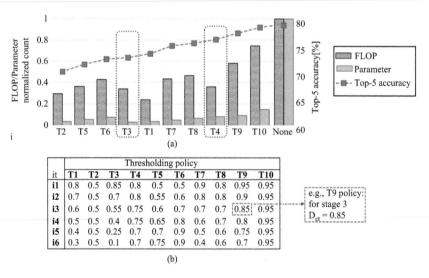

Figure 9.21   Variable thresholding policies: (a) the accuracy and average FLOP count, (b) the table including the $\bar{D}_{Ct}$ values in each iteration for each thresholding policy (for the last iteration all the remaining images are classified)

to the CONV layers in the ICNN structure. With the FC layers being smaller in the early iterations, significant drop in the parameter count is observed due to skipping the parameters in FC layers of last iterations as a result of early termination.

The complexity/accuracy trade-off suggests that by setting high values for confidence thresholds, and thus higher FLOP count, the accuracy increases from T1 to T10. However, extensive exploration of a large set of variable TPs with ICNN yields the TP to be more of a Pareto optimization question, where increased accuracy can be achieved with lower FLOP count through intelligent tuning of the D_{Ct} values. For instance, while the FLOP counts of T1 and T4 are significantly lower than T3 and T8, respectively, they yield higher accuracy.

9.10.4 Context-aware pruning policy for parameter reduction

9.10.4.1 Context-aware pruning policy for FC layer

Figure 9.22(a) shows the overall accuracy and average parameter count for various FC layer pruning policies, while the table in Figure 9.22(b) captures the setting of the pruning policy ($\bar{P}_{th}$) by listing the number of remaining classes after pruning the classes with low probability. The last bar shows the ICNN results when none of the classes are pruned in any of the iterations. P1–P8 are sorted based on their parameter count, with P1 having the lowest parameter count and P8 the highest.

Figure 9.22 shows that by increasing the number of pruned classes (i.e., lower P_{th}) the accuracy drops; however, intelligent selection of the pruning policy yields reductions in the parameter count, with negligible accuracy loss. For instance, P4 yields a 17% reduction in the parameter count with negligible accuracy loss. It should be noted that all the images go through all the iterations in this scheme. Thus, the only reduction in the FLOP count is due to the pruning of the last FC layer in each iteration.

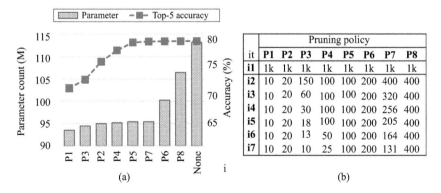

Figure 9.22   *Pruning policies: (a) the accuracy and average parameter count for FC layers, (b) the table including the number of labels not pruned in previous iterations. (The first iteration uses all the 1,000 labels as there is no feedback from the previous iterations.)*

Newer and deeper CNNs (e.g., VGGNet and GoogleNet) deploy a single FC layer as opposed to three FC layers in AlexNet. Hence, the application of pruning policy to deeper CNNs increases the rate of FLOP count reduction as well as parameter count reduction in their iterative version. Note that moving the large set of parameters required for the FC from the memory accounts for a significant energy and execution delay.

Caffe provides a set of tools to benchmark models by calculating layer-by-layer execution delay, which reports system performance and measures relative execution times for CNN models. Using these tools, the average delay of each operation (e.g., MAC) in CONV layers is calculated to be 10× lower than the same operation for an FC layer. As a result, while the reduction in the FLOP count through pruning is small, the reduction in the execution time and energy is significant.

9.10.4.2   Context-aware pruning policy for CONV layer

Figure 9.23 captures the result of filter pruning for the CONV5 layer in iterations 2–7. Note that the CONV5 of each iteration consists of 32 filters, and in each iteration, 5, 10 and 15 filters least affecting the top-5 classes from the previous iteration are pruned (i.e., $rm = 5, 10, 15$ and $P_{th} = 5$). The smart approach takes advantage of the feedback from previous iterations and depending on the remaining classes removes the least contributing filters, while the ignorant approach prunes filters based on how strongly each filter contributes to the overall accuracy of the network across all classes and all images in the training dataset. As illustrated in Figure 9.23, the contextual knowledge generated after each classification, and selective pruning of filters based on remaining classes significantly reduces the loss in classification accuracy when pruning filters.

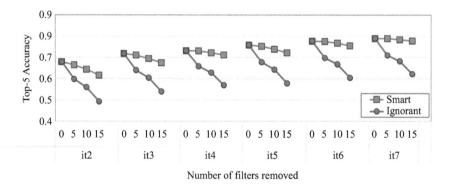

Figure 9.23   The accuracy of the CAPP$_{CONV}$ policy for the last CONV layer (i.e., CONV5) in iterations 2–7. The ignorant trend-line shows the results for pruning filters that least effect the accuracy for detection of all classes, while the smart trend-line shows the results for when feedback from previous iterations is used to prune the filters

9.11   Pruning and thresholding hybrid policy

Figures 9.24(a) and 9.25(a) show the accuracy, and normalized FLOP and parameter counts for the *PTHP* policies, while Figures 9.24(b) and 9.25(b) capture the setting used for experimented thresholding and pruning policies in the hybrid approach. The figures are divided into five sections, one for each TP. Each segment assesses the impact of five different pruning policies on total parameter and FLOP count when combined with thresholding in *PTHP*.

9.11.1   Fixed percentage PTHP

Figure 9.24(a) shows the normalized accuracy, FLOP and parameter counts for the $FTHP_{FP}$ policy. For each TP, we study how each $\bar{P}_{th}$ policy affects the FLOP and parameter counts by highlighting the increase and decrease in the average count by red and black colors.

An inverse trend is observed when both thresholding and pruning policies are aggressive (images with lower confidence are classified in early iterations, and more

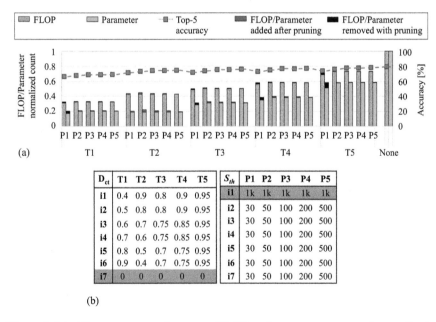

(a)

D_{ct}	T1	T2	T3	T4	T5	S_{th}	P1	P2	P3	P4	P5
i1	0.4	0.9	0.8	0.9	0.95	i1	1k	1k	1k	1k	1k
i2	0.5	0.8	0.8	0.9	0.95	i2	30	50	100	200	500
i3	0.6	0.7	0.75	0.85	0.95	i3	30	50	100	200	500
i4	0.7	0.6	0.75	0.85	0.95	i4	30	50	100	200	500
i5	0.8	0.5	0.7	0.75	0.95	i5	30	50	100	200	500
i6	0.9	0.4	0.7	0.75	0.95	i6	30	50	100	200	500
i7	0	0	0	0	0	i7	30	50	100	200	500

(b)

Figure 9.24   *The accuracy and average FLOP and parameter counts (normalized to ICNN with no pruning or threshold policy) for PTHP$_{FP}$. (a) Flop/Parameter count and accuracy, (b) Detection and selection thresholds for each iteration. For each thresholding policy (i.e., $\bar{D}_{Ct}$ vector), multiple pruning policies (i.e., $\bar{S}_{th}$ vector) are investigated. The red and black bars show the increase and reduction, respectively, in the number of FLOP and/or parameter counts of a thresholding policy due to pruning*

classes are pruned in each iteration), where the parameter and FLOP counts are increased by pruning. This is due to the fact that an aggressive pruning policy that keeps only a small number of classes might eliminate one or more classes in the top-5 classes of the next iteration, reducing the top-5 confidence of the next iteration and forcing ICNN to proceed to its next iteration, which increases the parameter and FLOP counts.

9.11.2   Confidence-tracking PTHP

As illustrated in Figure 9.25, with aggressive thresholding (e.g., T1), there are not many opportunities for pruning, and a significant drop in accuracy is observed. However, with moderate thresholding, some (but not all) of the applied pruning policies allow the parameter and FLOP count to significantly drop with only a little impact on the accuracy. This is mainly due to the fact that these pruning policies allow only the high probability classes (with accumulated probability of S_{th}) to proceed to the next iterations.

In the $PTHP_{CT}$, the classification would be terminated if (1) a top-5 confidence of D_{Ct} is reached or (2) the number of classes selected for the next iteration is no bigger

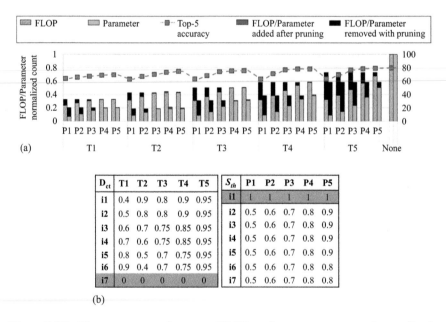

(b)

Figure 9.25   The accuracy and average FLOP and parameter counts (normalized to ICNN with no pruning or threshold policy) for PTHP$_{CT}$. (a) Flop/Parameter count and accuracy, (b) Detection and selection thresholds for each iteration. For each thresholding policy (i.e., $\bar{D}_{Ct}$ vector), multiple pruning policies (i.e., $\bar{S}_{th}$ vector) are investigated. The red and black bars show the increase and reduction, respectively, in the number of FLOP and/or parameter counts of a thresholding policy due to pruning

than 5. In the second case, proceeding to the next iteration does not increase the top-5 accuracy and ICNN is terminated, while the confidence threshold is not reached. The effect of this early termination is 2-fold: on the one hand, it identifies images that would never reach a high classification confidence, and for which processing of more iterations is a waste of resources, hence reducing computation with no accuracy loss. On the other hand, it prematurely terminates the processing of images that could have reached high confidences in the proceeding iteration, negatively affecting the accuracy. Hence, the selection of the best combination of $\bar{D}_{Ct}$ and $\bar{S}_{th}$ is an optimization problem. Figure 9.25 shows that when the value of $\bar{S}_{th}$ at each iteration is selected to be slightly higher than $\bar{D}_{Ct}$ of the next iteration, reductions in FLOP and parameter counts have the least impact on the accuracy (see T4-P5 hybrid policy).

It should be noted that the inverse impact of aggressive pruning and thresholding on parameter and FLOP count mentioned for Figure 9.24 is observed for Figure 9.25 too (see red bars in both the figures).

9.11.3   Run-time and overall accuracy

9.11.3.1   Pruning and/or thresholding

Adopting the pruning or TP creates a trade-off between average delay of classification, and the accuracy of classification. The pruning policy reduces the parameter count, and the TP reduces the average FLOP count. However, based on the results (see Figures 9.21 and 9.22), increased resources does not always translate into higher accuracy. The hybrid policies, which combine both pruning and thresholding, exhibit the same behavior, in which higher number of parameters and FLOPs does not always contribute to higher classification accuracy. Consequently, finding the optimal strategy in which the target accuracy is reached with minimal resources (in this case execution time), requires thorough exploration and tuning of the thresholding and pruning parameters.

Figure 9.26 captures the design space of the ICNN when trading the accuracy to reduce run-time through 5k combination of thresholding and pruning policies.

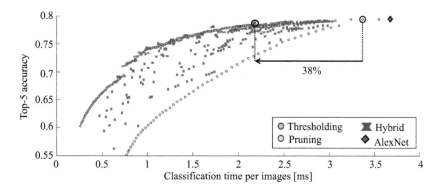

Figure 9.26   *The accuracy vs. average run-time per image of iterative AlexNet with a batch size of 1 for 50k validation images on K80 GPU. The diamond marks the original AlexNet. The policies on the top border of the diagram mark the most efficient ones in terms of accuracy and execution time*

In this figure, each point denotes a unique combination of thresholding and pruning policies. For the real-time applications, waiting for a whole batch to be processed significantly adds to the latency [39], thus a batch size of 1 was selected to target real-time streaming applications.

As illustrated, the stand-alone TP yields better run-time/accuracy trade-off compared to the stand-alone pruning policy. However, their combination in hybrid policy could lead to optimal solutions. Several optimization points for the hybrid policies in Figure 9.26 exhibit lower run-time compared to the stand-alone TP with the same accuracy. For instance, Figure 9.26 highlights a stand-alone TP and a hybrid policy derived by combining the same TP with pruning. Figure 9.26 shows that the hybrid policy reduces the classification time by 38% with only 1% accuracy loss.

9.11.3.2   Deadline-driven

Figure 9.27 shows the overall accuracy of *DD* policy for iterative AlexNet with a batch size of 1 for 50k validation images on K80 GPU for various time-budgets per image. As opposed to the pruning and/or TPs, all the images go through the same iterations for any given deadline. Thus, the accuracy is captured as a function of time-budget. It should be noted that higher time-budgets only increase the accuracy when it is sufficient for execution of the next iteration, which results in the step-like behavior observed in the figure.

Unlike the thresholding and pruning policies, the *DD* policy only executes the FC layer of one iteration, more specifically the last iteration given the time-budget. However, the pruning and/or TPs require the FC layers of all the iterations to be completed to draw conclusion about the early termination and pruning of class labels.

As a result, for higher accuracy values (i.e., high D_{Ct} and P_{th} and low S_{th} values in hybrid/thresholding/pruning policies, and large time-budget for the *DD* policy),

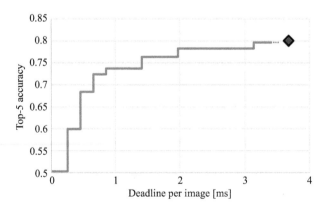

Figure 9.27   *The overall accuracy of DD for iterative AlexNet with a batch size of 1 for 50k validation images on K80 GPU. The diamond marks the original AlexNet. Higher time-budget only increases the accuracy when it is sufficient for execution of the next iteration*

where all images go through all the iterations, the *DD* policy yields lower execution time due to the fact that the computations in the FC layers of the preceding iterations are skipped in the *DD* policy. For instance, a top-5 accuracy of 79% is reached with a time-budget of 1.7 ms with *DD* policy, while the same average run-time yields at least 1% drop in the top-5 accuracy with the *TPHP* policies. The *DD* policy allows adjusting the run-time per images in the range of 0.3–3.2 ms based on the available time-budget by trading off accuracy.

9.12 Conclusions

In this chapter, an iterative architecture for processing CNN (ICNN) was introduced. As a case study, ICNN was used to break the large CNN network of AlexNet into a sequence of smaller networks (uCNN), each processing a subsample of the input image, providing the ability to terminate the classification early (when reaching a deadline in a real-time system or reaching a required classification accuracy in low-power systems), or carry the classification to the next iteration (if the deadline in a real-time system is not reached, or classification accuracy threshold is not satisfied in a low-power system). ICNN enables us to explore a wide range of complexity vs. accuracy trade-offs. To explore these trade-offs, a dynamic deadline-driven exit policy for real-time applications, a confidence TP for dynamic complexity reduction, a CAPP for parameter reduction and two hybrid pruning and TPs for simultaneous parameter and complexity reduction were introduced. Our simulation results show that with intelligent selection of the pruning and/or TPs, ICNN reduces the average FLOP and parameter counts, and execution time across 50K validation images in ImageNet database by more than 25%, 80% and 38%, respectively, with negligible accuracy loss. The reductions in the number of FLOP and parameter counts are directly translated to energy saving, motivating a power-aware CNN architecture. Moreover, the real-time systems could exploit the dynamic structure of the ICNN by reducing the execution time by up to $12\times$ by trading off accuracy with execution time.

References

[1]   J. Deng, W. Dong, R. Socher, L.-J. Li, K. Li, and L. Fei-Fei, "ImageNet: A large-scale hierarchical image database," in *Computer Vision and Pattern Recognition, 2009. CVPR 2009. IEEE Conference on*. IEEE, 2009, pp. 248–255.

[2]   G. A. Miller, "Wordnet: A lexical database for English," *Communications of the ACM*, vol. 38, no. 11, pp. 39–41, 1995.

[3]   A. Krizhevsky, I. Sutskever, and G. E. Hinton, "ImageNet classification with deep convolutional neural networks," in *Advances in Neural Information Processing Systems*, Curran Associates Inc. 2012, pp. 1097–1105.

[4]   K. Simonyan and A. Zisserman, "Very deep convolutional networks for large-scale image recognition," *arXiv preprint arXiv:1409.1556*, 2014.

[5] C. Szegedy, W. Liu, Y. Jia, *et al.*, "Going deeper with convolutions," in *Proceedings of the IEEE Conference on Computer Vision and Pattern Recognition*, 2015, pp. 1–9.

[6] K. He, X. Zhang, S. Ren, and J. Sun, "Deep residual learning for image recognition," in *Proceedings of the IEEE Conference on Computer Vision and Pattern Recognition*, 2016, pp. 770–778.

[7] M. D. Zeiler and R. Fergus, "Visualizing and understanding convolutional networks," in *European Conference on Computer Vision*. Springer, 2014, pp. 818–833.

[8] M. Liu, J. Shi, Z. Li, C. Li, J. Zhu, and S. Liu, "Towards better analysis of deep convolutional neural networks," *IEEE Transactions on Visualization and Computer Graphics*, vol. 23, no. 1, pp. 91–100, 2017.

[9] Y. LeCun, B. Boser, J. S. Denker, *et al.*, "Backpropagation applied to handwritten zip code recognition," *Neural Computation*, vol. 1, no. 4, pp. 541–551, 1989.

[10] Y.-H. Chen, T. Krishna, J.S. Emer, and V. Sze, "Eyeriss: An energy-efficient reconfigurable accelerator for deep convolutional neural networks," *IEEE Journal of Solid-State Circuits*, vol. 52, no. 1, pp. 127–138, 2017.

[11] C. Zhang, P. Li, G. Sun, Y. Guan, B. Xiao, and J. Cong, "Optimizing FPGA-based accelerator design for deep convolutional neural networks," in *Proceedings of the 2015 ACM/SIGDA International Symposium on Field-Programmable Gate Arrays*. ACM, 2015, pp. 161–170.

[12] M. Jaderberg, A. Vedaldi, and A. Zisserman, "Speeding up convolutional neural networks with low rank expansions," *arXiv preprint arXiv:1405.3866*, 2014.

[13] V. Lebedev, Y. Ganin, M. Rakhuba, I. Oseledets, and V. Lempitsky, "Speeding-up convolutional neural networks using fine-tuned CP-decomposition," *arXiv preprint arXiv:1412.6553*, 2014.

[14] B. Liu, M. Wang, H. Foroosh, M. Tappen, and M. Pensky, "Sparse convolutional neural networks," in *Proceedings of the IEEE Conference on Computer Vision and Pattern Recognition*, 2015, pp. 806–814.

[15] M. Rastegari, V. Ordonez, J. Redmon, and A. Farhadi, "XNOR-Net: ImageNet classification using binary convolutional neural networks," in *ECCV*. Springer, 2016, pp. 525–542.

[16] S. Yu, Z. Li, P.-Y. Chen, *et al.*, "Binary neural network with 16 Mb RRAM macro chip for classification and online training," in *Electron Devices Meeting (IEDM), 2016 IEEE International*. IEEE, 2016, pp. 16–2.

[17] J. H. Kim and S.-K. Park, "The geometrical learning of binary neural networks," *IEEE Transactions on Neural Networks*, vol. 6, no. 1, pp. 237–247, 1995.

[18] I. Hubara, M. Courbariaux, D. Soudry, R. El-Yaniv, and Y. Bengio, "Binarized neural networks," *Proceedings of the 30th International Conference on Neural Information Processing Systems*, Curran Associates Inc. 2016, pp. 4107–4115.

[19] M. Courbariaux, I. Hubara, D. Soudry, R. El-Yaniv, and Y. Bengio, "Binarized neural networks: Training deep neural networks with weights and activations constrained to+ 1 or-1," *arXiv preprint arXiv:1602.02830*, 2016.

[20] J. Wu, C. Leng, Y. Wang, Q. Hu, and J. Cheng, "Quantized convolutional neural networks for mobile devices," in *Proceedings of the IEEE Conference on Computer Vision and Pattern Recognition*, 2016, pp. 4820–4828.

[21] S. Zhou, Y. Wu, Z. Ni, X. Zhou, H. Wen, and Y. Zou, "DoReFa-Net: Training low bitwidth convolutional neural networks with low bit-width gradients," *arXiv preprint arXiv:1606.06160*, 2016.

[22] M. Courbariaux, Y. Bengio, and J.-P. David, "Low precision arithmetic for deep learning," *CoRR, abs/1412.7024*, vol. 4, 2014.

[23] S. Gupta, A. Agrawal, and P. Narayanan, "Deep learning with limited numerical precision," in *ICML*, 2015, pp. 1737–1746.

[24] D. D. Lin, S. S. Talathi, and V. S. Annapureddy, "Fixed point quantization of deep convolutional networks," in *ICML*, 2016, pp. 2849–2858.

[25] H. Tann, S. Hashemi, R. I. Bahar, and S. Reda, "Runtime configurable deep neural networks for energy-accuracy trade-off," in *Hardware/Software Codesign and System Synthesis (CODES+ ISSS), 2016 International Conference on*. IEEE, 2016, pp. 1–10.

[26] P. Panda, A. Sengupta, and K. Roy, "Conditional deep learning for energy-efficient and enhanced pattern recognition," in *Design, Automation and Test in Europe Conference, 2016*. IEEE, 2016, pp. 475–480.

[27] S. Teerapittayanon, B. McDanel, and H. Kung, "BranchyNet: Fast inference via early exiting from deep neural networks," in *Pattern Recognition (ICPR), 2016 23rd International Conference on*. IEEE, 2016, pp. 2464–2469.

[28] L. Deng, "The MNIST database of handwritten digit images for machine learning research [best of the web]," *IEEE Signal Processing Magazine*, vol. 29, no. 6, pp. 141–142, 2012.

[29] K. Neshatpour, F. Behnia, H. Homayoun, and A. Sasan, "ICNN: An iterative implementation of convolutional neural networks to enable energy and computational complexity aware dynamic approximation," in *Design, Automation and Test in Europe*, 2018.

[30] K. Neshatpour, F. Behnia, H. Homayoun, and A. Sasan, "Exploiting energy-accuracy trade-off through contextual awareness in multi-stage convolutional neural networks," in *ISQED*, 2019.

[31] C. S. Burrus, R. A. Gopinath, and H. Guo, *Introduction to Wavelets and Wavelet Transforms: A Primer*, Pearson. 1997.

[32] D. Nekhaev and V. Demin, "Visualization of maximizing images with deconvolutional optimization method for neurons in deep neural networks," *Procedia Computer Science*, vol. 119, pp. 174–181, 2017.

[33] M. D. Zeiler, G. W. Taylor, and R. Fergus, "Adaptive deconvolutional networks for mid and high level feature learning," in *Computer Vision (ICCV), 2011 IEEE International Conference on*. IEEE, 2011, pp. 2018–2025.

[34] W. Shi, J. Caballero, L. Theis, *et al.*, "Is the deconvolution layer the same as a convolutional layer?," *arXiv preprint arXiv:1609.07009*, 2016.

[35] J. Long, E. Shelhamer, and T. Darrell, "Fully convolutional networks for semantic segmentation," in *Proceedings of the IEEE Conference on Computer Vision and Pattern Recognition*, 2015, pp. 3431–3440.

[36]   A. Dosovitskiy, P. Fischer, E. Ilg, *et al.*, "FlowNet: Learning optical flow with convolutional networks," in *Proceedings of the IEEE International Conference on Computer Vision*, 2015, pp. 2758–2766.

[37]   A. Radford, L. Metz, and S. Chintala, "Unsupervised representation learning with deep convolutional generative adversarial networks," *arXiv preprint arXiv:1511.06434*, 2015.

[38]   S. Anwar, K. Hwang, and W. Sung, "Structured pruning of deep convolutional neural networks," *Journal on Emerging Technologies in Computing Systems*, vol. 13, no. 3, pp. 32:1–32:18, 2017. [Online]. Available: http://doi.acm.org/10.1145/3005348.

[39]   S. Han, H. Mao, and W. J. Dally, "Deep compression: Compressing deep neural networks with pruning, trained quantization and Huffman coding," *arXiv preprint arXiv:1510.00149*, 2015.

[40]   S. Han, X. Liu, H. Mao, *et al.*, "EIE: Efficient inference engine on compressed deep neural network," in *Proc. of the 43rd Int. Symposium on Computer Architecture*. IEEE Press, 2016, pp. 243–254.

[41]   Y. Jia, E. Shelhamer, J. Donahue, *et al.*, "Caffe: Convolutional architecture for fast feature embedding," in *Proceedings of the 22nd ACM International Conference on Multimedia*. ACM, 2014, pp. 675–678.

[42]   S. Mallat, *A Wavelet Tour of Signal Processing*. Burlington, MA: Academic Press, 1999.

[43]   H. Chu and Symas Corporation, "Lightning memory-mapped database manager (LMDB)," 2011. http://104.237.133.194/doc/.

[44]   "Pywavelets wavelet transforms in python," https://pywavelets.readthedocs.io/en/latest/#contents.

[45]   S. Zha, F. Luisier, W. Andrews, N. Srivastava, and R. Salakhutdinov, "Exploiting image-trained CNN architectures for unconstrained video classification," *arXiv preprint arXiv:1503.04144*, 2015.

Part V

Deep learning on analog accelerators

Chapter 10

Mixed-signal neuromorphic platform design for streaming biomedical signal processing

Sandeep Pande[1], Federico Corradi[1], Jan Stuijt[1], Siebren Schaafsma[1], and Francky Catthoor[2,3]

Streaming biomedical signal processing platforms should offer complex real-time signal-processing capabilities at very low energy consumption. Low-power operation and compact size requirements ensure that these platforms can be employed in *always-on* wearable devices with realistic size and battery usage. The signal-processing algorithms that can adapt in real time to individual patients will open new possibilities for the personalized health-care systems. Current biomedical signal processing systems lack this feature; whereas the neuromorphic computing paradigm is capable of offering this feature.

This chapter presents the mixed-signal design approach for the design of neuromorphic platforms for the biomedical signal processing. The proposed approach combines algorithmic, architectural and circuit design concepts to offer a low-power neuromorphic platform for streaming biomedical signal processing. The platform employs liquid state machines using spiking neurons (implemented on analog neuron circuits) and support vector machine (SVM) (implemented as software running on advanced RISC machine (ARM) processor). A dynamic global synaptic communication network realized using the ultralow leakage IGZO thin film transistor (TFT) technology circuit switch is also presented. The proposed architectural technique offers a scalable low-power neuromorphic platform design approach suitable for processing real-time biomedical signals.

The combination of biologically inspired learning rules on spiking neural networks (SNNs) offers a promising solution for the realization of adaptable biomedical signal processing. Thus, the proposed system architecture advances the current state-of-the-art toward designing the personalized health-care platforms.

[1]Stichting IMEC Nederland, Eindhoven, The Netherland
[2]IMEC Leuven, Heverlee, Belgium
[3]ESAT Department, KU Leuven, Leuven, Belgium

10.1   Introduction

Advances in biomedical sensing have enabled accurate measurement of biological data such as heart rate using electrocardiogram (ECG) and brain activity using electroencephalogram (EEG). Traditionally, these measurements are carried out by hospital for inpatients periodically and analyzed by physicians for deciding the treatment. Continuous, *always-on*, real-time biomedical signal processing and analysis has the potential for detecting the vital signatures that occur during the early stage of the disease. Real-time patient monitoring can help in better disease management avoiding adverse events such as heart attacks and strokes. Hence, in recent years, there is a growing research in the area of wearable and always-on biomedical signal analysis platforms.

Real-time biomedical signal processing platforms should have complex signal-processing capabilities while consuming very low energy. Low-power consumption and compact size requirements ensure that these platforms can be integrated into wearable devices that can work for weeks on single battery charge. One of the desirable requirements is the adaptable signal processing based on the individual patient data.

Traditional signal-processing techniques implemented on custom Application Specific Integrated Circuits (ASICs) can offer complex signal-processing capabilities but consume more power (due to their complexity) and they still cannot offer the desired adaptability. Neuromorphic computing is a promising alternative computational approach to standard von Neumann machines for dedicated adaptive signal processing, estimation and classification tasks. Neuromorphic systems or hardware SNN systems emulate cognitive abilities of the human brain by emulating the massive, dense and complex interconnection of neurons and synapses, where each neuron connects to thousands of other neurons and communicates through short transient pulses (*spikes*) along synaptic links. Brain-inspired deep learning systems aim to create neural network structures with a large number of (or deep) layers. This massive scaling poses a challenge for designing the global synaptic network for the neuromorphic architectures. This chapter discusses a circuit-switched network realized in 3D very large scale integration (VLSI) implementations that offer a compact scalable power efficient global synaptic communication network. Currently, we are applying and demonstrating this for medium-size applications like the streaming ECG classifier. However, our concepts are intended to scale this up to a much larger size, up to millions of neurons and billions of synapses, as required for deep learning applications. We believe the concepts exposed here are potentially reusable in that direction but their practical implementation is clearly future work.

The main design challenge for the realization of compact low-power biomedical signal processing neuromorphic platforms is efficient implementation of the following system elements:

- neural elements, including local synapse array
- global synaptic communication infrastructure
- efficient (on-line) learning techniques

The choices we have made for these components and their motivation will now be provided in the subsequent sections. Section 10.2 reviews various neuromorphic architectures and related research. The section also discusses the signal processing challenges for biomedical (specifically ECG) signal processing. Section 10.3 presents the proposed NeuRAM3 mixed-signal neuromorphic platform and Section 10.4 presents the ECG application mapping on the proposed platform. Results are discussed in Section 10.5 and the conclusions are presented in Section 10.6.

10.2 Related work

10.2.1 Mixed-signal neuromorphic architectures – brief review

Nervous systems are a special class of distributed information processing system that processes the information in a profoundly different manner than modern computer technologies that are based on the von Neumann architecture. The neurobiological systems exploit billions of slow, inhomogeneous, noisy and limited precision elements (neurons and synapses) and nevertheless still outperform computers in many tasks such as speech processing, symbolic reasoning, motor control and multi-sensorial integration. In recent years, there is an increasing interest in exploring alternative computing technologies that can go beyond the von Neumann architecture. Neuromorphic engineering is an active field of research in which the computational principles of biological systems are applied while developing artificial systems for practical applications, exploiting known physical properties of the silicon Complementary Metal-Oxide-Semiconductor (CMOS) technology or other materials and substrates. Within this context, many mixed-signal combinations of analog and digital implementations of neural processing elements have been proposed. That is mainly true because the analog nature of the part of the computation matches the low-power requirement and it is in line with the neurobiological counterpart.

Some of the recent projects aim at the development of hardware platforms for large-scale neural hardware emulators. This is done with the aim of simulating the largest possible number of neurons and synapses with the lowest possible power budget. The spiking Neural Network Architecture (SpiNNaker) project[*] has realized a digital platform, based on 18 mobile digital processors Advanced RISC Machine ((ARM)) into a single die that aims at simulating parts of the human brain in real time. This digital system recently reached a 1 million core milestone on a single machine able to model one billion leaky-integrate-and-fire (LIF) neurons in real time. The customized ARM9 chips include 18 general-purpose ARM9,[†] with 100 kByte local memory for each core (program and data) and 128 MByte shared dynamic random access memory used for storing synaptic weights or other internal variables. These cores provide a programmable platform for implementing arbitrary neuron models and learning algorithms, in which computation is based on a 16-bit fixed-point arithmetic. They are interconnected with a torus communication network which supplied reasonable bandwidth up to a medium scale range but when going to (many) millions of neurons also that torus provides strong synapse communication bandwidth limitations.

---

[*]Led by Prof. Steve Furber at the University of Manchester.
[†]ARM: a family of RISC-based processor designed and licensed by ARM holding. ARM9 is a 32-bit ARM mobile processor.

The NeuroGrid project[‡] uses analog subthreshold circuits as custom implementations of neurons and synapses. One of the main goals is to study some of the principles of operation of the mammalian cortex in a cost-effective hardware system. The Neurogrid system is composed of 16 neural core chips each containing 65k neurons in a silicon area of 12×14 mm [1]. The full system contains 1 million neurons, modeled as quadratic integrate-and-fire neurons. To enable the system to reach large scale (1 million neurons), there are several trade-offs. In particular, neural plasticity in Neurogrid is not implemented. Also, the asynchronous routing scheme supports a limited amount of traffic between neurons, especially when they are situated far from each other. In the past, the system has been used in conjunction with the Neural Engineering Framework [2], which is a theoretical framework to translate equations and dynamical systems into neural network dynamics. It has been shown reliable emulation of a distributed working memory dynamics using 4,000 neurons with 16M feed-forward and on-chip recurrent connections. Recently, the efforts in this direction have continued and a new neuromorphic mixed-signal system has been developed [3]. This system is the first one that can be programmed at a high level of abstraction. It comprises 4,096 spiking neurons in 0.65 mm^2 silicon area using a 28 nm FDSOI process. The main innovations are the sparse encoding via analog spatial convolution and weighted spike-rate summation via digital accumulation as well as a novel communication scheme that drastically reduces the event traffic and therefore results in the lowest power consumption per spike figure in these types of systems, i.e., 381 fJ per synaptic operation in a typical network configuration. Still, also these recent developments have not removed the synapse bandwidth at very large scales.

Another major neuromorphic project has been the Synapse [4] project led by IBM. It aims to overcome the memory bottleneck problem by using custom digital circuits that use virtualization and share resources to emulate a single neuron. The system architecture, called TrueNorth [5], is built from a multi-neurosynaptic core system. Each neurosynaptic core comprises 256 neurons and 256×256 finite-resolution synapses using a cross-bar array. The custom digital neurosynaptic core, named TrueNorth, comes with a software architecture (called Compass) that can be used to reproduce and simulate the behavior of the neurosynaptic core, their impressive results show simulations of $5.3 \times 1,010$ neurons interconnected by $1.7 \times 1,014$ synapses [6]. This cross-bar array allows a very high synapse communication bandwidth up to a certain size, but then it drastically reduces that bandwidth when passing a threshold. So, also this option is not matched to supporting millions of neurons.

The FACETS/BrainScale project led by Univ. Heidelberg aims to achieve integration by using an analog approach to computation, in which neurons are simulated from 103 up to 105 times faster than real time. The approach is based on a full wafer system composed of multiple analog neuromorphic dies communicating using a digital asynchronous protocol [7]. The system includes learning capabilities via spike-timing-dependent plasticity (STDP) learning circuits that involve computation of the STDP learning in analog circuits, while the synaptic update is delegated to

[‡]Led by Prof. K. Boahen at Stanford University.

additional digital external circuits. The large variability of the neurosynaptic cores limits the precision in the mapping of synaptic weights or network dynamics. Classification using a single die chip has been demonstrated in a model of the olfactory system, in which weights were programmed after an on-line procedure [8]. This wafer-scale system approach is fully aimed at emulating a large neuromorphic system and not at low-power implementation.

Field-programmable gate array (FPGA) digital circuits have had a large impact on the development of custom digital chips by enabling a designer to try custom design on easily reconfigurable hardware. In fact, FPGAs contain programmable logic blocks that are based on a large number of gates and local memory, and connections between blocks are configurable. This reconfigurability makes it possible to realize parallel systems such as SNNs in hardware [9–11]. The common feature of these SNN architectures is that memory is distributed among massively parallel configurations of elementary computational blocks: neurons and synapses. At present, current FPGA systems are capable of simulating up to 4k neurons in real time by exploiting time-multiplexed resources on the board (Virtex 6) as in [12], with the ultimate intent of simulating polychronous SNNs to store spatiotemporal spike patterns. Another alternative approach to reconfigurable hardware for neural network is the use of custom field programmable analog arrays. This approach is mainly pursued by a laboratory situated in Virginia. Their custom VLSI systems are based on low-power analog signal processing blocks. They successfully implemented a linear and nonlinear classifier based on a vector–matrix multiplication and a winner-take-all network [13]. The custom chip includes basic programmable amplifiers, filters, adaptive filters, multipliers and gain-controlling circuits. Interestingly, the same approach has also been applied in the field of neuroprosthesis and audio signal processing.

At the ETH in Zürich, a research laboratory led by Prof. Giacomo Indiveri is investigating neuromorphic spiking networks in a low-power analog and mixed-signal implementation. The laboratory, among other achievements, successfully demonstrated robust learning mechanisms for the formation of associative memories in relatively small and reconfigurable neuromorphic spiking hardware [14] that can also be used in the framework of deep neural networks [15]. However, these systems are still implementing a relatively small number of neurons (few thousands) [16] and the need of scaling up to large number of neurons is required to solve more complex tasks.

In 2018, Intel Lab presented its first SNN hardware architecture implemented in a custom VLSI chip. The research efforts are focused on mimicking bio-realistic neural and synaptic behaviors, including adaptation and self-learning. The implemented learning rule is bioinspired as it is based on the relative time of the asynchronous stream of spiking events. One of the main goals of this research is to achieve a highly efficient system that can be applied in tasks that require low latency with an ultralow power budget. The chip was fabricated in a 14 nm technology, it implements a 128 cores, each containing 128 spiking neurons. The architecture occupies about 60 mm^2 of die area reaching the impressive density of 2,184 neurons per square millimeter [17]. Since today this chip represents the highest integration of neurons with learning synapses in a single die.

Many more university groups are active in smaller scale neuromorphic projects. This overview is not aiming at an exhaustive overview.

10.2.2   *Biomedical signal processing challenges for ECG application*

ECG signals represent the electrical activity of heart, this electrical activity is recorded using the potential difference between a number of leads placed on the body. In hospitals, it is common to use 12 leads placed in a standard configuration, which provides spatiotemporal information about the heart's activity in approximately three orthogonal directions; left–right, superior–inferior and anterior–posterior. Each of the 12 leads represents a particular orientation in space. This configuration gives a practical advantage to trained cardiologist, which are able to examine the pathophysiological processes underlying ECG traces. An ECG beat is composed of four typical complexes P, QRS, T and U. The P-wave indicates a contraction of the atrial rooms of the heart and it represents the depolarization of the left and right atrium. The QRS complex includes Q-wave, R-wave and S-wave. These three waves occur in a short time interval and they depict the electrical impulse that quickly spreads through ventricles resulting in ventricular depolarization. In healthy adult patients, the duration of the QRS complex is usually around 0.06 and 0.1 s. The T-wave succeeds the QRS complex and it implies ventricular repolarization. The T-wave is slightly asymmetric and the peak of the wave is shifted toward the end. The T-wave indicates ventricular repolarization. When a T-wave occurs in the opposite direction, it is usually an indication of some sort of cardiac pathology. In addition, if a tiny wave occurs between the T and P-waves, it is referred to as the U-wave. However, the biological basis of the U-wave is still under investigation [18]. The shape and the size of the different complexes vary according to the different leads from which the signal is being observed. Different features can then be extracted by different leads, and this makes the diagnosis of certain types of irregularities much easier to be detected from a particular lead. The majorities of arrhythmia-related diseases can be identified exploiting a modified two-lead (ML-II lead) configuration, which is also compatible with wearable devices mostly for its smaller form factor. Automated arrhythmia classification and detection systems are usually based on the two lead ML-II configuration and follow a few standards steps: (a) recording and storing the ECG signal, (b) filtering and preprocessing of the stored ECG, (c) segmentation of the various ECG complexes, (d) feature extraction and (e) classification. The learning of the features and the optimization of the various parameters of the classifier are usually carried off-line and no on-line adaptation or personalization is commonly exploited.

In the specific case of ECG signal analysis for arrhythmia detection and classification, the second step is commonly carried out with wavelet transform, Kalman filtering or other standard signal-processing algorithms [19–21]. The segmentation and event detection is based on reliable algorithms for the detection of the QRS complex [22,23]. After this segmentation stage, feature extraction can be achieved using one of the standard signal processing methods, which include filtering, embeddings and wrapper methods. Filter methods rely on the statistical properties of the signal and are based on correlations matrix or linear decomposition with independent component analysis [24]. Embeddings and wrapper methods are more computationally expensive than filtering techniques as they require a trained classifier and their role is to optimize the output with a variety of feature sets. More recently, the classification of ECG signals has also been performed using SVM [25,26], neural network approaches [27,28] and feature-based clustering methods [29,30].

Our proposition is to exploit an alternative computational approach that is compatible with state-of-the-art spike-based neuromorphic processors and that contrasts the computational models based on the von Neumann machine. Our focus is on the development of computational models, in which memory and computation are co-localized in a massively parallel network of spiking neurons. These models can then be implemented with the neuromorphic processors that are currently under development by different companies and research institutions [4,17,31]. Our method is alternative as it exploits an SNN that operates on streaming data, without the need to use memory buffers for extra signal filtering steps, without segmenting the heartbeat and without a clever feature extraction method. In our approach, we directly convert ECG signals into digital pulses (i.e., spike trains). The ECG signal classification and detection problem are casted into a temporal spike patterns classification problem. This problem is still a major challenge in computational neuroscience and machine learning. Solving the problem with a massively parallel network of spiking neurons can have great influence in the design of a new generation of embedded electronic systems [32,33].

10.3   NeuRAM3 mixed-signal neuromorphic platform

The NeuRAM3 mixed-signal neuromorphic platform aims to benefit from the low-power consumption characteristics of the analog neural components while maintaining the classification accuracy offered by the digital neural networks. Figure 10.1 illustrates the organization of the NeuRAM3 mixed-signal neuromorphic platform. The platform comprises analog neural circuits implementing a recurrent SNN and the SNN classifier executing as software module on the ARM processor. The scalable

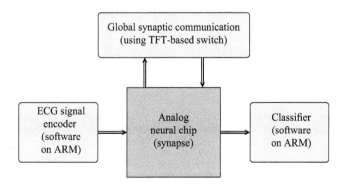

Figure 10.1   NeuRAM3 platform organization

global synapse network is realized by a dynamic segmented bus network implemented by means of ultralow leakage TFT switches. It provides the synaptic connectivity between the SNN cores on the Synapse analog neural chip. So many local synapse/neuron arrays can be communicating through a shared dynamic segmented bus network. As shown in [34], due to a special virtualization scheme, this approach allows an upfront-specified minimal spike bandwidth between these local arrays, even when the number of arrays grows to enable (many) millions of neurons.

We have demonstrated the usability of this parametrized platform architecture template with a small-scale instance executing a relatively small but representative application, namely, an ECG algorithm based on spike trains (see Section 10.2.2). This application does not yet emphasize the scalability of our platform as it requires less than thousand neurons, but it is intended to show the main features. Hence, the current instantiation of our platform is also not yet dimensioned to allow the potential scaling up described earlier. The prototype technology limitations for the noncommercial IGZO TFT technology would not allow us yet to demonstrate a huge hardware instantiation.

10.3.1   Analog neural components including local synapse array

The analog neural circuits are realized by means of the custom VLSI neuromorphic processor of ETH Zurich, the *CXQuad*. This custom neuromorphic processor is an asynchronous multi-neuron chip that includes analog neuron and synapse circuits, as well as supporting spike communication digital logic. The *CXQuad* analog neuron circuits are optimized for very low-power operation and consume a very competitive amount of energy per spike activity, namely, 2.8 pJ @1.8 V power supply [15]. Each *CXQuad* chip contains 1,024 neurons organized as four cores of 256 neurons and synapse blocks. The synapse is an analog linear integrator circuit, which integrates input events from 64 12-bit programmable content addressable memory cells. The log-domain differential pair integrator filters that emulate a bio-realistic temporal synaptic dynamics, with time constants in the range of tens of ms. The neural dynamics is emulated using subthreshold analog circuits, and the neuron model is a bio-realistic adaptive-exponential I&F neuron circuit.

The recurrent SNN using the ECG application has been implemented using the analog neural components of the *CXQuad* neuromorphic processor. The proposed recurrent SNN topology employs two cores of the *CXQuad* chip. The 256 excitatory neurons and their local synapse connections are mapped to one core and the 64 neurons inhibiting the excitatory population are mapped to the other core. The inter-core global synaptic connectivity is offered by the TFT-based global synapse communication switch.

10.3.2   Global synapse communication network realized with TFT-based switches

The SNN organization for large applications exhibits modular structure, where multiple localized densely connected cluster of neurons are interconnected using the global synapse network. For example, the ECG application SNN topology presented

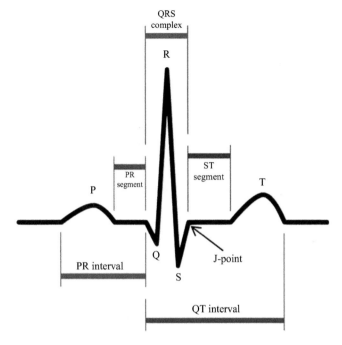

Figure 10.2   ECG complex

in Figure 10.2 comprises a cluster of excitatory neurons, a cluster of inhibitory neurons and a classifier. In the NeuRAM3 demonstrator, these are mapped on four different local arrays in the CxQuad board. A limited number of inter-cluster connections are then only present in this ECG instantiation. But this global synaptic connectivity strongly increases with the application size and can take up significant area on the chip and also consume a major amount of energy. So, to deal with this undesired area and energy explosion, we have proposed a novel scalable dynamic segmented bus inter-cluster synaptic communication network for large-scale neuromorphic platforms with a circuit-switched data plane and a control plane based on full virtualization [34]. The network architecture comprises run-time-controlled segmented buses interconnecting clusters. The segmented bus intersections are controlled by a novel lower power circuit switch implemented with TFTs. The selected TFT material exhibits ultralow-leakage power consumption. When scaled up, these devices reside between the metal layers in a many-layer back-end-of-line (BEOL) metal interconnection stack [35]. The proposed 3D-VLSI implementation scheme with segmented buses based on these BEOL circuits implemented with TFT devices results in a compact low-power global synaptic communication network.

When we return to our ECG demonstrator, the cluster communication can be mapped and scheduled in several ways on a segmented bus for global synapse communication, as discussed in the general approach of [34]. One interesting mapping is shown in Figure 10.3. The excitatory cluster is split in a top and a bottom part, and

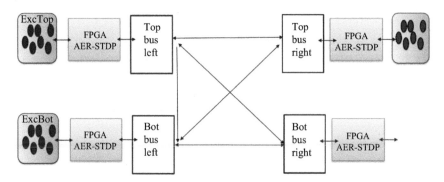

Figure 10.3   ECG mapping on CxQuad local arrays and FPGA board

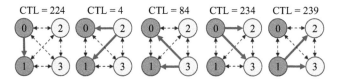

Figure 10.4   ECG routing on CxQuad local arrays and TFT global synapse communication IC

the same is true for the inhibitory cluster. These are assigned to different CxQuad arrays. Then, with the intermediate support of glue logic on the PFGA board of the NeuRAM3 demonstrator hardware setup, the synapse Address Event Representation (AER) streams are routed to the ports of the segmented bus IC. That latter one has 9 of the 12 possible unidirectional connections enabled, as shown also in the figure.

A feasible schedule for this can be obtained by routing the required global synapse communications (big arrows) sequentially on the segmented bus architecture, as illustrated in Figure 10.4. Note however that some of these synapse communications are mutually compatible with each other, so these can be and have then also been scheduled in parallel. One example of this is illustrated in Figure 10.5.

To scale this up for more local neural clusters, we have to split up the excitatory and inhibitory neuron groups further. That is illustrated in Figure 10.6. There it is also visible that the global synapse communication requirements (the number of big arrows) are increasing in a highly sublinear way, so they do not explode.

We have also implemented a prototype test chip for this global synapse communication functionality. The proposed NeuRAM3 mixed-signal neuromorphic platform instance demonstrates the functionality of this switch circuit in a not yet scaled up form so compatible with the mapping of Figure 10.3. To reduce both the fabrication cost and the related challenges, we have currently designed a prototype in IMEC's ultralow leakage IGZO TFT plastic technology. The switch provides connectivity between the excitatory and inhibitory neural clusters mapped on the CXQuad cores. It has been fabricated, packaged and measured.

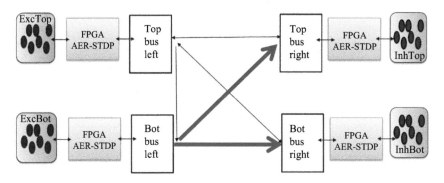

Figure 10.5 *ECG scheduling on CxQuad local arrays and TFT global synapse communication IC*

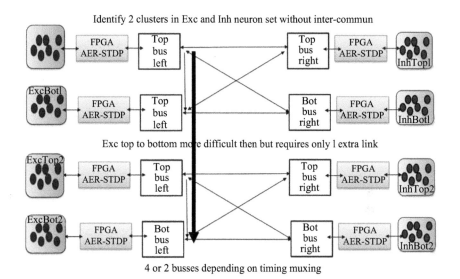

Figure 10.6 *Scaling up for twice as many cluster partitions of ECG scheduling on CxQuad local arrays and TFT global synapse communication IC. (AER: address event representation, STDP: spike-timing-dependent plasticity, ExcBot: bottom excitatory pool of neurons, ExcTop: top excitatory pool of neurons, InhBot: bottom inhibitory pool of neurons, InhTop: top inhibitory pool of neurons)*

The switch architecture illustrated in Figure 10.7 consists of four input and four output ports. Each output port (Y*n*) can be configured to connect to any input port except the input port with the same number (X*n*). Figure 10.8 shows the chip layout and the pinout. The chip uses single-bit input and output ports to save the number of pins on the die and package. The datapacket can be fed as a serial packet to the input port and is received as a serial packet at the output port. The AER packets from

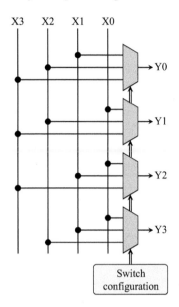

Figure 10.7   TFT switch architecture

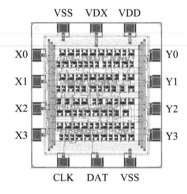

Figure 10.8   TFT switch chip layout (die size: 2.86 mm × 3.10 mm)

CXQuad are converted in serial datapackets using the UART protocol and routed through the switch.

10.3.3   NeuRAM3 mixed-signal neuromorphic platform FPGA architecture

The NeuRAM3 mixed-signal neuromorphic architecture is implemented as a multi-board platform. Figure 10.9 illustrates the organization of the platform and Figure 10.10 shows the actual platform photograph.

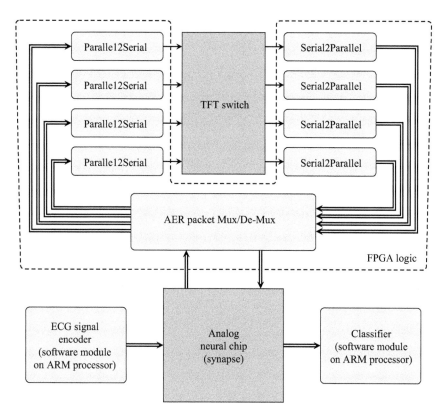

Figure 10.9   NeuRAM3 platform FPGA architecture

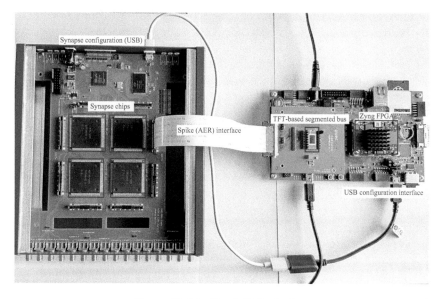

Figure 10.10   NeuRAM3 platform

The platform consists of a Zynq FPGA board that acts as the host board. The TFT switch and the AER interface are implemented on a custom board that fits on the FPGA Mezzanine Connector of the Zynq FPGA board. The Synapse (CxQuad chips) are located on a separate board that connects to the Zynq FPGA using USB cable and to the AER interface using a custom high-speed cable.

The Zynq FPGA is a combination of an ARM microprocessor and FPGA configurable logic and provides an ideal solution as a host board for the NeuRAM3 neuromorphic platform. The CxQuad has high-speed AER interface connectors that can send and receive the spike packets from in and out of the chip. The glue logic between the high-speed AER interface of the CxQuad and the TFT switch is implemented on the FPGA configurable logic. The outgoing spike packets from the high-speed AER interface are demultiplexed, serialized (using the UART protocol) and fed into the TFT switch. The spike packets (in the serial UART format) from the TFT switch are deserialized and multiplexed and sent to the destination neurons in the CxQuad chip. As discussed in Section 10.5.3, the speed of the TFT chip is high enough to time multiplex the spike data over multiple AER ports and the bits of the 8-bit words. So that task is assigned to the FPGA board. The ECG signal encoder, classifier and the overall system control are implemented as software modules running on the ARM processor inside the Zynq FPGA.

10.4   ECG application mapping on non-scaled neuromorphic platform instance

The mixed-signal neuromorphic platform exploits a fully event-driven approach for carrying biomedical signal processing. In the following application, the platform has been tuned to carry arrhythmia detection and classification employing a bio-inspired SNN. We have implemented a two-staged SNN topology which comprises a recurrent network of spiking neurons whose output is classified by a cluster of LIF neurons that have been (supervised off-line) trained to distinguish 18 types of cardiac patterns; of which 17 are actual cardiac patterns, and one class is used for unrecognized ECG signals due to excessive noise, movements or other adversities.

10.4.1   ECG classification and overall setup

The classification task is based on ECG recordings from the Massachusetts Institute of Technology and Beth Israel Hospital (MIT/BIH) dataset. The PhysioNet Arrhythmia Database is a publicly available dataset provided by the MIT/BIH. It comprises a number (see Table 10.1) of high-fidelity ECG signals that have been hand labeled by a pool of trained cardiologists. These signals are digitized at 360 samples per second per channel with a resolution of 11-bit over a 10 mV range. In our experiment, we have compressed such data exploiting a delta-modulator encoding scheme [36]. This type of signal preprocessing is compatible with the nature of the ECG signals as it offers several advantages for our neuromorphic platform; first it offers on-demand

Table 10.1 Number of single ECG complexes per class. The distribution of the dataset is highly unbalanced

Classification by expert (label)	Training	Testing
%N normal beat	10,882	2,714
%L left bundle branch block beat	1,050	266
%R right bundle branch block beat	860	250
%B bundle branch block beat (unspecified)	8	2
%A atrial premature beat	948	206
%a aberrated atrial premature beat	70	8
%J nodal (junctional) premature beat	28	4
%S supraventricular premature or ectopic beat (atr. or nod.)	1,128	300
%V premature ventricular contraction	10	2
%r R-on-T premature ventricular contraction	78	12
%F fusion of ventricular and normal beat	34	6
%e atrial escape beat	34	6
%j nodal (junctional) escape beat	11	11
%n supraventricular escape beat (atr. or nod.)	244	68
%E ventricular escape beat	154	22
%/ paced beat	64	24
%f fusion of paced and normal beat	106	44
%Q unclassifiable beat	64	10

signal compression and second it converts analog signal directly into a stream of asynchronous digital events that can be directly used to stimulate the SNN.

The proposed SNN architecture is illustrated in Figure 10.11. The architecture exploits spikes for both communication and computation, it consists of three main blocks.

1. Two delta modulators convert the ECG input signals into digital pulses (i.e., spikes). The output temporal spike patterns can be thought to be produced by four spiking neurons (plus and minus circles in Figure 10.11).
2. In a first stage, a recurrent SNN receives inputs stimulation from the delta modulators and performs a dimensionality expansion of the inputs via its recurrent connections.
3. In a second stage, a pool of LIF neurons has been supervised trained to classify the different temporal spike patterns produced by the recurrent SNN. The spikes from the LIF neurons are counted and the most active class is selected.

In the next subsection, we explain in detail all these blocks and we describe the supervised training algorithm.

10.4.2 ECG signal compression and encoding in spikes

The two leads ECG input signal is converted by two delta modulators in an asynchronous stream of digital events. Each delta modulator is simulated in software and

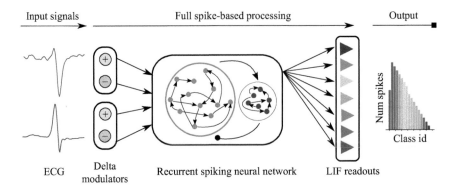

Figure 10.11   Processing pipeline architecture. ECG input signals are loaded from the MIT/BIH dataset. Two delta modulators convert signals into spike patterns, every ECG lead is encoded in two channels ON (+) and OFF (−). The recurrent SNN architecture is composed of two dense clusters of neurons interconnected with excitatory and inhibitory connections among themselves. Output spikes from the SNN are sent to an LIF neurons layer. These LIF neurons perform classification of the spike pattern by selectively firing when specific spike patterns are present

converts the high-fidelity ECG trace in two channels (ON and OFF) spiking outputs. Digital events from every channel signal the time at which the input signal has changed more (ON) or less (OFF) than a threshold (see [36] for more details on the encoding scheme).

The value of the threshold δ represents the single incremental or decremental change of the input signal that will cause a spike at the output. Given an ECG normalized input trace in range [0, 1], we set the threshold $\delta = 0.003$. Lower values of this threshold will result in higher rate of spikes and higher threshold values will result in lower spike rates. With this parameterization, an ECG complex is encoded in about 250 spikes in total. Once the signals have been converted, they can then be directly sent as a stimulus for mixed-signal neuromorphic platform.

In Figure 10.12, a trace is shown of an ECG signal that has been converted in spikes exploiting a delta modulator algorithm first introduced in [36]. This particle encoding is compatible with analog signal processing circuits and can be easily interfaced directly with neuromorphic spiking systems. The main benefits of this type of encoding are the sparsity of the spikes, the low-bandwidth requirements and the on-demand nature of the encoding (when input signal is not changing, no output spikes are produced). The bottom plot in Figure 10.12 shows a trace of spikes; when there is no change in the input signal, both output channels (ON/OFF) are active at very low rate. The encoding of the two ECG complexes, over the full period of [0.0 − 1.4] s, results in a total of 717 spikes. The top plot in Figure 10.12 shows the reconstruction of the original ECG trace carried using the spikes produced by the delta modulator.

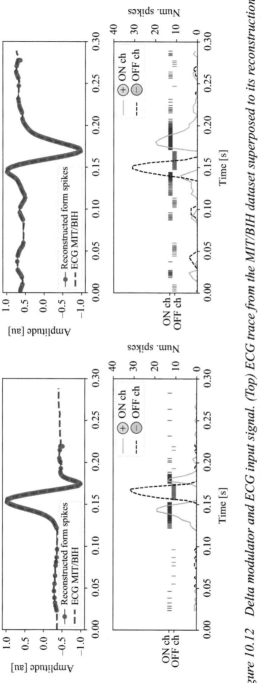

Figure 10.12 Delta modulator and ECG input signal. (Top) ECG trace from the MIT/BIH dataset superposed to its reconstruction after compression carried by delta modulator. (Bottom) delta modulator output. Spikes are shown as vertical bars (ON/OFF). The average number of spikes is shown as continuous and dotted lines, the time bin used to calculate the number of spikes has a size of 170 ms

The reconstruction achieves an average of 12 dB signal-to-noise error ratio (SNER) between the original and the reconstructed ECG signals. Previous work has demonstrated that these delta modulators are feasible to be implemented in VLSI hardware and are compatible with neuromorphic systems [36].

10.4.3 Recurrent spiking neural network

The mixed-signal neuromorphic platform is used in the paradigm of a spiking recurrent neural network. The characteristic feature of recurrent SNNs that distinguish them from any feed-forward neural network is the connection topology that allows for cycling activity. The existence of cycles has a tremendous impact on the computational properties of the network, which can then be described as a dynamical system. In fact, a recurrent SNN may develop a self-sustained temporal activation dynamics even in the absence of input; this is the indication of a type of attractor of the dynamics. In addition, when driven by external input signal, a recurrent neural network preserves its internal state as a nonlinear transformation of the input history, which is an indication of dynamical memory. Two main classes of recurrent neural networks exist: (a) model characterized by an energy minimizing stochastic dynamics and symmetric connections, (b) models that feature a deterministic update dynamics and direct connections. The first class of recurrent networks is Hopfield networks [38], Boltzmann machines, but also the deep belief networks. These types of networks can be trained in unsupervised and supervised fashion and the typical applications for these networks are distributed and associative memories, data compression, models of decision making, pattern classification [39]. In this first class of models, the network is run for a fixed period of time during which the dynamics of the system converges to an equilibrium state. The second class of recurrent neural network models usually implements nonlinear filters that are trained in a supervised manner. These filters are used to transform an input time series into an output time series that is usually projected into a higher dimensional space than the input one. In our implementation, we exploit this second type of dynamics and in particular, we took inspiration from the echo state network computational framework [40]. In this framework, a recurrent network of spiking neurons is generated randomly and only readout units are trained with high precision. This second type of neural network appears appealing for mainly three reasons: (a) cortical computational models always exhibit recurrent connection pathways, providing a hint that these models are powerful but at the same time are efficient because units are reused over time, (b) the mixed-signal nature of the hardware is compatible with random connectivity properties (i.e., it is easier to control efficacy distribution than single value of synaptic connections in an analog hardware) and (c) it can be shown that these types of recurrent neural networks are universal approximators [41].

10.4.4 Recurrent neural network implemented in VLSI spiking neurons

The recurrent SNN implemented in the mixed-signal platform is composed of 320 spiking neurons organized in two dense clusters. One cluster contains 256 excitatory

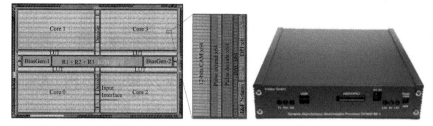

Figure 10.13   *(Top) Die picture of the multi-core neuromorphic processor used to implement the recurrent SNN, the die is a prototype chip designed by UZH and ETH Zürich, see [31] for more details. The multi-neuron chip is organized in four cores, each of which containing 256 neuron and synapse units. (Bottom) Dynamic asynchronous neuromorphic processors DYNAP-SE-1. This system hosts four neuromorphic processors and enables the use of them via a USB communication with a standard desktop computer (see [37])*

neurons, while the second cluster contains 64 inhibitory neurons (Figure 10.13). The SNN in the hardware neuromorphic processor achieves real-time performances. Upon different random initializations, the recurrent SNN expresses a wide range of network dynamics; this dynamics strongly depends upon the connectivity levels, the interaction among excitatory and inhibitory recurrent connections, as well as from the amount and distribution of input connections. By varying the connectivity levels, it has been possible to observe full synchronicity, cluster states, attractor states and asynchronous dynamics [42]. In our settings, network dynamics has been tuned to produce transient states that relate to the input patterns in a nonlinear manner, this can be achieved by making sure that the network dynamics does not collapse in any attractor states which would produce a dimensionality reduction of the input spike patterns. This can be measured by exploiting the effective transfer function measure [43,44] as a viable tool for exploring network dynamics point-by-point.

Configurations that exhibit stable states and ongoing activations even in the absence of inputs have been avoided by reducing the connectivity levels of the recurrent connection in the excitatory population, and by increasing the level of inhibitory connections from the inhibitory clusters of neurons. The use of the effective transfer measure enables us to tune the analog hardware parameters (biases) of the mixed-signal platform as synaptic time constants, mean synaptic efficacy, neuron's refractory period and neuron's firing threshold such that network dynamics does not fall in stable states. If the network dynamics would exhibit stable states, upon the presentation of an input stimulus network dynamics would relax into a prototypical pattern of activity performing a dimensionality reduction of the input stimulus [45]. On the other hand, if the network dynamics would be completely driven by the input, there would not be transient activity and reverberation, which is essential in discriminating temporal spike patterns. Therefore, we have selected to work in a state in which there is some balance among excitatory and inhibitory contributions and the network dynamics reverberates after the stimulus removal for about 0.3 s.

The hardware analog neurons behave accordingly to a bio-realistic adaptive exponential LIF neuron model. Description of the physical neuron model is given in detail in Section 10.4.6. More information about the hardware analog neurons and the neuromorphic processor is presented in [31].

The input layer of the network by the ON (+) and OFF (−) output channels of the delta modulators. These channels can be seen as four input neurons that emit spike patterns. These input neurons make fixed random connections to 20% of the synapses of the excitatory cluster of neurons. The weights of the input connections are drawn from a Gaussian distribution centered around zero ($\mu = 0$) with a standard deviation of $\sigma = 0.08$. Connectivity levels among the excitatory and inhibitory pools of neurons in the SNN are the followings: $Exc - Exc = 30\%$, $Exc - Inh = 20\%$, $Inh - Exc = 10\%$, $Inh - Inh = 20\%$. Connectivity levels refer to the probability that one neuron has to make a connection to any other neuron in the destination cluster.

Network implementation in the analog neuromorphic processor does not allow to store predefined high-resolution synaptic weights. For this reason, in the analog neuromorphic processor, the weights of the network have not been precisely mapped from the software simulation, but only the distributions and the average connectivity levels have been maintained. This has been necessary because of the inability of the current version of the neuromorphic analog processor to store predefined high-resolution synaptic weights. In the results section, we show the limited impact of this restriction on the overall performance of the system.

10.4.5 Training LIF classifiers

The output of the recurrent network has been used to supervise training (using software simulations) a pool of LIF neurons that would selectively fire when a spike pattern of the corresponding class is presented at the inputs.

In order to achieve such classification exploiting LIF neurons, we first trained in standard SVM and then we converted the numerical results into weights vectors for a pool of LIF neurons. The method that we have followed was first introduced in [46]; here, we report some of the mathematical steps and the details of our design.

Let us consider the pattern classes $P^p, p = 1, \ldots, 18$. Each spike pattern is composed of incoming spikes that are produced by the recurrent pool of 320 neurons over a presentation time T. Let t_{ij} be the time of the jth spikes of the ith neuron. We can consider the impact of a spike train at the postsynaptic site after the application of the constant kernel function $k(t)$. In other words, at each time t, we evaluate a vector $f(t) = (f_1(t), f_2(t), \ldots, f_n(t))$ where $f_i(t) = \sum_j k(t - t_{ij})$. This means that the spike pattern is transformed into a set of points $f_p = \{f(t_l)\}$ that is sampled at fixed intervals $t_l = \Delta_l$ (see $f(t_l)$ in Figure 10.14). The intent of the classification is to find a hyperplane $X(W, b)$ defined as

$$W_1 f_1 + W_2 f_2 + \cdots + W_N f_N - \rho = 0$$

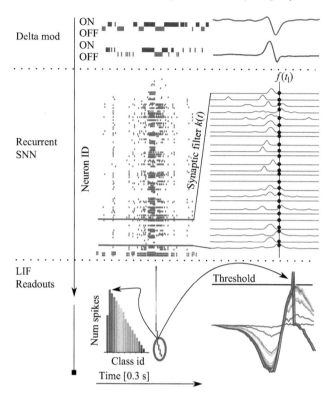

Figure 10.14   *Full spike-based processing pipeline. Processing flow is from top to bottom. (Top – delta mod) ECG input signals are converted in spikes by two delta modulators. (Middle – recurrent SNN) raster plot for the first 180 neurons in the recurrent SNN. Every dot represents one spike emitted by a neuron. Horizontal lines define the first 31 neurons. The blue traces on the right represent the effect of the spikes of the first 31 neurons to LIF readout neuron after the application of the synaptic kernel k(t) with time constant equal to $\tau_e = 3 \times 10^{-5}$. (Bottom – LIF readouts) raster plot for the 153 LIF neurons. Colors encode LIF neuron's id. The histogram groups spikes obtained for each class collected as a vote. On the right, it is shown the membrane potential for all LIF readout neurons. The threshold has been determined exploiting equivalent SVMs*

that separates at least one point from a pattern that is part of class P^q to all patterns in another class P^h. SVM can be used to solve this task. In our multi-class problem, we used the approach of one-against-one as originally proposed in [47].

We have used the solver provided by the open-source C library *libsvm* [48] that implements a one-against-one SVM approach for multi-class classification [47]. We have constructed $k(k-1)/2$ classifiers ($k = 18$ classes) and each one is trained with data from two classes. During the classification phase, we have exploited a voting strategy: each binary classification is considered to be a voting where votes are cast for all data points. In the end, a point is designated to be in the class with the maximum number of votes.

Training an LIF neuron readout means finding the optimal synaptic weights. In our approach, we convert every SVM into a single LIF neuron which solves a binary classification problem, we have constructed a pool of $k(k - 1)/2 = 153$ neurons. The synaptic weights for a neuron can be obtained by transforming the hyperplane coefficients W of the respective SVM. To achieve that one only needs to multiply the coefficients W with ϕ/ρ, where ϕ is the LIF firing threshold. The membrane potential of the LIF neurons is therefore described by the following dot product:

$$V_{LIF}(t) = \left(\frac{\phi}{\rho}\right) W \cdot f(t_i)$$

The result can be intuitively described as constraining the synaptic weights such that the membrane potential of an LIF neuron is below the firing threshold for patterns that are outside the desired class, and above (at least for one time t) for the desired target class (see LIF neurons in Figure 10.14).

A winner-take-all strategy on all LIF neurons can then be applied as a voting scheme. This process ensures a complete match between classification carried by SVMs and a pool of LIF neurons.

10.4.6 VLSI implementation of the recurrent spiking neural network

The recurrent SNN has been implemented in the custom VLSI neuromorphic processor, the "CXQuad" [31], which has been introduced earlier as a main component in our neuromorphic platform. In our experiment, we have used a USB communication port to connect the device to a host computer that has been used to convert ECG signals into spike trains by implementing in software the delta modulators (as described in Section 10.4.2). We have used the open-source library *libcaer* for communicating spike events to and from the "CXQuad." Our application has been fully written in C++ and performs in real time.

The learned support vectors are encoded as synaptic weights of the connections between each SNN neuron with all LIF readout neurons (153 in total). The support vectors are the points in the dataset, which are the closest to the decision boundaries, some of them represent examples that are wrongly classified (i.e., at the wrong side of the decision boundary) and for which a penalty is assigned during the learning process. This representation allows to retrieve the decision boundaries by simply calculating the dot product between input test patterns and weight connections. In our spiking implementation, this dot product is computed between the output spikes of the recurrent SNN, after the application of the synaptic filter $k(t)$, weighted by the synaptic input connections for all LIF readout neurons. Decision boundaries are the threshold values of the membrane potential of the LIF neurons; if an LIF neuron receives enough positive contributions, it will reach the threshold and will emit a spike. The spike will signal a vote for the selected class among the two of its own competence. Since the MIT/BIH dataset is highly unbalanced, the number of support vectors varies for each class, therefore every LIF has a different number of input synapses. Our training process results in a total of 3, 745 support vectors. The number of support vector per class varies from a maximum of 1, 219 (%N) to a minimum of 6 (%J). Each LIF neuron receives inputs via a number of synaptic contacts that depend on the number of support vectors. For example, the LIF neuron whose role is the decision among classes %N vs %J has a synaptic dendritic tree (input connections) composed of $1, 219 + 6 = 1, 225$ input weight vectors.

10.5 Results and discussion

10.5.1 Classification accuracy

Classification accuracy for the ECG application running on our neuromorphic plat-form is reported in Table 10.2 as the cross-validated performance on the full dataset that has been randomly split as in Table 10.1. The number under training and testing refers to the number of single ECG complexes selected. During the split, we kept constant the distribution of examples in each class as in the MIT/BIH dataset. The variation in Table 10.2 refers to the variation over a 5-fold cross-validation. Every line in the table refers to a different experiment. These results demonstrate the effect of the recurrent SNN on the performance of the system (i.e., classification accuracy).

The classification carried out with SVMs on the full resolution (320 Hz sampling rate) ECG signals is able to obtain a classification accuracy of 94.2%, this result is obtained without the use of any spiking neuron, only with the use of the dataset with a standard machine learning approach (implemented with *libsvm* as in Section 10.4.5). This requires about 6 h of training time in an 8 core *i*7 standard desktop computer.

If the signals are encoded into spikes and used to excite the recurrent SNN, the accuracy of the classification carried by a linear SVM increases up to 95.6%.

Table 10.2 *Classification results and ablative study. (1) Using high resolution ECG signals classified by an SVM. (2) Using ECG signals encoded by two delta modulators and classified by an SVM. (3) Fully spiking solution exploiting the multi-neuron neuromorphic processor. (4a/b/c) Fully spiking solution simulated in software*

Classification type	Accuracy
1. ECG full resolution	94.2 ± 0.3
2. ECG ENC	84.5 ± 0.6
3. ECG ENC + rSNN neuromorphic VLSI	93.8 ± 1.2
4.	
a. ECG ENC + rSNN digital 32 bit floating	95.6 ± 0.5
b. ECG ENC + rSNN digital 16 fixed	95.2 ± 0.7
c. ECG ENC + rSNN digital 8 fixed	93.2 ± 0.9

This performance can then be mapped one-to-one to a pool of LIF neurons. This requires only 20 min of training time in an 8 core *i*7 standard desktop computer. In addition, if the outputs of the two delta modulators (ECG ENC in Table 10.2) are used without the recurrent SNN but are applied directly to the synaptic kernel and then classified with an SVM, the performance drops significantly (only 84%). This is a confirmation of the fact that the recurrent SNN is performing interesting dimensionality expansion of the compressed ECG signals.

The three last rows in Table 10.2 show the performance of the system when a fixed-point representation is used for the synaptic weights in the SNN. By reducing the number of bits from 32 to 8 accuracy only drops with about 2.5% (Figure 10.15).

Interestingly, the performance of a fully digital implementation of a recurrent SNN with a fixed-point resolution of 8 bits for the synaptic weights is similar to the one of the mixed-signal analog/digital neuromorphic VLSI processor. The hardware processor is also the one that shows greater variation. This is not surprising given the analog nature of computation and the susceptibility to electrical noise, temperature and other factors that influence the subthreshold dynamic of the ultralow-power neurons and components in the device. Overall, this variability remains very well contained, however, showing that the analog implementation is very well suitable.

10.5.2 Discussion on results for ECG application

In this work, we propose a heartbeat classification system that exploits a two lead-ECG signals and then processes the information in a fully event-driven manner. We first compress and convert the ECG signals into temporal spike patterns. We then exploit a recurrent SNN in hardware and in software. We demonstrate by means of

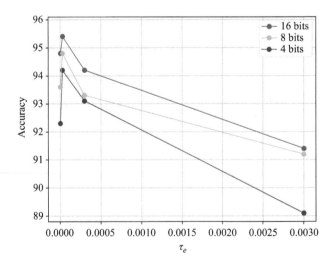

Figure 10.15   Synaptic decay constant exploration: a peak of accuracy is evident for $\tau_e = 3 \times 10^{-5}$ for all experiments

an ablation study the effectiveness of the recurrent SNN that enables the training of simple linear classifiers. We conclude that our approach of heartbeat classification is accurate as we achieve more than 95% accuracy on the 18 classes of arrhythmia provided by the MIT/BIH dataset. In addition, our system is compatible with spiking neuromorphic processors and could be easily mapped into an energy-efficient and accurate wearable device.

Many design choices have been made to simplify the neuron model of the recurrent SNN. These simplifications include the fact that the neuron model has no leak and it is devoid from a bio-realistic mechanism of membrane integration. Despite these remarkable simplifications, the role of the recurrent SNN is still proven to be useful in providing a high-dimensional expansion of the spiking input signals. After this expansion, the spike pattern can be classified by linear models with less parameters optimization [49]. These simplifications have been made to enable the design of a compact digital neuron circuit that is functional but at the same time has the less number of components. In this work, we have exploited standard machine-learning techniques to train SVMs, and then we have translated these results into optimized synaptic weights for robust spike pattern classification. This makes our results easily interpreted in terms of neural networks and still are based on well-known machine-learning techniques.

10.5.3 NeuRAM3 hardware platform results

The IGZO-TFT-based synapse communication IC has been measured to function up to about 1 MHz. This limited speed is mainly due to the use of the non-scaled devices in IMEC's ultralow leakage IGZO TFT plastic technology. As mentioned already, this has been decided to reduce both the fabrication cost and the related challenges to design this prototype. Still, due to the inherent nature of the spiking neuromorphic design paradigm, the speed requirements for the spiking neurons and related AER spike rates are very relaxed. For the ECG application, this implies that we need only around 8 kHz. In order to further reduce the cost, we have time multiplexed the 8 bits (see above) so that leads to a bit rate of 64 kbps on the now serial ports. Hence, we have quite some slack still with respect to the maximal rate of 1 Mbps which could be achieved.

When scaling up however to larger applications which higher spike rates, such as streaming imaging or video sequences, we will need to increase the bandwidth. Fortunately, that is easily achievable by parallelizing the AER spike streams. As already indicated in Figure 10.6 however, the amount of synapse communication required between the local synapse arrays will never explode in an exponential way for realistic and well-optimized spiking application mappings. It is not predictable beforehand where this communication will happen, but because of the virtual dynamic assignment of the activations on the segmented bus proposal with P parallel lanes, we will not face bandwidth problems as long as not more than P concurrent local arrays that are situated "close" to each other have to communicate. Moreover, due to the segmented nature, many of such array clusters can be simultaneously active on the overall architecture where each of these have up to P lanes available.

As we will go to the 3D-stacked monolithic realization where the TFT devices are sandwiched between the metal layers, when scaling up, the area footprint is expected to remain very reasonable as well. And the efficient 3D local routing patterns that are achievable in this 3D dynamic segmented bus topology will allow also the dynamic energy to remain very reasonable. The same is true for the leakage energy associated with the large majority of bus segments that are not active in a given event-driven execution cycle, and that hence remain "passive." The ultralow leakage IGZO TFT devices provide a material-level solution for this severe problem which faces scaled silicon CMOS circuits.

10.6   Summary and conclusions

Our main objectives in this chapter are to demonstrate that it is feasible to design real-time streaming biomedical platforms which enable on-line adaptive signal-processing capabilities for biomedical wearable systems. In order to arrive at a very low total system energy, we have introduced mixed-signal design spiking neuron circuits embedded in a local synapse array. That is combined with a dynamic global synapse network effectively supporting the spike communication between the local arrays. The latter enables the scalability we need to extend this platform to applications requiring millions of neurons and synapses.

The architecture concepts for the global synapse network are based on the use of dynamic segmented bus topology, optimized for the use in this neuromorphic context. This approach is illustrated here for a realistic ECG application. It enables a high scalability with a guaranteed minimal bandwidth across all the synaptic routes between neurons. And it also supports a very low dynamic energy due to the optimized use of the segmentation. That will be further enhanced when we use 3D stacked technologies to realize this synapse communication fabric. In order to further reduce the total energy, we have used an ultralow leakage IGZO TFT technology combined with the proper circuit techniques.

To enable algorithms that can adapt themselves on-line to individual patient data, we have used extended liquid state machines. All this is demonstrated for a realistic wearable ECG application. These features are not achievable with current algorithms nor platforms.

Acknowledgments

This work is supported in parts by EU-H2020 grant NeuRAM3 Cube (NEUral computing aRchitectures in Advanced Monolithic 3D-VLSI nano-technologies) and ITEA3 PARTNER project (Patient-care Advancement with Responsive Technologies aNd Engagement togetheR).

Authors also thank and acknowledge Prof. Giacomo Indiveri and his team at Institute of Neuroinformatics, UZH/ETH Zurich, for the significant contributions on the mixed-signal neuromorphic circuit and board design.

References

[1]   Choudhary S, Sloan S, Fok S, *et al.* Silicon neurons that compute. In: Artificial Neural Networks and Machine Learning – ICANN 2012. Springer. Springer Berlin Heidelberg; 2012. p. 121–128.

[2]   Eliasmith C, and Anderson CH. Neural engineering. (Computational Neuroscience Series): Computational, Representation, and Dynamics in Neurobiological Systems. 2002.

[3]   Neckar A, Fok S, Benjamin BV, *et al.* Braindrop: A mixed-signal neuromorphic architecture with a dynamical systems-based programming model. Proceedings of the IEEE. 2019;107(1):144–164.

[4]   Akopyan F, Sawada J, Cassidy A, *et al.* Truenorth: Design and tool flow of a 65 mW 1 million neuron programmable neurosynaptic chip. IEEE Transactions on Computer-Aided Design of Integrated Circuits and Systems. 2015;34(10):1537–1557.

[5]   Merolla PA, Arthur JV, Alvarez-Icaza R, *et al.* A million spiking-neuron integrated circuit with a scalable communication network and interface. Science. 2014;345(6197):668–673.

[6]   Wong TM, Preissl R, Datta P, *et al.* Ten to power 14. IBM, Tech. Rep. RJ10502; 2013.

[7]   Schemmel J, Briiderle D, Griibl A, *et al.* A wafer-scale neuromorphic hardware system for large-scale neural modeling. In: Proceedings of 2010 IEEE International Symposium on Circuits and Systems, Paris, France; 2010. p. 1947–1950.

[8]   Schmuker M, Pfeil T, and Nawrot MP. A neuromorphic network for generic multivariate data classification. Proceedings of the National Academy of Sciences of the United States of America. 2014;111(6):2081–2086.

[9]   Cassidy A, and Andreou AG. Dynamical digital silicon neurons. In: 2008 IEEE Biomedical Circuits and Systems Conference, Baltimore, MD; 2008. p. 289–292.

[10] Cheung K, Schultz SR, and Luk W. NeuroFlow: A general purpose spiking neural network simulation platform using customizable processors. Frontiers in Neuroscience. 2016;9:516.

[11] Maguire LP, McGinnity TM, Glackin B, *et al.* Challenges for large-scale implementations of spiking neural networks on FPGAs. Neurocomputing. 2007;71(1–3):13–29.

[12] Wang RM, Cohen G, Stiefel KM, *et al.* An FPGA implementation of a polychronous spiking neural network with delay adaptation. Frontiers in Neuroscience. 2013;7:14.

[13] Hall TS, Hasler P, and Anderson DV. Field-programmable analog arrays: A FloatingGate approach. In: International Conference on Field Programmable Logic and Applications, Monterey, CA. Springer; 2002. p. 424–433.

[14] Qiao N, Mostafa H, Corradi F, *et al.* A reconfigurable on-line learning spiking neuromorphic processor comprising 256 neurons and 128K synapses. Frontiers in Neuroscience. 2015;9:141.

[15] Indiveri G, Corradi F, and Qiao N. Neuromorphic architectures for spiking deep neural networks. In: 2015 IEEE International Electron Devices Meeting (IEDM), Washington, DC. IEEE; 2015. p. 4.2.1–4.2.4.

[16] Qiao N, and Indiveri G. Scaling mixed-signal neuromorphic processors to 28 nm FD-SOI technologies. In: 2016 IEEE Biomedical Circuits and Systems Conference (BioCAS), Shanghai, China. IEEE; 2016. p. 552–555.

[17] Davies M, Srinivasa N, Lin TH, *et al.* Loihi: A neuromorphic manycore processor with on-chip learning. IEEE Micro. 2018;38(1):82–99.

[18] Riera ARP, Ferreira C, Ferreira Filho C, *et al.* The enigmatic sixth wave of the electrocardiogram: the U wave. Cardiology Journal. 2008;15(5): 408–421.

[19] Li C, Zheng C, and Tai C. Detection of ECG characteristic points using wavelet transforms. IEEE Transactions on Biomedical Engineering. 1995;42(1): 21–28.

[20] Bahoura M, Hassani M, and Hubin M. DSP implementation of wavelet transform for real time ECG wave forms detection and heart rate analysis. Computer Methods and Programs in Biomedicine. 1997;52(1):35–44.

[21] Luz EJdS, Schwartz WR, Cámara-Chávez G, *et al.* ECG-based heartbeat classification for arrhythmia detection: A survey. Computer Methods and Programs in Biomedicine. 2016;127:144–164.

[22] Pan J, and Tompkins WJ. A real-time QRS detection algorithm. IEEE Transactions on Biomedical Engineering. 1985;32(3):230–236.

[23] Zong W, Moody G, and Jiang D. A robust open-source algorithm to detect onset and duration of QRS complexes. In: Computers in Cardiology, 2003. IEEE; 2003. p. 737–740.

[24] Wei JJ, Chang CJ, Chou NK, *et al.* ECG data compression using truncated singular value decomposition. IEEE Transactions on Information Technology in Biomedicine. 2001;5(4):290–299.

[25] Übeyli ED. ECG beats classification using multiclass support vector machines with error correcting output codes. Digital Signal Processing. 2007;17(3): 675–684.

[26] Melgani F, and Bazi Y. Classification of electrocardiogram signals with support vector machines and particle swarm optimization. IEEE Transactions on Information Technology in Biomedicine. 2008;12(5):667–677.

[27] Osowski S, and Linh TH. ECG beat recognition using fuzzy hybrid neural network. IEEE Transactions on Biomedical Engineering. 2001;48(11): 1265–1271.

[28] Dokur Z, and Ölmez T. ECG beat classification by a novel hybrid neural network. Computer Methods and Programs in Biomedicine. 2001; 66(2–3):167–181.

[29] De Chazal P, O'Dwyer M, and Reilly RB. Automatic classification of heartbeats using ECG morphology and heartbeat interval features. IEEE Transactions on Biomedical Engineering. 2004;51(7):1196–1206.

[30] Lagerholm M, Peterson C, Braccini G, *et al.* Clustering ECG complexes using Hermite functions and self-organizing maps. IEEE Transactions on Biomedical Engineering. 2000;47(7):838–848.

[31]   Moradi S, Qiao N, Stefanini F, *et al.* A Scalable Multicore Architecture with Heterogeneous Memory Structures for Dynamic Neuromorphic Asynchronous Processors (DYNAPs). IEEE Transactions on Biomedical Circuits and Systems. 2018;12(1):106–122.

[32]   Mitra S, Fusi S, and Indiveri G. Real-time classification of complex patterns using spike-based learning in neuromorphic VLSI. IEEE Transactions on Biomedical Circuits and Systems. 2009;3(1):32–42.

[33]   Mohemmed A, Schliebs S, Matsuda S, *et al.* Training spiking neural networks to associate spatio-temporal input–output spike patterns. Neurocomputing. 2013;107:3–10.

[34]   Catthoor F, Mitra S, Das A, *et al.* In: Mitra S, Cumming DRS, editors. Very Large-Scale Neuromorphic Systems for Biological Signal Processing. Heidelberg, Germany: Springer International Publishing; 2018. p. 315–340. Available from: https://doi.org/10.1007/978-3-319-67723-1_13.

[35]   Nag M, Chasin A, Rockele M, *et al.* Single-source dual-layer amorphous IGZO thin-film transistors for display and circuit applications. Journal of the Society for Information Display. 2013;21(3):129–136.

[36]   Corradi F, and Indiveri G. A neuromorphic event-based neural recording system for smart brain–machine interfaces. IEEE Transactions on Biomedical Circuits and Systems. 2015;9(5):699–709.

[37]   Corradi F, Pande S, Stuijt J, *et al.* ECG-based Heartbeat Classification in Neuromorphic Hardware. In: 2019 International Joint Conference on Neural Networks (IJCNN). IEEE; 2019. p. 1–8.

[38]   Hopfield JJ. Neural networks and physical systems with emergent collective computational abilities. Proceedings of the National Academy of Sciences of the United States of America. 1982;79(8):2554–2558.

[39]   Hinton GE. A practical guide to training restricted Boltzmann machines. In: Neural Networks: Tricks of the Trade. Second Edition. Berlin, Heidelberg: Springer Berlin Heidelberg; 2012. p. 599–619.

[40]   Jaeger H. Echo state network. Scholarpedia. 2007;2(9):2330.

[41]   Funahashi K-i, and Nakamura Y. Approximation of dynamical systems by continuous time recurrent neural networks. Neural Networks. 1993;6(6): 801–806.

[42]   Maass W, Natschläger T, and Markram H. Real-time computing without stable states: A new framework for neural computation based on perturbations. Neural Computation. 2002;14(11):2531–2560.

[43]   Camilleri P, Giulioni M, Mattia M, *et al.* Self-sustained activity in attractor networks using neuromorphic VLSI. In: IJCNN; 2010. p. 1–6.

[44]   Giulioni M, Camilleri P, Mattia M, *et al.* Robust working memory in an asynchronously spiking neural network realized with neuromorphic VLSI. Frontiers in Neuroscience. 2012;5:149.

[45]   Giulioni M, Corradi F, Dante V, *et al.* Real time unsupervised learning of visual stimuli in neuromorphic VLSI systems. Scientific Reports. 2015;5:14730.

[46]   Ambard M, and Rotter S. Support vector machines for spike pattern classification with a leaky integrate-and-fire neuron. Frontiers in Computational Neuroscience. 2012;6:78.

[47]   Hsu CW, and Lin CJ. A comparison of methods for multi-class support vector machines. IEEE Transactions on Neural Networks. 2002;13:415–425.

[48]   Chang CC, and Lin CJ. LIBSVM: A library for support vector machines. ACM Transactions on Intelligent Systems and Technology. 2011;2:27:1–27:27. Software available at http://www.csie.ntu.edu.tw/ cjlin/libsvm.

[49]   Barak O, Rigotti M, and Fusi S. The sparseness of mixed selectivity neurons controls the generalization–discrimination trade-off. Journal of Neuroscience. 2013;33(9):3844–3856.

Chapter 11

Inverter-based memristive neuromorphic circuit for ultra-low-power IoT smart applications

Arash Fayyazi[1,2], Mohammad Ansari[1], Mehdi Kamal[1], Ali Afzali-Kusha[1], and Massoud Pedram[2]

Nowadays, the analysis of massive amounts of data is generally performed by remotely accessing large cloud computing resources. The cloud computing is however hindered by the security limitation, bandwidth bottleneck, and high cost. In addition, while unstructured an multimedia data (video, audio, etc.) are straightforwardly recognized and processed by the human brain, conventional digital computing architecture has major difficulties in processing this type of data, especially in real time. Another major concern for data processing, especially in the case of Internet of Things (IoT) devices which do distributed sensing and typically rely on energy scavenging, is power consumption. One of the ways to deal with the cloud computing bottlenecks is to use low-power neuromorphic circuits, which are a type of embedded intelligent circuits aimed at real-time screening and preprocessing of data before submitting the data to the cloud for further processing. This chapter explores ultra-low-power analog neuromorphic circuits for processing sensor data in the IoT devices where low-power, yet area-efficient computations are required. To reduce power consumption without losing performance, we resort to a memristive neuromorphic circuit that employs inverters instead of power-hungry op-amps. We also discuss ultra-low-power mixed-signal analog-to-digital converters (ADC) and digital-to-analog converters (DAC) to make the analog neuromorphic circuit connectable to other digital components such as an embedded processor. To illustrate how inverter-based memristive neuromorphic circuits can be exploited for reducing power and area, several case studies are presented.

11.1 Introduction

The *Internet of Things* (IoT) is a computing concept that brings Internet connectivity to everyday life objects, such as smart thermostats, keys, wearables, health

[1]School of Electrical and Computer Engineering, College of Engineering, University of Tehran, Tehran, Iran
[2]Department of Electrical and Computer Engineering, University of Southern California, Los Angeles, CA, USA

monitors, tracking devices, etc. This is achieved by equipping the physical objects with microcontrollers, communicational transceivers, and proper protocol stacks [1]. The IoT concept commonly rely on embedded sensors. In Figure 11.1, two possible approaches to send the sensory data to the client over the IoT are illustrated [2,3]. In the first approach, the raw sensory data (e.g., temperature, humidity, image pixels) is converted to digital form and sent to the client side over the Internet. In the second approach, the sensory data is collected and processed in a local low-power processor and only summary (significant) data is transmitted over the Internet. While the first approach provides a more detailed information about the sensed environment, it is not suitable for applications where the energy and communication bandwidth are limited. The second approach is effective only in cases where the local processor has low-power (energy) consumption and can perform complex computational tasks (e.g., recognition).

There are several paradigms to implement processors to be used as part of IoT devices. Among the promising architectures for IoT designs, neuromorphic processors have received much attention [4, 5]. Neuromorphic processors, which are energy efficient, high speed, and scalable, have shown a great propensity for processing complex tasks such as recognition, clustering, and classification. Also, neuromorphic circuits have tolerance to error and variability sources, which makes them efficient for VLSI implementation [6]. In addition, due to the learning capability of the neuromorphic circuits, it is possible to train a single multifunction sensor for different applications such as analyzing the combination of traffic, pollution, weather, and congestion sensory data [7]. The most popular neuromorphic architecture is the one based on the artificial neural networks (ANNs) [8]. There are two implementations for the ANNs which are analog and digital. The analog ANNs are often faster and more power efficient compared to the digital implementations [8].

In-memory computing for accelerating ANN inference and training and the use of nonvolatile memory (NVM) arrays (for computing in analog domain) has been

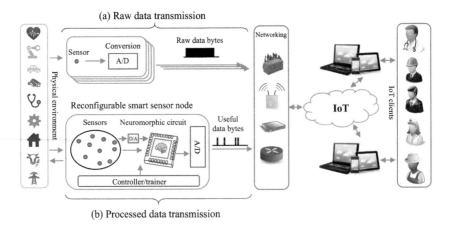

Figure 11.1   (a) Raw sensory data transmission, (b) reducing the communication traffic by transmitting meaningful data only

proposed [6,9]. In these circuits, despite the critical role of ADC and DAC at the input/output interfaces, few prior works have specifically addressed NVM-compatible scalable ADC (DAC) designs. The ability to support a flexible quantization scheme is a desirable ADC and DAC property that can benefit a variety of sensor frontend interfaces [10]. In addition, the ADC faces design challenges including reduced intrinsic device gain, decreased signal swing, and aggravated device mismatch when migrating to a smaller feature size technology node operating at a lower supply voltage [11,12]. Since DACs are used as a sub-block in the design of ADCs [13], all DAC design challenges also exist for the ADC design including switching glitches and device mismatches [14,15]. Therefore, conventional ADC and DAC circuits often require significant manual design iterations and re-spins to meet the desired performance specifications for a new fabrication process [14,16].

To address these issues, this chapter describes an inverter-based memristive neuromorphic circuit [17,18] for ultra-low-power IoT smart sensors. The proposed design consists of the following topics:

(1) A neuromorphic circuit that accepts digital I/O and utilizes inverters as neurons and memristive crossbar as synaptic weights.
(2) An analytical model of the inverter-based neuromorphic circuit to be utilized in the training phase.
(3) A memristive DAC structure without utilizing active elements to reduce the power consumption and boost the performance of the neuromorphic circuit.
(4) A scheme for merging the DAC into the neuromorphic circuit to achieve higher DAC resolutions.
(5) A modified backpropagation algorithm to train the neuromorphic circuit by considering the circuit level constraints imposed by the memristor technology.
(6) A fast and power-efficient memristive neural network-based ADC without oscillations or spurious states, while it has the flexibility of converting input voltages with different ranges and desired resolutions.

The rest of this chapter is organized as follows. Section 11.2 provides a comprehensive review of the researches and attempts on different aspects of this field for building an ultra-low-power memristive neuromorphic hardware. Section 11.3 discusses the details of the proposed neuromorphic circuit as well as DAC and ADC hardware implementations. The efficacy and accuracy of the proposed neuromorphic circuit is studied in Section 11.4. Finally, the chapter is concluded in Section 11.5.

11.2 Literature review

A neural network is realized using layers of neurons connected by synapses that link the output of one neuron to the input of another in the following layer. Each neuron represents an activation function where a weight is associated with each synaptic connection. A prior work has shown that the memristor is a highly desirable circuit element that can model the plasticity of synapses [19]. In particular, memristors can be fabricated densely in the form of memristive crossbar arrays [19]. The arrays can realize the synapses of an ANN by performing a weighted sum of their inputs. This is equivalent to a weight lookup and matrix multiply in digital ANN alternatives. This implementation enjoys from low power consumption and plasticity in resistance [19].

Memristor: Memristor, as the fourth fundamental passive two-terminal electrical component, relates the electric charge (q) and magnetic flux (φ) [20]. Initially physically realized in 2008 [21] by analyzing a titanium dioxide thin film, memristors are particularly well suited for the design of ANNs where matrix multiplications can be performed by consuming ultra-low amount of power. From that time, different teams have been working on the development of memristor based on a variety of other materials (see, e.g., [22,23]). In general, the memristor, also known as a resistance switch, is an electronic device whose internal states depend on the history of its experienced currents and/or voltages. The resistance of the memristor could be altered in a range between a minimum (e.g., 12.5 KΩ) and maximum value (e.g., 8.3 MΩ) by applying voltage pulses. The amplitudes and durations of the voltage pulses determine the amount of change in the resistance. Generally, the amplitude of the applied voltage should be larger than a threshold voltage (denoted as the write threshold voltage of the memristor, e.g., 4 V) to alter the resistance of the memristor [24]. The programming of a memristor (i.e., changing its conductance) requires only a small amount of energy, as the device can be extremely small ($<$2 nm) [25], and the switching speed can be very fast ($<$1 ns) [26]. Organized into large arrays, or stacked three-dimensionally (3D), the intermediate computing results (such as weights in a neural network) can be stored locally as conductance values in each single nonvolatile memristor during the computation.

Analog neurons: The activation function of the neuromorphic circuits with memristive crossbar could be implemented with different elements such as analog comparators [27], operational amplifiers (op-amps) [28], and CMOS inverters [29]. Among these implementations, the inverter-based network has the lowest power consumption and smallest delay due to its simplest structure. Table 11.1 compares the design parameters of the neurons in these implementations in a 90-nm technology. The reported numbers are achieved by simulating a single neuron with a 500 KΩ resistive load.

Memristive multilayer network: The results of extensive numerical simulations reported in prior works show that memristive neural networks would provide orders of magnitude higher speed–energy efficiency compared with the traditional

Table 11.1 Comparison of delay, power, and energy per operation of different implementations of a single neuron

Implementation	Number of transistors	Delay (ns)	Power consumption (mW)	Energy per operation (pJ)
Op-amp	24 × 2	3.394	2.455	44.85
Comparator	13	2.219	0.1996	4.294
Inverter	2 × 2	0.032	0.0031	0.0007

CMOS hardware platforms. The authors in [30] demonstrated pattern classification using a TiO$_{2-x}$-based memristive crossbar circuit by building a single-layer perceptron network. They trained the perceptron network by both in-situ and ex-situ methods. For ex-situ method, the synaptic weights were calculated using a software while for in-situ method, the synaptic weights were adjusted simultaneously in the memristive crossbar. The ex-situ method, which is easy to implement, may require a shorter training time and have a lower efficiency in synaptic weight updating. A 128 × 8 1T1R (1-Transistor-1-Resistor) array of HfAl$_y$O$_x$/TaO$_x$ devices was the first experimental implementation for face recognition [31], and a 128 × 64 Ta/HfO$_2$ 1T1R array was built and used for efficient analog signal and image processing and machine learning [32,33]. A 10 × 6 portion in an 12 × 12 array of Al$_2$O$_3$/TiO$_2$ memristors was used to recognize 3 × 3 pixel black/white images [34]. The experimental demonstrations, however, were limited to very small arrays which could solve only relatively simple problems. The reasons for using small arrays were mainly non-idealities in device properties (such as variability) and challenges in the integration of large array [35].

ADCs and DACs: The neural operations in the memristive crossbar circuit are basically performed using the analog signals of current and conductance. This requires ADCs and DACs for coupling the neuromorphic circuit to digital components. The conversions, however, make up a large portion of the total power consumption (e.g., see Figure 11.2) and chip area of the neuromorphic accelerator [6,36]. This mandates the use of efficient ADCs and DACs for different tasks, such as synapse readout in this mixed signal system. There are prior works (e.g., [37,38]) in which the capability of memristive structures for implementing the ADC and DAC has been shown. The neural network approach for implementing the ADC and DAC has some advantages over the conventional structures in terms of the area, power efficiency, and flexibility [37]. Some problems including spurious states and utilization of op-amp however reduce the efficacy of such converters. To overcome these problems, by relying on inverter-based

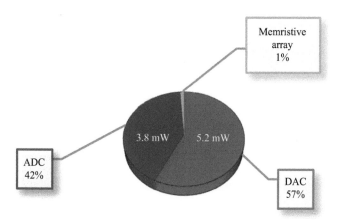

Figure 11.2   The power consumption breakdown of a neuromorphic circuit proposed in [36]

neuromorphic circuits, a DAC structure which employs memristors to generate the corresponding analog outputs is also discussed. This structure could be merged to the memristive crossbar of the neuromorphic circuit. In addition, a modified backpropagation algorithm which comply with the proposed structure is described. This structure is faster and more power efficient compared with the conventional DAC structure considered for using in neuromorphic circuits. Additionally, a neural network-based ADC which has the flexibility of converting input voltages with different ranges and desired resolutions is presented. It should be mentioned that the feedforward structure of the proposed ADC also eliminates the problem of spurious states of the conventional Hopfield ADCs.

11.3   Inverter-based memristive neuromorphic circuit

The block diagram of a two-layer ANN implemented by the proposed memristive neuromorphic structure is shown in Figure 11.3. This structure comprises an input interface, an output interface, a programming interface, and two layers of analog inverter-based memristive neural network. The weights of the ANN are calculated using our proposed training framework which is realized using a software in an off-chip machine. Before the first usage of the circuit, the calculated weights are written

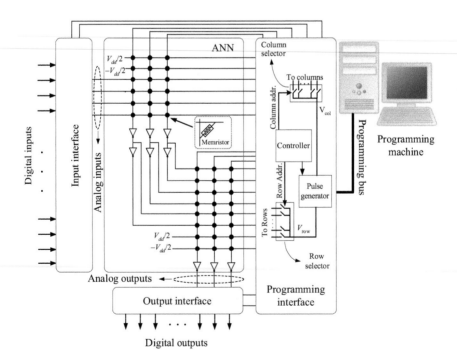

Figure 11.3   The block diagram of the inverter-based memristive neuromorphic circuit with its interfaces

to the memristive crossbar through the programming interface hardware. The programming interface also initializes the input and output interfaces. After the weights are written to the crossbar and the input/output interfaces are initialized, the programming interface is turned off and its outputs become float, the ANN is powered on, and normal operation mode of the circuit begins. The programming interface also includes switches (row and column selectors in Figure 11.3) to select the proper memristor to write and protect other memristors from unwanted write. In the rest of this section, the details of these components, as well as the method for training the neural network are discussed.

11.3.1 Neuron circuit with memristive synapse

Assume a neural network layer with V_{ip}, V_{in} ($i = 1, \ldots, N$) inputs and w_{ji_p}, w_{ji_n} synaptic weights. In this neural network layer, the input of the jth neuron (net_j) is

$$net_j = \sum_{i=1}^{N} (V_{ip} w_{ji_p} + V_{in} w_{ji_n}) \tag{11.1}$$

Based on (11.1), we propose the circuit of Figure 11.4 to implement a single neuron and its synaptic weights with two CMOS inverters and a column of the memristive crossbar. Each input of this circuit (e.g., x_i) is differential which contains inverted (V_{in}) and non-inverted (V_{ip}) signals. In this circuit, the voltage of the node net_j (the input of the inverter of column j) is

$$V_{net_j} = \zeta \sum_{i=1}^{N} (V_{ip} \sigma_{ji_p} + V_{in} \sigma_{ji_n}) \tag{11.2}$$

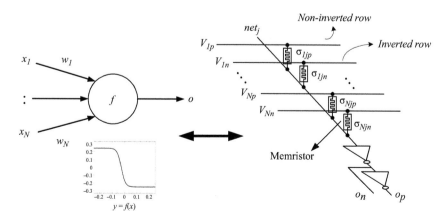

Figure 11.4 Implementation of synaptic weights for each neuron

where σ_{ji_p} (σ_{ji_n}) is the conductance of the memristor located in non-inverted (inverted) row i and column j, and V_{net_j} is the voltage of the node net_j and parameter ζ is defined by

$$\zeta = \frac{1}{\sum_{i=1}^{N}(\sigma_{ji_p} + \sigma_{ji_n})} \tag{11.3}$$

Based on (11.1), two memristors are employed per weight which enables implementing both positive and negative weights. In the inverter-based neuromorphic circuit, the first inverter acts as activation function and performs the nonlinear operation on the weighted sum. However, because in this implementation, both positive and negative values of the neuron output (the input of the neuron in the next layer) are needed, another inverter is utilized to generate the non-inverted output (O_p). Hence, all of the neurons of this structure, except the ones in the output layer, include two inverters. It should be noted that due to the much higher efficiency of the inverters compared with the op-amps, the inverter-based design, even with complementary, is more efficient. Since a neuron output in the output layer is considered as a primary analog output of the network, one inverter is utilized for this neuron. In this chapter, the operating voltage of the inverters is $\pm V_{dd}/2$. Note that the bias input of the neuron may be implemented by considering an additional constant input for the neuron. Also, in order to map the neural network weights to the neuromorphic circuit, we equate (11.1) and (11.2). Hence, the weights (w_{ji_p} and w_{ji_n}) can be calculated as

$$\begin{cases} w_{ji_p} = \dfrac{\sigma_{ji_p}}{\sum_{m=1}^{N}(\sigma_{jm_p} + \sigma_{jm_n})} \\ w_{ji_n} = \dfrac{\sigma_{ji_n}}{\sum_{m=1}^{N}(\sigma_{jm_p} + \sigma_{jm_n})} \end{cases} \tag{11.4}$$

and thus,

$$\begin{cases} w_{ji_p}\left(\sum_{m=1}^{N}(\sigma_{jm_p} + \sigma_{jm_n})\right) - \sigma_{ji_p} = 0 \\ w_{ji_n}\left(\sum_{m=1}^{N}(\sigma_{jm_p} + \sigma_{jm_n})\right) - \sigma_{ji_n} = 0 \end{cases} \tag{11.5}$$

The value of the fabricated memristor conductance is bounded between minimum ($\sigma_{\min}$) and maximum ($\sigma_{\max}$) values. Therefore, in this work, we use the memristor parameters of [39] where the maximum and minimum values are 7.9 and 0.12 $\mu\mho$, respectively, which are used when (11.5) is solved. Using (11.5) and based on the boundary values of the memristor conductance, one may write:

$$\begin{cases} \sigma_{\min} < w_{ji_p}\sum_{m=1}^{N}(\sigma_{jm_p} + \sigma_{jm_n}) < \sigma_{\max} \\ \sigma_{\min} < w_{ji_n}\sum_{m=1}^{N}(\sigma_{jm_p} + \sigma_{jm_n}) < \sigma_{\max} \end{cases} \tag{11.6}$$

Writing the equations of (11.5) for all of the weights of the column forms a system with $2N$ equations and $2N$ unknowns which should be solved to map the neural network weights to the conductance values of the memristors conductance. This system of equations which is utilized in the training process may be expressed as

$$
\begin{bmatrix}
w_{j1_p} - 1 & w_{j1_p} & \cdots & w_{j1_n} \\
w_{j1_n} & w_{j1_n} - 1 & & w_{j1_p} \\
\vdots & & \ddots & \vdots \\
w_{jN_n} & w_{jN_n} & \cdots & w_{jN_n} - 1
\end{bmatrix}
\begin{bmatrix}
\sigma_{j1_p} \\
\sigma_{j1_n} \\
\sigma_{j2_p} \\
\sigma_{j2_n} \\
\vdots \\
\sigma_{jN_p} \\
\sigma_{jN_n}
\end{bmatrix}
=
\begin{bmatrix}
0 \\
\vdots \\
0
\end{bmatrix}
\tag{11.7}
$$

Since (11.7) is a homogeneous linear equations system, it has a nontrivial solution only if the determinant value of its coefficients matrix is equal to zero. We have shown that applying the following condition results in zero determinant value for the coefficients matrix of (11.7) and hence a nontrivial solution:

$$
\sum_{i=1}^{N} (w_{ji_n} + w_{ji_p}) = 1
\tag{11.8}
$$

Assuming (11.8), and aggregating all of the rows of the coefficients matrix of (11.7) in the first row, the equations system could be rewritten as

$$
\begin{bmatrix}
\sum_{i-1}^{N}(w_{ji_n} + w_{ji_p}) - 1 & \sum_{i-1}^{N}(w_{ji_n} + w_{ji_p}) - 1 & \cdots & \sum_{i-1}^{N}(w_{ji_n} + w_{ji_p}) - 1 \\
w_{j1_n} & w_{j1_n} - 1 & & w_{j1_n} \\
\vdots & \vdots & \ddots & \vdots \\
w_{jN_n} & w_{jN_n} & \cdots & w_{jN_n} - 1
\end{bmatrix}
\begin{bmatrix}
\sum_{i=1}^{N}(\sigma_{ji_n} + \sigma_{ji_p}) \\
\sigma_{j1_n} \\
\sigma_{j2_p} \\
\sigma_{j2_n} \\
\vdots \\
\sigma_{jN_p} \\
\sigma_{jN_n}
\end{bmatrix}
=
\begin{bmatrix}
0 \\
\vdots \\
0
\end{bmatrix}
\tag{11.9}
$$

Since $\sum_{i=1}^{N}(w_{ji_n} + w_{ji_p}) = 1$, all of the elements in the first row of the coefficients matrix of (11.9) are zero. Therefore, the determinant of the coefficients matrix is equal to zero. Hence, the learning algorithm should train the neural network under these two constraints:

1. Weights must be positive and the conductance of all of the memristors must be in the range of $[\sigma_{min}, \sigma_{max}]$.
2. The sum of all the weights entering a neuron must be equal to 1 (based on (11.8)).

11.3.2 Input interface (DAC)

The input interface should convert the input digital signals to analog ones, hence a DAC is needed. There are several implementations for DAC (e.g., [36,37,40]). In order to reduce the power consumption while maintaining the performance, we suggest implementing the DAC without active components such as operational amplifier [17]. The suggested n-bit DAC structure is depicted in Figure 11.5. In this structure, the voltage of the digital inputs of the DAC ($D_0 - D_{2^{n-1}}$) are scaled and accumulated in the node $A0$ through the binary weighted resistors ($R, 2R, \ldots, 2^{n-1}R$) which could be implemented using memristors in a small area. The voltage of the analog output node may be found from the KCL equation:

$$\frac{nV_{A0}}{R_{Load}} + \sum_{i=0}^{n-1} \frac{V_{A0} - V_{Di}}{2^{n-1-i}R} = 0 \tag{11.10}$$

where V_{Di} is the voltage of the ith digital input, and R_{Load} is the equivalent load resistance of the memristive crossbar driven by the DAC. Using (11.10), one may calculate (real) V_{A0} as

$$V_{A0} = \frac{\left(\sum_{i=0}^{n-1} \frac{V_{Di}}{2^{n-1-i}R}\right)}{\frac{n}{R_{Load}} + \sum_{i=0}^{n-1} \frac{1}{2^{n-1-i}R}} \tag{11.11}$$

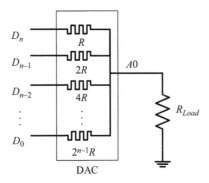

Figure 11.5   *Memristive DAC structure with resistive load (e.g., memristor crossbar)*

On the other hand, in the ideal DAC (without loading), input/output voltage relation is given by

$$\sum_{i=0}^{n-1} \frac{V_{A0_{\text{ideal}}} - V_{Di}}{2^{n-1-i}R} = 0 \tag{11.12}$$

which may be used to obtain ideal V_{A0} as

$$V_{A0_{\text{ideal}}} = \frac{\sum_{i=0}^{n-1} \frac{V_{Di}}{2^{n-1-i}R}}{\sum_{i=0}^{n-1} \frac{1}{2^{n-1-i}R}} = \frac{\sum_{i=0}^{n-1} 2^i V_{Di}}{(2^n - 1)} \tag{11.13}$$

Hence, the relative error between the ideal and real outputs of the DAC is expressed by

$$\text{Error} = \frac{V_{A0_{\text{ideal}}} - V_{A0}}{V_{A0_{\text{ideal}}}} = 1 - \frac{V_{A0}}{V_{A0_{\text{ideal}}}} = \frac{\frac{n}{R_{\text{Load}}}}{\frac{n}{R_{\text{Load}}} + \sum_{i=0}^{n-1} \frac{1}{2^{n-1-i}R}} \tag{11.14}$$

Assuming that the input error tolerance of the neural network is α, the maximum value of R (R_{max}) may be determined from

$$\frac{\frac{n}{R_{\text{Load}}}}{\frac{n}{R_{\text{Load}}} + \sum_{i=0}^{n-1} \frac{1}{2^{n-1-i}R}} < \alpha \tag{11.15}$$

Rearranging the above inequality, one finds

$$\frac{n}{R_{\text{Load}}}(1 - \alpha) < \alpha \frac{(2^n - 1)}{2^{n-1}.R} \tag{11.16}$$

and finally,

$$R < R_{\text{max}} = \frac{2^n - 1}{2^{n-1}} \times \frac{\alpha}{n(1 - \alpha)} \times R_{\text{Load}} \tag{11.17}$$

Therefore, in designing the DAC, the R value should be selected based on R_{Load} and α. In the cases where R_{max} is smaller than the minimum resistance of the available memristor, we should employ memristors with minimum resistance in parallel. It is noteworthy that due to the compactness and small layout size of the memristor, the overhead area of using parallel memristors is much smaller than the area occupied by the transistors of an op-amp.

The resistance of the binary weighted memristors grows exponentially when the resolution of DAC increases ($R, 2R, \ldots, 2^{n-1}R$). Since the resistance of the memristors are limited (bounded between the maximum and minimum resistances), a large number of memristors may be needed. To overcome this problem, for higher resolutions, we suggest that the memristive branches of DAC grouped into 4-bit (partial) clusters and use a second stage for combining the results of the partial clusters.

The second stage of the DAC (which is considered as the last stage) is merged into the first layer of the neural network as shown in Figure 11.6. In order to train the neural network, the model of the DAC circuit is extracted and the corresponding analog outputs to digital inputs are computed. In this approach, the outputs of

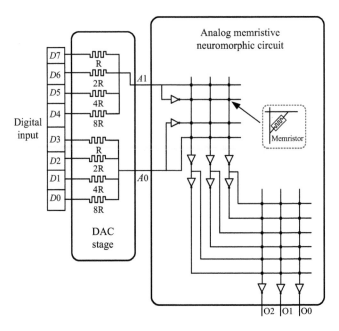

Figure 11.6   Dividing DAC into multiple parts and merging it into the
neuromorphic circuit for higher resolutions

DAC are considered as inputs for the neural network. Based on these inputs and target outputs, the neuromorphic circuit is trained by employing the backpropagation algorithm [41] and function mapped weights [42]. The training algorithm determines proper memristor states.

11.3.3   Training scheme

To train the neural network, we utilize a circuit aware training framework where the backpropagation algorithm of [41] is modified to consider the physical characteristics of the neuromorphic circuit. The pseudo code for the proposed algorithm is given in Algorithm 1 [18]. While the modified algorithm maintains the integrity of the gradient descent search in the backpropagation algorithm, it also effectively deals with the physical constraints in the memristive circuits, such as the limited range of memristor conductance.

The backpropagation algorithm employs the gradient descent optimization approach to minimize a loss function and thereby determine the network weights [41]. The cost function (i.e., J) may be defined by

$$J = \sum_{j}(t_j - O_j^L)^2 \tag{11.18}$$

Algorithm 1. Pseudo code for the proposed training algorithm

Input: Patterns

Output: Trained weights
1:    Initialize all weights with small random numbers
2:    **While** *(maximum number of iterations < than specified)* **or**
3:        *(Cost function J is > than specified)* **do**
4:    **For** every *pattern* **do**
5:      Present the *pattern* to the network
6:      // Propagated the input forward through the network:
7:      **For** each layer in the network **do**
8:        Calculate the *function mapped weights* using g_1 and g_2
9:        **For** every node in the layer **do**
10:       Calculate the weighted sum of the inputs to the node
11:       Calculate the activation for the node
12:      Calculate the Cost function *J*
13:      // Propagate the errors backward through the network:
14:      **For** every node in the output layer **do**
15:        Calculate the error signal $(t_k - O_k^L)$
16:      Update θ's in the output layer using (11.21) and (11.26)
17:      **For** all hidden layers **do**
18:        **For** every node *j* in the layer **do**
19:          Calculate the *j*th node's signal error $(\sum_{k\in(l+1)} \delta_k w_{kj_p}^{l+1})$
20:        Update θ's in that layer using (11.21) and (11.26)
21: **Return** *Thetas*

---

where t_j is the expected output of the *j*th neuron of the last layer and L represents the last layer of the network. In this case, the output of the *j*th neuron in the *i*th layer is defined by

$$O_j^i = f_j^i \left(\sum_k \theta_{jk_p}^i O_{k_p}^{i-1} + \theta_{jk_n}^i O_{k_n}^{i-1} + \beta_p^i b_p^i + \beta_n^i b_n^i \right) \tag{11.19}$$

where f_j^i is the activation function of the *j*th neuron in the *i*th layer and $\theta_{jk_p}^i$ ($\theta_{jk_n}^i$) is the weight from the positive (negated) output of the *k*th neuron in the $(i-1)$st layer to the *j*th neuron in the *i*th layer. Moreover, $b_p^i(b_n^i)$ denote the positive (negated) bias in the *i*th layer and $\beta_p^i(\beta_n^i)$ are the corresponding positive (negated) weights. In this work, $V_{DD}/2(-V_{DD}/2)$ is considered for the bias b_p^i (b_n^i) in all layers.

Now, in the following, we provide the details for extracting the update equations in the case of the positive weights. The updating rule and equations for the negative weights are also similar. For extracting the update equations, we use a method called function mapped weights that has been proposed in [18] (see Figure 11.7). To employ

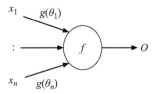

Figure 11.7   Constrained neuron model with weight mapping function

this method, the function which maps unconstrained ANN weights to implementation weights (memristor conductance in this work) is incorporated in the update rules of the backpropagation algorithm. For this purpose, the gradient parameter (∇) of the backpropagation algorithm is defined by [26]:

$$\nabla = \frac{\partial J}{\partial \theta} = \frac{\partial J}{\partial g\,(\theta)} \times \frac{\partial g\,(\theta)}{\partial \theta} \tag{11.20}$$

where θ is the unconstrained weight, $g: R \rightarrow R$

The weight updating rule (for the case of the positive weights) may be defined by

$$\theta^i_{jk_p \text{ new}} = \theta^i_{jk_p \text{ old}} - \eta \frac{\partial J}{\partial \theta^i_{jk_p}} \tag{11.21}$$

where $\theta^i_{jk_p \text{ new}}$ is the weight after updating, $\theta^i_{jk_p \text{ old}}$ is the weight before updating, and η is the *learning rate*. In order to address the first training constraint and since we need a continuously differentiable weight mapping function (which can be utilized by the updating rule), we utilize a biased binary sigmoid function g_1 defined as

$$g_1(\theta^i_{jk_p}) = \sigma_{\min} + \frac{\sigma_{\max} - \sigma_{\min}}{1 + e^{-\theta^i_{jk_p}}} \tag{11.22}$$

where $\sigma^i_{jk_p} = g_1(\theta^i_{jk_p})$.

Additionally, we utilize a second weight mapping function g_2 which is derived from (11.4) to ensure that the second training constraint is also satisfied. Hence, g_2 is defined by

$$g_2(\sigma^i_{jk_p}) = \frac{\sigma^i_{jk_p}}{\sum_{m=1}^{N}(\sigma^i_{jm_p} + \sigma^i_{jm_n})} \tag{11.23}$$

where N is the total number of neurons in the previous layer. Combining these mapping functions, the function mapped weights can be expressed as

$$w^i_{jk_p} = g_2(\sigma^i_{jk_p}) = g_2(g_1(\theta^i_{jk_p})) \tag{11.24}$$

For convenience, we consider $g(\theta^i_{jk_p})$ as $g_2(g_1(\theta^i_{jk_p}))$. Therefore, the output model of neuron (i.e., (11.19)) should be modified as follows:

$$O^i_j = f^i_j \left(\sum_k g\left(\theta^i_{jk_p}\right) O^{i-1}_{k_p} + g\left(\theta^i_{jk_n}\right) O^{i-1}_{k_n} + \beta^i_p b^i_p + \beta^i_n b^i_n \right) \tag{11.25}$$

Also, we define $net_j^i = \sum_k g(\theta_{jk_p}^i)O_{k_p}^{i-1} + g(\theta_{jk_n}^i)O_{k_n}^{i-1} + \beta_p^i b_p^i + \beta_n^i b_n^i$ as the weighted sum of the inputs of the jth neuron in ith layer. Therefore, the weight gradient by considering the proposed weight mapping functions is defined as

$$\frac{\partial J}{\partial \theta_{jk_p}^i} = \frac{\partial J}{\partial f_j^i} \cdot \frac{\partial f_j^i}{\partial net_j^i} \cdot \frac{\partial net_j^i}{\partial \theta_{jk_p}^i} \tag{11.26}$$

where

$$\frac{\partial net_j^i}{\partial \theta_{jk_p}^i} = \frac{\partial g(\theta_{jk_p}^i)O_{k_p}^{i-1}}{\partial \theta_{jk_p}^i} = \frac{\partial (g_2)O_{k_p}^{i-1}}{\partial g_1} \cdot \frac{\partial g_1(\theta_{jk_p}^i)}{\partial \theta_{jk_p}^i} \tag{11.27}$$

$$\frac{\partial g_1(\theta_{jk_p}^i)}{\partial \theta_{jk_p}^i} = \frac{1}{K} g_1(\theta_{kj_p}^i)[K - g_1(\theta_{kj_p}^i)] \tag{11.28}$$

$$\frac{\partial (g_2)O_{k_p}^{i-1}}{\partial g_1} = \frac{O_j^{i-1}}{\left[\sum_{m=1}^{N}(g_1(\theta_{km_p}^i) + g_1(\theta_{km_n}^i))\right]}$$

$$- \frac{1}{\left[\sum_{m=1}^{N}(g_1(\theta_{km_p}^i) + g_1(\theta_{km_n}^i))\right]^2} \sum_{m=1}^{N} O_m^{i-1} \times g_1(\theta_{km_p}^i) \tag{11.29}$$

After the training phase, the weights should be written to the memristive crossbar. In this chapter, the scheme of [43] is assumed to be implemented in the programming interface for writing the memristors. It solves the problems of device variation and stochastic write and has the relative accuracy of 1%. Also, the memristor model proposed in [24] for the device of [39] which has a good endurance and retention is utilized. In this model, the $I - V$ characteristic (and hence the conductance) of the memristor is determined by its state variable. Therefore, the extracted conductance values should be mapped to the corresponding state parameter of the memristor for the use in the SPICE simulations. The $I - V$ characteristic of the memristor model is formulated as [24]:

$$I(t) = \begin{cases} a_1.x(t). \sinh{(b.V(t))}, & V(t) \geq 0 \\ a_2.x(t). \sinh{(b.V(t))}, & V(t) < 0 \end{cases} \tag{11.30}$$

where b, a_1, and a_2 are the fitting parameters and $x(t)$ is the state variable. For this element, the $I - V$ relation is not linear making the mapping of the conductance σ to the state variable x not very easy ($\sigma(t) = I(t)/V(t)$). To simplify the extraction of x from σ, we suggest employing the first two terms of the Taylor series of (11.30). Based on this approximation which has a maximum error of only 0.1%, $I(t)$ may be expressed as

$$I(t) = \begin{cases} a_1 x(t)\left(bV(t) + \frac{b^3 V^3(t)}{6}\right), & V(t) \geq 0 \\ a_2 x(t)\left(bV(t) + \frac{b^3 V^3(t)}{6}\right), & V(t) < 0 \end{cases} \tag{11.31}$$

and $\sigma(t)$ as

$$\sigma(t) = \frac{I(t)}{V(t)} = \begin{cases} a_1 x(t)\left(b + \frac{b^3 V^2(t)}{6}\right), & V(t) \geq 0 \\ a_2 x(t)\left(b + \frac{b^3 V^2(t)}{6}\right), & V(t) < 0 \end{cases} \tag{11.32}$$

Since $\sigma(t)$ depends on $V(t)$ which is determined by the inputs of the neuromorphic circuit and memristor conductance values (weights), additional simulations are required to determine $V(t)$. In order to make $\sigma(t)$ independent of $V(t)$ and reduce the training time, here we suggest using $V_{max}^2/2$ instead of $V^2(t)$ where V_{max} is the maximum voltage which could be applied across each memristor. This voltage is smaller than the circuit operating voltage which is less than 1 V in current technologies. Since the parameter b is small (typically 0.05) [24], and hence $b^3 \ll b$, the error of this approximation is negligible. Using this explanation, (11.32) is rewritten as

$$\sigma(t) = \frac{1}{R(t)} = \begin{cases} a_1 x(t)\left(b + \frac{b^3 V_{max}^2}{12}\right), & V(t) \geq 0 \\ a_2 x(t)\left(b + \frac{b^3 V_{max}^2}{12}\right), & V(t) < 0 \end{cases} \tag{11.33}$$

Based on our experiments, the values of 200 KΩ for the R_{Load} and 0.1 for the parameter α is considered. Using these values in (11.17) yields R_{max} equal to 10.4 KΩ. Also, the memristors used in this work have the minimum resistance value of ~125 KΩ [39]. Thus, as mentioned earlier, to realize proper resistance values, the memristors with the minimum value may be used in parallel. More specifically, for implementing R, 16 memristors in parallel which provide a resistance value of 7.8 KΩ are utilized. Also, note that the voltage of V_{Di} is smaller than the write threshold voltage of the memristors to avoid unwanted write to the memristors during the D/A conversion. We also assume that the circuit of [43], which has the relative accuracy of 1%, is used for writing the memristors. Note that due to the using of feedback in this write circuit, the effects of memristors variations are compensated.

11.3.4   Output interface (ADC)

To transmit the generated analog outputs of the proposed ANN, they should be converted to digital form. Therefore, an ADC should be employed. We propose a memristive inverter-based implementation of neural network ADC [17]. The suggested structure is based on low triangle neural network ADC (LTNN ADC [44,45]) which avoids the problem of spurious states of Hopfield ADC. An n-bit LTNN ADC, which is shown in Figure 11.8(a), has n neurons and its design is based on the method of successive approximation. At the beginning, the most significant bit (MSB) is determined and then the approximation becomes finer, and finer as successive bits are determined continuing the sequence until the least significant bit (LSB) is determined. Thus, specifying the value of an output bit requires the information of the higher bits determined earlier. Therefore, the *ith* bit neuron has nonzero weights coming from only the higher bit neurons, and hence the weight matrix of the network is lower triangular.

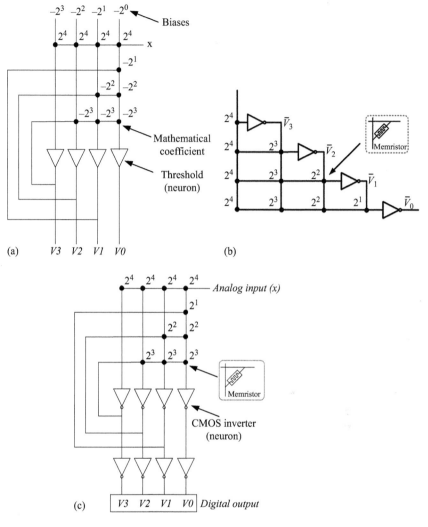

Figure 11.8 (a) LTNN ADC neural network model, (b) reconstructed LTNN structure to show its feedforward nature, and (c) the implementation of the LTNN ADC using memristor and CMOS inverter. Note that the biases are removed in this circuit by choosing differential supply voltage and modifying the weights of the neural network

The net weights for the LTNN weight matrix may be defined as

$$T_{ij} = \begin{cases} -2^j & \text{for } j > i \\ 0 & \text{for } j \le i \end{cases} \tag{11.34}$$

$$I_i = -(x - 2^i), \quad i = 0, 1, 2, \dots, n - 1 \tag{11.35}$$

where T_{ij} is the conductance of the memristor which connects the output of the jth neuron to the input of the ith neuron of ADC and x is the analog voltage to be converted. Also, I_i is the input bias current of the neuron i which could be provided through the memristor of (relative) conductance 1 connected to the input voltage x and through the memristor of conductance 2^i connected to a -1 V reference potential [46].

We use an inverter as the activation function for the neurons of the ADC network. This is due to its lowest power consumption and smallest delay among the conventional analog implementations of the activation functions (including comparator or op-amp). It switches when the voltage on their inputs equal to $(V_{dd} + V_{ss})/2$ where V_{dd} and V_{ss} are the positive and negative supply voltages, respectively. Note that V_{ss} equals $-V_{dd}$ in the differential mode. Therefore, the biases and their corresponding (connected) weights can be removed since inverter imposed a bias due to its switch point $((V_{dd} + V_{ss})/2)$. Also, since the analog input voltage range of the LTNN in [46] is $[0, 2^n - 1]$ while in the case of our neuromorphic circuit, the range of the input voltage (denoted by x) of the ADC is $[0, V_{dd}]$ (single-ended) or $[-V_{dd}/2, V_{dd}/2]$ (differential), the input weights must be multiplied by $2^n/V_{dd}$ where n is the resolution of the ADC. Therefore, for an n-bit proposed LTNN ADC (Figure 11.8(c)), the weights are determined by

$$T_{ij} = \begin{cases} -2^j & \text{for } j > i \\ 0 & \text{for } j \leq i \end{cases} \tag{11.36}$$

$$I_i = -(2^n/V_{dd})x, \quad i = 0, 1, 2, \ldots, n-1 \tag{11.37}$$

11.4 Results and discussion

In this section, first, the accuracy and performance of the proposed DAC and ADC which are used in input and output interfaces, respectively, are evaluated. Then, the efficacy of the proposed neuromorphic circuit utilizing the input/output interfaces under five applications is assessed. Next, the robustness of the proposed circuit in the presence of weight uncertainty (which is due to the memristor parameters variations and stochastic write operation) is studied. Finally, the effectiveness of the proposed neuromorphic circuit in a range of operating voltage levels is evaluated. All the HSPICE simulations of this section have been performed using the memristor model provided in [24] and in a 90-nm technology. Additionally, the parasitic effects of the write circuit switches were considered in the simulations by adding large inverters (5× larger than a minimum-sized inverter) to each row and column of the circuit. Note that the write circuit is off during the normal work of the neuromorphic circuit.

11.4.1 Input interface (DAC)

First, the delay and power consumption of the proposed 4-bit DAC structure are compared with the delays and powers of the DAC structure proposed in [36,37]. For the average power, we consider all the input combinations. The results, which are given in Table 11.2, show that the proposed memristive DAC consumes 278× lower power than the one in [37] with active components. Additionally, the proposed structure has a substantially lower delay compared with those of DACs proposed in [36,37]. The smaller delay may be mainly attributed to the small RC delays of the binary weighted memristors as well as the memristive crossbar and small parasitic capacitances of the inverters. Also, the differential nonlinearity (DNL) (the maximum deviation of an actual analog output step, between adjacent input codes, from the ideal step value of 1 LSB [47]) and integral nonlinearity (INL) (the maximum deviation, at any point in the transfer function, of the output voltage level from its ideal value [47]) of the proposed memristive DAC structure is depicted in Figure 11.9(a) and (b), respectively.

Table 11.2   Average delay and power consumption of the proposed DAC structure compared with the two state-of-the-art DAC

Design	Type	Average power (mW)	Delay (ns)
This work	Binary weighted memristors	0.009	0.0059
[37]	Binary weighted memristors with op-amp	2.5	3.394
[36]	Current steering	5.2	3

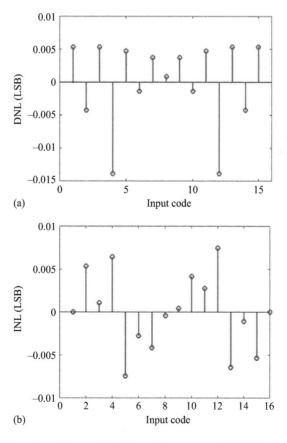

(a)

(b)

Figure 11.9   (a) DNL and (b) INL of the proposed 4-bit DAC structure

11.4.2   Output interface (ADC)

We perform HSPICE circuit simulations to validate the functionality of the proposed ADC by implementing a 4-bit LTNN ADC. The analog input voltage range in this experiment was from −0.25 to 0.25 V (corresponding to the considered inverter-based neuromorphic circuit) leading to the conversion step size of 0.03125 V. In this structure the maximum resistance is 8× larger than the minimum resistance, whereas in the circuit of [37] the maximum resistance is 64× larger than the minimum resistance. This ratio is important because the maximum and minimum resistance of the memristors are limited by the physical constraints and the minimum resistance in the circuit should be kept high enough to prevent excessive loading on the inverters. The input voltage and the corresponding digital output code of the neural-based ADC are shown in Figure 11.10. Also, the worst-case delay for the conversation was about 3.9 ns and the average total power (including leakage and dynamic power) was 6.4 μW for power supplies of +0.25 and −0.25 V. The power and delay measurements are performed using transient HSPICE simulation of the circuit by applying stepwise analog inputs ranging from V_{ss} to V_{dd} to the circuit.

Table 11.3 compares the average power consumption and conversion time of the proposed ADC with those of the ADC in [37] and some common nonneural structures used as ADC in [4,48]. The power consumption of the proposed circuit is at least 100× smaller than that of the other designs while its delay is only 0.9 ns higher than that of the flash ADC. Additionally, compared with the other ADC designs, our proposed

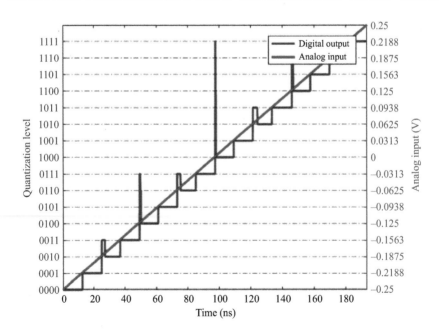

Figure 11.10   Transfer characteristics of the 4-bit memristive LTNN ADC

Table 11.3   Circuit level characteristics of the proposed ADC structure

Design	Type	Implementation	Average power (mW)	Conversion time (ns)
This work	4-bit LTNN	Memristor +CMOS inverter	0.0064	3.9
[37]	4-bit Hopfield NN	Memristor +CMOS op-amp	29.52	40.7
[36]	4-bit Flash	CMOS	3.8	3
[6]	3-bit SAR	CMOS	0.69	100
[6]	3-bit VCO	CMOS	5.6	2.2–10

ADC has the lowest area due to the fact that it has the lowest neuron area (using inverter instead of op-amp or comparator) as well as the lowest numbers of memristor among the state-of-the-art neural-based ADCs.

11.4.3   Inverter-based memristive neuromorphic circuit

In this section, the effectiveness of the proposed inverter-based neuromorphic circuits under several applications is evaluated. The system-level flowchart of the proposed training framework is depicted in Figure 11.11. First, the mathematical model of the neurons (i.e., inverters) is extracted by employing SPICE simulations for the TSMC 90-nm technology model. Then, the neural network is trained using the neuron and crossbar models as well as the training data by considering the physical limitations of the neural network circuit. After this phase, the extracted weights are converted to memristor states based on the physical characteristics of the memristor and deployed in the SPICE netlist. Finally, the neural network circuit is simulated employing SPICE simulation to measure the post-deployment accuracy and the circuit parameters (e.g., delay, power, and energy consumption).

This circuit was employed as a neuromorphic processor in a smart sensor node MNIST classification [49]. The kernel part of two approximate computing applications from Axbench package [50], a time-series regression application [51] and time-series mobile health (MHealth) dataset [52], were chosen to be run on the neuromorphic circuit. Input data provided in the Axbench package, MHealth, and Air Quality dataset for training (80% of data samples) and testing (20% of data samples) have been used. In the case of MNIST application, 1,000 of 14 × 14-pixel images, which were compressed forms of the 28 by 28 images in the MNIST database, were utilized for the training and testing. The MHealth dataset comprises body motion and vital signs recordings from ten volunteers of diverse profile while performing several

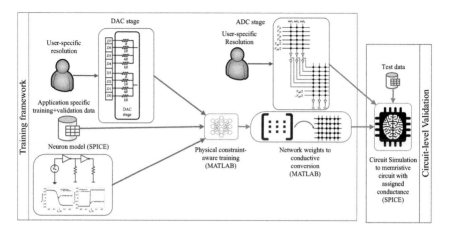

Figure 11.11   Proposed ex-situ training and validation framework

physical activities. Sensors placed on the subject's chest, right wrist, and left ankle are used to measure the motion experienced by diverse body parts, namely, acceleration, rate of turn, and magnetic field orientation [52]. The Air Quality dataset contains the responses from an array of five metal oxide chemical sensors embedded in an air quality chemical multisensor device deployed on the field in an Italian city. Hourly responses averages are recorded along with gas concentrations references from a certified analyzer [51].

Table 11.4 shows the configuration, delay, power, energy per operation, and accuracy of the extracted inverter-based memristive neuromorphic circuits in each studied application. The accuracy of the circuits for approximate computing applications (i.e., FFT, Sobel, and Air Quality) is reported in terms of the mean square error (MSE), while for the classification applications it is reported in terms of the classification accuracy (CA). Also, in the configuration column, the first and last numbers show the number of input and output bits of the neuromorphic circuit, respectively. The middle numbers represent the number of neurons of each layer of the neural network. Additionally, the delay and power consumption have been extracted by the HSPICE simulations for the supply voltage levels of ±0.25 V. The measured MSE of the HSPICE simulation output shows the accuracy of the proposed circuit. Also, note that the reported delays include DAC, neural network, and ADC delays. It should also be noted that in the classification applications, due to the fact that the desired outputs have only two values the ADC stage could be bypassed (see Figure 11.3) and turned off to save power.

As the results reveal, the neuromorphic circuit, which is trained for MNIST application, has the largest power consumption since it has the largest number of inputs and outputs. Also, the results show small delay, and very small power, and energy per operation for the designed neuromorphic circuits. Note that the number of the elements in the critical delay path of the memristive ANN is a function of the

Table 11.4 *Evaluated benchmarks, the trained neural network configuration, and HSPICE simulation results*

	Application	Type	Training dataset	Neuromorphic circuit configuration	Post HSPICE MSE/CA	Total power (μW)	Delay (ns)	Energy/operation (fJ)
Approximate Computing Applications	FFT	Signal processing	32,768 Random floating point numbers	$(8)^+ \to 2 \to 10 \to 2 \to (8)^*$	6.6×10^{-3}	70.1	5.6	142.7
	Sobel	Image processing	One 512×512 pixel color image	$(72) \to 18 \to 8 \to 1 \to (4)$	3.4×10^{-3}	300.8	8.9	114.1
	Air Quality	Air quality prediction	9,358 instances of hourly averaged responses from an array of five metal oxide chemical sensor	$(92) \to 24 \to 5 \to 1 \to (4)$	3.7×10^{-4}	337.2	6.3	89
Classification Applications	MHealth	Human behavior analysis	$10 \times 161,279$ time-series data from sensors placed on the subject's chest, right wrist, and left ankle	$(184) \to 46 \to 50 \to 13$	94.5%	1,592.2	5.6	305.8
	MNIST	Handwritten digit recognition	1,000 of 14×14 pixel images	$(1,568) \to 392 \to 100 \to 10$	98.0%	1,776.9	5.3	197.4
	Average	—	—	—	—	815.4	6.3	196.8

$^+$Digital input bit width, *Digital output bit width.

number of ANN layers (not the number of its neurons). As an example, for all of the ANNs in this work (which have one hidden layer), regardless of the size of the network, the delay path contains only two memristors and three inverters. Therefore, the delay of the circuit does not change considerably by changing the size of the network. Also, the total power consumption of the proposed neuromorphic circuit with DAC and ADC is even less than that of the previously proposed DACs and ADCs provided in Tables 11.1 and 11.2. On average, the delay, power, and energy per operation of the extracted neuromorphic circuits (including DAC and ADC stages) were 6.3 ns, 815.4 μW, and 196.8 fJ, respectively. It should be noted that the reported small MSE values have a negligible effect on the final output of the benchmark whose kernel part is performed by the proposed neuromorphic circuit. For instance, as shown in Figure 11.12, the error (image difference [36]) of the final image generated from the neuromorphic circuit (using the values from accurate HSPICE simulation) is only 7% compared with the original Sobel filter [50].

Next, in Figure 11.13, the delay and power of the memristive neuromorphic circuit are compared with those of the corresponding ANN ASIC implementation. For obtaining the power and delay results of the digital ASIC designs, Synopsys Design Compiler tool was used. The ASIC designs were fully combinational where 256×8-bit LUTs were used to implement the ASIC neurons. To make the ASIC design as similar as possible to the memristive ANN, one LUT is used for implementing each

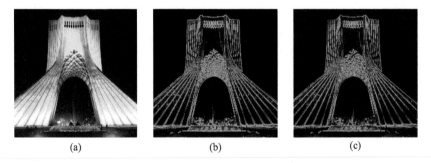

Figure 11.12   (a) The input image of the Sobel filter, (b) the original output of the Sobel filter, and (c) the output of the designed neuromorphic circuit

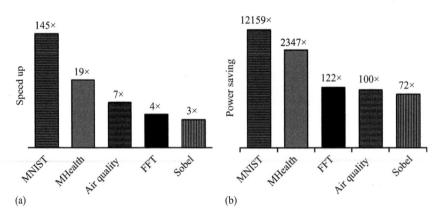

Figure 11.13   (a) Circuit speedup and (b) power saving of the designed neuromorphic circuits over their digital ASIC counterparts for different applications. Note that figures are depicted in logarithmic scale

Table 11.5   Comparison of write operation in memristive array
and SRAM cache

	32 × 8-bit SRAM cache [53]	32 × 8 memristive crossbar
Write time	1.719 ns	24 ns
Write power	6.381 mW	0.998 mW
Write energy	5.296 pJ	1.762 pJ

neuron to make the design completely parallel. The weighted sum of the inputs is considered as the 8-bit address input of the LUT which is programmed such that its 8-bit output is equal to the sigmoid function of its address input. The comparison reveals that using the proposed circuit results in considerable power savings while improving the performance over the fully digital ASIC design based on the 90-nm CMOS technology. It is noteworthy that due to consecutive write operations in the memristive ANN (which is needed for precise tuning of weights [43]), its initialization may be slower than that of the ASIC design. However, the initialization energy and power of the memristive design are still lower than those of the ASIC design. For instance, Table 11.5 compares the write operation of each weight in a 32×8-bit SRAM cache and a 32×8 memristive crossbar (considering an average of 12 consecutive writes for precise tuning of each weight [43]).

11.4.4   Impact of unideal condition

11.4.4.1   Process variation

For most of the applications, the output accuracy (e.g., MSE or CA) strongly depends on how accurately the resistive state can be set during the actual fabrication since there is considerable variability in this process [43]. Thus, to show the effect of this uncertainty on the accuracy of the neuromorphic circuit, we added random noises to the conductance of all of the memristors in the network and measured the network error in the presence of these changes. The varied conductance was defined by

$$\text{Conductance}_{\text{Noisy}} = (1 + \sigma X)\,\text{Conductance}_{\text{Normal}} \qquad (11.38)$$

where X is a random number that has Gaussian distribution with standard deviation of σ and mean of 0 ($X \sim N[0, 1]$). For this study, the considered memristor variations (i.e., σ) were 5%, 10%, and 20% of the nominal values of the conductance and 500 Monte Carlo samples were simulated. The values of the CA and MSE of the network outputs in the presence of memristor variation are illustrated in Figure 11.14. As the results show, with 20% memristor variation, the average MSE is still below 0.009 for all of the approximate computing applications. Also, the maximum CA degradation due to the considered variations for MNIST and MHealth applications is about 2%.

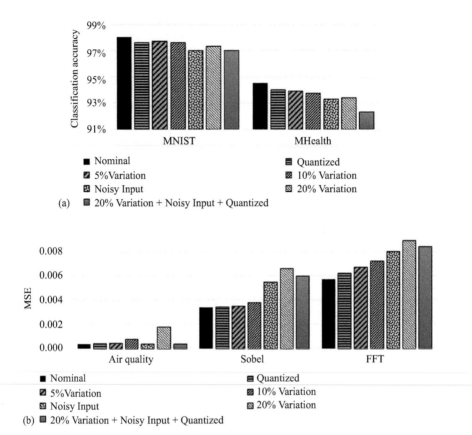

Figure 11.14   (a) CA and (b) MSE of inverter-based memristive neuromorphic circuits in presence of process variation, input noise, and considering limited write precision of the memristor

11.4.4.2   Input noise

Tolerance to electrical noise is one of the important characteristics of analog circuits. To assess the effect of the electrical noise on the analog parts of the circuit, we injected a random noise with $\sigma = 30$ mV at the analog inputs of the circuit (outputs of the DAC stage) and measured the accuracy of the circuits under this condition. The results, which are shown in Figure 11.14, reveal that even in the presence of the injected noise the accuracy of the circuit remains higher than 93%. Also, the MSE remains below 0.008 for all of the applications.

11.4.4.3   Limited write precision

After the weights of the ANN (conductance of memristors in ANN) are determined by the training algorithm, they should be uploaded to the memristive crossbar using a write circuit. The write circuit has a limited precision which may reduce the accuracy of the network. In order to examine the effect of the limited write precision of memristors, we quantized the conductance of memristors with 4-bit precision. As Figure 11.14 demonstrates, the limited write precision of the memristors has a very small effect on the accuracy of the circuit.

11.4.4.4 Combining unideal conditions

Finally, we combined all of the previously mentioned nonideal effects (process variation, limited write precision, and input noise), and measured the accuracy of the circuit. Figure 11.14 shows that even with considering all of these effects together, the accuracy of the circuit is still above 92%. Note that, as mentioned earlier, the error of writing on memristors by employing the circuit proposed in [43] is below 1%. Hence, the impact of the memristor variability on the output accuracy of the network is negligible. Also, there are some algorithms (e.g., [54, 55]) that could be used to decrease the effect of process variation not only in the memristors but also in the CMOS inverters. For example, in [55], the neurons (CMOS inverters) characteristics were extracted from the manufactured chip, and then the network weights of chip were adjusted based on the extracted information. Finally, to compensate the resistance shifting issue of the bias memristors, which is caused by their constant passing current direction [56], the low-cost inline calibration scheme of [57] may be implemented in the programming interface.

11.5 Conclusion

In this chapter, we presented an ultra-low-power memristive neuromorphic circuit that may be deployed in IoT. We also proposed mixed-signal interfaces which could be efficiently integrated into the proposed neuromorphic circuit. The proposed interfaces that consisted of memristive DAC and ADC reduced the area and power consumption. The effectiveness of the proposed neuromorphic circuit was assessed under datasets collected from wearable sensors, air quality chemical multisensor device, and several recognition and regression applications. The circuit level HSPICE simulations performed for the considered datasets showed that the proposed neuromorphic circuit with memristive crossbar and inverter-based neurons was on average 3×10^3 times more power efficient than its ASIC implementation counterpart in a 90-nm technology. We also investigated the effect of the memristor process variation and limited write precision on the circuit accuracy. The results revealed that the limited write accuracy had a small effect on the CA. Also, the classification accuracy of the circuit with a 20% memristor variation remained above 93%. In addition, the results of the HSPICE simulations of the proposed interfaces revealed that the power consumptions of the proposed structures for ADC and DAC were $5,267\times$ and $278\times$ smaller than those of the previously proposed design method.

References

[1]   Atzori L, Iera A, and Morabito G. The Internet of Things: A survey. *Comput Networks*. 2010;54(15):2787–805.

[2]   Barnaghi P, Sheth A, and Henson C. From data to actionable knowledge: Big data challenges in the web of things. *IEEE Intell Syst*. 2013;28(6):6–11.

[3]   Singh SK, Singh MP, and Singh DK. A survey of energy-efficient hierarchical cluster-based routing in wireless sensor networks. *Int J Adv Netw Appl*. 2010;2(2):570–80.

[4]   Merolla PA, Arthur JV., Alvarez-Icaza R, *et al*. A million spiking-neuron integrated circuit with a scalable communication network and interface. *Science*. 2014;345(6197):668–73.

[5]   Calimera A, Macii E, and Poncino M. Literature Review of articles in computing neural networks architecture as topic the human brain project and neuromorphic computing. *Funct Neurol*. 2013;28:191–6.

[6]   Wang Q, Kim Y, and Li P. Neuromorphic processors with memristive synapses. *ACM J Emerg Technol Comput Syst*. 2016;12(4):1–22.

[7]   Preethi DN. Performance evaluation of IoT result for machine learning. *Trans Eng Sci*. 2014;2(11):1–4.

[8]   Du Z, Ben-Dayan Rubin DD, Chen Y, *et al*. Neuromorphic accelerators. In: *Proc 48th Int Symp Microarchitecture*. New York, NY, USA: ACM; 2016. p. 494–507. (MICRO-48).

[9]   Chi P, Li S, Xu C, *et al*. PRIME: A novel processing-in-memory architecture for neural network computation in ReRAM-based main memory. In: *Proc 2016 43rd Int Symp Comput Archit ISCA*, Seoul, South Korea. 2016. p. 27–39.

[10]   LiKamWa R, Hou Y, Gao J, Polansky M, and Zhong L. RedEye: analog ConvNet image sensor architecture for continuous mobile vision. *SIGARCH Comput Arch News*. 2016;44(3):255–66.

[11]   Weaver S, Hershberg B, and Moon U. Digitally synthesized stochastic flash ADC using only standard digital cells. *IEEE Trans Circuits Syst I Regul Pap*. 2014;61(1):84–91.

[12]   Weaver S, Hershberg B, Kurahashi P, Knierim D, and Moon U. Stochastic flash analog-to-digital conversion. *IEEE Trans Circuits Syst I Regul Pap*. 2010;57(11):2825–33.

[13]   Zuch EL. Principles of data acquisition and conversion Part 1. *Micropro-cess Microsyst* [Internet]. 2009;3(10):467. Available from: http://www.ti.com/lit/an/sbaa051a/sbaa051a.pdf. Updated in April 2015.

[14]   Kim MS, Li X, Liu H, Sampson J, Datta S, and Narayanan V. Exploration of low-power high-SFDR current-steering D/A converter design using steep-slope heterojunction tunnel FETs. *IEEE Trans Very Large Scale Integr Syst*. 2016;24(6):2299–309.

[15]   Balasubramanian S. *Studies on High-Speed Digital-to-Analog Conversion*. Ph.D. dissertation, Dept. Elect. Comput. Eng., The Ohio State Univ., Columbus, OH, USA, 2013.

[16] Xu B, Li S, Sun N, and Pan DZ. A scaling compatible, synthesis friendly VCO-based delta–sigma ADC design and synthesis methodology. In: *Proceedings of the 54th Annual Design Automation Conference* 2017. New York, NY, USA: ACM; 2017. p. 12:1–12:6. (DAC '17).

[17] Fayyazi A, Ansari M, Kamal M, Afzali-Kusha A, and Pedram M. An ultra low-power memristive neuromorphic circuit for Internet of things smart sensors. *IEEE Internet Things J.* 2018;5(2):1011–22.

[18] Ansari M, Fayyazi A, BanaGozar A, *et al.* PHAX: Physical characteristics aware ex-situ training framework for inverter-based memristive neuromorphic circuits. *IEEE Trans Comput Des Integr Circuits Syst.* 2018;37(8):1602–13.

[19] Jo SH, Chang T, Ebong I, Bhadviya BB, Mazumder P, and Lu W. Nanoscale memristor device as synapse in neuromorphic systems. *Nano Lett.* 2010;10(4): 1297–301.

[20] Chua L. Memristor—The missing circuit element. *IEEE Trans Circuit Theory.* 1971;18(5):507–19.

[21] Strukov DB, Snider GS, Stewart DR, and Williams RS. The missing memristor found. *Nature.* 2008;453(7191):80–3.

[22] Miao F, Strachan JP, Yang JJ, *et al.* Anatomy of a nanoscale conduction channel reveals the mechanism of a high-performance memristor. *Adv Mater.* 2011;23(47):5633–40.

[23] Yakopcic C, Taha TM, Subramanyam G, Pino RE, and Rogers S. A memristor device model. *IEEE Electron Device Lett.* 2011;32(10):1436–8.

[24] Yakopcic C, Taha TM, Subramanyam G, and Pino RE. Generalized memristive device SPICE model and its application in circuit design. *IEEE Trans Comput Des Integr Circuits Syst.* 2013;32(8):1201–14.

[25] Pi S, Li C, Jiang H, *et al.* Memristor crossbar arrays with 6-nm half-pitch and 2-nm critical dimension. *Nat Nanotechnol.* 2019;14(1):35.

[26] Strachan JP, Williams RS, Lohn AJ, *et al.* High-speed and low-energy nitride memristors. *Adv Funct Mater.* 2016;26(29):5290–6.

[27] Yakopcic C, Hasan R, Taha TM, McLean MR, and Palmer D. Efficacy of memristive crossbars for neuromorphic processors. In: *Proceedings of the International Joint Conference on Neural Networks.* Beijing, China; 2014. p. 15–20.

[28] Hasan R, Yakopcic C, and Taha TM. Ex-situ training of dense memristor crossbar for neuromorphic applications. In: *Proceedings of the 2015 IEEE/ACM International Symposium on Nanoscale Architectures, NANOARCH 2015.* Boston, MA, USA; 2015. p. 75–81.

[29] Hasan R, and Taha TM. Enabling back propagation training of memristor crossbar neuromorphic processors. In: *Proc Int Jt Conf Neural Networks*, Beijing, China. 2014;21–8.

[30] Alibart F, Zamanidoost E, and Strukov DB. Pattern classification by memristive crossbar circuits using ex situ and in situ training. *Nat Commun.* 2013;4:2072.

[31] Yao P, Wu H, Gao B, *et al.* Face classification using electronic synapses. *Nat Commun.* 2017;8:15199.

[32] Li C, Belkin D, Li Y, *et al.* Efficient and self-adaptive in-situ learning in multilayer memristor neural networks. *Nat Commun.* 2018;9(1):2385.

[33] Hu M, Graves CE, Li C, *et al.* Memristor-based analog computation and neural network classification with a dot product engine. *Adv Mater.* 2018;30(9):1705914.

[34] Prezioso M, Merrikh-Bayat F, Hoskins BD, Adam GC, Likharev KK, and Strukov DB. Training and operation of an integrated neuromorphic network based on metal-oxide memristors. *Nature.* 2015;521(7550):61–4.

[35] Xia Q, and Yang JJ. Memristive crossbar arrays for brain-inspired computing. *Nat Mater.* 2019;18(4):309.

[36] Liu X, Mao M, Liu B, *et al.* RENO: A high-efficient reconfigurable neuromorphic computing accelerator design. In: *2015 52nd ACM/EDAC/IEEE Design Automation Conference (DAC).* San Francisco, CA, USA; 2015. p. 1–6.

[37] Gao L, Merrikh-Bayat F, Alibart F, *et al.* Digital-to-analog and analog-to-digital conversion with metal oxide memristors for ultra-low power computing. In: *Proceedings of the 2013 IEEE/ACM International Symposium on Nanoscale Architectures, NANOARCH 2013.* 2013. p. 19–22.

[38] Hu SG, Liu Y, Liu Z, *et al.* Associative memory realized by a reconfigurable memristive Hopfield neural network. *Nat Commun.* 2015;6:7522.

[39] Lu W, Kim KH, Chang T, and Gaba S. Two-terminal resistive switches (memristors) for memory and logic applications. In: *Proceedings of the Asia and South Pacific Design Automation Conference, ASP-DAC.* Pacifico Yokohama, Yokohama, Japan; 2011. p. 217–23.

[40] Kim CH, Lee JW, Kim J, Kim J, and Lee JH. GIDL characteristics in gated-diode memory string and its application to current-steering digital-to-analog conversion. *IEEE Trans Electron Devices.* 2015;62(10):3272–7.

[41] Rumelhart DE, Hinton GE, and Williams RJ. Learning internal representations by error propagation. In: Rumelhart DE, McClelland, JL, editors. *Readings in Cognitive Science: A Perspective from Psychology and Artificial Intelligence.* Cambridge, MA: MIT Press; 2013. p. 318–62.

[42] Wasserman PD. Neural Computing: Theory & Practice. New York, NY: Van Nostrand Reinhold, 1989.

[43] Alibart F, Gao L, Hoskins BD, and Strukov DB. High precision tuning of state for memristive devices by adaptable variation-tolerant algorithm. *Nanotechnology.* 2012;23(7):075201.

[44] Avitabile G, Forti M, Manetti S, and Marini M. On a class of nonsymmetrical neural networks with application to ADC. *IEEE Trans Circuits Syst.* 1991;38(2):202–9.

[45] Michel AN, and Gray DL. Analysis and synthesis of neural networks with lower block triangular interconnecting structure. *IEEE Trans Circuits Syst.* 1990;37(10):1267–83.

[46] Chande V, and Poonacha PG. On neural networks for analog to digital conversion. *IEEE Trans Neural Networks.* 1995;6(5):1269–74.

[47] AnalogDevices. 5—Testing data converters. In: *The Data Conversion Handbook*. Newnes: Analog Devices; 2005. p. 303–58.

[48] Adhikari SP, Yang C, Kim H, and Chua LO. Memristor bridge synapse-based neural network and its learning. *IEEE Trans Neural Networks Learn Syst*. 2012;23(9):1426–35.

[49] Lecun Y. THE MNIST DATABASE of handwritten digits [Internet]. html(MNIST dataset). 2010. p. 1–8. Available from: http://yann.lecun.com/exdb/mnist/

[50] Yazdanbakhsh A, Mahajan D, Esmaeilzadeh H, and Lotfi-Kamran P. AxBench: A multiplatform benchmark suite for approximate computing. *IEEE Des Test*. 2017;34(2):60–8.

[51] De Vito S, Massera E, Piga M, Martinotto L, and Di Francia G. On field calibration of an electronic nose for benzene estimation in an urban pollution monitoring scenario. *Sensors Actuators, B Chem*. 2008;129(2):750–7.

[52] Banos O, Garcia R, Holgado-Terriza JA, *et al*. mHealthDroid: A novel framework for Agile development of mobile health applications. In: *Lecture Notes in Computer Science (including subseries Lecture Notes in Artificial Intelligence and Lecture Notes in Bioinformatics)* [Internet]. 2014. p. 91–8. Available from: http://link.springer.com/10.1007/978-3-319-13105-4_14

[53] Thoziyoor S, Muralimanohar N, Ahn JH, and Jouppi N. "CACTI: An integrated cache and memory access time, cycle time, area, leakage, and dynamic power model," In Technical Report, HP Labs, 2008.

[54] Liu B, Li H, Chen Y, Li X, Wu Q, and Huang T. Vortex: Variation-aware training for memristor X-bar Beiye. In: *Proceedings of the 52nd Annual Design Automation Conference on—DAC '15*. San Francisco, CA; 2015. p. 1–6.

[55] BanaGozar A, Maleki MA, Kamal M, Afzali-Kusha A, and Pedram M. Robust neuromorphic computing in the presence of process variation. In: *Proceedings of the 2017 Design, Automation and Test in Europe, DATE 2017*, 2017. p. 440–5.

[56] Kadetotad D, Xu Z, Mohanty A, *et al*. Parallel architecture with resistive cross-point array for dictionary learning acceleration. *IEEE J Emerg Sel Top Circuits Syst*. 2015;5(2):194–204.

[57] Liu X, Mao M, Liu B, *et al*. Harmonica: A framework of heterogeneous computing systems with memristor-based neuromorphic computing accelerators. *IEEE Trans Circuits Syst I Regul Pap*. 2016;63(5):617–28.

Index

accuracy, defined 149–50
accurate-binary-convolution network (ABC-Net) 110–11
activation function (AF) 7–9, 46–8, 84–5, 148, 268, 282
activation sparsity 120–1
  supporting 125
adaline 15–16
ADAM optimizer 101
Address Event Representation (AER) streams 244
advanced RISC machine (ARM) processor 235, 237
Air Quality dataset 285–6
AlexNet 24–5, 123, 134, 162–3, 166–8, 187, 192, 198–200, 203–4, 218, 228
alternating direction method of multipliers (ADMM) technique 44
analog neurons 268
analog-to-digital converters (ADC) 265
application-specific integrated circuit (ASIC) 38, 119, 236
approximate computing 148, 285–6
ApproxNN 154–5
artificial neural networks (ANNs) 3, 6–7, 266, 286–7
  classification and regression, relation between 13
  in classification problems 11–12
  convolutional neural networks (CNNs) 20–1
    convolution layers 21
    examples 24–5
    learning in 23–4
    pooling layers 22–3
  multilayer and deep NNs 16
    autoencoders and stacked RBMs 17–18
    convolutional neural networks (CNNs) 18–19
    multilayer perceptron 16–17
    recurrent neural networks 19
  natural NNs 3–6
  preliminary concepts in 7
    feedforward and recurrent architectures in ANN 9–10
    Mcculloch and Pitz neuron 7–8
    supervised and unsupervised learning in ANN 10
    widely used activation functions 8–9
  in regression problems 12–13
  simple structure networks 14–16
autoencoders 17–18
automatic speech recognition (ASR) 44
autonomous driving 161
AxNN 154–5

back-end-of-line (BEOL) metal interconnection stack 243
backpropagation through time (BPTT) 19
backward propagation 97–8
batch normalization (BN) layer 101
battery-operated embedded systems 96
binarization 41, 43, 98, 102, 110
binary activation layer (BinActiv) 102
BinaryConnect 97–100

binary convolutional neural networks (BCNN) 112
binary neural networks (BNNs) 43, 95
  binarized and ternarized neural networks 100–8
  binary and ternary weights for neural networks 97–100
  hardware implementation of 111–12
  optimization techniques 108–11
binary weight networks (BWN) 102
biomedical signal processing challenges for ECG application 240–1
bitcount 100
Bit Fusion 55
bit-pragmatic 140–2
Bit-Tactical 125, 128
block random access memory (BRAMs) 161, 171–2, 182
Boltzmann machines 252
Boolean expression 100
brain-inspired deep learning systems 236
BranchyNet 196

C++ 154, 256
Caffe 112, 180–1, 218
Cambricon-X 125–8
CIFAR10 dataset 99–100, 107
classification accuracy (CA) 286
classification and regression, relation between 13
classification problems, ANNs in 11–12
clock gating 124
ClosNN 54–5, 57, 59
  collective communications on ClosNN 60–2
  customization and area reduction 62–4
  folded ClosNN 65–7
Clos topology 54–5, 57–8
clustering problem 154
Cnvlutin 125–6
ComPEND 140

Complementary Metal-Oxide-Semiconductor (CMOS) technology 237
compressed sparse column (CSC) 41, 132
compressed sparse row (CSR) 41
computation optimization and reuse 168
  design control variables 168
  partial sums and data reuse 169–70
  proposed loop coalescing for flexibility with high efficiency 170–1
computation reduction and accuracy, evaluation of 149
computation reuse 148–9, 156
  input redundancy, support for 152–3
  sources 152
  weight redundancy, support for 151–2
Concat layer 198
conditional deep learning network (CDLN) 196
confidence-tracking PTHP 216–17, 226–7
configurable logic blocks (CLBs) 39
context-aware pruning policy (CAPP) 214
  for CONV layer 215–16, 224
  for fully connected (FC) layer 214–15, 223–4
continuous weight space (CWS) 106
ConvEngine (CE) 178–9
CONV layer 194, 207–8
  context-aware pruning policy for 215–16, 224
  pruning filters in 211–12
convolutional neural networks (CNNs) 18–21, 84, 95, 121, 156, 161, 191–3
  bandwidth matching and compute model 171
  analyzing runtime 174–6
  resource utilization 171–2

unifying off-chip and on-chip memory 172–4
Caffe integration 180–1
computation optimization and reuse 168
   design control variables 168
   partial sums and data reuse 169–70
   proposed loop coalescing for flexibility with high efficiency 170–1
convolution layers 21
efforts on FPGA-based acceleration of 162–3
examples 24–5
inference phase 96
learning in 23–4
library design and architecture implementation 176
   concurrent architecture 176–8
   ConvEngine (CE) 178–9
   other layers 180
   restructuring fully connected layers 179
   zero overhead pooling 179–80
life cycle of 96
network structures and operations 163
   convolution 163
   inner product 163–5
   operations 166
   pooling 165
optimizing parallelism sources 166
   acceleration strategies 167–8
   identifying independent computations 166
performance evaluation 181
   architecture comparison 185–7
   onboard runs 182–4
   optimizer results 181–2
pooling layers 22–3
training phase 96
convolution layers (CLs) 21, 163
CORN 148–9
   16-bit fixed-point numbers in 155

architecture 150–1
weight and input redundancy extraction 155
CXQuad 242–3, 245–6, 248, 256

DaDianNao architecture 125–6, 140–1
data storage units (DSUs) 128, 131
deep neural networks (DNNs) 95–6, 119
dense accelerator, advantages of sparsity for 124–5
design variable optimization 182
deterministic low-discrepancy bit-streams 82–4
differential nonlinearity (DNL) 283
digital signal processors (DSPs) 161, 171, 184
digital-to-analog converters (DAC) 265
directed acyclic graph (DAG) 194
direction memory access (DMA) streaming unit 45
discrete state transition (DST) 105
discrete wavelet transform (DWT) 196
discrete weight space (DWS) 106
discretization of weights 105
DNNWeaver 112
Dragonfly 57
drone surveillance 161
DropConnect 99
Dropout 99
dual MAC Arrays (dual-MAAs) 128, 131
dynamic complexity reduction, thresholding policy (TP) for 213
   fixed thresholding policy 214, 220–2
   variable thresholding policy 214, 222–3
dynamic deadline (DD) policy for real-time applications 212–13, 219–20
dynamic precision 124

eDRAM bank 125
efficient inference engine (EIE) 131–3
efficient RNN (E-RNN) framework 44
electrocardiogram (ECG) 156, 236
   ECG application mapping on
      non-scaled neuromorphic
      platform instance 248
      ECG classification and overall
        setup 248–9
      ECG signal compression and
        encoding in spikes 249–52
      recurrent neural network
        implemented in VLSI spiking
        neurons 252–4
      recurrent spiking neural network
        252
      training leaky-integrate-and-fire
        (LIF) classifiers 254–6
      VLSI implementation of the
        recurrent spiking neural network
        256–7
electroencephalogram (EEG) 236
EMBRACE interconnection 56
end-to-end automation 161
exploration strategy 182
Eyeriss 124, 132, 137

FACETS/BrainScale project 238
feedforward and recurrent architectures
     in ANN 9–10
feedforward neural networks on
     massively parallel architectures
     53
   ClosNN 59
      collective communications on
        60–2
      customization and area reduction
        62–5
      evaluation 68
        neural network size, sensitivity to
          72–3
        power comparison 71–2
        realistic workloads, performance
          evaluation under 70–1

synthetic traffic, performance
     comparison under 69–70
folded ClosNN 65–7
   leaf switch optimization 67
   preliminaries 57–9
   scaling to larger NoCs 67–8
FICaffe 167–8, 171, 174,
     180–1
field-programmable gate arrays
     (FPGAs) 39, 112, 119, 161,
     239
FINN framework 112
First in First out (FIFO) 176, 195
fixed percentage PTHP 216, 225–6
fixed thresholding policy 214, 220–2
floating point operations (FLOPs) 192,
     227
folded ClosNN 65–8
full-precision memory 104
fully connected (FC) layers 121, 162–4,
     179, 194
   context-aware pruning policy (CAPP)
     for 214–15, 223–4
   improving bandwidth for 168
   pruning neurons in 211

gated recurrent units (GRU) model 19,
     36–7
Gaussian distribution 200, 208, 219,
     254
GoogleNet 24–5, 162–3, 166–8, 182–4,
     192
graphics processing units (GPU) 38,
     147
GXNOR-Net 104–7
   multiplication operation in 106

hard pruning 122
hardware description language (HDL)
     39, 88
Hebb Net 14
high-radix networks 59
H-NoC 56, 68–71
Hopfield networks 252
HSPICE circuit simulations 284

hybrid binary-bit-stream design 85
  multiplications and accumulation 86
  negative weights, handling 86–7

Ifmaps 195, 203
ImageNet 96, 99, 109–11, 191
ineffectual output neurons (iEON) 139
inner product layers 163
input feature maps (IFMs) 163, 166,
        175
  first strategy 169–70
input interface (DAC) 269–70, 274–6,
        282–3
input redundancy
  computation reuse support for 152–3
  extraction 155–6
input redundancy table (IRT) 152–3
integral nonlinearity (INL) 283
Intel Lab 239
interactive speech recognition 161
Internet of Things (IoT) platforms 96,
        119, 265
interneurons 5, 54–5
intra-channel parallelism 167
intra-filter parallelism 166–7, 187
inverter-based memristive
        neuromorphic circuit 265
  input interface (DAC) 274–6, 282–3
  inverter-based memristive
        neuromorphic circuit 285–9
  neuron circuit with memristive
        synapse 271–4
  output interface (ADC) 280–2,
        284–5
  training scheme 276–80
  unideal condition, impact of 289
    combining unideal conditions 291
    input noise 290
    limited write precision 290–1
    process variation 289
iterative convolutional neural network
        (ICNN) 191
  background on 194–5
  CNN visualization, background on
        204

complexity analysis 203–4
contextual awareness in 208
  CONV layers, pruning filters in
        211–12
  fully connected (FC) layers,
        pruning neurons in 211
  prediction rank (PR) 209–11
implementation results 218
  context-aware pruning policy for
        parameter reduction 223–4
  dynamic deadline policy for
        real-time applications 219–20
  implementation framework
        218–19
  thresholding policy for dynamic
        complexity reduction 220–3
iterative learning 196
  iterative AlexNet (case study) 199
optimization of 195–6
policies for exploiting
        energy-accuracy trade-off in
        212
  context-aware pruning policy
        214–16
  dynamic deadline (DD) policy for
        real-time applications 212–13
  pruning and thresholding hybrid
        policy (PTHP) 216–17
  thresholding policy (TP) for
        dynamic complexity reduction
        213–14
  variable and dynamic bit-length
        selection 217–18
pruning and thresholding hybrid
        policy (PTHP) 225
  confidence-tracking PTHP 226–7
  fixed percentage PTHP 225–6
  run-time and overall accuracy
        227–9
training schemes 200
  parallel training 200–3
  sequential training 200
visualizing features learned by
        204–8

kernels 163
k-means clustering algorithm 154

laconic architecture 142–3
latency estimation model 181–2
leaf switch optimization 67
leaky-integrate-and-fire (LIF) neurons
       237, 254–6
lightning memory-mapped database
       (LMDB) format 219
load balance-aware pruning method
       41–2
long short-term memory (LSTM) 19,
       27, 30–1, 156
    hardware implementation of 39
       datatype and quantization 44–6
       memory 46–8
       model compression 40–4
    main concept of 31–2
    steps in 32–4
    variants on 35–6
Lookup Tables (LUTs) 112
low-discrepancy (LD) bit-streams 79

MATLAB 82, 88, 154
matrix-by-vector multiplication (MVM)
       operation 128
matrix–vector multiplication 38, 45–7,
       85
matrix–vector product accumulation 45
Mcculloch and Pitz neuron 7–8
mean absolute error (MAE) metric 83
mean square error (MSE) 286
memory access stall cycles 166
memristive multilayer network 268–9
memristive synapse, neuron circuit with
       271–4
memristor 267–8, 275
mixed-signal neuromorphic platform
       design 235, 237–40
    biomedical signal processing
       challenges for ECG application
       240–1
    classification accuracy 257–8

ECG application mapping on
       non-scaled neuromorphic
       platform instance 248
    ECG classification and overall
       setup 248–9
    ECG signal compression and
       encoding in spikes 249–52
    recurrent neural network
       implemented in VLSI spiking
       neurons 252–4
    recurrent spiking neural network
       252
    training LIF classifiers 254–6
    VLSI implementation of the
       recurrent spiking neural network
       256–7
electrocardiogram (ECG) application,
       discussion on results for 258–9
NeuRAM3 hardware platform results
       259–60
NeuRAM3 mixed-signal
       neuromorphic platform 241
    analog neural components
       including local synapse array
       242
    FPGA architecture 246–8
    global synapse communication
       network realized with TFT-based
       switches 242–6
MNIST dataset 43, 88, 99, 107
mobile health (MHealth) dataset 285
Moore's law 119
motor neurons 5
MSB 140
multilayer and deep NNs 16
    autoencoders and stacked RBMs
       17–18
    convolutional neural networks
       (CNNs) 18–19
    multilayer perceptron 16–17
    recurrent neural networks 19
multilayer perceptron (MLP) 100, 148
multiplication operations 86–7, 98, 148
multiply-and-accumulate (MAC)
       operations 95, 124, 166

Multistage Interconnection Network
    (MIN) topology 54–5
MUX-addition 111

natural language processing (NLP) 27
natural NNs 3–6
network-on-chip (NoC) 54, 57
network-specific runs 182–4
Neural Engineering Framework 238
neural networks (NNs) 3, 79, 147–8
    baseline architecture 150
        input redundancy, computation
            reuse support for 152–3
        weight redundancy, computation
            reuse support for 151–2
    experimental results 154–6
    future work 156
    motivation 148–50
    multicore neural network
        implementation 153
    more than *K* weights per neuron
        153
    more than *N* neurons per layer
        153–4
    sensitivity to size of 72–3
neural processing unit (NPU) 125, 128
NeuRAM3 mixed-signal neuromorphic
        platform 241
    analog neural components including
        local synapse array 242
    FPGA architecture 246–8
    global synapse communication
        network realized with TFT-based
        switches 242–6
    hardware platform results 259–60
NeuroGrid project 238
neuromorphic computing 236
neuron circuit with memristive synapse
        271–4
next-generation CNNs 164
nonvolatile memory (NVM) arrays 266
normalization (NORM) layer 195
N-to-1 multiplexer (MUX) 128
NullaNet 100

efficient realization of a neuron in
        101
Nvidia 125

off-chip and on-chip memory, unifying
        172–4
    effective bandwidth latency 173–4
    impact of unmatched system
        172–3
off-chip memory bandwidth 162
Ofmap pixel 195, 203, 212
on-chip bandwidth 162, 167, 180, 182
OpenCL 162–3, 166, 168, 170, 172,
        176, 181
optimal DRAM access 178–9
output feature maps (OFMs) 163
    first strategy 170
    parallelism 168
output interface (ADC) 269–70, 280–2,
        284–5
output sparsity 121
    supporting 137–40

parameter reduction, context-aware
        pruning policy for 223
    CONV layer 224
    FC layer 223–4
Perceptron rule 15
PhysioNet Arrhythmia Database 248
pooling (*POOL*) 165, 194–5
pooling layers, in CNN 18, 20–3
power comparison 71–2
power consumption, in neural networks
        156
Pragmatic tile 140–2
prediction rank (PR) 209–11
principal component analysis (PCA) 17
processing element (PE) 123
    architecture 162
    PE Efficiency 185
pruning, software approach for 122
    hard pruning 122
    questioning pruning 122–3
    soft pruning, structural sparsity, and
        hardware concern 122

pruning and thresholding hybrid policy (PTHP) 216, 225
  confidence-tracking PTHP 216–17, 226–7
  fixed percentage PTHP 216, 225–6
  run-time and overall accuracy 227
    deadline-driven 228–9
    pruning and/or thresholding 227–8
pruning technique 40
P-wave 240

quantized back propagation 98
questioning pruning 122–3
Q-wave 240

realistic workloads, performance evaluation under 70–1
real-time biomedical signal processing platforms 236
ReBNet 112
rectified linear unit (ReLU) function 102, 120–1, 166
recurrent neural networks (RNNs) 9, 19, 27–30, 121
  gated recurrent units (GRU) model 36–7
  hardware acceleration for RNN inference 37
    hardware implementation 38–9
    software implementation 37–8
  hardware implementation of LSTMs 39
    datatype and quantization 44–6
    memory 46–8
    model compression 40–4
  long short-term memory (LSTM) 30–1
    main concept of 31–2
    steps in 32–4
    variants on 35–6
  software implementation 37–8
Register-Transfer Level (RTL) 62
regression problems, ANNs in 12–13

residual neural network (ResNet) 25, 95, 163, 166, 192, 204
resistive random-access memory (ReRAM) 56
restricted Boltzmann machine (RBM) 17–18
Ristretto 161, 181
run-length encoding 124
R-wave 240

sensory neurons 5
sequence learning 27, 48
simple structure networks 14–16
singular value decomposition (SVD) 41–2, 140
SnaPEA 137–8, 140
Sobol sequences 82–4, 86, 88, 90–1
soft pruning 122
sparse convolutional neural network (SCNN) 56, 131, 134–7
sparse deep neural networks 119
  hardware support for 123
    advantages of sparsity for dense accelerator 124–5
    supporting activation sparsity 125
    supporting both weight and activation sparsity 131–7
    supporting output sparsity 137–40
    supporting value sparsity 140–3
    supporting weight sparsity 125–31
  software approach for pruning 122
    hard pruning 122
    questioning pruning 122–3
    soft pruning, structural sparsity, and hardware concern 122
  types of sparsity methods 120–1
SparseNN 140
sparse ternary connect (STC) 100
spike-timing-dependent plasticity (STDP) learning circuits 238
spiking Neural Network Architecture (SpiNNaker) project 237
spiking neural networks (SNNs) 235–6, 239, 253
spiking neurons 235, 241, 248

SpiNNaker 56, 237
SqueezeNet 162–4, 168, 184
state-of-the-art neural networks 147,
   154
static random access memory (SRAM)
   132
stochastic-binary convolutional neural
   networks 79
   convolutional neural networks 84
   deterministic low-discrepancy
      bit-streams 82–4
   experimental results 88
      cost comparison 90–2
      performance comparison
         88–90
      proposed hybrid binary-bit-stream
         design 85
      multiplications and accumulation
         86
      negative weights, handling 86–7
   related work 84–5
   stochastic computing (SC) 79–82
stochastic gradient descent (SGD)
   training 97
Stratix V GXA7 FPGA 162, 181, 185
Stripes 55
structural sparsity 122
supervised and unsupervised learning in
   ANN 10
support vector machine (SVM) 235
SVHN 107
S-wave 240
synapse buffer (SB) 125
synthetic traffic, performance
   comparison under 69–70
system-on-chip (SoC) 54

TCL 125, 128–9
teacher–student methods 103
TensorFlow 37
TensorFlow Lite 37
ternary–binary network (TBN) 104
ternary neural networks (TNN) 97, 103
ternary weight neural (TWN) networks
   97, 99

ternary weight space (TWS)/binary
   weight space (BWS) 106
Theano 37
thin film transistor (TFT) technology
   235
thresholding policy (TP) for dynamic
   complexity reduction 213
   fixed thresholding policy 214, 220–2
   variable thresholding policy 214,
      222–3
TOT-Net 106–7
   multiplication operation in 106
T-wave 240

unified serial PE structure 139
Uniform Serial Processing Element
   139–40
U-wave 240

value sparsity 121
   supporting 140–3
variable and dynamic bit-length
   selection 217–18
variable thresholding policy 214, 222–3
very large scale integration (VLSI)
   236, 239
   recurrent neural network
      implemented in VLSI spiking
      neurons 252–4
   recurrent spiking neural network,
      VLSI implementation of 256–7
VGG 162, 182, 185, 187, 192
VGGNet 24

wearable devices 96, 235–6, 240, 259
weight and activation sparsity,
   supporting 131–7
weight buffer bandwidth, reducing 167
weight redundancy, computation reuse
   support for 151–2
weight redundancy table (WRT) 151
weight sparsity 121
   supporting 125–31
weight table (WT) 150
Winograd Transformations 161, 187

XNOR 41, 43, 100–2
XNOR-bitcount 111
XNOR network (XNOR-Net) 102,
    104–6, 110
XNOR Neural Engine (XNE) 112

YodaNN 112

ZeNA 131–2, 134–5
    PE organization 134
zero-free neuron array format (ZFNAf)
    125
zero overhead pooling 179–80